The Genocidal Mentality

Other Books by Robert Jay Lifton

The Future of Immortality and Other Essays for a Nuclear Age

The Nazi Doctors: Medical Killing and the
Psychology of Genocide

The Broken Connection: On Death and the Continuity of Life

Death in Life: Survivors of Hiroshima

In a Dark Time (with Nicholas Humphrey)

Indefensible Weapons: The Political and
Psychological Case against Nuclearism (with Richard Falk)

Six Lives/Six Deaths: Portraits from Modern Japan
(with Shuichi Kato and Michael Reich)

The Life of the Self: Toward a New Psychology

Living and Dying (with Eric Olson)

Home from the War: Vietnam Veterans—
Neither Victims nor Executioners

History and Human Survival

Boundaries: Psychological Man in Revolution

Revolutionary Immortality: Mao Tse-tung and
the Chinese Cultural Revolution

Thought Reform and the Psychology of Totalism:
A Study of "Brainwashing" in China

Books Co-edited by Eric Markusen

Nuclear Weapons and the Threat of Nuclear War (with John B. Harris)

Death and Dying: Challenge and Change (with Robert Fulton, Greg Owen, and
Jane Scheiber)

Science and Ethical Responsibility (with Sanford Lakoff, Ronald J. Bee, and
Jeffrey Leifer)

The Genocidal Mentality

NAZI HOLOCAUST AND NUCLEAR THREAT

Robert Jay Lifton
and Eric Markusen

MACMILLAN
LONDON

This book derives in part from the
Peter B. Lewis Lectures of the Center of International Studies,
delivered at Princeton University by
Robert Jay Lifton in 1988.

First published in the United States of America 1990
by Basic Books, Inc., Publishers, New York

First published in the United Kingdom 1991 by
MACMILLAN LONDON LIMITED
Cavaye Place, London SW10 9PG

Associated companies in Auckland, Delhi, Dublin, Gaborone,
Hamburg, Harare, Hong Kong, Johannesburg, Kuala Lumpur,
Lagos, Manzini, Melbourne, Mexico City, Nairobi, New York,
Singapore and Tokyo

ISBN 0-333-55201-6

A CIP catalogue record for this book is available from the British Library

Designed by Vincent Torre and Ellen S. Levine

Printed by Billing & Sons Ltd, Worcester

Your lacerations tell the losing game
You play against sickness past your cure.
How will the hands be strong? How will the heart endure?

—Robert Lowell

To the memory of Raphael Lemkin,
whose one-man crusade focused the attention of the world
on the crime of genocide—and to all those
who continue his struggle.

Contents

Preface by Robert Jay Lifton

LONG BEFORE embarking on a study of Nazi doctors in the late 1970s, I had been much concerned with psychological and moral dimensions of nuclear threat. By the time I published *The Nazi Doctors: Medical Killing and the Psychology of Genocide* in 1986, I was convinced that certain forms of behavior in German society during the Nazi period had relevance for American and Soviet behavior in connection with nuclear weapons. To bear witness as a scholar to these Nazi actions required looking back to confront them and looking ahead to apply what I could learn from them.

During the early 1980s, Eric Markusen and I were in active dialogue about these matters. He was assisting me with research on Nazi doctors and at the same time teaching courses on nuclear weapons and completing his dissertation connecting strategic bombing during the Second World War with certain themes of the Nazi Holocaust. It was he who suggested that we collaborate on a book; and, over time, we came to our particular way of doing that.

We noted that many people were invoking comparisons with the Holocaust in discussing nuclear dangers, but we felt that these comparisons needed to be made more systematically and in ways that stressed differences as well as parallels. The form our book came to take, as worked out together, emerged primarily from my discussion of general themes of genocide at the end of my study of Nazi doctors. And the book's conceptual principles derive mostly from my earlier work. Markusen provided insight from his studies of various forms of governmental mass killing as well as specific analyses of American nuclear-weapons policies. We met frequently in both New York City and Wellfleet, Massachusetts, to discuss in detail the structure and content of each chapter, and many ideas developed in dialogue. I then wrote the chapter, and we continued our dialogue with each of my subsequent drafts.

We make use of a research method I have developed over the years for the psychological study of contemporary or recent historical events. It is influenced by the work of Erik Erikson, who was the first to combine a depth-psychological approach with full intellectual immersion into the historical era studied. While Erikson's approach focused on the great person in history, mine centers on *shared themes,* on psychological characteristics of a particular group of people centrally involved with significant historical forces of their era.

Thus, an early study dealt with Chinese and Western groups exposed to "thought reform" (or "brainwashing"), a problem I viewed as by no means exclusively Chinese but related to wider tendencies toward absolutism or "ideological totalism" in our time. Similarly, I related my work on Hiroshima to psychological issues surrounding worldwide nuclear threat, and at the end of the study compared Hiroshima survivors and those of Nazi camps. My work with Vietnam veterans had to do not only with their war but with a person's psychological capacity, upon confronting death, to undergo significant change in the direction of renunciation of violence. And my study of Nazi doctors suggested the extent to which certain psychological mechanisms, notably that of "doubling," could be called forth by ordinary people in the service of evil.

For all of these studies, I conducted extensive interviews, as a way of getting directly at the mind-sets of the people involved, of learning (in Isaiah Berlin's phrase) "what it must have been like [for them] to think, feel, act." I obtained an empirical body of data from which I could draw the shared themes in question, and then raised further questions about the social and historical significance of these shared psychological themes.

I also made use of interviews in the present study, in this case with scientists who have done weapons work, nuclear strategists, and retired military officers of high rank. I interviewed six former strategists, two of whom had been presidential advisers, and four of whom were scientists as well; six physicists who had been involved with weapons work; and three retired admirals. Beyond what they revealed about psychological involvement with nuclear weapons, these interviews raised larger psychological and moral questions that Markusen and I could further explore.

Some readers will be offended by the use of a Nazi model, however we qualify that use and emphasize "disanalogies" as well as analogies. I well understand that sentiment. The Nazis, after all, probably came as close as any group in history to something on the order of naked evil. But that does not mean that they have nothing to tell the rest of us. Having immersed myself, over the past three decades, in a number of highly destructive events, I am convinced that we must confront this dimension of the human psychological and historical repertoire.

The approach is a hopeful one. It assumes that such intellectual and moral confrontation can help open the way to alternative possibilities in the direction of human realization. Eric Markusen and I carried out the work described in this volume in precisely that spirit of hope.

Acknowledgments

DIFFICULT JOURNEYS require good companions. We had invaluable discussions with Charles Strozier, Jerome Bruner, Ron Bee, and Betty Jean Lifton, all of whom read the manuscript and made suggestions that were sensitive and important. Henry Bienen was a wonderful intellectual host at Princeton for the Lewis Lectures. Richard Falk, as always, contributed much to the dialogue, as did Kent Lee. We also benefited greatly from many exchanges at meetings of the Wellfleet Psychohistory Group.

Loving support was offered throughout the work by our families—Betty Jean, Kenneth, and Natasha Lifton, and Randi and Maria Markusen.

At Basic Books, we received enthusiastic support and editorial guidance from Martin Kessler and Jo Ann Miller, extraordinary manuscript editing from Phoebe Hoss, and valuable additional help from Suzanne Wagner and Michael Wilde. Lucy Silva prepared the manuscript and contributed to the work in more ways than we can describe.

Chapter 1

"If Deterrence Fails": Confronting Nuclear Entrapment

> Once upon a time it happened to my people, and now it happens to all people. And suddenly I said to myself, maybe the whole world, strangely, has turned Jewish. Everybody lives now facing the unknown. We are all, in a way, helpless.
>
> —Elie Wiesel

THIS IS a book about the threat nuclear weapons pose to the human future, about the cast of mind that created and maintains the threat, and about an alternative, hopeful direction. In its exploration of the sequence from a genocidal mentality to a species mentality, the book first confronts the general nature of nuclear entrapment and then seeks insight from a major genocide that has already taken place.

*The sources for all quotations and research findings can be found in the notes keyed to the individual text page and beginning on page 281.

Ultimate Absurdity

As we enter the last decade of this century, almost everybody is aware that nuclear weapons pose unprecedented peril. Even the governments of the two superpowers, long behind their people on such matters, have agreed that there can be "no winners" in a nuclear war, and seem to be moving toward unprecedented cooperation. And both express support for the liberating revolutions taking place before our eyes in most of Eastern Europe. Yet the weapons remain dangerously in place because of a mode of thought that is considerably less understood, a set of attitudes and policies that can be called nuclear absurdity.

The absurdity consists of our detailed arrangements, in concert with the Soviet Union, for our extinction and theirs. In the name of national security, we and they threaten actions that could destroy the world. The absurdity is a matter not of a philosophical stance but rather of deep unreason and loss of ethical bearings in maintaining a situation of ultimate danger.

The term *deterrence,* central to nuclear discourse, is the basis of a fundamental confusion. Deterrence has two very different meanings—as a word, and as a body of theory and policy specific to nuclear weapons. The original verb, *to deter,* literally means "to frighten from" or to restrain by fear. From the time of the sixteenth century, the word has been associated with legal policy, with the idea of imposing strong punishments in order to prevent evil or criminal behavior. To be sure, there was a longstanding military tradition of maintaining sufficient strength to discourage or prevent one's enemy from attacking, as in Theodore Roosevelt's famous use of the adage "Speak softly and carry a big stick." But deterrence as an elaborated military policy took shape mainly with nuclear weapons.

For instance, when John Foster Dulles, secretary of state under Eisenhower, announced the American deterrence policy of the early 1950s, he drew an analogy to the legal arrangements of local communities "to punish any who break in and steal." The analogy has been shown to be misleading: there is no overall world legal system to establish, and limit the violence of, the "punishment." Rather, an assumed transgression could lead to a world-destroying punishment—the entire process dependent upon psychological signals and interpretations (see chapter 7).

The United States and the Soviet Union have constructed vast genocidal systems, which they justify by the claim of "deterrence." A genocidal system is not a matter of a particular weapons structure or strategic concept so much as an overall constellation of men, weapons, and war-fighting plans which, if implemented, could end human civilization in minutes and the greater part of human life on the planet within days or even hours. Unlike any previous weapons or natural disasters, nuclear weapons could destroy much of the earth's animal and plant life as well, whether by the effects of the explosions, by the subsequent deadly radiation, or by creating a "nuclear winter" brought about by changes in the earth's climate owing to debris in the atmosphere which would block out the sun's rays. This genocidal system, then, could mean terminal genocide—recently labeled "omnicide," or the destruction of all life.

For the "credibility," or believability, of deterrence policy, as its proponents emphasize, requires *genuine willingness to use the weapons* under certain conditions, such as actual or imminent enemy attack. Hence, deterrence policy gives rise not only to a genocidal system but to a "genocidal mentality," which can be defined as a mind-set that includes individual and collective willingness to produce, deploy, and, according to certain standards of necessity, use weapons known to destroy entire human populations—millions, or tens or hundreds of millions, of people. And that genocidal mentality can become bound up with the institutional arrangements necessary for the genocidal act.

Deterrence policy also requires that we constantly "modernize" the genocidal system by means of "new generations" of nuclear weapons and equally new strategic plans for their potential use. Even with greatly improved relations with the Soviet Union and much official talk on both sides of extensive arms control (late 1989), there are at the same time reports of improved weapons "so devastating that they could penetrate the deepest underground [Soviet] bunkers," combined with "calls for advanced new Stealth

reconnaissance planes capable of flying more than four times the
speed of sound to ferret out critical Soviet targets, including mobile missiles." We seem as entrapped as Sisyphus in his perpetual,
vain endeavor to push a heavy rock to the top of a steep hill. At
the top of our steep hill, never quite reachable, is genuine "national security" in the nuclear age. Thus, George Kennan speaks
of our

> piling weapon upon weapon, missile upon missile, new levels of de-
> structiveness upon old ones . . . helplessly, almost involuntarily: like
> the victims of some sort of hypnotism, like men in a dream, like lem-
> mings heading for the sea, like the children of Hamelin marching
> blindly along beside their Pied Piper. And the result is that today we
> have achieved, we and the Russians together . . . levels of redundancy
> of such grotesque dimensions as to defy rational understanding.

Kennan conveys the blindly compulsive way in which we have
sought safety from the weapons and at the same time avoided
taking in what the weapons would do when used. Our difficulty is
that we cannot or will not (in Martin Buber's phrase) "imagine the
real." That deficiency in imagination is reflected in the bland circumlocution "if deterrence fails . . ." One need only contrast the
innocuous implication of the phrase (that if one thing fails, we try
something else and, in one way or another, manage) with what
would actually result: millions of incinerated human bodies surrounded by rubble. Moreover, as General Brent Scowcroft, a leading authority on national security, has pointed out, "Deterrence is
a very ambiguous notion. It cannot be demonstrated unless it fails,
in which case you knew it was not there." To which we would add
that if deterrence (as prevention) fails, it will be because of deterrence (as policy),
Nuclear absurdity becomes eerily manifest in the dangerous
contradictions surrounding what is called "command and control," the arrangements for maintaining communications and for
conveying orders in the event of war or near-war crisis, including
the behavior of the president as commander in chief. This is, so
to speak, the final common pathway of the genocidal system. But
simply putting the command-and-control mechanism on alert—
that is, systematically "preparing for" nuclear emergency—can

send the very signals to one's adversary that will bring on that emergency. For, as one observer put it, dangerous "brinkmanship" is not just rhetoric but "an inherent feature of opposing strategic forces that are programmed for first strikes."

Each American president since the Second World War has had to be briefed about his role as the ultimate decision maker in a nuclear crisis. But each has been in some way odd or inadequate—whether having "an almost morbid" interest in the process (Carter), showing extreme avoidance as "the great neglecter" (Nixon), or acting "like an automaton" and "saying things like, 'What do I do now? Do I push the button?' " (Reagan). All too appropriate here is George Kennan's 1981 admonition to superpower leaders: "You are mortal men. You are capable of error. You have no right to hold in your hands—there is no one wise enough and strong enough to hold in his hands—destructive powers sufficient to put an end to civilized life on a great portion of our planet. No one should wish to hold such powers."

A central danger of command and control is the inevitable emphasis on speed—on launching one's weapons before they are destroyed on the ground. That emphasis, in turn, creates increasing reliance on technology that approaches "launch on warning," or all-out retaliation in response to a warning signal of nuclear attack. A writer on nuclear issues, Daniel Ford, was struck by the absurdity of command and control, its grossly inadequate telephone arrangements recalling the scene in the 1964 film *Dr. Strangelove* in which Peter Sellers (as Captain Mandrake), desperate to contact the Pentagon to advise it to recall U.S. nuclear bombers on their way to Russia, has to break into a Coca-Cola machine to get the necessary coins. Our helplessness before our own technology of destruction, caricatured in that scene, was more or less confirmed by the highest authority on the U.S. command system, Air Force Lieutenant General Robert Herres, when he spoke of "the so-called hair-trigger posture": "The technology put us in this posture. We don't like it at all." Whether we like it or not, that posture includes arrangements for firing the weapons in the absence of anyone surviving at central command so that "the decapitated United States and Soviet military establishments would be reduced to the status of pea-brained dinosaurs."

In 1960, Herman Kahn wrote of a hypothetical "Doomsday Machine": that is, "a device whose only function is to destroy all human life," which it could do by means of a computer programmed "so that if, say, five nuclear bombs exploded over the United States, the device would be triggered and the earth destroyed." Even Kahn, no opponent of nuclear weapons, ultimately rejected the Doomsday Machine because it was not sufficiently controllable and killed too many people too automatically. He also doubted whether NATO or the United States or the Soviet Union would be willing to spend billions of dollars "to give a few individuals this particular kind of life and death power over the entire world." Here Kahn was wrong. The parties involved have been willing to do just that: we have the equivalent of a Doomsday Machine in place right now. The claim could be made that its function is not *only* "to destroy all human life," since the weapons are supposed to serve deterrence—but, then, so was Kahn's original, then hypothetical, Doomsday Machine.

At the heart of nuclear war planning is ignorance and fantasy. As a former member of the Joint Chiefs of Staff stated, "Nobody can come up with any realistic situation as to what would happen during a nuclear war. We are groping in the unknown." Strategists and decision makers have created a surreal universe in which warfighting scenarios give rise to elaborate regulations concerning "emergency action messages" in the midst of a nuclear holocaust, including the status and available numbers of nuclear weapons and the relaying of "significant event[s] or incident[s]"; accompanying civil defense plans include careful arrangements for the forwarding of mail; and the weapons continue to proliferate beyond any possible advantage or use. There is a special, self-enclosed logic to it all—the logic of social madness.

Despite great hopes for an improved relationship between the United States and the Soviet Union, the danger of our weapons arrangements persists as both countries continue to devote prodigious resources to the improvement of nuclear weapons and to the militarization and nuclearization of space. The danger expands, moreover, as the weapons proliferate to other countries with no clear limits in view. Great Britain, France, and the People's Republic of China acknowledge their possession of usable nuclear weapons; India, Pakistan, South Africa, and Israel either possess weapons or could quickly produce them; and Brazil and Argentina will soon reach that capacity. Third World countries are racing to acquire both ballistic missiles to "deliver" conventional, chemical, or nuclear warheads (about twenty of these countries are thought to possess them now); and "the poor man's nuclear weapons," the term applied to chemical weapons because of their relative cheapness (it is believed that somewhere between fourteen and twenty nations throughout the world have chemical arsenals). There is the added specter of bacteriological weapons, also easy to acquire and, although difficult to control, as lethal as nuclear weapons. Finally, what is called "conventional" weaponry is proliferating, in advanced forms, throughout the First, the Second, and the Third worlds.

Much attention now shifts, and with good reason, to the Third World, where relatively unstable governments are acquiring powerful weaponry. Such recognition all too often assumes that the superpowers are "stable" and no longer the problem. The truth is that, with arsenals approaching fifty thousand weapons, they remain very much the hub of the problem, and their example energizes all other weapons races, especially in the Third World. Thus, any conflict anywhere holds the potential of ending in the destruction of the human species.

A grave danger is the potential loss of control over the enormous worldwide man-weapons constellation. One authority, referring most specifically to the command-and-control apparatus, speaks of "systems of incomprehensible complexity" and adds, "Our intuitive, gut reaction is that the operation of anything so large and complicated must be dangerously unstable." Or, as he goes on to state, "The war systems of the United States and the Soviet Union are now so jumpy and apprehensive, so quick and potentially incontinent in response, so convinced that they know what must be done, that they have the capacity to leap from crisis to war all by themselves. Such a war would be 'accidental' only in the sense that it was not what the belligerents 'wanted.'" "The mechanism does not perform as expected; the slave will not obey," is the way a general student of technology puts it in referring specifically to the command-and-control system.

Herbert York, one of America's most experienced weapons makers and arms control advocates, directly describes, in his *Race to Oblivion,* two "absurd situations" in regard to our weaponry: The first is that, although our military power has been steadily increasing, "at the same time our national security has been rapidly and inexorably decreasing"; and the same thing is happening to the Soviet Union. And the second,

> not yet so widely recognized[,] . . . lies in the fact that in the United States the power to decide whether or not doomsday has arrived is in the process of passing from statesmen and politicians to lower-level officers and technicians and, eventually, to machines.
>
> Thus, we seem to be heading for a state of affairs in which the determination . . . will be made either by an automatic device designed for the purpose or by a pre-programmed President who, whether he knows it or not, will be carrying out orders written years before by some operations analyst. Such a situation must be called the ultimate absurdity.

That "ultimate absurdity" is also reflected in a saying among strategists and commentators: "Nobody believes it [the possibility of carrying out arrangements for fighting and winning a nuclear war] but the system believes it."

Learning from Nazi Genocide

> I say with a deep consciousness of these words that
> Trident* is the Auschwitz of Puget Sound.
>   —ARCHBISHOP RAYMOND G. HUNTHAUSEN

If we are to grasp what is really involved in the genocidal mentality, we would do well to look at another historical situation in which it led to actual genocide. We might then be in a better position to take steps to prevent that outcome.

Among modern genocides—recently in Cambodia, Africa, and

*The name of both the base and the nuclear submarines; each of the latter carries the destructive equivalent of 2,040 Hiroshima bombs.

the Indian subcontinent, as well as earlier in Turkey and the Soviet Union—the one from which we have most to learn is that of the Nazis during the fifth decade of the twentieth century. Nazi genocide is particularly relevant to us as it was perpetrated by an advanced Western Christian nation and because it was linked with the beginnings of nuclear threat during the Second World War.

Among the writers, scientists, and religious leaders who have suggested parallels between the Holocaust and nuclear danger, consider Samuel Pisar's deeply troubled commentary on the production of weapons throughout the world:

> Everything seems poised for the apocalypse. It is as if an Auschwitz fever has taken hold of mankind, pushing it irresistibly toward the precipice, an Auschwitz ideology, characterized by rapid devaluation of the ultimate human right—the right to life. The combination of high technology and high brutality, which I had seen practiced on a pilot scale not so long ago, shows that man is quite capable of resorting to both the ideological premises and the scientific means for wholesale annihilation.

And the physicist I. I. Rabi ("And now we have the nations lined up, like those prisoners of Auschwitz, going into the ovens, and waiting for the ovens to be perfected, made more efficient") as well as Elie Wiesel and the Catholic archbishop of Seattle (see the epigraphs on pages 1 and 8).

All spoke from considered reflection, three from direct knowledge: Wiesel and Pisar are Auschwitz survivors, and Rabi was one of the physicists who contributed to the work at Los Alamos on the atomic bomb. None of these commentators would equate the Nazi Holocaust with nuclear threat; nor would we. But we, and they, believe that in these very different historical situations there are certain parallels having to do with levels of destruction and casts of mind.

It is neither easy nor pleasant to invoke the Nazis for comparison with groups within our own democratic society. Our image of the Nazis tends to be that of thugs and murderers, an image they did much to earn. But students of Nazi genocide have long stressed what recent work on the Nazi doctors has confirmed: namely, that ordinary Germans became involved in killing, people who had previously shown no particular inclination toward violence. These findings are especially troubling because they bring the Nazis closer to the rest of us. We are much more comfortable viewing them as a separate tribe of demons. But the painful truth is that they are more part of our century, more involved in historical and psychological questions that still bedevil us, than we have wished to acknowledge. In our present genocidal predicament, responsibility lies in seeking to draw from the Nazi project lessons that might head off the ultimate nuclear Auschwitz.

To use the Nazis comparatively in this manner is in no way to deny the uniqueness of their Holocaust. No other historical genocide has been so systematically carried out against an entire people, even to the attempt to round up Jews from virtually all over the world in order to kill them. We therefore reject the "revisionist" position of some German historians to the effect that the Holocaust is just one of the many examples of cruelty that dominate human history, and should be given no special emphasis. We would, in fact, insist upon stressing differences or "disanalogies" between the Nazi and the nuclear situations. As Charles S. Maier explains, while exploring similar questions, "Comparison is a dual process that scrutinizes two or more systems to learn what elements they have in common, and what elements distinguish them. It does not assert identity; it does not deny unique components."

The most fundamental difference, of course, is that Nazi mass killing is a matter of historical record, so that (as one observer put it) even if nuclear-weapons arrangements are viewed as "an Auschwitz waiting to happen, no one is being gassed or cremated." The distinction is between the actual and the potential. Another fundamental difference has to do with intent. The Nazis killed designated victims—primarily Jews, but also Gypsies, Poles, Russians, mental patients, and homosexuals. In contrast, the stated nuclear intent is to prevent war, and the killing would take place only with a failure of that structure of deterrence. Still another difference is the reality of a dangerous adversary: the Jews posed no threat to the Nazis, but the Soviets pose a real military threat to us. And many more differences would emerge with a fuller exploration of the complexities of German history. There is a final, sobering difference having to do with victimizers and victims. There was a clear-cut distinction between the Nazis themselves as perpetrators and those they decided to kill. In the nuclear case, should the weapons be used, there would be no such distinction: everybody would become a victim. At Nuremberg, after the Second World War, there was an attempt to hold individuals and groups accountable for their role in killing. There can be no nuclear Nuremberg; hope lies only in establishing responsibility for genocide *prior* to its occurring—responsibility for participating in a genocidal system and a genocidal process.

When one probes these differences more carefully, as we shall do in later chapters, they turn out to be far from absolute. Concerning potential versus actual, a leading authority has argued that a nuclear genocide has already occurred with the bombings of Hiroshima and Nagasaki; and others have claimed that the larger nuclear genocide has also begun via our planning for it because " 'an' act . . . like omnicide . . . is begun in the preparations of thousands." And while the distinction in terms of adversary definitely holds, nuclear-weapons advocates have frequently exaggerated if not falsified the threatening postures of the Soviet Union. Even the difference concerning victimizers and victims can be qualified in relation to Hitler's final "scorched earth" orders for Germany, which, if carried out, would have been a form of self-genocide.

But these basic differences between the Nazi and the nuclear situations should nonetheless be kept constantly in mind. One can then focus on the issue of how comparison, if it has "a plausible basis in fact" and goes "beyond mere taxonomy," can "add . . . to knowledge" and "offer perspectives that the single case might not suggest . . . [and] help reveal a wider historical process at work." Such comparison can enable the observer "to discern a common causal mechanism otherwise unrevealed—to diagnose, in a sense, a human illness." Hence, in deriving principles of behavior from a specific historical event, that of Nazi genocide, we do not question the specificity of that event. What we do claim is that different historical events can include parallel features and related forms of behavior. It is because the Nazis were so extreme that they become useful in epitomizing certain destructive patterns that may operate—less visibly, more subtly—in nuclear weapons policies.

It was the Nazis who provided the impetus for the legal naming of a very old crime. The word *genocide* was coined (from the Greek *genos,* "race, tribe," and the Latin *cide,* "killing") in 1944, and defined by the United Nations General Assembly in 1946 as "a denial of the right of existence of entire human groups." The Convention on Genocide, passed by the U.N. General Assembly in 1948, and finally approved by the United States Congress in 1988, associated the concept with killing, seriously harming, or interfering with the life continuity of "a national, ethnical, racial or religious group." The distinguished legal scholar Raphael Lemkin fought hard to establish the concept. He spoke of it as "an old practice in its modern development," and clearly meant the principle to apply everywhere. We believe that our efforts here to explore common patterns in Nazi genocide and potential nuclear genocide are in the spirit of Lemkin's work.

One such common theme is that of a genocidal ideology: in the case of the Nazis, the ideology of racism or of the "biomedical vision" (the idea that a cure for the sickness of the Nordic race lies in destroying the infecting agent—namely, the Jews); and in the case of the weapons, the ideology of nuclearism, the exaggerated embrace of the weapons, and dependency on them for security, peace, and something close to salvation. Both ideologies were embraced as a resolution or "cure" for a severe historical trauma: the humiliating defeat in the First World War in the case of the Nazis, and the appearance of atomic weapons and their use in Hiroshima and Nagasaki in the nuclear case (see chapter 3). Both of these ideologies, moreover, include near worship of science and technology and the claim of breakthrough in these areas (Nazi versions of biology and technocratic attitudes of nuclear strategists [see chapter 4]). Another parallel lies in the overall participation of professionals in the genocidal system: for example, physicians and biologists in the Nazi case, and physicists and strategists in the nuclear (see chapter 5). And still another parallel is the vast societal involvement in a genocidal project, creating dangerous forms of bureaucratic momentum that can carry one across the threshold into genocide—as happened in the Nazi case, and threatens to happen in the nuclear situation (see chapter 6).

In both cases, these tendencies create a compelling narrative, one focusing on heightened collective life rather than on mass killing. The narrative takes on heroic dimensions, and those who play leading roles in it can come to wear the mantle of the individual hero. It becomes the master narrative for those in power and for many others, to the extent that alternative views can find little expression.

Both Nazi and nuclear narratives are crucially sustained by certain psychological mechanisms that protect individual people from inwardly experiencing the harmful effects, immediate or potential, of their own actions on others. These mechanisms, all of which blunt human feelings, include dissociation or splitting, psychic numbing, brutalization, and doubling. "Dissociation," or "splitting," is the separation of a portion of the mind from the whole, so that each portion may act in some degree separately from the other. "Psychic numbing" is a form of dissociation characterized by the diminished capacity or inclination to feel, and usually includes separation of thought from feeling. "Doubling" carries the dissociative process still further with the formation of a functional second self, related to but more or less autonomous from the prior self. When numbing or doubling enables one, with relatively little psychological cost, to engage in sustained actions that cause harm to others, we may speak of "brutalization."

Nazi doctors, for instance, required extreme forms of psychic numbing to avoid experiencing the pain of their victims. As the doctors, over time, participated in killing, they underwent progressive brutalization. That brutalization could also be enhanced by their experience of doubling: the formation of an "Auschwitz self" adapted to the murderous work of that environment, while making use of their prior self in periodic visits with wives and children. Various bureaucratic procedures, by divesting the individual of a sense of responsibility for destructive collective behavior, could greatly enhance numbing and doubling as well as brutalization. In the nuclear case, the domination of technology makes the numbing all the easier. Patterns of doubling are observable in certain physicists and strategists, including the formation of a "nuclear-weapons self," but in a much less extreme psychological form than in the Nazi situation. They also undergo what could be called "silent technological brutalization," an increasing capacity to take actions that could result in enormous destruction, the entire process so distanced by the technology that one must assert one's moral imagination to reconnect cause and effect. From that definition, the policy of nuclear deterrence is a form of silent brutalization and depends upon various forms of dissociation in those who promulgate it (see chapter 7).

These dissociative tendencies—numbing and doubling and brutalization—are part of the mind's repertoire. Likely to be called forth in connection with any expression of cruelty, they are certainly required for any form of mass killing or genocide. That is why the historian Charles S. Maier, when reflecting on the Holocaust, suggests that human beings may function with "a fragmented self," and that "the psychologist and moralist as well as the historian must deal with the issue of how men and women can be apparently normal and yet killers."

A Species Future

R. G. Collingwood, the British philosopher of history, declared that "the chief business of twentieth-century philosophy is to reckon with twentieth-century history." We would claim that the same is true of twentieth-century psychology, with the added requirement that we begin to anticipate twenty-first-century history as well. We must bring what Isaiah Berlin spoke of as "imaginative insight" to bear on the "possible world" of the future. For there is still time to reverse the genocidal mentality of those promoting the nuclear project *once we recognize it clearly.*

There is a generational discrepancy here. People born after the development of nuclear weapons have never known a world from which these were absent. The weapons come to be viewed as more or less given, and may even be perceived psychologically as something close to elements of nature. It then may become as difficult to imagine getting rid of them as it is to imagine, say, getting rid of a river or a mountain. Yet that sense of resigned acceptance of the weapons has also shown itself to be increasingly vulnerable to truths about what the weapons are and do. Those truths are painful but they unite the generations in reasoned evaluation and in the capacity to act.

When one recognizes the nature of our present threat—that it is not primarily to a particular group or nation but to the human species itself—one's relationship to enemy nations and people radically changes. One becomes aware of the principle of shared fate. An American can say to an individual Soviet counterpart, "If you die, I die"—who can respond in turn, "If I survive, you survive." As that awareness takes shape, enemies no less than friends feel compelled to collaborate on behalf of their common survival. Each takes on a measure of species consciousness. The sense of self—one's way of symbolizing one's own organism—becomes bound up with every other self on the planet. One can then begin to identify oneself with the rest of humankind—to give shape to a species self (see chapter 9). That is what Lewis Mumford tried to tell us more than three decades ago:

> Man's principle task today is to create a new self, adequate to command the forces that now operate so aimlessly and yet so compulsively. This self will necessarily take as its province the entire world, known and knowable, and will seek, not to impose a mechanical uniformity, but to bring about an organic unity, based upon the fullest utilization of the varied resources that both nature and history have revealed to modern man . . . a new vision of a self capable of understanding and cooperating with the whole.

Here Mumford was referring to a species self, and to the beginnings of species politics and species ethics. But in order to enhance that shift, we must first take a hard look at the evolution of the genocidal mentality.

Chapter 2

The Evolving Genocidal Mentality

> You press a button and death flies down. . . . How can there be writhing, mangled bodies? . . . It is like listening to a radio account of a battle on the other side of the earth. It is too far away, too separated to hold reality.
>
> —CHARLES LINDBERGH

HOW HAVE we come to this readiness to destroy ourselves and our species? Mind-sets have histories, and the history of this one includes struggles with the twentieth-century emergence of, first, aviation technology, then atomic weaponry, and finally the hydrogen bomb. From the American side, that history can be traced in relation to attitudes and policies of the presidential administrations from the time of the Second World War to the present. Faced with formidable problems and threats, kind and intelligent men were subject to "an accretion of large fears, thoughtless assumptions, and incremental decisions"; and the emerging mentality came to be associated with necessity, loyalty, and psychological health.

The Brutalizing Power of Technology

> Never viewed solely as a weapon, the airplane was
> the instrument of flight, of a whole new dimension
> in human activity. Therefore it was uniquely capa-
> ble of stimulating fantasies of peacetime possibili-
> ties for lifting worldly burdens, transforming man's
> sense of time and space, transcending geography,
> knitting together nations and peoples, releasing
> humankind from its biological limits. Flight also
> resonated with the deepest impulses and symbols
> of religious and particularly Christian mythology—
> nothing less than Christ's ascension. Its realization,
> then, served as a powerful metaphor for heavenly
> aspirations and even, among the literal-minded, as
> the palpable vehicle for achieving them.
> —MICHAEL S. SHERRY

We have mentioned the relationship between brutalization and
numbing, and the silent brutalization that can be associated with
weapons of high technology. If airmen themselves were "too far
away, too separated" from "writhing, mangled bodies" to "hold
reality," that process held even less reality for those making decisions from the ground. The people involved, though by no means
inherently brutal or bloodthirsty, were in the grip of a rationale for
the weapons' use, a rationale that allowed them to separate themselves emotionally from the human consequences of that use—as
in the practice of strategic bombing which set the stage for the use
of atomic weapons.

The Strategic Bombing of the Second World War

Strategic bombing is part of an overall policy or strategy, such as
destroying the enemy's industrial capacity or general morale, as
opposed to *tactical bombing* employed as part of an immediate battle
or effort to defeat an enemy force or take a city. In practice, strategic bombing involved the systematic killing of hundreds of thousands of people, the overwhelming majority of whom were non-
combatants.

The area bombing of civilians had begun almost with the discovery of the airplane at the turn of the century, strategic bombing having been attempted even with the primitive flying machines of the First World War.* The results were inconclusive: but given the horrors of ground fighting, air power came to be seen as *not only a technical but a moral advance.* It was viewed as "a merciful substitute for the hell of the trenches" and even, at least to many observers, as an escape from, rather than an extension of, the slaughter of modern war. As the ranks of the air visionaries increased (to include Billy Mitchell in the United States and Basil H. Liddell Hart and Hugh Trenchard in England), all came to stress the potential of air warfare to demoralize populations together with its relative humanity.

"Of all the belligerents of World War II," a leading American historian of area bombing tells us, "only Great Britain and the United States had made a strong commitment to the strategic air offensive *before* the conflict started, and only they were able to mount and sustain such offensives once the war began" (italics added). In spite of their favorable response to Franklin Roosevelt's appeal of 1 September 1939 to all belligerents in the Second World War to avoid the bombing of civilians, the British, with Trenchard now their leading air theorist, clearly had contingency plans for implementing strategic bombing. For the British, as later for the Americans, there was a "piecemeal evolution of air war," as it became possible for the Allies to bomb German cities.

There was an attempt, especially on the part of the Americans, to maintain a concept of "precision bombing"—aiming bombs not randomly, but at specific military and industrial targets—a concept that proved to be extremely difficult to realize. Moreover, daytime raids, necessary for even a modicum of precision, resulted in devastating losses of planes and airmen. America gradually adopted the policy of area bombing it had initially resisted upon joining the European air offensive in mid-1942; earlier policies of discrimination or precision in targeting gave way to "blind" bombing by means of radar, which "depended for effectiveness upon drenching an area with bombs." Yet the concept of precision could serve as a justification for strategic bombing.

*As early as 1910, Giulio Douhet, the Italian air-warfare visionary, had declared, "From above one can see well and from above one can strike easily."

Nazi evil did play an important part in the overall dynamic. In their early strategic bombing, the British saw themselves as retaliating for Nazi bombing of civilian populations—in Warsaw in late 1939, and in 1940 in Rotterdam, a London residential area, and the small city of Coventry. But it turned out that the Nazi air actions, cruel as they were, tended to be in support of ground operations or to result from communication confusions (both factors affected the bombing of Rotterdam), accidental (the London residential area), or as a form of limited Nazi reprisal (switching from military to civilian targets in raids over London, and the killing of five hundred civilians in Coventry). In the case of the British, however, there was a clear directive to Bomber Command in February 1942 that "the primary objective of your operations should now be focused on the morale of the enemy civil population and, in particular, of the industrial workers." But Churchill and other British leaders, in going ahead with this policy, were affected by their increasing sense of Nazi malignancy and threat (and the Germans were to employ, toward the end of the war, their own indiscriminate civilian-targeted weapons, the V-1 and V-2 rockets). There followed massive incendiary attacks on virtually all major German cities, culminating in the joint British and American attack on Dresden of 13 February 1945. Within that sequence, the "four furious assaults" on Hamburg in late July and early August 1943 had resulted in the first great firestorm of the war and in the abandonment of even a pretense of industrial targeting in the systematic bombing of residential areas, so that any destruction of factories was only "a bonus."

American theorists were ready to transfer these techniques to the Pacific war, long aware that, as Billy Mitchell had put it, "towns, . . . built largely of wood and paper, . . . form the greatest aerial targets the world has ever seen"; and "Incendiary projectiles would burn the cities to the ground in short order." "With an eye to the bombing of Japan," American experts studied the Hamburg firestorm carefully. There was some reluctance about area bombing on the part of the person first designated to be in charge, Brigadier General Haywood S. Hansell Jr.: he did it when ordered, but without great enthusiasm or effect. While it is uncertain whether this reluctance derived solely from his commitment to the doctrine of precision bombing, which he had helped to formulate, or from moral reservations as well, he was soon replaced by General Curtis E. LeMay, who clearly had no such reservations. Then, and subsequently, LeMay was to prove himself a zealous, even fanatic, advocate of air warfare in general and strategic bombing in particular. He also demonstrated tactical ingenuity in combining several new bombing methods—keeping the B-29s at low altitudes and making extensive use of incendiary bombs—to produce the success of the large Tokyo raid on 9 and 10 March 1945. But while that raid was LeMay's greatest Second World War moment, it cannot be understood as merely a product of his personal energies and style. It resulted, as the historian Michael Sherry tells us, from "pressures upon and within the Air Force to secure an incontrovertible success, and to do so before invasion closed the opportunity."

That bureaucratic pressure was supported by impulses for revenge upon the Japanese for their bombing of Pearl Harbor and extreme abuse of American prisoners of war. Also of great importance were ongoing technological advances involving bombers, targeting, and incendiary materials. These technological advances expanded what was operationally possible, so that "bombing forces, British or American, did what they could do best, not necessarily what it was best to do." Contributing greatly to the technological breakthroughs was early collaboration between Air Force authorities and civilian scientists and technologists, and a "civilian militarism" that involved professionals of all kinds. Military officer and civilian alike then found themselves "concentrating their energies on the perfection of technique rather than the enemy." Freeman Dyson, himself a talented physicist enlisted for the British war effort, noted later how "the more technological the war becomes, the more disastrously a bad choice of means will change a good cause into evil"; and how "science and technology . . . made evil anonymous."* The technological distancing of combat airmen, as Lindbergh observed, rendered the evil unreal (see the epigraph, page 16). Americans at home were, of course, radically removed

---

*Inadvertently, Dyson revealed how that kind of evil begets more evil, as he concluded that "once we had got ourselves into the business of bombing cities, we might as well do the job competently and get it over with."

from the bombing—a "distance . . . [that] not only enhanced its attractiveness in the immediate struggle, but blinded awareness of future perils"; while many high-ranking American and British air officers had similar "difficulty viewing the air war any more realistically than did the general public . . . especially when that war intensified in 1944."

In their drive to destroy an evil enemy in any way possible and to achieve vengeance for enemy cruelties, Allied planners preferred not to see the reality of the bombings of Dresden, Hamburg, and Tokyo. At Dresden at least 40,000 people were killed (estimates go as high as 250,000) in a city virtually undefended and teeming with civilian refugees; the firestorm was visible to bomber crews two hundred miles away.* At Hamburg, where it is also believed that more than 40,000 Germans died, people had a sense of "a world-ending event, one 'transcending all human experience and imagination . . . a speechless horror, one usually identified later only with the victims of atomic bombing.' " In the Tokyo raid, as many as 130,000 people were killed. Improved incendiary materials and techniques created an even more furious firestorm which was "rapaciously expansive, . . . a giant bellows to super heat the air to 1800 degrees Fahrenheit," so that "entire block fronts burst into flames before the main body of fire reached them." That American raid on Tokyo, a city with an extraordinary population density, caused greater devastation and killed more people than any single air attack in human history, including the atomic bombings of Hiroshima and Nagasaki.

The Atomic Bombings

For many military and political leaders, the atomic weapons were simply more efficient vehicles for the continuing policy of strategic bombing; by that time, "the distinction between 'military target' and 'city' had totally collapsed." In a sense, the brutalization during the war had already settled the matter: the Stimson

*The American novelist Kurt Vonnegut, a prisoner of war in Dresden at the time, described the city as having been made into "one big flame" that "ate everything organic, everything that would burn," so that when he and others came out of a shelter, "Dresden was like the moon . . . nothing but minerals. The stones were hot. Everything else in the neighborhood was dead."

Committee charged with making decisions about the use of the atomic weapon never really considered *not* using it. Indeed, such restraint during wartime would have been remarkable, though a good case has been made for the special opportunity for such restraint created by the Japanese surrender overtures already received. President Truman himself, enraged by the Japanese attack on Pearl Harbor and their extreme abuse of American prisoners of war, declared, "When you have to deal with a beast, you have to treat him as a beast." To be sure, many American decision makers genuinely believed that use of the weapons would save lives by ending the war quickly. There is also evidence that strengthening the American position vis-à-vis the Soviet Union was an important factor, as was the impulse to make use of something produced with such great cost and effort (and the difficulty of explaining to a congressional investigation committee why it was not used), as well as everyone's enormous curiosity to see whether the device would "work."

Was racism a factor in the American use of the atomic bomb on the Japanese? Work on the bomb had originated from specific fear that the Germans would make it first, and had continued as a secret portion of the general war effort. But the Japanese, more than the Germans, were seen as alien, as fanatical (in their willingness to die or kill for the emperor), and as murderously cruel (in their treatment of American prisoners of war). The Japanese were more readily dehumanized, viewed as "animals" or as "rats and apes," so that an atmosphere was created in which the chairman of the War Manpower Commission could favor "the extermination of the Japanese in toto." There were surely racist attitudes on the part of Americans—and, indeed, of the Japanese toward Americans as well; and there is no doubt that these influenced political and military attitudes and policies. But rather than serving as a primary reason for the bomb's use, they probably blended with the factors already mentioned in the irreversible momentum toward that use, a momentum fueled by the escalation of violence in general and by strategic bombing in particular.

American scientists involved in making the bomb at the Los Alamos laboratory or contributing to the process from the MET laboratory in Chicago or from Oak Ridge, Tennessee, thought little about mass killing or genocide; they mostly understood themselves as contributing their special knowledge to their country's need to defeat an evil and formidable enemy and end a terrible war.* Hovering over the entire Manhattan Project, however, was the possibility of the weapon's capacity for uncontrollable destruction. As early as 1942, during exchanges among the leading scientists prior to the formation of the Los Alamos laboratory, the Hungarian-born physicist Edward Teller raised the question whether there was danger of the bomb's igniting the nitrogen in the atmosphere or the hydrogen in the oceans sufficiently to burn up the world. Although Oppenheimer came to conclude, with considerable relief, that such an uncontrollable, even world-ending explosion was impossible, apprehension about it never entirely left the project. During the hours just preceding the Trinity test explosion of 16 July 1945, Fermi offered to take bets from scientific colleagues "on whether or not the bomb would ignite the atmosphere, and if so, whether it would merely destroy New Mexico or destroy the world." Fermi was undoubtedly engaging in gallows humor (either of those two outcomes would have allowed little prospect of collecting on a wager) that barely covered over anxiety about the weapon's potential for destruction. And although General Leslie Groves, the military head of the project, was "annoyed" with Fermi's behavior, he himself took precautions against unforeseen effects by ordering the preparation of a public statement explaining the sudden death of a large number of scientists and by informing the governor of New Mexico that he might have to declare martial law.

To be sure, there were expressions of resistance to this overall pattern of numbing: Chicago scientists petitioned against the bomb's use, and Assistant Secretary of the Navy Ralph Bard urged restraint in the form of a preliminary warning about the bomb in order to preserve America's standing "as a great humanitarian nation." But these were cries in the night.

*Such was the extent of wartime callousness among scientists, however, that in April 1943, the brilliant Italian physicist Enrico Fermi suggested to the project director, Robert Oppenheimer, that radioactive fission products might be used to poison the German food supply. Oppenheimer, after considering the proposal seriously and discussing it with others, came to the conclusion that strontium 90 "appears to offer the highest promise," but recommended holding back because "we should not attempt a plan unless we can poison food sufficient to kill a half a million men."

The consequences were unprecedented. The single Hiroshima bomb exploded, with a force equivalent to 20,000 tons of TNT, 1,800 feet in the air near the center of a flat city built mainly of wood. Totally destroyed were an area (including residential, commercial, industrial, and military structures) extending 3,000 meters (about 2 miles) in all directions; and 60,000 of 90,000 buildings within 5,000 meters (over 3 miles), an area roughly encompassing the city limits. Flash burns from the heat generated by the release of an enormous amount of radiant energy occurred at distances of more than 4,000 meters (2½ miles), depending upon the type and amount of clothing worn and the shielding afforded by immediate surroundings. Injuries from the blast, and from splintered glass and falling debris, occurred throughout the city and beyond.

The number of deaths, immediately and over a period of time, will probably never be fully known. Variously estimated from 63,000 to 240,000 or more, the official figure is usually given as 78,000; but the city of Hiroshima estimates 200,000—or between 25 percent and 50 percent of the city's daytime population. The enormous disparity is related to the extreme confusion that then existed, to differing methods of calculation, and to emotional influences at times affecting the estimators. What is clear is that from the moment of the explosion, *all of Hiroshima immediately became involved in the atomic disaster*—a disaster that had, and has, no end point. Delayed radiation effects, mainly in the form of leukemia and cancer, are still being recorded; and fears of these effects extend over a survivor's lifetime and, given the possibility of their hereditary transmission, into future generations. A sense of the totality of the experience never left survivors' minds, as they later reported: "I thought this was the end of Hiroshima, of Japan, of humankind"; "Hiroshima had disappeared. . . . That was mainly what I saw—Hiroshima just didn't exist"; and "My body seemed all black, everything seemed dark, dark all over. Then I thought, 'the world is ending.' " This devastation and sense of the end of the world resulted not from thousands of firebombs and hundreds of attacking bombers as in Tokyo, Dresden, and Hamburg; rather, it was one plane, one bomb, one city.

When American leaders learned about the effects of the atomic bombs on Hiroshima and Nagasaki, they were able, at least at first, to continue to view the use of the new weapon as merely a continuation of strategic bombing, or of what has been called "the science of city-burning." And this numbed view could be maintained by justifying the use of the bomb. That was done, almost lyrically and salvationally, by no less a figure than the British prime minister, Winston Churchill: "To avert a vast, indefinite butchery, to bring the war to an end, to give peace to the world, to lay healing hands upon its tortured peoples by a manifestation of overwhelming power at the cost of a few explosions, seemed, after all our toils and perils, a miracle of deliverance." Yet at the same time, Americans most closely involved (decision makers and scientists) and eventually everyone else came to recognize that this time things had gone much further, that strategic bombing had transcended itself. But that second view has never been fully able to displace the first, the sense of the bomb as another weapon in the strategic sequence, as a basis for policy.

The Hydrogen Bomb

> The fact that no limits exist to the destructiveness of this weapon makes its very existence and the knowledge of its construction a danger to humanity as a whole. It is necessarily an evil thing considered in any light.
> —ENRICO FERMI AND I. I. RABI

The destructive power of the hydrogen bomb was as revolutionary in respect to the atomic bomb as was the latter to conventional weaponry. The atomic bomb involves the release of energy through the *fission,* or splitting of the nuclei, of such heavy atoms as uranium or plutonium; it requires the existence of a certain amount—a *critical mass*—of fissionable material in order to produce the necessary "chain reaction" that creates the explosion. The hydrogen bomb, in contrast, produces energy from the joining together, or *fusion,* of lighter elements into heavier ones, by means of a reaction produced under very high temperatures.* No critical mass is required; and once the fusion has begun, the energy released promotes additional burning or explosive power so that "a fusion can . . . be made arbitrarily large, as a fire can be made arbitrarily large, by piling on more fuel." The hydrogen bomb was revolutionary in a moral sense as well. Now no one could plead ignorance of its effects. What the new weapon could do was known. The human power to destroy had now become, in the precise meanings of the words, *limitless, infinite.*

That was the essence of the report of 30 October 1949 issued by the General Advisory Committee (chaired by J. Robert Oppenheimer) to the Atomic Energy Commission. The report not only advised "strongly" against an all-out effort to make the hydrogen bomb, but also made clear that the new weapon would be "in a totally different category from an atomic bomb," with "no inherent limit in the destructive power that may be attained." It pointed out that the weapon's use "would involve a decision to slaughter a vast number of civilians," so that "a super bomb might become a weapon of genocide." Such warning voices as in the minority report signed by the physicists Enrico Fermi and I. I. Rabi (quoted in the epigraph to this section) could not be heard in the agitated atmosphere of the cold war. In their distrust of the Soviet Union, American decision makers had vividly in mind the Greek civil war of 1946–48, the communist coup in Czechoslovakia in 1948, the Berlin crisis of 1948–49, and the communist victory in China in 1949. Stalin replaced Hitler as a looming figure of evil. But the key event was the Soviet testing of an atomic bomb in the summer of 1949, which in turn intensified American fears that the Soviets could, before long, make their own "super" or hydrogen bomb. Four days before President Truman's decision to go ahead with the hydrogen bomb, Klaus Fuchs, who had been greatly involved in early British-American work on the super, was arrested for espionage. To suggest ethical considerations under those conditions was, as one participant in the deliberations put it, "like saying 'no' to a steamroller."

---

*A fusion, or hydrogen, bomb requires an optimal temperature of 1 billion degrees, though it can proceed at 10 million to 100 million degrees, the temperature required for the fissioning of plutonium.

With the development of the hydrogen bomb, the genocidal mentality took shape. That is, a weapon was being made that was known to be capable of destroying entire human populations—millions of people; and policies were formulated for its potential use. That mentality had, as we have seen, evolved slowly through the strategic bombing of the Second World War, to the making and using of atomic bombs in 1945, and to the progressive postwar weapons development (by December 1948, warplan Trojan called for dropping 133 atomic bombs on 70 Soviet cities in ways that would result in tens of millions of immediate deaths). But the commitment to the hydrogen bomb in the face of knowledge that it involved a completely new dimension of destruction—and at a time when there was no war but only fear of an enemy—was a quantum leap in this genocidal connection between mind and weapon. In the United States and the Soviet Union, which quickly plunged ahead with its own hydrogen bomb development, the genocidal mentality took shape in decision makers, weapons designers and strategists, and large portions of the general population. So powerful had become the forces shaping that mentality that to refuse it became an act of resistance.

Crude Deterrence versus Flexible Response

Over subsequent administrations and decades, the genocidal mentality has been extended, routinized, and translated into a series of nuclear postures that include war-fighting plans. These postures have taken on a certain rhythm that has sustained itself through all the shifts and changes in policies, administrations, secretaries of defense, and nuclear strategists. There is first the policy of crude retaliatory deterrence, of threatening the enemy nation with nuclear attacks on its most heavily populated areas, its largest cities, should it attempt to strike first with either nuclear or conventional weapons or assume a stance we could view as one of imminent attack. (Crude deterrence could include a policy of a "pre-emp-tive" first strike in response to perception of enemy preparation for attack, as revealed publicly by Curtis LeMay in 1957.) In the alternative, more "flexible" policy, adopted partly in revulsion from the very crudeness of the first stance, there is an attempt to focus potential nuclear war fighting more precisely on military targets, often the enemy's weapons, and generally on specific and limited areas. While this policy is seen as more "restrained," "ap-propriate," and "humane," it actually tends to make nuclear holo-caust more likely—more of a tactical consideration—and would produce casualties so enormous as to approach those of the seem-ingly crude policy. This second approach also tends to be based on the highly dubious assumption that both sides, were they able to do so, would carefully confine themselves to these focused, limited targets.

Assured, and Mutually Assured, Destruction

An example of the first posture of crude deterrence was the doctrine of "massive retaliation" developed during the Eisen-hower administration (1953–61) and articulated by Secretary of State John Foster Dulles. The United States would respond "in-stantly" and "massively" by "means and at places of our own choosing" to what was deemed threatening behavior by other na-tions anywhere in the world. The chairman of the Joint Chiefs of Staff, Admiral Richard Radford, made clear that the policy meant that "atomic weapons are . . . our primary forces," and that "nu-clear weapons, fission and fusion, will be used in the next major war." This policy was remarkable for its public declaration of a genocidal response, at least under certain conditions, as the official policy held out to the American public for its support. Massive retaliation, then, was massive brutalization. While planners had to be numbed in relation to the highly theoretical projections of such policies—to the paperwork of genocide—they could also have a certain crude awareness. Under Curtis LeMay, it was not unusual for high-ranking Air Force officers to express themselves in the language of male macho: "Goddammit . . . there is only one way to attack the Russians, and that's to hit them hard with everything we have and (at that point pounding his fist on the top of a huge Bible on an end table) knock their balls off!"

While there were also contingencies, under Eisenhower, for the use of smaller tactical nuclear weapons designed for battlefield use, "just exactly as you would use a bullet or anything else," it was not until the Kennedy-Johnson era (1961–69) that massive retaliation was fundamentally criticized in favor of Robert McNamara's policies of "flexible response" and "multiple options." This defense secretary's band of strategists, many of them from the influential RAND think tank, stressed "rational" use of the weapons, with gradations according to circumstances, or "controlled escalation." McNamara had been "stunned" when, during a military briefing at NORAD (North American Air Defense Command) held soon after his taking office, he had first "looked the subject of nuclear war down the throat": that plan would have killed 350,000,000 Russians, Chinese, and Eastern Europeans within hours, with lethal radiation enveloping not only "enemies" but neutral and friendly European countries as well. McNamara was soon urging President Kennedy to set up arrangements for preventing all this from happening, arrangements for restraint and a more measured response.

But McNamara came to realize that this more measured and flexible response meant unlimited demands by the military for weapons and targeting, and was consistent with the Air Force's inclination toward preparation for a first strike. So in 1963 he put through a "new" policy termed *assured destruction*—a policy that stressed deterrence with a capacity to wreak sufficient destruction on the enemy as to discourage any attack. After the transition from the radical crudeness of massive retaliation to the more refined "flexibility" (but even greater danger) of multiple options, McNamara brought us back to what was again essentially crude retaliation, though now presented as a little less crude than the original version. His eventual doctrine of assured destruction required the American capacity and—under certain circumstances, willingness—to destroy the Soviet Union as a nation by destroying at least half its industry and killing between 20 percent and 25 percent of its population. The acronym MAD (mutual assured destruction) was created by a RAND strategist, Donald Brennan, as a way of ridiculing the policy's lack of flexibility and its ostensible preference for "dead Russians" over "live Americans."

Throughout, the process of silent technological brutalization was bilateral, as demonstrated by the Cuban missile crisis of 1962. There was an escalation of risk all around: by the Soviets in bringing missiles into Cuba to create the immediate crisis; by the Americans in previously threatening to invade Cuba (which turned out to be a major reason for the Soviet action); by both superpowers during the six-day crisis following the American decision to apply a naval quarantine to prevent Soviet ships from bringing in additional missiles, and by the military moves and countermoves during that period until an agreement was made whereby Premier Nikita Khrushchev agreed to remove the missiles. These were actions of major powers risking the destruction of human civilization under claims of national danger and national security.

Aggressive Vulnerability

During the Nixon-Ford era (1969–76), there was a re-enactment of the crude–flexible–semi-crude deterrence policy sequence. By prefacing the McNamara legacy of "assured destruction" with the word "mutual," the acronym MAD could be "used . . . like a club" to denounce that policy. While critics—many of them from RAND or its offshoot, the Hudson Institute—minced no words in denouncing the doctrine as "a policy of genocide" which "rests on a form of warfare universally condemned since the Dark Ages—the mass killing of hostages"—once again their alternative was "flexibility" in targeting and in "limited" nuclear options and war fighting. And once again administration officials (notably James Schlesinger, secretary of defense) came to realize that this war-fighting strategy created incentives for unlimited weapons production beyond the capacity of the defense budget.

During this era was also a trend toward what could be called "aggressive vulnerability." Now the Soviets underwent a surge in weapons production and apparently sought no less a first-strike capacity than what the United States already possessed. The vulnerability, in the most fundamental sense, was real; but those experts aggressively articulating that vulnerability insisted on intensified nuclear-weapons development and stockpiling as a means of overcoming what could not be overcome. This era, then, was characterized by an aggressive pursuit of the illusion of security via ever-improved and expanding nuclear stockpiles together with a manifest awareness of the weapons' genocidal qualities. With that combination the genocidal mentality itself, while largely unacknowledged, moved closer to the surface.

Protracted Nuclear War and Ethnic Targeting

Most notable about the Carter administration (1977–80) was the sequence from deeply humane intent to draconian policies. In his inaugural address, President Jimmy Carter promised to "move this year toward our ultimate goal—the elimination of all nuclear weapons from this earth." Committed to immediate, deep cuts, he "astonished" the Joint Chiefs of Staff during a pre-inaugural briefing with the suggestion that we needed a retaliatory force of no more than 200 nuclear weapons. Yet in 1978 and 1979, Carter signed several presidential directives ordering preparations for the United States to fight, survive, and win not only a brief and decisive but also a "protracted" nuclear war. The task required elaborate buildups not only in weapons—including approval of the production of 200 MX missiles, widely considered to be as wasteful as they were dangerous—but in command-and-control structures.

During the Carter administration, there also emerged what has come to be known as *ethnic targeting.* The doctrine is best illustrated by a series of questions asked by Zbigniew Brzezinski, the national security adviser, while he and other high-ranking officials were receiving a military briefing. To Brzezinski's question "Where are the criteria for killing Russians?" the briefer, a bit puzzled, first gave the standard response to the effect that the policy is not to target "population per se," but that since Soviet workers tend to live close to the factories where they work, an attack would kill a large number of Soviet citizens, the estimate being about 113,000,000. Brzezinski retorted, "No, no, I mean *Russian* Russians." Brzezinski's point was that it was the ethnic Russians (or Great Russians) who essentially ran the Soviet Union, and who consequently were the main enemy—the group you had to "deter" or, if deterrence failed, the group you had to kill. The stunned briefer "felt that he was listening to the voice of 600 years of Polish history" (Brzezinski, Polish-born, is thought to harbor traditional Polish anti-Russian sentiments). But Brzezinski and others gave what they considered the practical argument that this kind of targeting could "speed the breakup of the Russian empire," since ethnic Russians are afraid of the antagonisms of non-Russian, mostly Asian, populations within the Soviet Union. In answer, an observer made the point that in the same way "the Russians might target white neighborhoods in a segregated American city . . . because whites are afraid of blacks."

Ethnic targeting has been called "genocide as a substitute for massive retaliation" and "would strike Europeans as behavior more typical of the defendants than the prosecutors at Nuremberg." In other words, ethnic targeting meets the precise definition of genocide because it singles out for destruction a specific group on the basis of its ethnic background.

The whole issue reveals in a special way the lethal paradoxes of our nuclear-weapons stances. An act that is most concretely genocidal—ethnic targeting—turns out to kill fewer people than would the more diffuse targeting in the war-fighting plans associated with traditional policies of assured destruction. And the deadly hypocrisy of the latter, more "ordinary" policy is revealed in the reply initially given to Brzezinski by the briefer: "It is a kind of unwritten rule among the strategic planners that one does not target 'population per se' "—which is "another circumlocution characteristic of the Pentagon, like the phrase 'if deterrence fails.' " Even as cities are targeted, policy makers need to imply that their focus is on military targets.

Carter had become a victim of, among other things, the powerful image of vulnerability. To be sure, he was also affected by aggressive Soviet behavior in weapons development and by the Soviet invasion of Afghanistan. But ultimately, as one commentator put it, "the logic of the situation" turned him around, that situation being the preoccupation with vulnerability and the self-defeating struggle against it. This aggressive focus on vulnerability, especially by strategists from RAND and related think tanks, became known as the "new orthodoxy" in nuclear strategy.

In 1976, out of the vulnerability issue had emerged the Committee on Present Danger, which was to become an even greater force in the subsequent Reagan administration. The message of this group, buttressed by a study made by a special Central Intelligence Agency "B-team" (called in by George Bush, the new CIA director, to re-examine prior agency estimates), was that the Soviets think they can fight and win a nuclear war while we are permitting ourselves to become weak and vulnerable. We will have more to say in the next chapter about the part played by the institutionalization of the weapons-centered ideology of nuclearism, but here will note the extent to which an existing genocidal system and mentality have absorbed people in power who originally advocated humane antinuclear policies.

War Fighting and Peace-Mindedness

During the Reagan administration (1981–88), and in Reagan himself, there occurred a surprising sequence from extreme weapons-mindedness and aggressive war-fighting scenarios to a receptivity toward species consciousness, to an awareness of overall needs of humankind. The weapons-mindedness was greatest during the early years, which were characterized by a fierce emphasis on one-sided American vulnerability. The obsession was that America was weak and getting weaker, while the Soviets were strong and getting stronger; the solution to the grave danger lay in building more weapons, becoming strong and *in*vulnerable, and being "ready" to fight a nuclear war if necessary. Brutalization was apparent in the increasing emphasis on nuclear weapons as a source of national power and in the increasingly "enthusiastic frame of mind" concerning RAND scenarios for war fighting. "To Reagan and his national security managers, counterforce [targeting of enemy nuclear weapons, especially missile silos] and its various accoutrements were to be celebrated, not rhetorically qualified." The war-fighting doctrine was by no means new—it had been carried quite far by the Carter administration; but now there was a general release from restraint in contemplating nuclear holocaust.

Strategists were drawn from among the most belligerent:

"Crazier analysts have risen to higher positions than is normally the case." Among this second generation of strategists (or third, depending upon how one counts), some, such as Colin Gray, could complain that his predecessors suffered from the "Armageddon syndrome"—that is, being so preoccupied with the extent of nuclear destructiveness that their analyses seemed "to stop when the buttons are pushed." Gray's articles, for instance, insisted that "victory is possible" and made a case for "a theory of victory." Policy makers followed suit. The "watershed" in strategic thinking (according to a physicist who had formerly been a high-ranking Air Force civilian) was that "a lot of people . . . in charge look at counterforce not as a broader deterrent but as part of the acceptability of war"; and that for many, nuclear war fighting "is not only possible but very probable."

Reagan himself seemed to wish to hedge that attitude with a wishful vision—that of "Star Wars," or the Strategic Defense Initiative—of a "shield" that would rid the world of the "scourge" of nuclear weapons by rendering them "impotent and obsolete." In that way Star Wars expanded and totalized the illusion of overcoming vulnerability and achieving security; few people other than Reagan himself (and possibly Edward Teller) seemed to believe in the vision, and it greatly confused Reagan's cabinet members and European allies. In actuality, the Star Wars project has contributed to perpetuating the arms race by suggesting an endless action-reaction sequence: you build a shield, I build improved weapons that can break through your shield and work on improvements in my shield, you build better weapons, and so on. In that sense, we can say that Star Wars is a vision of an alternative to nuclear weapons which, in its combination of illusion and provocation, actually furthered their aggressiveness. All nuclear-weapons–related aggressiveness tends to be hidden by its distancing technology; Star Wars has the added veil of claimed liberation from the weapons themselves.

Yet after a record of almost total disdain for arms control efforts, President Reagan shocked everyone by virtually agreeing, at the Reykjavik summit with General Secretary Gorbachev in 1986, to a proposal for eventually eliminating *all* strategic nuclear weapons. That proposal failed because of American insistence on, and Soviet rejection of, an accompanying right to build and deploy the Strategic Defense Initiative. But the subsequent Intermediate Nuclear Force (INF) agreement between the two countries, whatever the complex political motivations of the two leaders, surely contained elements of species consciousness on the part of both. One may assume that even in the belligerent Reagan there had lurked a latent tendency to think in terms of humankind. That concern might well have been present in the revulsion he expressed toward the weapons in connection with his Star Wars advocacy, as might have been his earlier promise of "deep cuts" once the weapons buildup had proceeded to the point where he and his advisers could "negotiate from strength." All this suggests that people in general, and especially high officials when close to retirement, are capable of maintaining simultaneously two radically divergent sets of nuclear-weapons–related images, with a relatively separate sense of self for each. This dual capacity bordering on doubling, perhaps most marked in Reagan among American presidents but by no means limited to him, is further evidence of the absurdity of the genocidal structure and the accompanying genocidal mentality, both of which still prevail.

Threat and Use

A manifestation of the genocidal mentality transcending any specific administration has been the "use" of nuclear weapons as a specific, powerful threat, "In the precise way that a gun is used [according to Daniel Ellsberg, strategist turned peace activist] when you point it at someone's head in a direct confrontation, whether or not the trigger is pulled." Almost every president, from Truman through Reagan, with the possible exception of Ford and Carter, have "used" the weapons in that way—from Truman's June 1948 deployment of B-29s at the outset of the Berlin blockade of that year to Reagan's threat in 1981 to use the weapons to prevent Soviet incursion in the Middle East as well as subsequent statements by members of his administration concerning the possibility of fighting and even winning a nuclear war against the Soviet Union. Ellsberg makes an additional important point: "In *every one* of the half-dozen cases when U.S. or allied tactical units were surrounded or cut off and in danger of defeat—at the Chosin Reservoir, Dien Bien Phu, Berlin, Quemoy, Khe Sanh*—the administration secretly gave consideration, far more seriously than was ever admitted to the public, to the use of tactical nuclear weapons to defend them."

It is not that American leaders are necessarily more callous or immoral than leaders of other states. Rather, the existence of a genocidal system, made possible by mere technological capacity and commitment to the weapons, *invites* and helps sustain the genocidal mentality. The Soviets have made similar threats—at the time of the British and French invasion of Suez in 1956 and in various statements and writings about the possibility of *their* fighting and winning a nuclear war—many of their threats undoubtedly also made secretly.

Arms Control versus the Genocidal Mentality

Coexisting with the genocidal mentality has been an impulse to overcome it by means of arms control agreements. Of special importance here are the Limited Test Ban Treaty of 1963; the SALT (Strategic Arms Limitation Talks) I agreement of 1972 banning antiballistic missiles and limiting defensive weapons in general; the nonproliferation treaty of 1968; the SALT II agreement signed by President Carter in 1979 (but never ratified by the Senate) which only slightly limited the number of MIRVed† missiles and bombers capable of firing air-launched cruise missiles and limited some other weapons as well; and the 1987 INF agreement to destroy nuclear missiles with a range between 500 and 5,500 kilometers. Part of the importance of these agreements, and of many efforts at negotiation that did not result in treaties, has been the development of principles larger than the perceived national

*These places represent, respectively, a battle during the Korean War, the defeat of the French in the Indochinese War, the 1961 Soviet blockade of Berlin and the American airlift, the small island between Taiwan and mainland China, and a Vietnamese city where American marines were under siege. While it matters enormously that in all these cases the decision was made not to use nuclear weapons, one can say that the serious consideration of the possibility of using them is itself a manifestation of the genocidal mentality.

†MIRV is the acronym for "multiple independently targetable re-entry vehicle"; a missile is "MIRVed" when it has attached to it more than one warhead, each of which can be directed to a different target.

interests of the two superpowers. But unless part of a larger disarmament process, these agreements run the danger of legitimating the continuing arms race so long as it remains within the prescribed guidelines.

The genocidal mentality, then, not only can coexist with inclinations toward species consciousness but has continued to dominate the weapons arrangements. That mentality—the willingness, under certain condition, to take steps that could kill hundreds of millions of people—has become both an everyday matter and part of the various structures of society—both routinized and institutionalized. While no one sees oneself as an advocate of genocide, the genocidal mentality is increasingly identified with service, or even loyalty, to the state. And the great majority of ordinary citizens raise no objections.

Nuclear Normality

Living with nuclear weapons is our only hope.
—HARVARD NUCLEAR STUDY GROUP

From 8:15 A.M. on August 6, 1945, Hiroshima time, the human imagination has been struggling with an almost insurmountable problem. How is one to comprehend dimensions of destruction that, in their extremity, seem to have little relationship to anything the mind has previously confronted? Hiroshima survivors themselves have described how, at the moment of the bomb and afterward, they simply ceased to feel, a form of psychic numbing that served as some protection against the impact of the grotesque images that assaulted them. There is much evidence that the rest of us, in relation to the threat of nuclear devastation, undergo a milder version of that diminished capacity or inclination to feel.

A valuable study of the generation subjected to the "duck and cover" nuclear air-raid drills in American schools during the 1950s and 1960s brings out a characteristic psychological sequence: initial anxiety or even terror give way to long periods of suppression or numbing, punctured in turn by outpourings of anxiety and nightmares evoked by events inwardly associated with nuclear danger. In a real way we all lead something of a "double life": we are aware at some level that in a moment we and everyone and everything we have ever touched or loved could be annihilated, and yet we go about our ordinary routines as though no such threat exists.

Given the nature of the threat, some of that duality is inevitable. But there are social and historical currents that specifically contribute to this business-as-usual stance, currents that can be lumped together under the idea of "nuclear normality." What takes shape is a generally perceived obligation to view the weapons in certain ways because it is morally right, politically necessary, and personally mature to do so. The criteria for nuclear normality have generally been handed down by leaders and ostensible experts, though they are also influenced by the fear, mystery, and technological claims surrounding the weapons. Nuclear normality, then, becomes a cultural assumption, partly manipulated and at times so urgently put forward and embraced as to obscure the bizarre ideological and psychological assumptions contained in it.

Three waves of prescribed normal behavior can be identified: the first having to do with supporting the idea of fighting and winning nuclear wars; the second with accepting and "living with" the weapons; and the third with effective defenses to combat the weapons.

The First Wave

In the halcyon days or "Golden Age" of early nuclear strategy (late 1950s and early 1960s), Herman Kahn and a few other strategists and political leaders presided over the first great public wave of nuclear normality. They articulated attitudes and assumptions that haunt us even now. While the stated goal was prevention of war, the "reasonable" and "normal" man or woman was to join in a "rational assessment" of how to prepare for and win nuclear wars. To protest or in any way refuse that stance was to be "emotional" and poorly adjusted to "reality." "Rationality" was a key, and Kahn once declared that "the word 'rational' means that five or ten years after the war is over the country will not look back on the war as a mistake." And that, in order to be clear and "credible," we should acknowledge and make known that under certain conditions "going to war is rational."*

Parallel criteria were prescribed for individual behavior during and right after a war. Kahn focused on the danger of hypochondriacal responses: "Almost everyone is likely to think he has received too much radiation," and "If one man vomits, everybody vomits." As a remedy, Kahn recommended that everyone be provided with radiation meters: "Assume now that a man gets sick from a cause other than radiation. Not believing this, his morale begins to drop. You look at his meter and say, 'You have received only ten roentgens, why are you vomiting? Pull yourself together and get to work.' " This is nuclear normality at its most delusional. (On one occasion after a lecture, Kahn was asked by a member of the audience whether the information available on death and suffering in Hiroshima did not cause him to question some of his assumptions. His answer was that the Hiroshima work was "soft" (meaning insufficiently statistical) and appealed mainly to people's "emotions"—in other words, interfered with nuclear normality.)

Kahn's way had been paved by a "quasi-official campaign to soothe the public's atomic-bomb fears." A leader in that campaign was Rear Admiral William S. Parsons, a naval officer who had been a member of the Manhattan Project and responsible for the final assembly of the atomic bomb on board the *Enola Gay* during the flight to Hiroshima; he was also deputy commander of the 1948 atomic tests at the Pacific island of Eniwetok. Parsons railed against the "atomic neurosis" caused by "scientific propaganda" which warned of the bomb's destructive power and pushed people toward "a state which could well border on hysteria." He feared that this "neurotic approach . . . could make the United States vulnerable to a war of nerves," and said so in a series of magazine articles, some of which were aimed at the young and appeared in *Boy's Life*.

---

*Kahn went so far as to suggest a dialogue in which the president says to his advisers, "How can I go to war—almost all American cities will be destroyed?" And they answer, "That's not entirely fatal, we've built some spares." To be sure, actual presidents and their advisers in such situations have demonstrated much more restraint. But Kahn had considerable influence in policy circles, and his attitudes and tone did much to shape public discourse.

Recent release of a 1956 document makes clear that there were official efforts to involve professionals, notably psychiatrists and other physicians, in formulating and imposing nuclear normality. William F. Vandercook, a historian of that period, tells of the formation of a special panel in early 1956 by the National Security Council and the Federal Civil Defense Administration in order to evaluate the willingness of the American people "to support national policies which might involve the risk of nuclear warfare." The panel was charged with determining how a nation's civilian population was affected by a general awareness that an enemy "has the technological capability of annihilating [the] . . . nation," and by the possibility that the two nations in question "could produce mutual annihilation." The panel, to be made up of "wise and mature individuals" with professional knowledge of human behavior, came to include eleven white males, among whom were five physicians (several had been actively involved either in the Manhattan Project or at later nuclear-test sites), three of them psychiatrists; the rest were either social scientists with a military background or one in studies of morale, or retired military officers.

In the report "Human Effects of Nuclear Weapons," which the panel presented in November 1956, the members declared their "firm belief" that it was "possible to prepare effective psychological defenses" for nuclear attack, so that "both the war effort and the National Government would be effectively supported." Moreover, such preparation would enable the populace to overcome their lack of "knowledge and real understanding of basic national security considerations," and not "accept . . . wild exaggerations and misinterpretations." The panel recommended an extensive grass-roots discussion program in an atmosphere of "calm deliberation with less emphasis on the symbols and images of disaster that so often characterize the emergency approach to attention getting." The members pointed out that too much stress on "awareness of annihilation" was harmful, because it leads to "attitudes and behavior of the majority . . . attuned to the avoidance of nuclear war, no matter what the cost," and tends to "weaken public support of policies that involve any substantial risk of nuclear war." The report appealed to "our pioneer background and inheritance [which] predispose us to find hardships a challenge and fortify us against complacency." The discussion groups never came to much, but what is significant is the official (in this case, the Eisenhower administration) effort to enlist members of healing professions (psychiatry and medicine) to work with military representatives to establish concrete principles of nuclear normality.

This involvement of professionals is troubling but not surprising. For professionals tend to work from, rather than to question, social norms. By exclusively stressing their technical function, they create what William Blake called "mind-forged manacles." They can then apply their skills on behalf of any project sponsored by the prevailing power structure. The healing professions—psychology, psychiatry, social science, medicine, and religion—are especially vulnerable to this collusion because standards for physical or spiritual health tend to be greatly influenced by existing social currents. When those currents come to include officially sanctioned national illusion, healing professionals can all too readily be recruited to support that illusion. Moreover, they can apply their skills to undermine efforts to expose unpalatable truths: one can recall the gossip of psychiatrists—when one of their talented colleagues, Jerome Frank, took an early interest in nuclear-weapons questions—about the "personal problems" or "childhood trauma" responsible for this strange preoccupation. It was inevitable for the conventional arbiters of normality to be enlisted to maintain nuclear normality.

Nuclear normality was to be instilled early in life—as was done in the 1950s and early 1960s by combining nuclear air-raid drills with an educational program. These were held throughout the United States, typically once a month but sometimes as often as once a week, and became so standard that in 1952 a survey revealed that 95 percent of elementary schools in cities of 50,000 or more provided civil defense education, as did the overwhelming majority of secondary schools. These were the "duck and cover" drills for protection against nuclear attack. We know now that many children were terrified of the danger, but the message given to them was to suppress that fear and take on "faith . . . [the] ability to survive, no matter what the danger." Again, psychologists and psychiatrists were called upon to articulate and legitimate the message "that it was not normal to fear the bomb." The same principle applied, of course, outside the drills. When a twelve-year-old boy, after hearing an explosion, looked out of his window and remarked, "No mushroom cloud," and "returned to his homework with a pleasant and reassuring smile at his mother," that behavior was described by one psychiatrist as "well adjusted." But as an astute later observer put it, "perhaps a mental health professional could conclude that a twelve-year-old's immediate association of an explosion with an atomic bomb was perfectly normal only in an era when a pleasant and reassuring smile amounted to Federal policy."

Civil defense has always been integral to nuclear normality. In the 1950s and 1960s, Kahn and Edward Teller, a gifted physicist and extreme nuclear-weapons advocate, gave it enormous stress and did much to bring about the shelter-building craze, the nuclear air-raid drills in the schools, and the elaborate civil-defense propaganda. Teller, in his civil-defense fanaticism, constantly minimized the danger of fallout, at one point even declaring that it might be good for us. On another occasion he declared that more mutations have resulted from dressing men in trousers, and thereby increasing the temperature of male reproductive organs and adversely affecting sperm cells, than from nuclear testing; he added that we need such mutations anyhow for the evolution of the human race. His message has always been that civil defense can protect us from radiation problems.

Teller took on the role of national psychological adviser and therapist as well. He denounced the "psychological barrier" and "monstrous anxiety" which interfered with "the necessary preparation for limited nuclear warfare." To resist that course was "to seek refuge in a make-believe world" and replace "rational behavior . . . by anxiety, by feelings of guilt, by fears of improbable and fantastic calamities." And Teller fiercely advocated an expansive national program of shelter building for civil defense arrangements which, he wildly insisted, would "save perhaps 90 percent of our population."

But the American people have had the wisdom to question this crass and perverse concept of nuclear normality. They—and the Soviet people as well—have especially rejected claims of effective civil defense, and have simply been unable to believe that evacuation plans would smoothly and safely remove them from nuclear danger or that shelters would do the same. But with all of our doubts, we are hardly free, even now, of the deadly illusions of this first wave of nuclear normality.

The Second Wave

Moreover, a second wave of nuclear normality may have been much more influential through having been asserted in ways that are more restrained and seemingly "balanced." This wave is epitomized by the book entitled *Living with Nuclear Weapons,* published by the Harvard Nuclear Study Group. By 1983, when the volume was published, nuclear weapons had become ensconced both in their stockpiles (there were by then some 50,000 nuclear weapons in the world) and in our collective minds. And that is the order of things, we are told. The authors urge, at the end of the book, that we persevere in "reducing the likelihood of war even though we cannot remove the possibility altogether." But the clear message is that "our only hope" lies in living with the weapons (see epigraph, page 37). Committing oneself to drastic nuclear disarmament is to this group a "form of atomic escapism," "a dead end." They disdain "absolute solutions— either holocaust or disarmament"; and while they acknowledge that nuclear war would be catastrophic, they go to some lengths to insist upon the right of envisioning, under certain circumstances, a moral use of nuclear weapons and upon the necessity of living with some "risk of nuclear war." The tone of the book is one of calm authority; its goal (as stated in the foreword by Derek Bok, president of Harvard) to "inform the people"; its stance that of a reasoned middle ground between "denying that nuclear dangers exist" and "finding refuge in simplistic, unexamined solutions."

But the book's sensibility is best revealed in its treatment of nuclear-holocaust–related humor. Stanley Kubrick is chastised for rendering *Dr. Strangelove,* originally "a serious book about how a nuclear war might begin," into "an absurd fantasy."* The film is

---

*The film *Dr. Strangelove* was adapted from a novel by Peter George (with the pseudonym Peter Bryant), *Two Hours to Doom* [American edition, *Red Alert*]. Terry Southern, in writing

labeled as an expression of "denial"; concerning its subtitle, "Or How I Learned To Stop Worrying and Love the Bomb," the authors' comment is: "One way to stop worrying was black humor." Tom Lehrer is put in the same category, his satirical lyrics dismissed as another form of denial and mere release of tension—that is, as an undesirable alternative to the healthier "search for better understanding of the vast problems nuclear weaponry creates." But can these "realists" truly believe that Tom Lehrer was simply releasing tension when he sang, "We'll all go together when we go," or, "So long, Mom, I'm off to drop the Bomb"? Or that the film's subtitle was meant as a prescription to learn to stop worrying and love the bomb? In actuality, both Lehrer and the creators of *Dr. Strangelove* made brilliant use of mocking humor to expose our genocidal system and mentality in their full absurdity and to prod us to take basic steps to free ourselves from that nuclear entrapment. In contrast, the authors of *Living with Nuclear Weapons* ask that we stay within the structure, that we equate reason and adaptation with remaining entrapped.

This second wave of nuclear normality argues for (and reveals itself in) a set of aviary subdivisions—"Hawks, Doves, and Owls" (also the title of a book by some of the same men who wrote *Living with Nuclear Weapons*). Admittedly caricatures, they clearly convey a message. Hawks and Doves are more or less balanced against one another. Hawks fear "one-sided weakness—their classic example is Munich . . . appeasement"—and seek "a position of superior military strength" in order "to make our deterrent threat credible." Doves worry about steps that make the arms race "provocative" and about the "irresistible momentum of military preparations"; they "prescribe a policy of conciliation and accommodation." And "if provocation is the potential fatal flaw in the Hawk's approach, ineffectual appeasement is the equivalent flaw in the dovish prescription." Into the breech step the Owls, who concern themselves with "organizational routines, malfunctions of machines or of

the film script, converted the "serious book" into a black comedy; then the novel closely based on the film, with the same title, was again written by George.

minds, misperceptions, misunderstandings, and mistakes," as well as with "loss of control and nonrational factors."

But these subdivisions turn out to be little more than a reinforcement of second-wave nuclear normality, with the Owls playing the part of management birds who maintain the genocidal system. To be sure, their management function is meant to minimize dangers of inadvertent use of the weapons. But putting forth that owlish role as true wisdom requires a balancing act that understates the genocidal mentality of Hawks (their advocacy of first-strike capability, of plans for "victory," and at times even of "preventive" nuclear war). It also misrepresents the Doves' advocacy of *mutual* nuclear disarmament and of measures to control nonrational factors. The Owl position, it turns out, tends to focus heavily on a "credible nuclear deterrent" requiring constant improvement of nuclear weapons and a rejection of a no-first-use agreement or policy. In addition, Owls are wary of "overselling arms control" because that "runs the risk of lulling the public and elected officials into complacency, so that they are unwilling to invest adequately in defense." Owls, then, maintain and preside over our nuclear entrapment.

The second wave of nuclear normality is reinforced by a more or less formally reasoned claim of "ethical" justification. Joseph Nye, in his *Nuclear Ethics,* recognizes that "deterrence depends upon some prospect of use," and goes on to explain, in monumental understatement: "And use involves some risk that just war limits [especially that of killing large numbers of noncombatants], will not be observed." Yet his resolution of this dilemma is to alter policies of targeting and war fighting to include "a limited counter-city doctrine . . . a counter-combatant [enemy armies] rather than a counter-silo [enemy weapons] approach to counterforce [military] targeting." Nye warns against "the emotivist approach" because "outrage generally prevents reasoning." In this way, the second wave adds an ethical claim, ostensibly grounded in philosophical logic, to its support of our genocidal system and genocidal mentality. Nuclear absurdity is rendered necessary and good; nuclear normality is deepened and solidified. Thus, this second wave of nuclear normality—in claiming objectivity, rationality, and ethical reasoning—supports and extends our genocidal system and genocidal mentality.

The Third Wave

The third great wave of nuclear normality, more or less simultaneous with the second and interwoven with it, is that of the Strategic Defense Initiative, or Star Wars (SDI). If wave 1 of nuclear normality can be characterized as "Be ready to fight, defend, and survive," and wave 2 as "Learn to live with the weapons, with the mutual terror of deterrence, and the willingness to use the weapons if necessary, all calculated rationally and morally," then wave 3 is "Depend on the technology of the nuclear shield to protect you and be willing to spend trillions of dollars for it." We should not be surprised to learn that wave 3 draws upon the first two waves in fundamental if somewhat hidden forms.

Star Wars perpetuates—indeed, radically expands—the central illusion of the first wave of nuclear normality: namely, that one can defend oneself against nuclear weapons and recover from nuclear holocaust. In that important sense, Star Wars becomes "the ultimate civil defense project," one in which "the sky itself is to be converted into one vast schoolroom desk, under which we will collectively huddle while teacher hurls erasers at the marauding invaders."

During the early 1980s, the Reagan administration revived and extended Herman Kahn's concept of radiation meters, now advocating "radiological defense kits" as standard equipment for shelters. That in turn was part of a vast scheme of "crisis relocation," with elaborate plans for evacuation and allocation of shelters. The new civil defense propaganda barrage included an animated film, *Protection in the Nuclear Age,* produced in English and Spanish versions and with captions for the deaf. The message was that "protection is possible"; that nuclear war "would not mean the end of the world, the end of our nation"; that "we can survive." But as in the past, Americans simply could not believe that civil defense arrangements would really protect them, and responded with laughter. The butt of most of the laughter was T. K. Jones, a Defense Department official concerned with the Federal Emergency Management Agency, who was to be forever haunted by the words he chose in advising Americans, in the event of nuclear attack, to "dig a hole, cover it with a couple of doors and then throw three feet of dirt on top. . . . If there are enough shovels to go around, everybody's going to make it." Jones and these elaborate evacuation plans, with their arrangements for mail forwarding, were something of a gift to cartoonists and humorists of all kinds. So much so that he had to be quickly removed from the lecture circuit and hidden from view—as did most of the civil defense program. But he did not lose his high-ranking Pentagon position, and the Reagan administration continued to advocate shelter building and to distribute its plans for evacuation and protection from radiation.

Star Wars resurrects civil defense in the form of a visionary technology. Nuclear normality now calls for faith in technological brilliance, especially American technological brilliance. That faith is meant to help people dispel doubts—to numb themselves to what they intuitively know—about the efficacy of civil defense arrangements in protecting people from nuclear holocaust. As those in authority have been forced to become modest in their public statements about what SDI could actually do, and to admit that there is no prospect of its offering genuine protection against nuclear weapons, the drum beating has switched to the miraculous technological spinoffs of the program: in computer modeling, weather forecasting, mapping the ocean floor, talented robots, electron beams useful to combat malignant tumors, synthetic crystals that can revolutionize silicon chips in computers, and so on. But even those claims turned out to be reminiscent of similar promises during the first wave of nuclear normality: "To anyone who has pored over hundreds of late-1940s descriptions of the exciting spinoffs to be expected from the invention of the atomic bomb, such rhetoric produces a profound sense of *déjà vu*, and a profound sense of depression."

The heart of the ethical claim to this third wave of nuclear normality lies in President Reagan's initial vision of rendering nuclear weapons "impotent and obsolete," and in his assumption that "it is better to protect lives than to avenge them." When it began to become clear that "the Reagan version [was] unobtainable," the claim shifted to the system's usefulness in contributing to deterrence by means of the ironic principle of protecting valuable military assets rather than people. Generally speaking, Star Wars is dangerously destabilizing on a number of counts. Its claim of "damage limitation" is the kind that renders nuclear war fighting more acceptable. The same claim could signal "first-strike intention" to an adversary who may interpret the SDI buildup as protection from the retaliation that would follow such a first strike. The adversary, then, might be tempted to a "preventive" first strike of its own.

The nuclear-normalizing role of Star Wars is bound up with American popular culture, with video games and movies that have "helped condition the public, especially the young, to imagine nuclear war as a high-tech game played by computers, with minimal human risk and involvement." In this way, the fantasies of mass culture and government weapons programs form a vicious circle: "The fantasies lay the psychic groundwork for the weapons programs; the weapons programs in turn stimulate new fantasies." Indeed, there is reason to suspect that the former president's enthusiasm for Star Wars was influenced by a 1940 Warner Brothers film, *Murder in the Air,* which featured an SDI-like secret weapon called the Inertia Projector, whose rays could strike down incoming enemy aircraft from miles away. The star of that film was a twenty-nine-year old actor named Ronald Reagan. The very name "Star Wars" (taken from the 1977 George Lucas hit movie), which the project cannot shake, suggests science fiction fantasy and more than a hint of mockery, but at the same time provides a feeling of comfort and familiarity.

Yet also present in the Star Wars constellation is the American principle of self-reliance, the idea that "in a world of nuclear menace and 'evil empires,' we must take our fate into our own hands." In actuality, though, the very opposite of self-reliance prevails. With Star Wars, the technology is literally asked to replace human responsibility. Much of the system is to function automatically, its sensors and computers activated by the enemy's technology—all in the absence of anything resembling the human hand, eye, or heart.

All these features contribute to the highly wishful quality of this third wave of nuclear normality, put forward by a president who may well have been the embodiment of American wishfulness:

> This is a President who is well attuned to the American viscera. Somewhere in the American viscera we don't want to believe that some son of a bitch on the other side can destroy us. He's offering us that wonderful defense in the sky. It has nothing to do with military planning. Anyone who takes a serious look at this knows that the Reagan version is unattainable. It's just this gut reaction that comes from the deepest recesses of the American viscera that Reagan is attuned to.

While none of these three waves of nuclear normality has been sustained fully, each has played an important part in promulgating dangerous illusions. The first wave established illusions of preparation (one can take effective steps to get ready for nuclear war), of protection (via shelters and evacuation), of limited nuclear war (one can stop the "exchange" at a certain point), and of viable recovery or even victory (one can "raise the flag on Mt. Suribachi"* and then rebuild). The second wave of nuclear normality focuses on the beneficence of the weapons (they are a necessity for preventing war) and of human helplessness before them (our only choice is to learn to "live with them"). The third wave puts forward the illusion of nuclear invulnerability (the idea that we can reverse the fundamental truth of the nuclear age—that of absolute, universal vulnerability).

Although the assumptions within the various waves may contradict one another (President Reagan, in advocating Star Wars, characterized the superpowers as "people facing themselves across the table each with a cocked gun, . . . no one knowing whether someone might tighten the finger on the trigger"), the constellation of all three waves takes on a certain unity of assumption that rationality and mental health require that we accept the permanance of a nuclear-weapons–dominated world. The widespread acceptance of overall nuclear normality dissipates what would be a more appropriate sense of urgency and threat in relation to nuclear weap-

*Colin Gray was referring to the mountain on Iwo Jima where the victory flag was actually raised, as a model for the desired outcome of nuclear war.

ons and, by giving agency to the weapons themselves, undermines constructive human action on behalf of life enhancement. Nuclear normality also helps maintain a world of "organized peacelessness" and legitimates the rhetoric and policies of nuclearism (see chapter 3) as the only ones available to us. Moreover, whenever fundamental questions are raised about such assumptions, there tends to be a reassertion, in whatever guise, of these ostensibly normative principles. And nuclear normality, when in effect, becomes associated with genocidal readiness.

Chapter 3

Genocidal Ideology: Trauma and Cure

There are some remedies worse than the disease.
—PUBLILIUS SYRUS

This great iridescent cloud and its mushroom top
. . . is actually a protective umbrella that will forever
shield mankind everywhere against the threat of
annihilation in any atomic war.
—WILLIAM LAURENCE

GENOCIDE, or its potential, can only be understood as occurring within a particular historical context. And we shall be at pains to note the enormous differences between the historical situations of Nazism and of nuclear threat. But we need also to explore the degree to which each calls forth imagery of trauma or sickness on the one hand, and resolution or cure on the other. Isaiah Berlin sees nationalism as emerging from a "wound to group consciousness" and as including "a new vision of life" which helps to heal that wound. The Nazis have taught us that a nation's potential for genocide depends greatly upon how it defines its collective trauma and upon the kind of ideological response brought forth as relief and cure.

The Nazi Biomedical Vision: Racial Therapy

> We more than deserved this defeat [of the First
> World War]. It is only the greatest outward symp-
> tom of decay among quite a series of internal ones.
> —ADOLF HITLER

Prior to embracing Hitler, the German people felt themselves to be in the grip of an intolerable affliction. The ending of the First World War involved much more than military defeat. It was associated with a sense of national humiliation, economic chaos from catastrophic inflation, and near civil war. Loss on the battlefield was trauma enough to a nation that had prided itself on its military; but the trauma entered into still deeper social and psychological layers of dislocation and demoralization. For individual Germans, the world fell apart. They experienced a sense of personal disintegration and despair about their individual and collective future.

The general atmosphere of the time, political and otherwise, was described by one historian as "oppressive with doom, almost eschatological." For in 1918, the Germans had become survivors of killing and dying on an unprecedented scale, and of the death of resplendent national and social visions, of meaning itself. The First World War, entered into with extraordinary enthusiasm, had been seen as the means of overcoming the deep confusions or and "cultural despair" accompanying German historical struggles with modernization and unification from the mid-nineteenth century. The war had been a miserable failure, and the Versailles Treaty, with its requirement of reparations and assumptions of German guilt alone for the war, came to symbolize, and serve as an exaggerated focus for, the entire spectrum of national humiliation.

Germany's defeat in the First World War was in this sense an additional "wound" to an existing nationalism whose intensity belied its vulnerability. The result was a fierce new assertion of nationalism, drawing upon and contributing to some of the most dangerous ideological currents, political and racial, of its time. Crucial to these ideological responses was the meaning given to the wound—the collective survivor formulation of what had occurred. That formulation came to include victimization from without (Germany was suffering because of unfair treatment by the other Western nations at Versailles) but more powerfully from within (the legend of the "stab in the back" by political and racial enemies, especially Jews) in ways that resulted in profound internal decay (as Hitler expressed in the epigraph on page 52). Cure, then, required extensive purification in order to achieve regeneration of nation and self—or, one might say, of national and racial self.

Collective trauma seeks resolution and cure, and the key to that process is ideological. The healing ideology must, above all, promise new collective energy or life power—a vision of collective revitalization. Hitler's national success was undoubtedly related to his claim of a deeper "diagnosis" of Germany's affliction. That diagnosis, while put forward as political doctrine, claimed ultimate *biological* truth. Hitler wrote in *Mein Kampf,* in the mid-1920s, "Anyone who wants to cure this era, which is inwardly sick and rotten, must first of all summon up the courage to make clear the causes of this disease." Those causes were biological and, specifically, racial: The Aryan race, the only race that was "culture-creating," had permitted itself to be rendered weak and its survival endangered by the one "culture-destroying race," the Jews. The agent of "racial pollution" and "racial tuberculosis," "the Jew" was a form of "bacteria" or "parasite" which brought about the "infection" and become "a maggot in a rotting corpse." This medical imagery was no mere colorful metaphor: it was a social theory of collective decay, a social diagnosis containing a clear direction of treatment. As early as 1920, Hitler had made clear that the only solution for the Aryan malady was "the removal of the Jews from the midst of our people." The vision, then, was not just biological but biomedical.

The sole purpose of the Nazi state Hitler then projected was to bring about this racial cure: "The state [is] only a means to an end, and as its end it considers the preservation of the racial existence of man." The state, that is, was merely a vehicle for the "mission of the German people on earth," which was that of "assembling and preserving the most valuable stocks of basic racial elements in this [Aryan] people . . . [and] . . . raising them to a dominant position." The state was an extension of race, subsumed to a biological mission of propagating "those Aryan elements" that would bring about "the beauty and the dignity of a higher humanity." This focus alone, Hitler believed, could be the means of transforming racial demise into new racial vitality: "From a dead mechanism which only lays claim to existence for its own sake, there must be formed a living organism with the exclusive aim of serving a higher idea."

Nazi racial thought and policy were wildly visionary and romanticized on the one hand, and narrowly technocratic and scientistic on the other. These two seemingly contradictory patterns were, in fact, inseparable. Consider two comments by Nazi doctors. A leading medical administrator for the regime reported that he had joined the Nazi party the day after hearing a speech by Rudolf Hess in which the deputy party leader had declared, "National Socialism is nothing but applied biology." And a still more malignant comment was made by a Nazi doctor in Auschwitz when asked by a prisoner physician how he could reconcile the smoking crematoria they viewed in the distance with his Hippocratic oath: "Of course I am a doctor and I want to preserve life. And out of respect for human life, I would remove a gangrenous appendix from a diseased body." Both of these statements are visionary in the extreme: the one, a claim to have discovered the means to reduce all political and historical process to biological principles; the other, invoking a higher therapeutic purpose to justify the mass murder of Jews. What the Nazis called "scientific racism" or "racial hygiene" was in actuality a mystical and lethal approach to biology in particular and to science in general.

We can speak, then, of the biomedical ideology as "totalistic"—as containing an all-or-none set of assumptions which are equally absolute in their claim to truth and in their rejection of alternative claims. Parallel to the psychological principle of totalism is what the Nazis themselves called their "political principle of totalitarianism," according to which any differing political ideas were to be "ruthlessly dealt with, as the symptom of an illness which threatens the healthy unity of the indivisible national organism." That monitoring of the environment for potential opposition in order to suppress it is an expression of *milieu control,* always fundamental to ideological totalism.

Also characteristic of a totalistic environment is the kind of *sacred science* we have been discussing. While ideas of race had been of scientific interest from the time of the eighteenth century, it was the emergence of physical anthropology during the late nineteenth and early twentieth centuries that gave rise to claims of "scientific racism." Within that tradition, not only physical but also psychological and moral characteristics could be attributed specifically to race. Developing principles in genetics and biology in general also entered the constellation. Particularly important was the emergence of *eugenics,* a term coined by the eccentric English scientist Francis Galton, who had in mind a science for improving human stock by giving "the more suitable races or strains of blood a better chance of prevailing speedily over the less suitable." Eugenics had enormous appeal for a wide variety of thinkers and nonthinkers in Europe and the United States but, despite its evolutionary claims and later reference to genetic laws, has never had genuine scientific standing. These haphazard racial ideas took on special passion when they became associated with the idea of nation, when "racism and nationalism began to fuse." And "the fear which haunted racial thought after the mid-nineteenth century was that of degeneration."

Thus, Fritz Lenz, a leading German physician-geneticist who was later to become a prominent Nazi biomedical ideologue, prefigured some of Nazi racial thought and had direct influence on Adolf Hitler. As early as 1917, Lenz was writing about the duty of the state and the individual to "serve the race," and expressed fear that without a radical eugenics project, "our race is doomed to extinction." The Nazis were to claim that theirs was a *scientific* resolution of the problem, and that "the final solution of the Jewish question"—the murder of every Jew they could lay their hands on—was part of their "applied biology." For the Nazis brought to their biology emotions resembling those of millenarian movements of the Middle Ages whose ideological sources tended to derive mainly from the Book of Revelation and, to a lesser extent, from Old Testament sources such as the Book of Daniel. Like these movements, the Nazis sought purification and cleansing of their version of evil, but for them the biologically demonic source of evil was the Jews. The Nordic race, because of the influence of that evil, had become "biologically fallen," in need of redemption. This biological dimension of millenarian mysticism contributed strongly to Nazi totalism: Jews were absolutely and unredeemably evil; and the Nordic race, through its representative, the Nazi movement, was the source of all virtue.

That biological and millenarian polarization contributed directly to the ultimate feature of totalism—the *dispensing of existence.* When good and evil are absolute and clear, and particularly when they can be readily identified in biological terms, it is a relatively easy step to decide that biological evil should perish and only biological good survive. That ideological dichotomy pervaded the institutions and policies of Nazi Germany in ways that went beyond the beliefs of any individual. Nazi doctors in Auschwitz, for instance, varied greatly in their ideological convictions; but belief in that dichotomy made it psychologically easier for them to take part in the killing.

To embrace this ideology and work from it could be a heady experience for biologists and doctors. The medical administrator mentioned earlier told how, between 1934 and 1939, he made hundreds of speeches to colleagues as well as general audiences presenting the Nazi biomedical vision as a fundamental truth about humankind, and advocating a Nazi version of "biological socialism"; he emphasized that dealing with the Jews had nothing to do with old-fashioned anti-Semitism but only with "the aim of self-fulfillment, *völkisch* self-fulfillment." It was, he declared, "a beautiful time for me." He was referring to nothing short of a "high state," an experience of transcendence, afforded those living out this visionary biological claim. Those high states could be experienced by others in the movement who had little to do with biology as such. The central ideological principle, the promise of revitalization, offered individual people surges of immediate vitality and a sustained state of the shared immortality of the movement. It was, at bottom, a biological promise.

The ideology exerted its power over those who believed only bits and pieces of it. Among Nazi doctors, for instance, even partial beliefs, or "ideological fragments," contributed greatly to their participation in the projects of the regime. The typical Nazi doctor was not a fanatical ideologue but a conservative or reactionary nationalist drawn to the movement by its promise of collective revitalization; could laugh at the more extreme claims of Nazi racial theory while being attracted to the general biological emphasis and to certain principles of "scientific racism"; had fuzzy convictions about superior features of the Germanic or Nordic race and was worried about "racial mixing"; considered himself a "rational" rather than a fanatical anti-Semite; pointed critically to the number and prominence of Jewish doctors, especially in large German cities, and associated them with socialized medical insurance schemes which he detested; had not marched in the streets with the Nazis but was willing to offer them obedience and service in exchange for high social, economic, and military standing; and brought to the enterprise a certain opportunistic careerism and corruptibility.

A kind of apocalyptic biology led, perhaps inevitably, to a vision and practice of killing to heal. The Nazi cure was as literal as it was murderous and consisted of ridding the world of "life unworthy of life" by means of five identifiable steps: coercive sterilization, the killing of "impaired" children, the killing of "impaired" adults (these latter two steps erroneously called "euthanasia"), the selection and killing of "impaired" inmates of concentration camps, and finally the mass killings of Jews in the extermination camps themselves. The two "euthanasia" programs, though initiated by the regime, were conducted within medical jurisdiction and can therefore be described as "direct medical killing." This first Nazi genocide of more than 100,000 people was directed mostly at German non-Jews who had been given psychiatric diagnoses. The mass murder of Jews in extermination camps could also have a medical aura, notably in Auschwitz, and can therefore be described as "medicalized killing." While many divergent forces contributed to the sequence, these steps were consistent with one another. They were all expressions of biological purification, of destroying "bad" genes and "bad" racial elements in order to revitalize the Nordic race and the world at large. Had the Nazis named their institutions according to their ideological concepts, a "euthanasia" institution might well have been referred to as a "Center for Therapeutic Genetic Killing," while Auschwitz would have been called a "Center for Therapeutic Racial Killing."

Much of the cure was either coordinated or carried out by the élite SS corps (the letters stand for *Schutzstaffel* which literally means "protection" or "guard detachment"), initiated by Hitler as his bodyguard, the protector of his personal security, which was in turn equated with the security of the Nazi state. Heinrich Himmler built the SS into an all-encompassing police, intelligence, and military network that had elements of both a state within a state and a vast religious order. The mystical dimension was essential, since the SS was itself to epitomize the ultimate racial mission. Its members themselves were to have pure Aryan family trees in order to carry out a sacred function, which was "to ensure the eternal existence of the Germanic people of Germany." The SS was meant to be not just a vanguard but an ideological essence, a realization, in what it did and what it was, of the Nazi vision of murderous purification.

Killing as a project took on the quality of a religious ordeal, as expressed by Himmler in his infamous speech at Posen in October 1943:

> Most of you must know what it means to see a hundred corpses lie side by side, or five hundred, or a thousand. To have stuck this out and— excepting in cases of human weakness—to have kept our integrity, this is what has made us hard. In our history, this is an unwritten and never-to-be-written page of glory.

One must, that is, make sacrifices—or, as some SS officers put it, "overcome" oneself—for the sake of the higher therapeutic purpose. One has taken one's place in an ideological narrative within which the murderers are virtuous, the victims evil, and the killing necessary.

The Atomic Trauma

> Seldom if ever has a war ended leaving the victors
> with such a sense of uncertainty and fear, with such
> a realization that the future is obscure and that
> survival is not assured.
> —EDWARD R. MURROW

With nuclear weapons, the collective trauma has been very different. Rather than the loss of a war, the trauma stemmed from military victory—more precisely, from the weapon associated with that victory. The terrifying reverberations of the atomic bombings of Hiroshima and Nagasaki were experienced not only in Japan but throughout the world, and perhaps particularly strongly in the United States. Contributing greatly to that impact in this country were memories of Pearl Harbor having to do with unpreparedness, surprise, and deeply troubling vulnerability. These anxieties about nuclear vulnerability, moreover, became quickly related in American minds to antagonism to the Soviet Union.*

Early Fear of the Power of the Atom

> Some fool in a laboratory might blow up the universe unawares.
> —ERNEST RUTHERFORD

From the time of its appearance—and, in fact, well before then—the atomic bomb was responded to as more than a mere weapon, but as a device for potentially destroying the world. Ernest Rutherford, the great New Zealand–born British physicist, who did pioneering work on radioactivity at the turn of the century, used to "joke" about its dangers, once suggesting that "it was just conceivable that a wave of atomic disintegration might be started through matter, which would indeed make this old world vanish in smoke." His colleague, the chemist Frederick Soddy, took the issue seriously, and wrote a great deal about it, including discussing the

*This somewhat lost history of Hiroshima-related *American* fear has recently been valuably rendered by Paul Boyer in his *By the Bomb's Early Light.*

possibility that it could become sensible to "possess a weapon by which [one] could destroy the earth." H. G. Wells, having read Soddy, published in 1914 one of his notable science fiction novels, *The World Set Free*, in which he anticipated and named the atomic bomb and described how because of its use "most of the capital cities of the world were burning."

By the early 1930s, when Leo Szilard, the great Hungarian physicist, became interested in such matters, the idea of "breaking down the atom" was scientifically in the air. But reading Wells's *The World Set Free* seemed to make the idea of the atomic bomb more real to him; and in September 1933, while stepping off a curb to cross a London street, Szilard had his now-famous vision of how a nuclear chain reaction might take place. Szilard had just fled Nazi Germany; and from the beginning, his and others' fearful atomic imaginings took place in the direct context of Nazi threat. With Otto Hahn's discovery in 1938 that the uranium atom could be split, the issue became more immediate, and Szilard declared, "Hitler's success could depend on it." So fearful was he of Nazi acquisition of the weapon that he had a few years earlier attempted, ultimately unsuccessfully, to convince fellow physicists throughout the world to cease publishing papers on related scientific issues. It was the same fear that motivated him to approach his old friend Albert Einstein to prepare together the Einstein letter in 1939 to President Franklin Roosevelt that was to initiate the Manhattan Project. Yet even while sounding the alarm, Szilard was keenly involved in the scientific problem; and it was he, together with Enrico Fermi, who succeeded in creating the first atomic chain reaction on a University of Chicago squash court in 1942. Whatever his pleasure at that scientific success, Szilard felt at the time that it was a "bleak day in the history of mankind." The nuclear arms race, already three years old, was to remain for another three years a struggle between the United States and Germany (it was later learned that Japan was somewhere, though far back, in the race) to be the first to make the bomb. Only toward the end of the war in late 1944 was it learned that Germany had never come close.

Fear at Los Alamos

> You could tell at once they had had a strange expe-
> rience. You could see it on their faces. I saw that
> something very grave and strong had happened in
> their whole outlook on the future.
> —STANISLAW ULAM

The terror reflected in scientists' response to the first atomic bomb test (known as Trinity) has also been insufficiently recognized. Emilio Segrè combined a sense of awe ("I was flabbergasted by the new spectacle") with an insistent end-of-the-world image ("I believe that for a moment I thought the explosion might set fire to the atmosphere and thus finish the earth, even though I knew that this was not possible"). Kenneth Bainbridge combined fear and self-condemnation when he spoke of an unforgettably "foul and awesome display," and declared, "Now we're all sons of bitches." Oppenheimer's famous image from the *Bhagavad-Gita* ("Now I am become Death the destroyer of worlds") contains a quality of terror somewhat covered over by its literary-mythological aspect. I. I. Rabi described "a chill" of a personal kind concerning the fragility of "my wooden house in Cambridge and my laboratory in New York, and of the millions of people living around there." And Fermi, who had been seemingly cool in his wagers and calculations, experienced so severe a delayed reaction that he was unable to drive home from Trinity because his car seemed to be "jumping from curve to curve, skipping the straight stretches in between." No wonder the mathematician Stanislaw Ulam, who encountered the physicists upon their return to Los Alamos, "could see it in their faces."

Perhaps most revealing of all were the reactions of Brigadier General Thomas Farrell. In his *official* report (made to General Groves, who forwarded it to Secretary of War Henry L. Stimson and President Harry Truman at the Potsdam Conference) Farrell sounded less like a tough, high-ranking military engineer than an awed religious supplicant who felt himself overwhelmed by a vast supernatural force:

The effects could well be called unprecedented, magnificent, beautiful, stupendous and terrifying. No man-made phenomenon of such tremendous power had ever occurred before. . . . Thirty seconds after the explosion came, first, the air blast pressing hard against the people and things, to be followed almost immediately by the strong, sustained, awesome roar which warned of doomsday and made us feel that we puny things were blasphemous to dare tamper with the forces heretofore reserved to The Almighty. Words are inadequate tools for the job of acquainting those not present with the physical, mental, and psychological effects. It had to be witnessed to be realized.*

One who did witness it—Robert Lewis, the co-pilot of the *Enola Gay*—said, "Where we had seen a clear city two minutes before, we could now no longer see the city."

Hiroshima: Imagery of Extinction

While early American reactions to the news of Hiroshima and Nagasaki were considerably muffled by celebrations of victory and by an inclination to justify the use of the new weapon, there was an immediate trauma which has probably influenced American feelings and behavior ever since. On 8 August 1945, Anne O'Hare McCormick declared in the *New York Times* that the atomic bomb had caused "an explosion in men's minds as shattering as the obliteration of Hiroshima." In actuality, the effect was probably more in the nature of a fearful shadow, of a danger described by the *New York Herald Tribune* on 7 August as "weird, incredible, and somehow disturbing" so that "one forgets the effect on Japan or on the course of the war as one senses the foundations of one's own universe trembling." There was instant awareness of American vulnerability, as the leading news broadcaster of the time, H. B. Kaltenborn made clear on the night of 6 August: "We must assume that with the passage of only a little time, an improved form of the new weapon we used today can be turned against us." The next night another broadcaster, noting that the bomb had "destroyed the entire Japanese city of Hiroshima in a single blast," added, "It would be the same as Denver, Colorado, with a popula-

*He also had a more immediate, nakedly fearful response, which echoes to this day: "The longhairs have let it get away from them!"

tion of 350,000 persons being there one moment, and wiped out the next."

There were more extreme images of human extinction. The *St. Louis Post-Dispatch,* on 7 August, declared that science may have "signed the mammalian world's death warrant and deeded an earth in ruins to the ants." And a little later the *New York Times* referred to our capacity to "blow ourselves and perhaps the planet itself to drifting dust."

Those early responses conveyed the traumatic recognition of our own absolute vulnerability—recognition, that is, of the fundamental truth of the nuclear age. That recognition of vulnerability had been partly prepared by the earlier trauma of Pearl Harbor. At Pearl Harbor, less than four years earlier, a major part of the American Pacific fleet had been, with stunning suddenness, destroyed or severely damaged. Although later investigation revealed that there had been ample reason to anticipate such an attack, it was perceived by Americans as an act of cruel deception ("a day of infamy," in Roosevelt's words). More than that, it initiated the loss of what historians had called America's "free security"—the safety granted by the two great oceans distancing us from hostile forces on other continents. Even if Hawaii was not the American mainland, the attack, as the writer Marquis Childs commented at the time, "seared deeply into the national consciousness" and "tore at the myth of our invulnerability . . . at the precious legend of our might . . . [and] seemed to leave us suddenly naked and defenseless." Now, with Hiroshima, that nakedness and defenselessness had become stark. The American people, who in the past "had no reason to be concerned with their security," had been "uniquely situated far from any powerful state, easily supreme on their own continent, and protected by oceans on two sides," were now to become obsessed with "national security." *It is probably accurate to say that the American preoccupation with national security began with our own atomic bomb.*

From the beginning, the trauma caused by nuclear weapons has been associated with imagery of extinction—with the possibility of annihilating ourselves as a species by means of our own technology and by our own hand. There are parallels with religious end-of-the-world imagery, of humankind being destroyed by a higher power for reasons of sin or necessity. H. G. Wells clearly grasped the man-made technological dimension in his brilliantly prophetic fiction. But since the Second World War that imagery has been, so to speak, universalized, available to everyone. Certainly Nazi mass murder has, by means of the technology of the gas chamber, demonstrated the real possibility of human beings annihilating millions of their own species, "that henceforth the systematic, bureaucratically administered extermination of millions of citizens or subject peoples will forever be one of the capacities and temptations of government."

Thus, after the Second World War, we were left with profound doubts about our own human future. Our symbolization of immortality, of larger human connectedness, was put under duress. We were confronted with imagery of the "end"—of our own individual lives, to be sure, but also of our human groups, our cultural creations or "works," our religious or spiritual continuity, even of eternal nature, the organic environment we share with other animals. Most of these elements of imagery of extinction were unspoken and only periodically in our conscious awareness. But since 1945, that overall constellation of futurelessness, as at least a real possibility, has entered the human mind, and perhaps especially the American mind.

The Cultural Crisis

"A time of cultural crisis" was the way Paul Boyer characterized the overall post–Hiroshima and Nagasaki period, one involving "a new and threatening reality of almost unfathomable proportions," for which "the dominant . . . response was confusion and disorientation." There was the sudden emergence of a movement for world government as an alternative to collective doom, a movement whose political failure has obscured the psychological and moral authenticity of its impulse toward species politics and a species self (see chapter 9). The scientists' movement, responding to the same threat, had more success in influencing American consciousness and bringing about a measure of civilian control over the weapons and their energy sources.

Americans were aware that they were afraid: an important sociological survey done in 1946–47 concluded that Americans "know that the atomic bomb is terrible and to be feared." It quoted such comments as: "The bomb seems to be so powerful that it can destroy anything"; and, "I know the bomb can wipe out cities." Science fiction writers reflected this fear in offering end-of-the-world images of a third world war: "Every major city will be wiped out in 30 minutes. . . . New York will be a slag heap. . . . Radioactive energy . . . will leave the land uninhabitable."

There was an additional array of cultural responses in the uneasy, often trivializing efforts to absorb the new situation. Children began to incorporate atomic bombs into their play; and 750,000 of them, by returning cereal boxtops, obtained from General Mills Corporation mystical "atomic 'bomb' rings" with "sealed atom chambers." The bomb became a metaphor for sexual intensity, as in the 1947 pop song "Atom Bomb Baby" and the "Atom Bomb Dancers" featured in Los Angeles burlesque houses. Hollywood made spy thrillers about Nazi agents seeking the atomic bomb. In country music, atomic power was seen as coming from "the mighty hand of God" and as a source of sudden annihilation ("We will not know the minute, and will not know the hour") that threatened everyone ("They're sending up to Heaven to get the brimstone fire"). And there were the inevitable atomic-bomb jokes of dubious mirth (Bob Hope: "Will you be my little Geranium, until we are both blown up by Uranium?").

Boyer summed up the cultural dimensions of fear, "Years before the world's nuclear arsenals made such a holocaust likely or even possible, the prospect of global annihilation already filled the national consciousness."

Fear of the Soviet Union

> We cannot ignore the lessons of history, and we must always be ready for preemptive actions against the perfidy of the aggressors.
> —MAJOR GENERAL NIKOLAI TALENSKY

An important part of American atomic-bomb trauma was its early association with fear of the Soviet Union. Intense animosity had developed between the two allies during the latter stages of the Second World War and, indeed, contributed to the American decision to drop the bomb on Japan. During the early postwar years, American fears were accentuated by aggressive Soviet actions: the occupation of most of Eastern Europe and the use of the Red Army to install governments controlled by local communist parties in East Germany, Hungary, Rumania, Poland, and eventually Czechoslovakia. The cold war was intensified by disputes involving communist groups in Turkey and Greece in 1947, and in 1948 by the Soviet-engineered coup in Czechoslovakia and, after a currency dispute, the unsuccessful Soviet attempt to blockade West Berlin. While the United States and its Western European allies made their own contributions to the conflict, during that Stalinist era the Soviet Union could readily be seen as a dangerous totalitarian society. Indeed, there took shape a particular American fear that the closed totalitarian society of the Soviet Union would acquire its own atomic bombs. Some advocated threatening to drop atomic bombs on the Soviet Union unless it agreed to open up its society; even Bertrand Russell, generally associated with a vigorous antinuclear position, was to make a similar proposal. The Soviets would later come up with their own "preventive" projections, as in the 1953 declaration by Major General Nikolai Talensky, quoted in the epigraph to this section.

Americans became obsessed with the atomic-bomb "secret" and, above all, with preventing the Soviet Union from learning it. It was, as the leading American wartime scientific administrator, Vannevar Bush, put it, as if "there was an atomic bomb 'secret,' written perhaps on a single sheet of paper, some sort of magic formula": "If we guarded this, we alone could have atomic bombs indefinitely." Anxiety about the secret was intensified by actual Soviet espionage efforts in relation to the bomb, revealed in early 1946 in the case of the Canadian "atom spies." Knowledgeable observers concluded that the case had greater importance in generating a national American atom-spy hysteria than it did for the Soviet atomic-bomb project. As Boyer put it, "a population that for a year and a half had been in the grip of atomic fear was now told to turn its fear in a new direction: not vaporization but communization was the great menace confronting mankind."

The shocking August 1949 explosion of the Soviets' first atomic bomb intensified American suspicions of them as "stealers of secrets." Many Americans, including those in high places, had great difficulty believing that the Soviets could achieve such a technological feat on their own. President Truman himself, at first dubious, took the word of scientists at the time and made his announcement of the Soviet bomb. The idea that the Soviets had succeeded by stealing the American secret was further reinforced by the revelation, in January 1950, that Klaus Fuchs, a physicist with the wartime British team at Los Alamos, had, since 1942, been passing information to the Soviet Union. And during that 1949–50 period, a series of additional events inflamed American fears of the Soviet Union and of world communism—further consolidation of Soviet power in Eastern Europe, the stunning victory of the Chinese communists, the invasion of South Korea by communist North Korean forces initiating the Korean War, and the arrest and eventual trial in the United States of Julius and Ethel Rosenberg for atomic-bomb espionage activities. There is still doubt whether the Rosenbergs were actually involved in atomic-bomb espionage; the irregularities of the trial and the extremely harsh sentence, death in the electric chair, could well have been manifestations of American fear.

Further manifestations of that fear were evident in the politics of paranoia during the 1950s—the blacklisting of writers, the widespread demand for loyalty oaths, and waves of official and unofficial communist hunting. The culmination was the "Great Fear" of the McCarthy period. All of this must be understood in the context of atomic terror, the concept of the "secret," and the emergence of the Soviet threat. These interrelationships were brilliantly suggested by Edward Shils in an early (1956) study, appropriately entitled *The Torment of Secrecy: The Background and Consequences of American Security Policies.* Shils described how Americans found it "infuriating" to feel that they and their country were "rendered insecure by hidden enemies" who "would give away the secrets on which survival rests." Shils further equated these fears with tendencies toward polarizing the world between "the children of light and the children of darkness," so that "the atomic bomb was a bridge" over which extreme fantasies related to religious and political fundamentalism, ordinarily marginal, "entered the larger society which was facing an unprecedented threat to its continuance." With McCarthyism, the "secret" became not so much the bomb but a matter of "hidden Communists" and their equally hidden machinations—so that much of the inquisitorial hearings dealt with "revealing communist secrets" and "naming names." Now Americans could see "communism" as the source of the danger of annihilation and take active steps toward combating that "danger from within," rather than remain passively vulnerable to a worldwide nuclear-weapons structure that no one seemed able to alter. The "secret"—first of the atomic bomb and then of the communist danger—had come to serve as an effective psychological displacement for the primal fear of the bomb itself.

Hence, Americans found it devastating to learn, in October 1957, that the Soviets had launched Sputnik, the first "artificial earth satellite," into space. Sputnik was specifically associated with nuclear-launch capacity (the satellite could be replaced by a nuclear warhead of considerable weight and explosive power) and with Soviet technological achievement in general. Sputnik evoked not only "a sense of alarm, exasperation, humiliation, and confusion, but also a new dimension of fear." Indeed, "the very word was enough to send shivers up just about every American's spine. . . . The very notion that the Russians, previously thought of as primitive Asiatics when it came to advanced technology, could beat the United States of America in something so ultimately technological as the launching of an object into outer space was absolutely horrifying, a threat to national security in its own right." The resulting national "state of near panic" contributed greatly to dire official warnings of Soviet might, including that of the Gaither Committee (a special National Security Council commission which produced a highly influential report) that within two years (by 1959) "the USSR may be able to launch an attack with ICBMs [Intercontinental Ballistic Missiles] carrying megaton [explosive force equal to 1,000,000 tons of TNT] warheads, against which SAC will be almost completely vulnerable under present programs."

Cycles of Fear and Numbing

Since 1945, there have been cycles of nuclear fear and numbing—the latter generally preferred by governments in general lest the fear be turned into antinuclear activism. The early agitation about atomic bombs lasted from 1945 through 1950, at which time there seemed to take shape a "mood of diminished awareness and acquiescence in the developing nuclear arms race." But by the mid-1950s there was again a wave of fear, much of it now centered on the dangers of fallout, with particular alarm being roused by American H-bomb tests in 1955 which spread radioactive ash over 7,000 square miles of the Pacific, requiring evacuation of nearby islanders and bringing illness and death to Japanese fishermen 80 miles away. A rush of novels and films depicted nuclear danger and fear, and the Eisenhower administration was sufficiently worried about the film *On the Beach* that in December 1959 it was declared by the Office of Civil and Defense Management "very harmful" because of the "feeling of utter hopelessness" it produced, "undermining efforts to encourage preparedness." This wave of fear culminated in the Cuban missile crisis of October 1962, during which a large number of Americans, with considerable justification, thought nuclear war imminent.

Yet from September 1963 and through most of the 1970s, overt fear and activism declined to the point of near invisibility. Possible reasons that have been suggested include perception of diminished risk due to the Limited Test Ban Treaty of that year, the gradual adaptation to a world of nuclear weapons, the widespread embrace of the "peaceful atom" or nonmilitary atomic energy, the sense that the matter was being "taken care of" by reliable "experts," and the emerging claim on political and social passions of the Vietnam War. As a result, from the early 1960s to the late 1970s "most Americans . . . seemed oblivious to a danger that many in earlier years, and many others in the years to follow, considered the most urgent ever to confront the nation, and indeed the entire human race."

But in the late 1970s fearful agitation was once more renewed. Again, the causes are far from clear, but the important point is that

nuclear fear never entirely disappears but rather goes slightly underground, blunted by psychic numbing, only to be re-evoked by
nuclear saber rattling by either of the superpowers or even by
aggressive behavior by one of them (the Soviet invasion of Afghanistan late in the Carter administration, for instance) or by any
international crisis. By the early 1980s, psychological and social
studies began to demonstrate nuclear fear more or less throughout
the American population, but in forms that might be indirect,
bound up with numbing, and unpredictable.

Nuclearism: The Ideological Cure

> What is the only provocation that could bring
> about the use of nuclear weapons? Nuclear weap-
> ons. What is the priority target for nuclear weap-
> ons? Nuclear weapons. What is the only established
> defense against nuclear weapons? Nuclear weap-
> ons. How do we prevent the use of nuclear weap-
> ons? By threatening to use nuclear weapons. And
> we can't get rid of nuclear weapons, because of
> nuclear weapons.
>
> —MARTIN AMIS

The ideological cure for atomic trauma had, then, to treat not
military defeat or alleged "racial sickness" but the threat of extinction. And here we did something fateful and deeply ironic: we
seized upon the weapons themselves as a means of alleviating the
searing threat to existence created by those same weapons. Nuclearism, then, is an exaggerated dependency on nuclear weapons
for strength, protection, and safety, whatever the evidence that
they themselves are the instruments of genocide. The weapons are
passionately embraced as a solution to death anxiety and the threat
of extinction and a means of restoring a lost sense of immortality.
Nuclearism can take the form of a secular religion, a total ideology
in which grace and even salvation—the mastery of death and evil—
are achieved through the power of the new technological deity.

And that deity is then seen as capable not only of apocalyptic destruction but also of unlimited creation.

In the series of questions and answers in the epigraph to this section, the novelist Martin Amis has captured, with only minimal caricature, the self-enclosed logic by which, whatever the question, nuclear weapons provide an answer. They become for us existentially necessary objects.

In specific content, nuclearism bears no resemblance to the Nazi biomedical vision: it has nothing to do with race or any clear-cut social or political principle and focuses only on *things,* physical entities, that are supposed to render us powerful, safe, and free. But like the Nazi biomedical vision, nuclearism as an ideology is charismatic, overarching, anchored in "logic," and inherently genocidal. Again, there is the claim of diagnosis and cure: the diagnosis, vulnerability to annihilation by another power; and the cure, the means to annihilate one's potential annihilator. A psychological principle here, which occurs in many life situations, is to embrace that which we overwhelmingly fear in order to take on the power of the feared object. So great was this tendency in the areas of politics and the military that by 1950 "the dread destroyer of 1945 had become the shield of the Republic."

Nuclearism involves a false reliance on "strategy" and a radical neglect of efforts at improving human arrangements (diplomatic, political, and broadly social) that would be commensurate with the danger. All such considerations have been subsumed in an elaborate discourse about tactical military questions and strategic assumptions—in the claim of an all-purpose military science in connection with these genocidal devices. This claim leads to "the questionable assumption that strategic problems and war lend themselves to cool and confident prior calculation, apart from broader, random variables of personality, history, ambiguity, change, and chance." That assumption in turn confuses our perception of the genocidal devices themselves, which are sometimes viewed as mere weapons and at other times as virtual deities in protective reign over us, both images dangerous in the extreme. The commitment to nuclear weapons can become absolute. A scientist colleague characterized Edward Teller's attitude toward arms control as "always unabashedly hostile to the whole idea. If we were behind, we had to test to catch up, and if we were ahead, we had to stay there. There was no circumstance under which a test ban could be in our interest." Teller extended that attitude into potential scenarios of threat and conflict, involving various "appropriate" levels of use of nuclear weapons, and insisted, "We cannot and must not try to limit the use of weapons."

Robert Oppenheimer's tragic life illuminates much about nuclearism, in terms of both disease and cure.* In brilliantly leading and coordinating the Los Alamos project which produced the first atomic bombs, Oppenheimer became immersed in nuclearism. Beyond immediate military victory, he came to associate the use of the bomb with a higher purpose—that of "shaking mankind free from parochialism and war." As head of a scientific advisory group for the Stimson Interim Committee on the weapon, he argued against any nonlethal demonstration of the weapon. He justified this view further by adopting the great Danish physicist Niels Bohr's concept of "complementarity"—the idea that two findings in physics can, though different from and unrelated to one another, be equally true—applied morally (by Bohr and Oppenheimer) to the atomic bomb as both highly destructive and dangerous and potentially contributing to a deeper human relationship to peace. And when a group of Chicago scientists attempted to distribute at Los Alamos their petition against use of the weapons without warning on a human population, Oppenheimer prevented them, insisting that scientists were ill equipped to consider such matters and that more knowledgeable people were dealing with them at higher levels. After the bomb's use and the end of the war, though he spoke of the physicists' relation to "sin," he continued to consult on weapons and even opposed his fellow scientists' crusade against placing the new weaponry under complete military control.

But from about 1949, when he and others were considering the possibility of the "super" or hydrogen bomb—Teller's bomb, not his—Oppenheimer began to recognize, and express with great insight, the dangerous psychological essence of nuclearism: "What concerns me is really not the technical problem . . . but that this

*The complex issues at each stage of this life trajectory of Oppenheimer are discussed on pages 111–13.

thing appears to have caught the imagination, both of the congressional and military people, as *the answer* to the problem posed by the Russians' advance." He expressed the fear that Americans would "become committed to it as the way to save the country and the peace," and stressed that "our atomic bomb will not do all things," and, "the least we can conclude is that our twenty-thousandth bomb . . . will not in any deep strategic sense offset their two-thousandth." Here Oppenheimer was getting at the American psychological and political relationship to the weapon, the growing dependency upon it to achieve "all things." As a highly articulate man emerging from his own nuclearism—undergoing what may be called "nuclear backsliding"—he could expose from within this weapons-centered ideology and thereby mount a major conceptual critique of its function and influence.

When immersed in nuclearism, Oppenheimer was a national hero, the embodiment of the awesome but demonic power of destruction tapped by scientists. When he painfully extricated himself from that nuclearism, he was summarily crucified at a scandalous security hearing and became something of a "divine victim."

Nuclearism, especially in relation to ostensibly defensive weapons, has created strangely contradictory positions. A weapons scientist for the Strategic Defense Initiative, for instance, could deny that he fell into the category described by Pope John Paul II of those who worked on "weapons of death," and declared, "We're working on weapons of life, ones that will save people from the weapons of death. It's a moral decision and I believe in it very strongly." Similar distinctions were made by ideological factions of the Japanese peace movement when gathering in Hiroshima during the 1960s: factions favoring the Chinese could see their nuclear bombs as "weapons of peace" and those of the Soviets and the United States as "weapons of death"; while a faction supporting the Soviet Union reversed the Chinese and Soviet sides of things. But atomic-bomb survivors, who knew the weapons best, tended to have no truck with these distinctions.

Nuclearism and National Security

There is no such thing as security, and the word
should be stricken from our dictionary.
                                        —JAMES FORRESTAL

Just as the Nazis could never achieve their desired security against
"racial death" by persecuting and killing Jews, the nuclear quest
is equally fruitless in the perpetual struggle against vulnerability.
But there is also a major difference. The Jews were never, in
actuality, a military or political threat to the Nazis. The Soviet
Union and the United States, in their nuclear-weapons policies, are
indeed grave dangers to each other—more accurately, to the
world. Nuclearism begets nuclearism in one's adversary, in a grotesque back-and-forth process of mutual planning for genocide.
The quest for a psychological sense of security, which we work
hard to achieve in raising our children, is in a nuclear world constantly frustrated—which is why James Forrestal (secretary of defense during the 1940s) could, in a rare moment of candor and
insight, declare against the word altogether (see section epigraph).
*Indeed, Americans became preoccupied with national security at the moment
it ceased to exist.*

The actual term *national security* came into general American use
in 1947, partly in response to what was perceived as the failure of
international (United Nations) efforts at "collective security." In
July of that year, the concept was formalized with the passage of
the National Security Act, which provided for the beginning of the
Central Intelligence Agency (derived from the wartime Office of
Strategic Services) and for the National Security Council as a direct
advisory group to the president. But as the writer Marcus Raskin
has pointed out, the term *national security* was left undefined, "even
as all manner of policy is justified in its name." Raskin describes
an ideology of "the national security state" which stresses state
power, a strong military, and the inevitability of "constant conflict
with other states." As that ideology of the national security state
merged with nuclearism, three place names—Hiroshima, Pearl
Harbor, and Munich—took on special significance. Each of these

became part of a survivor legacy, tied to "lessons" learned from the death immersion of the war. Such lessons are part of survivors' collective quest for meaning; however dubious their application to new historical situations, they can become part of a passionately expressed survivor mission. Hiroshima, as we have seen, meant that we had to take steps against the danger of our extinction. Pearl Harbor meant military preparedness in the face of the possible "infamy" (President Roosevelt's term at the time) of devious enemies. Munich meant having the courage to "stand up" to one's enemies—or what the historian Martin Sherwin calls "appeasement phobia," in which Nazi-like purposes can be attributed to every Soviet action, and diplomacy of any kind is deeply feared lest it result in advantages for the Soviet Union and danger to ourselves.

A related survivor legacy of the Second World War was the extraordinary power America had come to possess and our sense that such dominant power was right and necessary. As the historian Ronald Steel put it, "America became not only a great world power, but *the* world power." That extraordinary power, together with largesse toward the shattered economies of former enemies and allies alike, enabled American leaders to experience "a certain omnipotence and hubris." So strong was the feeling of entitlement to that power that every American president since the Second World War has said words to the effect that the security of America and of the world depends upon our remaining the strongest nation in the world. That goal, of course, has required a "burgeoning reliance on atomic weapons." We have had to rely on our technological superiority: "A qualitative edge in nuclear weaponry seemed to be the surest, safest, cheapest—and perhaps even the only—way to maintain the security of our country and its allies." This was all part of what C. Wright Mills called "a military definition of reality." Moreover, "the country had no choice but to plan for the use of atomic weapons."

The first Single Integrated Operational Plan (SIOP), developed in 1960–61—according to Herbert York who, as director of defense research and engineering, was involved in its review—"made use of nearly a million times as much explosive power as was used at Hiroshima, perhaps 5,000 times that used in all of WW II." And the momentum had been established for increasingly destructive war-fighting plans, since the national security state had continuously to "propagate its version of reality" in relation to the desperate quest for what was unattainable. The domestic consequences of that contradiction were obsessions with "violators of national security," or "national security risks," and "security hearings" such as Oppenheimer's and the infamous congressional McCarthy and McCarren investigations during the 1950s. In early 1960, Herbert York concluded, after careful study of evidence, that the Soviets were not cheating on the then-existing nuclear test moratorium, and was told by the chairman of the Atomic Energy Commission, John McCone, that "my saying that was tantamount to treason." For just as the Nazis needed a concept of "the Jew" as the embodiment of absolute evil ("if the Jew did not exist, we would have had to invent him," is the way Hitler himself was said to have expressed the matter"), so was it necessary for the national-security state to construct an image of near-total Soviet evil in order to justify the planning of the nuclear destruction of the Soviet Union—as did the Soviets in relationship to the United States.

Nazi and nuclear ideologies have in common an impulse to slaughter human beings in numbers that can only be termed infinite, and to do so in the name of preserving the security of one's own group. In both cases, the final assertion of "security" readily becomes total self-destruction. In the case of nuclearism, that translation of security into absolute power can seem relatively innocent: there is no overt intent to victimize a particular people. Yet the potential consequences—and it must be noted that they are still just potential—could be absolute for the world at large.

Chapter 4

Science, Technology, and Totalism

The dynamo became a symbol of infinity . . . a moral force, much as the early Christians felt the cross. . . . Before the end, one began to pray to it.
—HENRY ADAMS

No Emperor or fiend from the past—not Caesar, not Alexander the Great, not Attila the Hun—ever claimed the sovereign right to determine the life and future of the entire universe. Yet that power is now claimed by every graduate engineer who steps into a nuclear weapons laboratory.
—E. L. DOCTOROW

NUCLEARISM EMERGES directly from physics and high technology, following upon genuine scientific discovery and significant technological breakthrough. By contrast, the Nazi biomedical ideology was based on no genuine biological breakthrough, the Nazis claiming such a breakthrough where none existed. Yet scientific claims have been greatly distorted in relation to nuclearism, and actual science was made use of by Nazism. Despite their differences, that is, the two ideologies exhibit certain common patterns in relationship to science and technology.

In both, the ideological vision encompasses a version of the existing science and technology. The Nazis started from the physical anthropology, genetics, and, to some extent, evolutionary theory of their time and then carried that theory into the realm of lethal fantasy by means of their particular biomedical vision and quest for a biocracy;* they found a bridge, as we have suggested, between existing science and science-connected fantasy in the slippery realm of eugenics. In nuclearism, the physics and technology have been brilliantly authentic. But extensions of scientific claims into strategic thought and nuclearistic ideology—extensions often made by physicists and engineers as well as social scientists—move quickly into their own lethal fantasy. The excesses of both ideologies are related to the central place science holds in modern cosmologies (as we shall discuss in relation to individual professionals in the next chapter).

The near worship of weapons emerged, as did the claims of scientific racism, from collective attitudes involving science and technology that have taken shape over the past two centuries. At the heart of the matter is the impulse to find in science and technology not just objects of worship but an immortalizing principle to replace the threatened and waning religious sources of eternal life. Scientific and technological achievement become substituted for spiritual and ethical ideas and for human arrangements in general. In that way science becomes not so much a religion as a fulcrum for extreme mystification. This is not to say that either Nazi or nuclearistic ideologies were inevitable twentieth-century developments, but rather that their embrace and mystification of science have significant historical roots. That kind of embrace and mystification, moreover, seem to be a requirement of contemporary genocide.

---

*A *biocracy* is a state claiming a divine mandate derived from biological principles. The term is meant to suggest a parallel to *theocracy,* a state ruled by priests. The biological priests (scientists and theorists) need not rule directly, but their biological ideology serves as the basis for those who do.

Technology as Destiny

> Evidently technological accomplishment has be-
> come a temptation that no person can reasonably
> be expected to resist. The fact that something is
> technically sweet is enough to warrant placing the
> world in jeopardy.
>
> —LANGDON WINNER

Lewis Mumford stresses science's early exclusion of the human
presence in favor of a "mechanical world-picture," within which
"human culture itself became a collective artifact." And even the
recent advances in physics that question a mechanical world view
have not succeeded in altering the " 'classic' scientific *Weltanschauung,* which imputed objectivity only to measurable data and repeat-
able experiments and denied the constant interplay between the
world of nature and the world of human culture, as both come to
a focus in a human personality." Mumford speaks of entire socie-
ties becoming vast machines, or "megamachines," on the basis of
combining this form of science with various social institutions, and
sees Hitler as "the chief agent in the modernization in the
megamachine," by means of "utilizing aspects of the available
science, plus the latest behaviorist advertising techniques, to condition the entire population." Moreover, our present megamachine—our structure of technical knowledge and institutions—
"wears the magic cloak of invisibility" so that "even its human
servitors are emotionally protected by their remoteness from the
human target they incinerate or obliterate." Strangely, it was an
Air Force general, Tommy White, who mocked the image of the
"defense intellectual" as conveying "a nice, cozy . . . feeling
. . . as though modern war could be settled on a chess board in an
ivy-covered Great Hall."

Over the course of the late nineteenth and early twentieth centuries, there took place in German historical experience what Fritz
Stern has called a "silent secularization." Passions formerly expressed in a Protestant religious context were transferred to inter-
pretive secular world views, notably that of science. Hence the
overall German tendency toward what can be called *romantic scien-*

tism, particularly in relation to evolutionary concepts and biology in general. The Nazis seized upon this tendency and imbued it with their own erratic expressions of mysticism—so that they could view their whole project as "nothing but applied biology."

We can similarly speak of a parallel process (occurring first in Western countries, and perhaps most strongly in the United States, but to a degree everywhere in the world), in which passions formerly associated with religion are applied to technical pursuits. As writers such as Jacques Ellul and William Barrett have pointed out, technique is made to transcend itself and become, so to speak, its own mystical truth. Hence, nuclearists can reduce the most complex human questions to "matters of physics." If the Nazi version of science was a bizarre expression of "biology as destiny," then the nuclearists' is one of "technology as destiny." (The Nazis also embraced technology, so much so that their regime has been aptly characterized as a form of "reactionary modernism.")* Nuclearism takes no account of the unpredictability of technological developments or of the unmanageability of the process of "technological dynamism," which creates in turn "uncertainty and unintention."

The idea of technological destiny is a further mystification of the principle of technological imperative. If an individual weapons scientist experiences a sense of technological imperative, he feels that any weapon that can be made should be made; if he experiences a sense of technological destiny, he takes on a world view in which technology represents a great force for human good, larger than any individual group, that will somehow deliver us from sin and destruction.† Thus, Werner Heisenberg, the world-renowned physicist who led the German atomic-bomb project, claimed that "the worst thing about it all [the building and use of atomic bombs] is precisely the realization that it was all so unavoidable."

The decision to go ahead with the hydrogen bomb might well

---

*Michael Sherry, in discussing pioneering interwar attitudes about civilian and military use of aircraft, speaks of "a combination of reactionary politics and technocratic idealism [which] provided another distraction from contemplation of future horrors."

†That attitude of technological deliverance was encountered by Stephen Kull in his interviews, by William Broad in his study of "Star Warriors," and in the interviews for this book. It is an expression of what Winner called "an atom-space-computer age Moira"—a fate that employs the free action of men to bring about ends that carry an aura of necessity.

have been equally affected by a sense of technological destiny. For Edward Teller, the bomb's most fierce proponent, the most passionate of his motivations (according to a formerly close colleague), even stronger than his antagonism toward the Soviet Union, was "to have technology evolve." When Oppenheimer and other physicists who had opposed the hydrogen bomb learned that a "technically sweet" way of making it had been found, their opposition tended to decline and many of them (Bethe and Fermi, among the most famous) agreed to work on the weapon.

Here science enters what has been called "rhetoric of the technological sublime"—and, indeed, of the "nuclear sublime." The weapons become exalted products of exalted enterprises. And the individual scientist or strategist can feel exalted in relation to them, can feel his own "destiny" to be bound up with theirs. In that way, the weapons become an integral part not only of his sense of self but also of his larger cosmology or immortality system. And the rest of our entire society—and Soviet society as well, we suspect—takes on some of that mind-set.

Nuclearism, then, contains an illusion of technological wisdom—the sense that the impressive achievements and esthetic elegance of its breakthroughs confer on technology a mystical goodness and even sagacity. Nuclearism enables believers to assume that nuclear technology is both beneficent and controllable. Those dangerous assumptions from the minds of nuclearists are expressions of *psychism*—the attempt to achieve control over one's external environment through internal or psychological manipulations, through behavior determined by intrapsychic needs no longer in touch with the actualities of the world one seeks to influence. An example of still more blatant Nazi psychism was the visionary idea, in the minds of SS ideologues, that killing every possible Jew took priority over considerations of the German war effort, because once the Jews had been completely destroyed all would go well in the world. In this relationship between mind and technology, the technology is asked to fill a contemporary "cosmic emptiness," to substitute for our waning modern and postmodern sense of the reliability and continuity of life. But the technology meant to fill the void is all too capable of rendering our planet into nothing but cosmic emptiness.

Ultimate Power

> It is also possible that if the first man could have
> been present at the moment of Creation when God
> said, "Let there be light," he might have seen
> something very similar to what we have seen.
> —WILLIAM LAURENCE

The essence of nuclearism is the identification—even merging—
with what is perceived as an ultimate form of power. While the
weapons actually possess overwhelming death power, they can all
too readily be psychologically perceived as possessing life power.
That reversal, however appalling, is an old story. Zeus in Greek
mythology and the Old Testament God of the Judeo-Christian
tradition could either destroy all human life or sustain it, depending upon either their whim or considered judgment at a given
moment. We worship such a figure, according to classical psychoanalysis, because it becomes the recipient of emotions associated
with deep dependence originally experienced during childhood
toward our parents. But worship is more fundamentally involved
with our continuing struggle to master death and with our awe
before those figures (or objects) possessing the power to inflict
death on a massive scale—and who, by not exercising that power,
seem to maintain life or, at least, permit it to continue.

Henry Adams could observe his own experience of religious awe
when contemplating a 40-foot dynamo at the Great Exposition in
Paris in 1900 (see chapter epigraph, page 77), but also expressed,
in another famous commentary, his sense of the danger of precisely that power of science: "Man has mounted science and is now
run away with. . . . The engines he will have invented will be
beyond his strength to control." With nuclearism, the "ultimate
energy" and "symbol of infinity" Adams spoke of, though bearing
on destruction, are worshiped nonetheless.

The strong impulse within nuclearism to convert ultimate destruction to ultimate creation was expressed by William Laurence,
the *New York Times* science editor who was chosen to be the official
military spokesman for the new weapon. Laurence's description of

the Trinity bomb focused strongly on a vision of rebirth—much like William James's descriptions of religious conversion—and contained such phrases as "One felt as though he had been privileged to witness the Birth of the World," and, "The big boom" became "the first cry of a newborn world." Laurence's further comment about "the first man . . . present at the moment of Creation" (see section epigraph, page 82) was in response to a more jaundiced observation by the chemist and later presidential science adviser George Kistiakowsky: "In the last millisecond of the earth's existence—the last man will see something very similar to what we have [seen]."

Laurence reacted with similar spiritual enthusiasm eleven years later to the explosion of America's first airborne hydrogen bomb in the northern Pacific: after being "momentarily staggered" by thoughts of what the weapon would do to the great cities of the world, he came to the "more reassuring thought" of the weapon as a perpetual shield (see chapter epigraph, page 51) and that "this rising supersun seemed to me the symbol of the dawn of a new era" in which the weapons would form a "world-covering, protective umbrella" until such time as "mankind will be able to beat atomic swords into ploughshares, harnessing the vast power of the hydrogen in the world's oceans to bring in an era of prosperity such as the world has never even dared dream about." The sequence is from total destruction to total protection to total salvation—in psychological terms, from annihilation to renewal to embrace and dependent worship. The deity is awesome, dreadful in its apocalyptic potential, but also the savior of humankind. The arbiter of immortality must be both.

Another version of nuclearism, as expressed by Edward Teller, is what may be called *heroic scientism*. Teller writes of the "spirit of spontaneity, adventure, and surprise" in pursuing thermonuclear problems with colleagues, some of whom, while strongly opposing his views, have spoken of his decades of dedication and phenomenal energy as nothing short of "heroic." In this way nuclearism becomes linked with elements of the myth of the hero: the "call to greatness" followed by the "road of trials" on the way to inevitable triumph. References to Teller as "the apostle of the Super" suggest his religious dedication to thermonuclear weapons, as do some of the chapter headings of his *The Legacy of Hiroshima:* "The Renaissance of Alchemy," "The Lure of Infinity," and "The Seeds of Tomorrow." The intensity of Teller's nuclearism leads him to make claims that are technologically and scientifically false (see page 42): the claim that the effects of nuclear war could be easily mitigated by fallout shelters and by an elaborate version of the strategic defense initiative; and the even more outrageous statements that radiation from test fallout "might be slightly beneficial."

Laurence the journalist and Teller the physicist represent a vanguard of visionary nuclearism, and come close to what William James called a "faith-state" in which "various dogmatic beliefs suddenly . . . acquire a character of certainty, become a new reality, become an object of faith." There is evidence of that kind of "faith-state" of "knowledge beyond reasoning" in certain strategists and decision makers who can, as William James also wrote, "see themselves as channels through which the infinite intelligence and power can work." This mystical dimension is at the heart of both Nazi and nuclearist ideology and extends outward in less intense forms through the bureaucracy and the rest of the population. In the Nazi case, the mysticism was overt; while in the nuclear case, it tends to be hidden by the focus on technical matters and apparent scientific detachment. But behind that apparent detachment lies a faith-state no less intense or "beyond reasoning" than those of the most ardent religious believer.

In this way, nuclearism resembles a secular religion, one that veers in the direction of fundamentalism. What is rendered sacred is not the literal word of the Bible or of a political movement but the literal entity of the all-destructive weapon. That literal "thing" plays the part of the "word," to be invoked as the answer to every question—whether concerning politics or morality, strategy or policy, nation or world, life or death, body or spirit. To understand these fundamentalist attitudes toward possession of the weapons, we need to turn for a moment to the more familiar form of nuclear fundamentalism having to do with their *effects.* In recent decades in America, we have been hearing more and more about a nuclear-weapons–related "end-time" theology within which ultimate virtue derives not from the preservation of the world but from proper spiritual preparation for its destruction. As a Pentecostal preacher put it, "if the [hydrogen] bomb dropped today, it wouldn't bother me one bit [because] the whole world would come into a knowledge of Jesus Christ, and . . . we would have peace." Nuclear Armageddon becomes a means of fulfilling the biblical prophesy of the Second Coming or the Kingdom of God. The central biblical document is the Book of Revelation ("almost an exact description of thermonuclear blast") with its description of world destruction and Christ's return to reign one thousand years, the Millennium, after which the virtuous—who will have been "raptured up" to heaven during the period of destruction—can dwell in a literal heaven on earth devoid of sorrow, pain, and death.*

The historian Norman Cohn has described a series of fierce, often murderous millennial movements during the Middle Ages, and he and others have suggested parallels to Nazi impulses. The political scientist James Rhodes, for instance, considers the Hitler movement, "a millenarian-gnostic revolution . . . [within which] the Nazis believed that their reality was dominated by fiendish powers and that they experienced revelations or acquired . . . knowledge . . . that made them want to fight a modern battle of Armageddon for a worldly New Jerusalem." An even closer Nazi relationship to the Book of Revelation has been suggested by recent work on the influence of Lanz von Liebenfels, a mystical racist who was obsessed with that book and felt himself its only true interpreter. And recently there has been a not inappropriate joining of Nazi and end-time nuclear ideologies in several American right-wing fringe groups, including those known as the Aryan Nations and the Order. The nuclear ideology provides "survivalist" impulses (arming and training in remote areas for ostensible survival) and end-time imagery (arming oneself spiritually for the events prophesied in Revelation), while Nazi ideology provides doses of vicious racism and crude elements of the biomedical vision. These fringe groups avidly prepare for, often welcome, nu-

*In a study of "Nuclear Threat and the American Self," being conducted at the Center on Violence and Human Survival at the John Jay College of Criminal Justice of the City University of New York, and headed by Robert Jay Lifton and Charles B. Strozier, psychological interviews with fundamentalists suggest that, although nuclear threat is absorbed into their end-time theology, they nonetheless do not welcome nuclear holocaust and "simply keep separate in highly complex and dissociative ways the logic o` their theology and their human decency."

clear holocaust and stand ready to impose by force in its wake a Nazi regime, all of which they see as somehow in the service of establishing a Kingdom of Saints and facilitating the Second Coming. Underneath the absurdity and mixed historical and spiritual metaphors, there is a certain perverse logic here that has to do with the regenerative fundamentalism common to elements of Nazi thought and response to nuclear threat. However at the edge of the mind's psychological repertoire such groups may be, they undoubtedly distill and caricature ideas and feelings held by much larger numbers of people in this country and elsewhere.

Armageddonist imagery can also be held by those close to the weapons, and may include impulses to purge the world of its evil by means of nuclear holocaust. Certainly the *actions* of many nuclear strategists and defense intellectuals in seeking nuclear confrontation that comes close to the brink (as in carrying out what is sometimes called "nuclear chicken," and waiting for the adversary to be the first to step back) suggest a secular impulse toward world destruction. While that should not be seen as the dominant inclination, there is interview evidence that at least some strategists may not be free of the lure of Armageddon—a temptation given fictional expression by Arthur Kopit in his drama *The End of the World: With Symposium to Follow.* These "secular Armageddonists," like their religious counterparts, renounce responsibility for the holocaust they anticipate and may press toward bringing about. Secular Armageddonists may view nuclear holocaust as an inevitable outcome of our time and technology which is pointless to resist, or as preferable to an assumed alternative of "giving in to the Russians." Secular and religious Armageddon images tend to merge in many minds, having in common their relationship to mystical expressions of nuclearism.

Anticommunist Totalism

> The great Golem we have made against our ene-
> mies is our culture, our bomb culture—its logic, its
> faith, its vision.
> —E. L. DOCTOROW

More than has been generally realized, the Nazis also put forward totalistic expressions of anticommunism, but subsumed to their overarching racial vision; and their totalism was much more extreme and more visible in their images of "Jewish bolshevism" and of bolshevism as "the highest stage of Judaism."

As a millenarian ideology, nuclearism also needed a source of pure evil to combat. This source was all too readily available in the form of "communism," the Soviet Union having engaged in massive killing and suppression of its people (Stalin killed more people than Hitler). In blending with a kind of sacred anticommunism, a religion in which devil hatred subsumes anything in the way of positive belief, nuclearism took on totalistic qualities, became associated with thought and feeling that was absolute and completely polarized. "Communism" at home and abroad became the repository for all evil; and America, by means of an insistent symmetry, the repository of good. Relations with the Soviet Union could then be understood in biblical terms; and a later American president could describe "communists" as "godless monsters," and the Soviet Union as the "focus of evil" and the "evil empire."

That totalistic quality of anticommunism associated with nuclearism reached an official apogee in 1950 in a report to the National Security Council by a special committee of leading figures from the departments of State and Defense. The report, known as NSC-68, dwelled extensively on Soviet evil and justified any means on our part, "covert or overt, violent or non-violent," that might "serve the purposes of frustrating the Kremlin design." The report contrasted Soviet duplicity and willingness to "strike a surprise blow"—with its nuclear weapons against us or our allies anywhere in the world—with something close to American pure virtue: with "the essential tolerance of our world outlook, our generous and constructive impulses, and the absence of covetousness in our international relations." While the language was "deliberately hyped" for the sake of gaining support for American weapons buildup, the overall statement was "amazingly incomplete and amateurish" in its exaggerated portrait of "the monolithic and evil nature of the Communist bloc." The overall report, however, was consistent in content and tone with highly ideologized American sentiment at the time.

This totalistic quality prevailed in official American circles. Herbert York tells how, during decades of weapons work in laboratories and in the Defense Department, "I never heard a single suggestion that there might be people inside the Soviet nuclear establishment who were pressing for moderation." York admits, "In retrospect this seems astonishing, but the picture of the Soviet Union as being, in effect, a vast prison camp simply did not allow room for such an idea," and concedes, "We might have made slightly different and perhaps better policy decisions had we known about even one such voice."

Nuclearism, then, has become totalistic in its relationship to science, to ultimate power, and to the American religion of anticommunism (and the Soviet religion of anticapitalism). Totalistic projects seek to "stop history" by means of a once-and-for-all resolution of problems of death and human continuity. They seek to cut off the flow of changing images and forms that make us, as human beings, the historical animal. While America, as an open society, has nothing comparable to the Nazis' milieu control, the inner councils of decision making concerning nuclear weapons have been dominated by nuclearistic attitudes and images to the exclusion of alternative views. And even popular discourse on the weapons has been essentially contained within "metaphors of power, the historical metaphor of a new industrial revolution, metaphors of the sun, [and] metaphors of transcendental religion." Thus, nuclearism controls the milieu through official secrecy and radical restriction of language and concepts.

It is only relatively recently that alternative attitudes and concepts have found acceptance in various American intellectual environments; and even to date, these alternative views are rarely permitted within official or semiofficial ones. Nuclearistic environments in various ways follow other themes of ideological totalism, including manipulation of guilt and shame in those who reject its assumptions and a cult of confession to permit such "deviants" to admit their errors (as in the security hearings of the 1950s), and the principle of "doctrine over person" (as when Herbert York was called a "traitor" for accepting the clear evidence that the Soviets were not cheating on an arms control treaty, rather than insisting that they were). And, as we have noted, nuclearism tends to claim the status of a "sacred science" even in situations where true data do not exist. There is no dispensing of existence in the Nazi sense: critics of nuclearism are not put to death. But they have been excluded from positions of influence and in various ways ignored or marginalized in what could be called a symbolic dispensing of existence. Moreover, should the weapons be used, the dispensing of existence and nonexistence would be on a scale that is, to put things quietly, unprecedented.

The Need for Mystification

Unlike overt Nazi victimization of Jews and others, the claim of nuclearism is always prevention, the weapons to be used only "if deterrence fails." This *contingent* aspect of genocidal intent enables us to resist recognizing it *as* genocidal intent. It would be hard for us to make that recognition and continue to see ourselves as an open democratic society proud of its moral claims. Indeed, one plausible theory concerning Oppenheimer's dismissal from public life was that he exposed nuclear genocidal intent when he prepared and signed the 1949 General Advisory Committee report which explicitly stated that hydrogen bombs are "weapons of genocide," and, as Thomas Powers points out,

> implicitly accused the Joint Chiefs of Staff of having both committed and prepared for genocide because *(A)* conventional and nuclear bombing during WWII constituted indiscriminate murder on the grand scale, and *(B)* JCS plans for war with Russia in October of [19]49

called for all-out attacks on Soviet civilian populations with no limit imposed beyond our capacity to ferry nuclear weapons from New Mexico to Eurasia.

As in the case of the Nazis, the nuclearists cannot publicly acknowledge—or, at least, not quite—the degree of brutalization—of genocidal intent, contingent or otherwise. There is for the nuclearists, as there was for the Nazis, a dark "secret," only partially and ambivalently kept, but crucial to the endeavor. The Nazis went to great lengths to conceal their mass murder: first, the direct medical killing of the "euthanasia" project; and then, the systematic genocide of the death camps. The direct medical killing, mostly of mental patients, was administered from Hitler's own Berlin chancellory, with the implication that he understood himself to be a prophet whose racial vision outdistanced the ordinary state structure and bureaucracy. Similarly, the Final Solution—the policy to murder all Jews—was considered a matter to be officially known by few other than the élite SS perpetrators, as again suggested in Himmler's proud declaration concerning the murder of Jews: "In our history, this is an unwritten and never-to-be-written page of glory." *Only* the SS was sufficiently ideologically advanced, in Himmler's judgment, to be entrusted to "carry the burden for our people," a "burden" that was both the killing and the secret of the killing. Others could not be told the secret because they had not been sufficiently numbed by the ideology and its practice either to practice or even accept the killing. In the nuclear case, there is also a special élite able to embrace the nuclearistic ideology sufficiently to accept the secret—that is, not the design of the weapon but the intent ("should deterrence fail") to make genocidal use of it. The callousness itself is more abstract; theoretical projections of millions of dead require a good deal less numbing than the actual killing of a single person.

Nuclearism's hold on American society is closely bound up with mystification, in the sense of both obfuscation and veneration. Military units associated with the weapons, think tanks projecting their use, and scientific and corporate contributors to their design and production all take on a certain aura, a *mystique* that renders them transcendent and beyond ordinary criticism, in a sense untouchable. Even with domestication—the bland-sounding principles of "living with nuclear weapons"—the mystique does not disappear but can be said to be "routinized," accepted into everyday life. The American institutions of nuclear genocide never approach the mystical public drama featured by the Nazis and epitomized by the Nuremberg rallies, though the Soviets have done some of that in connection with their May Day parades. Rather, our nuclear-age mysticism maintains a misleading quietude in its almost silent falsifications concerning our threatened existential state, while drawing upon the aura of all-powerful destruction.

The bizarre nuclear "scenarios" (the word derives from Italian and Latin terms for stage and scene) become mythic tales and morality plays about nuclearistic wisdom. These scenarios contribute greatly to nuclear mystification in their alleged control of the narrative—in their denial of the terrible truth that "most of the scenarios were far-fetched and even preposterous" precisely because their outcome in actuality was uncontrollable. But these scenarios may come to be perceived by both their creators and their audiences as containing a special psychic truth—a form of knowledge emanating from the priests and shamans of the nuclear cult.

The general mystification contributes also to the idea of nuclear-weapons work as a demanding, even heroic ordeal. Strategists and weapons designers can see their work as difficult, even unpleasant, but as something, as Bethe put it, "we have to do." Part of the ordeal is coping with thoughts that break through about what the weapons could do to human beings. A former missile combat crew deputy commander spoke of the special ordeal of men in the silos, of their "near maddening conditions of isolation, boredom and frustration . . . similar to a prisoner's life in solitary confinement," except for the presence of a second person. A crew member "is not supposed to have a conscience," and part of his ordeal is to "tr[y] . . . not to think about his ultimate responsibility, which could lead to the killing of millions of people." (Nazi doctors and technicians had a parallel ordeal.) A senior strategist spoke similarly about his painful feelings as an adviser during the Cuban missile crisis: "You just do not know where it's going to lead. You're just looking down an abyss."

Thus totalized and mystified, the ideology extends its claim everywhere so that even partial belief in it can exert considerable influence. Nuclear scientists and strategists, for instance, can oppose the extremities of nuclearism while accepting some of its more "reasonable" components such as "maintaining our deterrent," countering the Soviet Union, and advancing military technology in general. There is an ideological continuum, with relatively "pure" nuclearism (Edward Teller and William Lawrence) at one end and more "moderate" advocates of deterrence (such as the authors of *Living with Nuclear Weapons*) at the other—the entire continuum existing within and, in fact, maintaining the ideology of nuclearism. And there can be shifts within individual minds at various points of the continuum (see chapter 7). But as with Nazi ideology, nuclearism provides our society with a master narrative, a powerful source of meaning and self-definition for our collective existence—an ideological glue as potentially dangerous for our era as Nazism was for its time.

Ideological Ethics

Genocidal ideologies make ethical claims. Indeed, it is impossible to kill extremely large numbers of people without a vision of higher purpose. Many Germans came to feel that the Nazi project was right, fair, and just. Even the hatred and direct violence called forth could be seen as either justified or as excessive zeal in what was an ennobling political and social enterprise on behalf of national and racial rebirth.

Even among the highly educated, an ideological ethic could support brutal behavior. For instance, a German medical professor with an international scientific reputation, while attending a military medical conference, had the courage to rise in protest when it became evident that a paper being presented was based on human experiments. Shortly afterward, he was called to see the leading Nazi medical administrator, who explained to him in a friendly manner—more or less in the tone of one reasonable man to another—that the experiments were regrettable but necessary because they were part of an extremely important effort to develop a serum for treating or preventing the form of typhus that was endangering German troops. The professor, who was also an ardent Nazi and a leading military consultant, immediately withdrew his opposition, and not long afterward was himself implicated in similar human experiments. It was his commitment to the "higher purpose" of a total ideology and its war effort that enabled him to violate his own prior professional ethics.

The ethical claims of Nazi ideology could be quickly exposed by the critical observer as justifications for large-scale murder and vicious cruelty. While nuclearism could result in consequences even more extreme, its immediate ethical claims can seem much more reasonable. The very effort to create the atomic bomb was, as we have seen, understandably perceived as a desperate scientific race against an evil Nazi adversary. It is frequently claimed (though much new evidence calls the claim into question) that the bomb saved hundreds of thousands, even "millions" of lives that would have been lost in an invasion of Japan—a moral justification that set the stage for the development of later full-blown nuclearism. Over the post–Second World War era, nuclearism came to make two additional powerful claims: the bomb serves as a powerful buttress against expanding communism—that is, against another manifestation of the spread of evil; and the bomb—nuclear weapons in general—keeps the peace by means of the mutual threats contained in "deterrence." There could thus take shape an American "folk culture of nuclear weapons," according to which "the bomb could be used only for Good because the society that developed it represented the Good. The bomb would further democracy because it protected the democratic way of life."*

---

*Oppenheimer's celebrated declaration that "the physicists have known sin," frequently thought of as moral self-criticism, was understood differently by many observers. Herbert York, for instance, interpreted him as saying that the bomb, however "immediately harmful and regrettable," was one of those actions "that occasionally become . . . unavoidable in the slow and often fitful march of civilization." York went on to explain that, within official councils, there developed considerable resistance to any ethical approach. So much so that the moral statements in the General Advisory Committee (of the Atomic Energy Commission) report written by Oppenheimer in 1950 concerning the hydrogen bomb as a "weapon of genocide" worked against his position: "In the eyes of many people the introduction of ethical arguments . . . definitely undermined whatever effectiveness it might otherwise have had."

From within the discourse of nuclearism, systematic ethical exploration can become odd and contradictory. For instance, Joseph Nye, taking issue with a position put forward by Jonathan Schell, insists that simply because a policy entails a "tiny probability" of human extinction does not mean that it is wrong to pursue it or "that our generation has no right to take risks." He goes on to reject what he takes to be an exaggerated focus on our "obligations . . . to future generations"; and insists that we can know little about the values of those generations, so that to assume that those values must constrain our policies and prevent us from taking necessary risks would be to "establish a dictatorship of future generations over the present one." Without attempting an overall ethical refutation of Nye's position, it is enough to say here that one can indeed impute at least one value to future generations—the right to come into existence.

The general point here is that the genocidal ideology, given its totalistic claims, must press toward ethical justification. That ethical justification may be put forward as a step-by-step exercise in mainstream reasoning, as in the case of Joseph Nye's *Nuclear Ethics*. Or it can reach the absurdity of a contention by the right-wing antifeminist activist Phyllis Schlafly: "The atomic bomb is a marvelous gift that was given to our country by a wise God." At that point the means of extinction becomes, almost literally, God's grace.

Legitimation

If ideological claims are considered absolutely true, then their consequences must be viewed as equally absolutely legitimate. Thus Nazi Germany, contrary to many impressions, placed great stress on legitimacy, of which there were two levels, the overt and the hidden. Overt legitimacy consisted of official laws and decrees presented as outgrowths of Nazi ideology, publicly stated, and carried out by visible administrative groups. Hidden legitimacy involved secret orders emerging from the radical edge of the ideology, which were likely to involve killing and generally came from the highest Nazi authorities, such as Hitler himself (the *"Führer order"*) or Party or SS leaders claiming to speak in Hitler's name. That was the case with both the "euthanasia" projects of direct medical killing mostly of mental patients, and of the still greater genocidal projects victimizing Jews in particular but also Gypsies, Poles, Russians, homosexuals, and political enemies. These secret orders not only had full legitimacy but were generally given greater priority than overt ones.

In the case of nuclear weapons, there are also overt and covert ideological relations to legitimacy. On the one hand, the prevailing nuclearism enables the weapons to be openly and legally built, tested, and deployed: that is, legitimated both by official sanction and by moral claim of "national security" and "deterrence." But nuclearism also creates covert areas of legitimation: the secret plans for fighting and winning nuclear wars and for decisions to use the weapons, under various circumstances, at different levels of command, as well as the elaborate targeting of virtually all Soviet cities. Thus we can say that nuclearism is responsible for a "legitimation crisis" within which the political authorities of both the United States and the Soviet Union have official sanction, under certain conditions, to act in ways that could bring about human extinction. Specific doctrines, such as that of mutual assured destruction (MAD) are "formal statements" of "the de facto legitimacy of indiscriminate killing."

Killing to Heal

Nazi killing in the name of healing was specific and concrete, the sick Nordic race to be cured by killing the "infecting" forces. The principle was made still more literal by the medicalized approach to the killing, and the whole project had a spectacular naïveté. In the case of nuclearism, the principle of killing to heal is still there but in much more muted, indirect form. It is buried under claims of beneficent influence without actual use, of prevention of killing via deterrence; and rendered distant and unreal by unprecedentedly elaborated technology and bureaucracy. Yet this very insidiousness has a particular danger. For that healing-killing ethos—the idea of actually exploding the bomb for the sake of ultimate peace—was present almost from the beginning.

Secretary of War Henry Stimson, the person with greatest responsibility concerning use of the first atomic bombs, with the possible exception of the President, believed that through "the proper use of this weapon [it would be possible] to bring the world into a pattern in which the peace of the world and our civilization can be saved." Like many after him, Stimson felt that "the more frightful [the bomb] seemed as a weapon of war, the more useful it appeared as an instrument of peace."*

That moral equation—that by killing, or threatening to kill, the bomb would heal—has been extended to our conflicts with the Soviet Union, to the idea of destroying an enemy and eliminating Soviet evil on behalf of purifying the world. We hesitate before this "purification," just as many fundamentalists hesitate before the claim of their own theology that nuclear holocaust can serve as part of the cleansing force of end time. It was our struggle with such imagery that Robert Lowell had in mind in his post-Hiroshima lines, "And I am a red arrow on this graph/of Revelations."

Lowell later captured directly the healing-killing principle in stressing the long-standing American ideal of "saving the world," which "comes close to perhaps destroying the world." Should we act in such a way, "it would come in the guise of an idealistic stroke . . . the Ahab story of having to murder evil, and you may murder

---

*Even Leo Szilard, who was to become an outspoken leader of the antinuclear scientists, held that same view at least briefly. Early in 1944 he wrote, "It will hardly be possible to get political action along that line unless high efficiency atomic bombs *have actually been used in this war* and the fact of their destructive power has deeply penetrated the mind of the public." And for President Truman and the political and scientific leaders around him—including James Byrnes, Robert Oppenheimer, Edward Teller, and James Conant—the general view was that "not only the conclusion of the war but the organization of an acceptable peace seemed to depend . . . on the success of the atomic attacks against Japan." Containing the Soviet Union was part of that "acceptable peace."

all the good with it." Nuclearism makes this claim, described here by Lowell, to achieve collective vitality and a sense of purification by killing others—indeed, to achieve an intense form of shared immortality while pressing for arrangements that could end all life. Killing to heal is both the extreme edge and the essence of nuclearism.

Chapter 5

Professionals

So you see, love for a job well done is a deeply ambiguous virtue. It animated Michelangelo. . . . Rudolph Höss, the Auschwitz commander, boasted of the same virtue.

—PRIMO LEVI

You see what happened to me—what happened to the rest of us, is we started for a good reason, then you're working very hard to accomplish something, and it's pleasure, it's excitement. And you just stop thinking, you know, you stop.

—RICHARD FEYNMAN

GENOCIDE REQUIRES well-educated professionals. They are necessary for its technology, its organization, and its rationale. In the Nazi case, members of all of the professions—physicians, scientists, engineers, military leaders, lawyers, clergy, university professors, and school teachers—were effectively mobilized to the ideological project. In the nuclear case, a wide variety of professionals have also become involved with the genocidal system, especially those with skills consonant with the highly technical nature of that system. Despite the differences, troubling parallels emerge in the Nazi and nuclear situations, parallels having to do with socialization of overall professions, and of individuals within those professions, to the genocidal system and function, and with psychological mechanisms that enable people to view, as a form of authentic professional activity, work that is actually or potentially genocidal.

Nazi Professionals: Socialization and Doubling

The syringe belongs in the hands of a physician.
—NAZI "EUTHANASIA" MOTTO

When the Nazis took power, German medicine was reconstituted according to Nazi political and biomedical ideology by means of the Nazi policy of *Gleichschaltung* ("coordination" or "synchronization"; see chapter 6), which combined putting trusted ideologues in control with infusing the entire profession with Nazi ideology. The reconstituted profession thus focused strongly on "racial hygiene" and "scientific racism," and the process of *Gleichschaltung* was observed to have taken place even "more rapidly and obligingly" than in most other professions.

In Nazi genocide, there was an important distinction between professional killers and killing professionals. The professional killers were the "hit men"—usually members of the SS—who did the shooting and inserted the gas pellets. The killing professionals, our main concern, tended to formulate, supervise, and provide the technology for the killing.

For many doctors, embrace of the Nazi cause was a way of resolving pre-existing conflicts in a profession that had known great distinction but had undergone a series of crises. Conflicts included widespread anti-Semitism directed in particular toward the many Jewish doctors in large cities, some of whom had achieved great prominence; political struggles between social democrats and the conservative and right-wing tendencies of the majority of physicians, including special resentment by the latter of medical insurance programs; profound financial problems and a glut of young doctors, leading to poverty among many of them after the depression of 1929; and considerable competition from nonmedical "healing practioners" who focused on the natural life. Doctors were notably authoritarian and nationalistic, rallied to the colors in the First World War, joined right-wing paramilitary units after the war in considerable numbers, and during the middle and late 1920s formed a small group of early National Socialist physicians (which was to expand in 1929 into the National Socialist

Physicians' League), whose members joined in street rallies and sometimes in street combat with communists and others.

Much of early Nazi ideological doctrine on racial revitalization came from physician-geneticists such as Fritz Lenz, the latter specifically influencing Hitler (see chapter 3, page 55). Lenz, though not without some reservation about the way his work was used, declared enthusiastically in 1931 that "Hitler is the first politician of truly great influence who has recognized racial hygienics as a central objective of politics and who will vouch for its realization."

The emerging Nazi medical profession made use of extreme ideologues, loyal Party members, intense anti-Semites, and power-focused bureaucrats. As a group, however, it was the "decent Nazis"—well educated, competent, proper in their behavior, often in opposition to the more primitive Nazis, but themselves drawn to the ideology and loyal to the movement—who ended up doing most of the professional work of the regime.

They could do this task only by continuing to see themselves as professionals, as physicians, as scientists. And leaders of the profession were able to draw upon reputable German medical tradition, including that of the German Society for Racial Hygiene, formed in 1904 as a scientific body with its own journal. Indeed, Nazi physician-scientists could see themselves as not only bona-fide professionals but as antagonists to the "charlatans" within the Nazi movement. Konrad Lorenz, then an ardent Nazi and also a recipient of a prestigious chair, was able to attack those fellow Nazis who refused to accept the Darwinian view of evolution, arguing that it should be the core of the Nazi creed. At the same time, Lorenz used his Darwinism to extend and legitimate the Nazi bio-medical vision, and declared that the racial hygiene project should, in effect, take over the evolutionary process to bring about "a more severe elimination of morally inferior human beings" and "literally replace" the natural forces of elimination of prehistoric times. Once more, the "decent Nazi"—in this case, a young scientist of impeccable credentials along with his Nazi convictions—could have the greatest value for the regime.

Doctors could become *biological managers* by means of their university institutes for racial hygiene, which attempted to develop a national card index of people with hereditary taints. That management function could combine with harmful expressions of medical idealism: the central theorist of the coercive sterilization program was described as "not so much a fanatical Nazi as a fanatical geneticist" with "the aim of his life" that of establishing the genetic basis for psychiatric illness. And another leading advocate of eugenics and "racial hygiene" expressed the exuberance scientists could feel at the recognition given them by the regime: "What a special and rare joy for theoretical research, when it falls into a time, where the world view *(Weltanschauung)* is favourable, and where even its practical results are used instantaneously as a basis for measures to be taken by the state."

The "euthanasia" project—in which doctors took charge of killing their own patients—was a large step from ligating spermatic cords or ovarian tubes. While this *direct medical killing* was a secret project, many German doctors had to come to know something about it, given the wide net of medical facilities involved (including, especially, psychiatric hospitals and departments, other hospitals and homes for adults and children, and many individual physicians, nurses, and health workers who came to be concerned with the registration of mental patients and other chronically ill people for the project). However fragmentary their knowledge at first, and whatever the systematic efforts at deception by means of medicalization (including even referring to killing centers as places of advanced therapy), many doctors were in a position to recognize the increasing evidence of mass murder.

This project, too, had been scientifically prefigured in a work published in 1920 by two distinguished German professors—Alfred Hoche, a psychiatrist, and Karl Binding, a jurist—which provided the Nazis with their concept of "life unworthy of life." That study advocated the use of rigorous medical criteria in choosing patients for mercy killing, but revealed its medical hubris in the claim that doctors could determine incurability with "one hundred percent certainty of correct selection."

Leading doctors in the program combined their medical science with their political and biomedical ideology. The man who was mostly in charge of running it was an extreme Nazi enthusiast who was both a professor of psychiatry and a competent clinician on the one hand and on the other a person with little compunction about working with the Gestapo and the SS on intelligence questions and probably torture methods. Another was a prominent academic psychiatrist, also an ardent Nazi, who had developed an enlightened program of work therapy for the treatment of schizophrenia, and is thought to have acted with a certain amount of psychiatric idealism in wishing to end the scandal of poorly treated, regressed, back-ward psychiatric patients.

Young doctors brought into a killing role in the project could have some of their uneasy feelings assuaged by contact with professional luminaries, who could speak from "scientific tradition." These young doctors could make further use of science as a means of adapting to the killing project in the form of post-mortem studies of the brains of patients killed. One took advantage of the visits of a leading German neuropathologist to arrange to work with him on brain dissections. And in Auschwitz, an important motivation for conducting experiments on prisoners was the doctors' desire to keep a hand in scientific work. Research could be officially sponsored in relation to goals associated with the biomedical ideology, as was the case with the notorious sterilization experiments. A leading experimenter was a civilian professor who was internationally known for his work on infertility and, through meetings and correspondence with Heinrich Himmler, decided to reverse the procedure and investigate means of sterilizing large numbers of people designated as racially inferior.

But the main activity of Auschwitz doctors was supervising the overall killing process from beginning to end. They conducted "selections" of Jews at the ramp where the trains arrived (sending the great majority immediately to the gas chambers and a small minority of relatively intact adults to the camp for slave labor) and then transported the gas, together with the corpsman, in an open vehicle over the mile or so to the gas chambers where a doctor was in charge of both installing the gas and, when it had done its work, declaring the people inside dead (though the process became so routine that it was mostly carried out by corpsmen). Doctors also did selections at various places in the camp when it was decided that sick and weak prisoners had to be weeded out and their places given to somewhat more intact new arrivals. And they selected on medical blocks, where prisoner physicians were permitted to do a certain amount of actual therapeutic work: over a period of a week or two, the Nazi doctors would make ordinary visits during which they would discuss medical questions, and then on the eighth or fifteenth day would announce that selections would be held on the ward, meaning that the sicker patients would be killed.

Auschwitz doctors also did a certain amount of direct killing by means of phenol injections into the bloodstream or heart, though after developing these methods they tended to turn the task over to assistants or brutalized prisoners. And they gave technical advice on such matters as the most efficient way to burn bodies (when there were too many victims for the crematoria to handle) or the most psychologically effective way to conduct selections (for instance, whether it was better to separate mothers from children before or after the selections).

To do all this and still feel themselves to be doctors, they gave everything a highly technical focus. As one of them said, "Ethical . . . the word does not exist (in Auschwitz)," so that participation in killing became "purely a technical matter." Some also came to see themselves as maintaining their medical function by arranging for the killing to be as "humane" as possible in a situation they themselves did not create.

Apart from doctors themselves, both the gas chambers and the gas were created by disciplined professionals: the former by engineers who had to calculate and design for killing, and the latter by chemists who had to create and maintain the conditions and mixtures within which Zyklon-B could be stored, shipped, and then converted into its deadly gaseous form. For all these reasons the contemporary physician-historian Benno Müller-Hill could speak of Auschwitz as "a monument of science and technology."

We still need to ask what went on in the minds of Nazi doctors that enabled them to take the extreme step of reversing their professional relationship to healing and killing. Here our first stress must be on ways in which they internalized on at least three levels: the original socialization to the Nazification of medicine; the *Gleichschaltung* or "coordination" of the profession; and, finally, the socialization of people who were already Nazi doctors to the medical killing function, whether at "euthanasia" centers or at Auschwitz. In this last adaptation, the individual doctor was, without much reflection, strongly inclined to do what he came to understand doctors at Auschwitz or Brandenberg (a "euthanasia" killing center) were expected to do.

Much of this socialization to killing was achieved by medical mentorship: for example, in briefings at "euthanasia" killing centers, an arriving doctor, inexperienced in both medical work and medical killing, could be authoritatively led into a blending of the two. Young doctors were often given an awesome briefing by one or two of Germany's leading psychiatrists, now identified with the program, concerning its professional justification in relationship to the concept of "life unworthy of life." At Auschwitz, this mentorship would include special guidance by a more experienced colleague in the conduct of selections, including particular attention to helping the newcomer to be "strong" enough to overcome his initial squeamishness (one or two doctors collapsed during their first selections and were put through a kind of rehabilitation process). A new arrival might have a transition period of several weeks during which he experienced symptoms of anxiety and drank especially heavily, before his socialization took hold.

The extent to which German doctors in high places—and much of German medicine in general—became socialized to killing is revealed by two highly significant professional consultations. The first, conducted in early 1940, took the form of a clinical comparison between the killing efficiency of carbon monoxide gas and injection of lethal substances (various combinations of morphine, scopolamine, curare, and prussic acid). Two leaders of Nazi medicine, Karl Brandt and Leonardo Conti, made a point of administering the injections personally in order to demonstrate the highest "responsibility" to the Führer's order. The gas chamber, after being demonstrated by an SS chemist, was operated by the head of the "euthanasia" institution at which the demonstration took place, Dr. Irmfried Eberl, also to demonstrate "his own responsibility." The gas method proved superior, killing people "very quickly . . . [without] scenes or commotion," while the injections caused them to die "only slowly" or in some cases not at all until a second injection was given. Brandt considered the gas method more "humane," and ordered that "only doctors should carry out the gassings." Although gassing became the method used in the killing of adults, the motto put forward in the project (see epigraph, page 99) was a means both of accentuating physicians' responsibility for killing and of maintaining an aura of medical function, of medical "as if."

The second consultation took the form of a question put by Heinrich Himmler a few months later to his chief SS doctor, Ernst Grawitz, concerning the best method of mass killing. Grawitz recommended the gas chamber. In both consultations and in many Nazi situations, medical "responsibility" became associated with carrying through the killing work.

That "medical responsibility" prevailed also in Auschwitz, and the order that only doctors perform selections was said to have been handed down from Grawitz. One doctor, Eduard Wirths, demonstrated his own sense of responsibility by insisting that he himself perform selections, in order to share that ordeal with others, although as chief doctor he would not have been required to do so. Wirths also jealously guarded the doctors' prerogative concerning selections, insisting that they would perform them more "humanely" than others. Still another socialized expression of this responsibility was the medical insistence on avoiding even greater overcrowding in Auschwitz, which meant advocating that more Jews be killed on arrival. The language used in Auschwitz reflected the socialization of medicine to killing: "ramp duty" for assignment to selections; "special treatment" for killing; and even the word "selections" with its Darwinian associations, suggests a kind of positive biological activity.

To the extent that doctors took an interest in actual medical concerns, such as sponsoring treatment programs run by prisoner doctors or engaging in certain kinds of surgery or laboratory studies or, for that matter, clinical experiments, these were, as one of them put it, essentially "hobbies." And even insofar as doctors succeeded in bringing modest improvements into the diet or other aspects of life in Auschwitz, these served to better the efficiency of the killing machinery. Auschwitz life in these ways became normalized, as one doctor put it, "just the way it is in a civilian community, with all the human squabbling. . . . And the extraordinary [nature] of those . . . actions [the killing], . . . that was not a matter of debate.

. . . The problem of the crematorium and its capacity . . . was equal to the ordinary problem of sewerage or the like elsewhere." Doctors thus developed a double sense of Auschwitz: on the one hand, it became an ordinary place where you carried out your daily routine; and on the other, it was, as one of them put it, "a separate planet" where everything was so extreme that what you did there did not count in the ordinary world.

The psychological mechanism of *doubling* is a key to understanding how Nazi doctors managed to do the work of killing. Doubling involved the formation of an Auschwitz self, by which one internalized many of the patterns and assumptions of the Auschwitz environment: the reversals of healing and killing, the operative Nazi biomedical vision, the extreme numbing that rendered killing no longer killing, struggles with omnipotence (deciding who would live or die) and impotence (being a cog in a powerful machine), maintaining a medical identity while killing, and somehow finding meaning in the environment.

While we will discuss doubling as a form of dissociation in more detail in chapter 7, here we would stress the division of the self into two functioning wholes, so that a part-self acts as an entire self. The Auschwitz self took shape over months or years as an adaptation to that murderous environment, while the individual doctor's prior self was operative when he visited his wife, children, and parents when on leave for a few days every month. The Auschwitz self had an impressive autonomy from the prior self and was sufficiently inclusive to enable the individual doctor to adapt to the entire Auschwitz environment. It had a life-death dimension and protected the doctor from his own death anxiety while enabling him to avoid experiencing strong feelings of guilt. Some of the doubling was consciously desired in order for the doctor to overcome the conflict of a newcomer, but much of the doubling process took place outside of awareness.

Auschwitz as an institution ran on doubling. For an individual doctor it created an external environment so powerful that it could set the tone for much of his "internal environment." He perceived that the institution wanted him to bring forth a self that could adapt to killing without feeling himself a murderer. In that sense, doubling became not just an individual enterprise but a shared psychological process, the group norm, part of what one doctor called "the Auschwitz weather." Yet, however it happened and at whatever level of awareness, Nazi doctors were responsible for their choice of evil.

Nuclear-Weapons Professionals

It's a terrible thing but we have to do it.
—HANS BETHE

It should sound strange to speak of nuclear-weapons professionals as a category, given what we know about the weapon's power to destroy. We have, in fact, become quite used to the idea in relation to two groups: weapons scientists and nuclear strategists. Members of both groups must be understood in terms of how they came to their profession and how they function within it.

The Rise of American Nuclear Physics

American physics at the time of the Second World War was not an old profession in some decline, as had been the case with German medicine, but a young profession on the rise. A still younger category within the profession was that of nuclear physics.

During the late nineteenth century, American physics developed slowly and, as compared with European practice, tended toward mechanical reductionism and the downgrading of original research. With the early twentieth century emergence of Max Planck's quantum theory and Albert Einstein's principles of relativity, along with the early work by Ernest Rutherford on atomic structure and Niels Bohr's development of quantum mechanics, American physicists began to become painfully aware of their own shortcomings.

The First World War, although sometimes called a "chemist's war" (because of chemists' and chemical engineers' work on optical glass, nitrates for explosions, and poison gases), also enabled American physics to gain a certain prestige. Robert Millikan was in the foreground of demonstrating to the military the systematic scientific effort that led physicists to develop crucial submarine-detection devices, aeronautical instruments, and airborne photographic devices. Army and Navy projects made their way to about forty American university campuses and established a tradition of academic involvement in secret war research. In Europe the involvement of physicists in the First World War included participation in gas warfare.*

During what Oppenheimer later called the "heroic time" for nuclear physics of the mid-1920s, he and other American physicists made intellectual pilgrimages to Rutherford at Cambridge, Bohr at Copenhagen, or Max Börn and Werner Heisenberg at Göttingen (especially for the latter's new formulation of quantum mechanics and development of the uncertainty principle). Oppenheimer returned from Cambridge and Göttingen to become, in the early 1930s, "the most captivating, commanding and worshipped teacher of theoretical physics of his generation." At the same time, American science was expanding radically, aided by the mobilization of quintessentially American philanthropic and organizational energies. The profession, having overcome earlier anti-Semitic practices, had admitted many Jews (Oppenheimer himself and I. I. Rabi were prime examples), and, during the 1930s, received many Jewish émigrés. Because of all these developments, *Newsweek* could declare in 1936 that "the United States leads the world in physics." And with Ernest Lawrence's award of $1,150,000 from the Rockefeller Foundation in 1940 for his giant cyclotron, the United States pioneered a new kind of scientific practice, the "big physics" of "expensive machines and massive organizations." The news, in early 1939 (about seven months before the Second World War began), that Otto Hahn and Fritz Strassmann had succeeded in splitting the uranium nucleus, as confirmed by Lise Meitner and

---

*Fritz Haber, a talented German-Jewish chemist and a fierce German patriot, set up a special gas warfare unit and persuaded the physicists James Franck and Otto Hahn to join him. (All three were later to win Nobel Prizes.) Haber and Hahn actually directed gas attacks. Haber's wife, Clara Immerwahr, was in a sense a casualty of gas warfare. A scientist herself, she had become depressed by her domestic situation and much more so by her husband's gas-warfare work. After an argument following her unsuccessful attempt to persuade him to leave it, she killed herself.

Otto Frisch, was received by American physicists with great intellectual excitement along with inevitable elements of professional envy, followed by deep foreboding about the possibility of a Nazi atomic weapon.

By the spring of 1940, Vannevar Bush, an engineer who became the leading American scientific administrator, was consulting with others on "how best to mobilize science generally for national defense." He and other physicists did just that, most notably in the radar project and the building of the atomic bomb. The radar project, centered at the "radiation laboratory" of MIT,* brought together fifty physicists, among them many leaders of the profession, and helped create a model of elaborate cooperation that carried over into atomic-bomb work. The group followed up on British radar achievements in producing both the theoretical principles and practical devices necessary for detection, by means of radar-equipped aircraft, of the enemy submarines that were so decimating Allied shipping as to fundamentally threaten the war effort. So important was this work that a man familiar with both major projects could say in retrospect, "The atom bomb only ended the war. Radar won it."

The Manhattan Project, the name given to the overall atomic-bomb effort, was much larger and more complicated than the radar project, including not only the bomb laboratory at Los Alamos, but the uranium-enrichment plant at Oak Ridge, Tennessee (which Ernest Lawrence coordinated with his work at Berkeley), the plutonium-production plant at Hanford, Washington, and the Metallurgical Laboratory in Chicago, where scientists continued with basic research on the nuclear chain reaction.

Robert Oppenheimer was chosen to head the Los Alamos project because he was to other physicists an American intellectual hero and had a mastery unique among Americans of the emerging nuclear physics that made the bomb possible—attributes that outweighed his left-wing political background and his lack of previous administrative experience. Few physicists resisted the call to join him. The race to produce the bomb before the Germans did in-

*The name, ironically, was to "mislead outsiders into thinking that its resident physicists were working on something then considered so remote from military needs as nuclear physics."

spire both émigré scientists, many of whom had first-hand experience with the Nazis, and their American colleagues. Hans Bethe
hesitated briefly because of his wife's moral qualms: she wished
him to "go back to MIT and do radar that contributes to our war
effort and doesn't bring a new destructive device." But he nonetheless believed that "it had to be done, especially because the
Germans, after all, had discovered fission," and that "Heisenberg,
we knew, was working on it." Indeed, it was, of course, the possibility of German scientists making the bomb available to Hitler that
had spurred Leo Szilard and a small group of émigré colleagues
to take the first steps toward prodding American authorities to
launch what turned out to be the Manhattan Project. Herbert York,
as a patriotic young American physicist, welcomed the opportunity
to join Ernest Lawrence in bomb work at Berkeley: "It was time for
me to join the war effort with everyone else." Even a pacifist like
Robert Wilson came to the same conclusion in joining the Los
Alamos group: it was a matter of "the survival of the Nazi world
or the survival of the democratic world" (though he added, in that
same interview, "I'm not sure I would do it again").

That fear of the Nazis being the first to get the bomb haunted
the Los Alamos physicists, as Bethe recalled, "absolutely . . . from
the first day on." Psychic numbing, or the "half-conscious closing
of the mind," mentioned earlier, was nearly total (again, in Bethe's
words): "I had no feelings. I was only concentrated on the job."
More than that, there was intense camaraderie in the goal of ending the war: "We worked very much together. [It was] very cooperative" was the way Bethe put it. Also haunting the scientists was
the specter of failure, of being unable to make a bomb that
worked—a combination of elements summed up years later by
Richard Feynman (see epigraph, page 98). But the "thinking" he
saw as having "stopped" began again for many with Hiroshima.
Bethe reported how a small group of scientists viewing the photographs of the bombing "were really horrified." It was one thing to
make calculations about fire and destruction but quite another "to
see the pictures directly, with that whole city in ruins," and that
"was an awful impression." People came away with the strong
feeling of "never again," meaning that "we must see to it that these
weapons never [are] used again."

Oppenheimer and the Bomb

> The bomb for Bohr and Oppenheimer was a
> weapon of death that might also end war and re-
> deem mankind.
> —RICHARD RHODES

Robert Oppenheimer came to exemplify the overall experience of physics at that time. The man who did most to bring the new physics to America was, at Los Alamos, not just an outstanding leader but the soul of the entire enterprise. Even Edward Teller—later to clash with and, in many colleagues' eyes, betray Oppenheimer—told later how "Oppie knew in detail what was going on in every part of the laboratory," how "he knew how to organize, cajole, humor, soothe feelings—how to lead powerfully without seeming to do so," so that "disappointing him somehow carried with it a sense of wrongdoing." Outside of Los Alamos, Oppenheimer could be arrogant, impatient, "make people feel they were fools." But during the Manhattan Project, as Bethe put it, "I don't remember any occasion at Los Alamos in which he was nasty to any person." And Bethe, himself surely one of the greatest physicists of the twentieth century, said of Oppenheimer, "It was clear at Los Alamos that he was intellectually superior to us."

Yet this gifted man did not, as many colleagues have noted, make original contributions to physics commensurate with his brilliance, some would say genius. He did write important papers, and his overall achievements in mastering and teaching physics were formidable and enabled him to overcome severe forms of psychological disturbance he had undergone earlier in life. Yet it was only at Los Alamos that he could pull together his many-sided talents, that his sense of self cohered in a way that permitted full expression of his intellectual and broadly human capacities. Oppenheimer's special historical—one might say psychohistorical—tragedy was to have realized himself most completely in the creation of the atomic bomb.

This kind of charismatic leader, as Erik Erikson has taught us, makes profound contact with a fundamental conflict of his group and manifests his greatness by providing a resolution, both historical and psychological, for that conflict. The fundamental conflict for Oppenheimer and his times was the atomic bomb—first the difficulties in making it, and then the troubling question of subsequent ethical stance toward what had been made. Oppenheimer could mobilize his gifts to solve the first part of the question but not, much as he tried, the second.

At the time of the making of the bomb, Oppenheimer apparently engaged in extended discussion with Niels Bohr, who clearly exerted a profound influence upon him. He embraced not only Bohr's focus on openness and international cooperation even prior to the use of the bomb, but was taken also with Bohr's stress on complementarity (see page 72) as a basis for a moral stance toward the bomb. That translation of physical into ethical principle meant that the bomb could be seen as both destructive and redemptive (as suggested in the epitaph on page 111).*

But one could come to an opposite conclusion in relationship to complementarity and the bomb by examining a careful definition of the principle put forward by Emilio Segrè, an Italian physicist who did important work at Los Alamos: "Two magnitudes are complementary when the measurement of one of them prevents the accurate simultaneous measurement of the other. Similarly, two concepts are complementary when one imposes limitations on the other." The definition seems to suggest that one can simultaneously imagine the bomb as destructive and evil on the one hand and as a means of human redemption on the other, but that the two positions cannot be combined or reconciled with one another, because that would lead to the mismeasure or distortion of one of them. Yet such is the mind's way of functioning—Bohr's, Oppenheimer's, anyone's—that the very holding of the two images simultaneously causes one to create or assume precisely that reconciliation. Indeed, there readily takes place a *blending* of ultimate destruction and human redemption, resulting in the mystical expressions of nuclearism we are all too familiar with.

*The atomic-bomb historian Richard Rhodes associates Oppenheimer's choice of the term *Trinity* for the first test explosion to this version of a principle of complementarity; Oppenheimer himself connected that choice with lines from John Donne dealing with death and resurrection.

Oppenheimer's personal tragedy was also his profession's. For that profession came, as he did, to the making of the bomb shortly after its brilliant arrival on the international intellectual stage. The fact that American nuclear physics largely realized itself in the creation of nuclear devices has in no way prevented magnificent subsequent achievements in many different areas. But it has contributed to the inseparable ties persisting to this day between a significant minority of American physicists and the great weapons laboratories. They maintain these ties in the name of their own versions of ethical complementarity—of finding, in the building of these terrible devices, a means of ultimate benefit to humankind. And since physicists are far from the only ones to continue to invoke that principle, Oppenheimer's unsolved dilemma has become the world's.

Nuclear Physicists after the Second World War

American nuclear physicists emerged from the Second World War as heroes. For the public at large, they took on some of the transcendent qualities of the bomb they had made. Indeed, "Oppenheimer became a symbol of the new status of science in American society. His thin handsome face and figure replaced Einstein's as the public image of genius." To be sure, some of that legacy included a taint. *Time* magazine spoke of them as "the world's guilty men," but that judgment was something on the order of a distant murmur drowned out by the celebratory tones.

On a pragmatic level, physicists were profoundly involved with the American military, especially the Air Force. These cooperative efforts included not just the atomic-bomb project but also radar work, overall participation in Air Force targeting, and, more generally, the development (first in Britain and then the United States) of the concept of *operations research,* which makes use of laws of physics and mathematics in approaching military problems of any kind—whether artillery fire, bomber formations, or locating submarines. So much had war become scientific, and scientists warriors, that the relationship could hardly be ended by a peace treaty. Many physicists, therefore, retained their bomb-related military connections even as they happily returned to their peacetime laboratories.

There was also a significant trend away from weaponry, as expressed by the scientists' movement initiated during the war. At that time, James Franck, Leo Szilard, Eugene Rabinowitch, and their Chicago colleagues tried unsuccessfully to persuade the American government not to use the weapon on a populated city and even to stop short of fully testing the weapon so that the world would be left "without definite knowledge that the 'whole thing does work.' " After the war, Szilard and Rabinowitch, joined by many other scientists, took their crusade for restraint, openness, and civilian control of atomic weaponry and technology to universities, churches, Elks clubs, and whatever groups would hear them throughout the country—and created the still highly influential *Bulletin of the Atomic Scientists.* Antithetical to that crusade, physicists like Edward Teller and Ernest Lawrence remained immersed in nuclearism and preoccupied with building new weapons systems. Most physicists were undoubtedly, morally and psychologically, somewhere between these two tendencies.

Oppenheimer was outspoken in his personal desire, and advice to others, to return to academic life. He did that, but at the same time remained a prominent consultant at many levels of government and the military. And while he advocated international arrangements concerning the weaponry, he shocked many colleagues by favoring continued military rather than civilian control of atomic energy and by his active support for nuclear weapons development—until (as noted in the previous chapter) the hydrogen bomb.

Bethe, for instance, shared both the revulsion from the weapon felt by many colleagues and their eagerness to get back to academic life: "Well, my main wish was to go back to physics, pure physics. Let's get away from weapons." He, too, did so, with great enjoyment and enormous accomplishment; and during that "very exciting time in physics . . . I could mostly forget about atomic bombs." Yet within two years he began to consult on weapons developments at Los Alamos, mostly during summers, because he "had so many friends there" as well as out of his concern about the Russians, particularly after their rejection of the Baruch plan* for the sharing of atomic energy, and his general sense "that we had to stay ahead." But he also stressed the human nexus: "I certainly felt related to the effort, they were such nice people, it was a pleasant place, . . . and, I think this personal feeling of well-being was part of the story."

The Hydrogen-Bomb Paradox

The fateful step for American physics as a profession was the hydrogen bomb. We have noted the early opposition to the hydrogen bomb by scientists serving on an advisory committee chaired by Oppenheimer, and their awareness that it "might become a weapon of genocide." Yet, so paradoxical was their relationship to weapons making that a short time later, when actual work on the hydrogen bomb was under way, there was an impressive scientific ingathering that included many of the physicists who had been outspoken in their opposition to the weapon. American physicists, at this key moment, *voluntarily* affirmed their link to the government and the military. Herbert York later noted the "veritable *Who's Who* of American physics either consulting or working full-time with the group designing the weapon, including J. Carson Mark, Edward Teller, Hans Bethe, Gregory Breit, George Gamow, Enrico Fermi, Emil Konopinski, John von Neumann, and John Wheeler," as well as "a very special student, Richard Garwin." York could have added Luis Alvarez, Harold Brown, Robert Jastrow, and others. The ingathering was partly a product of the energies of Edward Teller (whose fiercely consistent advocacy of the hydrogen bomb from the earliest Second World War Los Alamos days is well known) and Ernest Lawrence (whose enormous influence and persistent political activities on behalf of weap-

*The Baruch plan was an American proposal to the United Nations for the international control of atomic energy. Bernard Baruch, the financier and frequent presidential adviser, had modified an earlier proposal bearing the names of Dean Acheson, then a high-ranking State Department official, and David Lilienthal, then chairman of the Tennessee Valley Authority, with a considerable contribution from Robert Oppenheimer. Among the differing views on why the plan failed—the Russians strongly rejected it—were the general feelings of distrust on both sides, the Soviet fear that the plan was a means of the United States maintaining a monopoly on the weapons (there was a provision that it could continue stockpiling them for several years after the approval of the plan), Baruch's influence in hardening the American position and dubious qualifications for the task, and general Soviet suspiciousness during the Stalinist era.

ons has been insufficiently appreciated outside of immediate scientific and governmental circles).

In speaking of his mentor's enthusiasm for the kind of crusade he had found satisfying at the time of the making of the atomic bomb, York made an observation about Lawrence that applies to other nuclear physicists: "I think that in one sense he welcomed it . . . [as] not only a matter of duty but . . . a personal opportunity" to return to the "kind of high" experienced in the making of the atomic bomb, the sense that "you were really part of a great movement, doing things which were interesting and consequential."

But it is Hans Bethe whose involvement illustrates the ambivalence of a man struggling to be both compassionate and responsible. After his major contribution to the making of the atomic bomb and subsequent consulting at Los Alamos, Bethe came to be deeply troubled by the idea of a hydrogen bomb. In the early fall of 1949, shortly after the Soviet atomic explosion, Edward Teller visited Bethe and told him, "Now you will agree that we have to go for the H-bomb—and you have to come to Los Alamos to lead the work." Bethe felt himself "very doubtful," and told Teller that he had to think about it. Bethe's wife again opposed his participation (this time much more strongly than she had the atomic bomb), as did such antinuclear colleagues as Leo Szilard and Victor Weisskopf. At a conference at Princeton, Teller and Bethe went together to talk to Oppenheimer, who was "very cagey," expressing no clear opinion about what Bethe should do while at the same time showing the two men a letter from James Conant strongly opposing the weapon. Bethe then went on a long walk with Weisskopf, who "asked me to visualize the effect of hydrogen bombs"—and "we thought of 100 to 1,000 times Hiroshima . . . one bomb would destroy a big city like Boston and suburbs, [but] not quite . . . destroy New York." Hence, "at the end of that talk [with Weisskopf] I decided not to go." In February 1950, following Truman's announcement of his decision to go ahead with the weapon, Bethe appeared at a press conference of scientists opposing it, and later that year published an article in *Scientific American* (reprinted in the *Bulletin of the Atomic Scientists*) describing the hydrogen bomb as "this weapon of total annihilation."

But Bethe had a change of heart, brought about by at least two important developments. With the outbreak of the Korean War, "I was . . . rather shocked . . . and misinterpreted this as meaning that the Russians were really aggressive wherever they could be." Bethe then "relaxed" his opposition to the hydrogen bomb and began to consult cautiously on the possibility of its being made. In those early consultations, he "still was hoping to make sure that it wouldn't work," and actually did some calculations attempting to demonstrate that. But when, during the spring of 1951, Stanislaw Ulam, in collaboration with Teller, formulated the general principle that enabled the bomb to be made, Bethe came to feel that it would have to be (see epigraph, page 107).

He adapted to the situation by focusing on "just the technical issues" and not giving "much further thought to the consequences." And even while working on it, he continued to wish that somehow the group would not succeed in making the bomb "because I still hated the thing." But that adaptation was threatened by an official visit of a group of high-ranking military officers with whom the leading scientists were asked to meet: "That was more difficult because there was this complete enthusiasm [among the military officers], and I was very reluctant [negative toward, and worried about, the hydrogen bomb], so I tried to be as technical as possible. . . . It was obvious that I shouldn't tell them what a horrible thing we were working on. And so I had to conceal my feelings."

This great physicist and good man, working as he did on a weapon he "hated" and knew to be annihilative, reveals the extent of his profession's immersion in a potentially genocidal enterprise—and perhaps also the extent to which human beings in general are capable of dissociating action from feeling (see chapter 7).

Generations of Physicists

In the profession of physics, the "Los Alamos generation" could, with its heroic image, transmit certain attitudes and involvements concerning weapons to subsequent professional generations. Talented students could be drawn by their mentors into weapons work. Oppenheimer brought several of his students—

notably Glenn Seaborg, Robert Serber, and Philip Morrison—into important positions in the original Los Alamos enterprise. And Bethe became the much admired mentor of "a large fraction of the entire Los Alamos gang," including Morrison, Robert Wilson, and Richard Feynman, who made "endless talk about the Los Alamos days . . . through [which] shone a glow of pride and nostalgia . . . [about] a great experience, a time of hard work and comradeship and deep happiness."

For the overall post–Los Alamos period, however, it was Robert Oppenheimer who emerged as the main spokesman for the older generation of American physics. Oppenheimer's convoluted messages to his professional sons epitomized the situation of physicists at the time: overt advice to return to the campus after the war, the need to reflect on threats and opportunities presented by the weapons, a personal model of a high-level weapons consultant, and, most powerfully, an ambivalent aura of collective professional greatness and more or less honorable "sin."

Lawrence, of the same generation as Oppenheimer, had an alternative, much less ambiguous message. In response to Oppenheimer's famous remark, "The physicists have known sin; and this is a knowledge which they cannot lose," Lawrence defiantly replied, "I am a physicist and I have no knowledge to lose in which physics has caused me to know sin." Lawrence was predominantly responsible for connecting "big science" with weapons work, and brought advanced students such as Alvarez and York into the atomic-bomb and hydrogen-bomb projects. York became aware, through Lawrence, that "there was a world one could intervene in," and then embarked on an influential career, in academic life and government, in weapons development and policies. But in its course he took a highly significant step away from his mentor's influence by becoming a prominent critic of nuclearism and advocate of arms control—yet echoed his mentor in declaring, "I don't have any apologies either for me or my generation." Alvarez took on Lawrence's lifelong commitment to weapons development, defying his mentor only once in going through with testimony against Oppenheimer in 1954 (Lawrence had been persuaded that such testimony would be harmful to the development of their own laboratory), and in summation made a declaration completely in Lawrence's spirit: "I am enormously proud of my part in the development of the atomic bomb and in the revitalization of the thermonuclear program."

A very important generational sequence that connected the atomic bomb with the hydrogen bomb involved Richard Garwin, who had been in high school during much of the Second World War, received his Ph.D. in physics in 1949 at the University of Chicago under Enrico Fermi, and followed his teacher to Los Alamos in 1950. Garwin had additional professional reasons: "It was a large laboratory which had things that I didn't know about that I wanted to learn." But there was also a suggestion of the mythic-heroic lure of the place for a young physicist: "I was seven years late at Los Alamos." Garwin distinguished himself quickly by writing an important paper on an aspect of weapons work and found himself talking to Edward Teller (who had also been his teacher at Chicago) about "this great idea" that Teller and Ulam had for making the hydrogen bomb. Teller told Garwin that he "wanted an experiment"; but the younger man surprised his teacher by producing for him (as Teller later remarked) "not an experiment but a design for the first hydrogen bomb." For Garwin was no ordinary physicist but, as Bethe put it, "a wizard" whose extraordinary talent lay in applying concepts of physics to difficult problems in technological design. Garwin mentioned a number of satisfactions he and other younger physicists experienced at Los Alamos—challenging work, good pay, a nice place to live and bring up children—but the greatest reward was that of "high-intensity involvement . . . with people such as Fermi, Bethe, and Teller, some of the more brilliant scientific minds of the twentieth century."

Reverberating down through subsequent generations of physicists was Edward Teller's highly influential and important testimony against Oppenheimer at the 1954 hearing. Most of the profession identified with Oppenheimer, with the exception perhaps of a number of professional "sons" and "grandsons" of Teller and Lawrence. Partly as a result of that division, the pro-Oppenheimer group tended to stay away from weapons laboratories and later to oppose the Strategic Defense Initiative, while the pro-Teller group continued to work with weapons and became the nucleus for SDI.

The latter generation extends from Teller to Lowell Wood, a charismatic and zealous organizer-manager-father of the "O-group" (the key unit in SDI and related weapons research) at Livermore (the second weapons laboratory, which was associated with Edward Teller), to younger scientist-"grandsons." These three generations have in common a combination of scientific talent, technological zealotry, and unbridled weapons enthusiasm.

Strained personal bonds between the generations can conflict with affection associated with weapons work. Theodore Taylor, now one of the most antinuclear of former weapons scientists, was taught and helped a great deal by Edward Teller while working at Los Alamos. Teller was "very kind, . . . very supportive," and in general can be "very good with students, very attentive." While Taylor could not forgive Teller for his role in the Oppenheimer hearings, he did retain "this feeling of gratitude." On one occasion, when the two men were taking opposite sides on a two-city television debate, Teller, during a break, declared, "We need you back!" Taylor experienced emotional pain, "mixed feelings, . . . a rush of memories . . . toward him, . . . good feelings." He was very much like a man who has come to view what his father was doing as morally reprehensible and yet cannot cease to feel affection and gratitude in relation to childhood love and guidance.

The New Profession of Nuclear Strategist

Sustained national involvement with potential nuclear killing has resulted in a new profession, that of nuclear strategy, and in a new group of professionals, later termed "defense intellectuals." The profession of nuclear strategy may be said to have begun on the morning of 7 August 1945, when the Yale political scientist and naval strategist Bernard Brodie, upon reading a newspaper account of the atomic bombing of Hiroshima, declared to his wife, "Everything I have written is obsolete." He was saying, in effect, that he and others had suddenly been deprofessionalized, rendered inexpert, even ignorant, in their own discipline. His way of reasserting his capacity as a professional was to recast military strategy to include the radically new development. With equal if not superior intellectual justification, he might have done so by expressing doubt about the possibility and desirability of developing reliable strategic thought in respect to the new weapon—a position he actually came to in his last years. But such doubt at the time would have raised considerable opposition and could well have undermined Brodie's status as a professional concerned with military strategy.

Brodie became the first to wrestle intellectually with deterrence and to live out its fundamental contradiction. In his early writings he declared: "Thus far the chief purpose of our military establishment has been to win wars. From now on its chief purpose must be to avert them." Yet he also soon stated that the international situation "requires appraisal of the atomic bomb as an instrument of war—and hence of international politics—rather than as a visitation of a wrathful diety." Brodie became a central figure among an influential group of scholars that formed at the Yale Institute of International Studies, then moved to Princeton, there to create the Center of International Studies. He and others were later to defect to the RAND Corporation.

RAND had been set up by the Air Force as a civilian think tank to serve its expanding intellectual needs in relation to high-technology weaponry; and the movement of strategists between universities and official military sponsors paralleled that of physicists working in weapons areas. Observant Air Force generals, notably Henry Harley ("Hap") Arnold, impressed by the contribution of science to the conduct of the Second World War, set up project RAND in late 1945 and early 1946 as "a continuing program of scientific study and research on the broad subject of air warfare with the object of recommending to the Air Force preferred methods, techniques, and instrumentalities for this purpose." Originally enlisting mainly physicists, mathematicians, and engineers, RAND, after a year of function, added two divisions, economics and social science. The latter division was needed to extend *game theory*—the search for mathematically determined patterns between "players," in which each is assumed to seek maximum gain while minimizing the gain of opponents—but in a way that subsumed social science to mathematical analysis. This search for "useful quantitative indices for a gadget, a tactic or a strategy" became a hallmark at RAND and was equated there with "the rational life."

The impulse in RAND was always to render strategy a technical and statistical matter. There was a two-stage process: first, the reduction of nuclear-age dilemmas to strategic ones; and then the reduction of strategic dilemmas to mathematical principles. The boldness of the venture and its well-supported interdisciplinary pursuit engendered great intellectual excitement, a "freewheeling almost anarchic atmosphere." Having special access to secret information, one could feel oneself in rebellion against, and free from the restraints of, the academic establishment and on a special cutting edge of human knowledge. One could almost playfully explore nuclear annihilation.

Crucial to the RAND process, and to the emergence of nuclear strategists in general, was the shift from operations research to *systems analysis.* While operations research entailed relatively clear-cut physical and mathematical evaluation (of weapons function, trajectories, velocities, and such), systems analysis (with weapons, as opposed to its use in other areas) has no such precision or even data. It turns the problem around by asking what kinds of equip-ment—in actuality, what kinds of and how many nuclear bombs—would be needed to fulfill an indeterminate range of hypothetical missions—with the analyst himself now free to speculate on such missions and needs as necessary for a version of national security. The exercise is conducted with minimal data and with extremely dubious assumptions about human behavior in relation to events that could kill hundreds of millions of people.

This approach became enormously influential as RAND became the hub of the new profession. RAND offshoots and attitudes ex-tended widely into official and nonofficial environments, so that significant numbers of people, mostly men, could converge from the professions, academia, and public life to join the ranks of the "defense intellectuals." Resulting think tanks could be nonprofit organizations, such as RAND, and later for-profit organizations, both types developed mainly for serving the intellectual needs of the military. With strategists moving to and from universities, think tanks, and government, there have emerged from this group national security advisers, undersecretaries and secretaries of defense, and secretaries of state. In the process there is also a considerable sharing of functions between weapons designers and professional strategists. Physicists like Oppenheimer and Teller have had much to say about nuclear strategy, as have laboratory directors at Los Alamos and Livermore. Similarly, strategists like Bernard Brodie, a political scientist, Herman Kahn, a physicist, and Colin Gray, perhaps simply a strategist, have had much to say about which nuclear weapons are considered necessary to design and possibly to use. Also, the generational sequence among nuclear strategists has, at least until recently, moved in an increasingly nuclearistic direction. Bernard Brodie developed fairly broad intellectual perspectives as a political scientist before becoming a RAND strategist; Herman Kahn, not much younger than Brodie but a member of the subsequent RAND generation, was more radical both in his embrace of the weapons and in his general reductionism; and Colin Gray, originally Kahn's disciple at the Hudson Institute (which Kahn founded upon leaving RAND) is still more nuclearistic and weapons focused than Herman Kahn.*

In this way there developed in American strategy a group that considered itself a breakthrough élite—physicists and mathematicians, economists and political scientists, psychologists and social scientists—who "would attempt to impose a rational order on . . . nuclear war," invent a whole new language in the process, and "condition an entire generation of political and military leaders to think about the bomb the way that the intellectual leaders of RAND thought about it." Over time, the work came to deal more and more with "intractable uncertainties" associated with *future* weapons systems so that "realistic tactical experience grew thinner and thinner," and dataless projections were put forward under the cloak of mathematical science. In the very different Nazi situation,

---

*Gray, in developing his more radical policy of war fighting, accused the earlier generation of strategists of suffering from "an Armageddon syndrome," by which he meant that their analyses did not extend beyond the point "when the buttons are pushed." Gray acknowledged the influence of Donald Brennan, who, under the tutelage of Herman Kahn at the Hudson Institute, changed from an advocate of arms control to one of aggressively "flexible" policies that included antiballistic missiles (ABM), extensive civil defense, and war-fighting plans. Brennan killed himself in 1980, shortly after having served as an adviser in Reagan's campaign. It should be added that some of this sequence of increasingly narrow weapons focus could be found in generations of involved physicists as well. But in neither group is this sequence inevitable.

biologists and physicians also imagined themselves a breakthrough élite, in their case concerning racial theory and practice
rather than the mathematics of nuclear strategy. What is common
to the two is the false claim of cutting-edge scientific knowledge—
to say nothing of the extraordinary potential for human killing.

The "Decent Nuclearists"

As in the case of Nazi doctors, there is a continuum in the
ideological and behavioral stance of nuclear physicists toward
weapons making. At one end have been those most opposed (at
various times Szilard, Franck, Weisskopf, and Rabi) and at the
other end those most passionately committed to the weapons (notably Teller, but also Alvarez, Lawrence, and John von Neumann,
the brilliant mathematician). Somewhere in the center of the continuum are the concerned men who were drawn into weapons
making in the ways we have described, but sought always to maintain some balance and to counter the extreme weapons advocates.
This middle group of "decent nuclearists" has included such distinguished men as Bethe, Garwin, York, and Harold Brown, former secretary of defense. It may well be the most important group
of all from the standpoint of contributions to weaponry from the
end of the Second World War until the present. For within the
overall dynamic, the most intense advocates—the Edward Tell-
ers—press forcefully toward a visionary extreme, outdistancing
general acceptance but greatly influencing the terms of discourse.
The iconoclastic opponents of the project may have some impact
but are essentially dismissed because they are in conflict with the
prevailing nuclear ideology. That leaves only the seemingly reasonable middle group to provide a consistent, acceptable, and
"professional" means of keeping everything going.

Moreover, a passionate ideologue such as Teller can have enormous influence even on those who come to disagree with him—for
example, Theodore Taylor's uneasy encounter with Teller years
after having defected from the weapons-making community (see
page 120). Former colleagues stress Teller's fierce energies on
behalf of weaponry—six trips to Europe in one year during his late
seventies, according to York, which is why "words like Messiah"

come to mind. In addition, York was unsettled by Teller's accusation that he, in turning toward advocacy of arms control and a test ban, had "sold out to those people" in Washington.

Similarly, a nuclear strategist, a man known to have been relatively "moderate" in that community, was highly critical of former RAND colleagues who spun out belligerent scenarios and talked about "surgical strikes" with "clean weapons." He, too, used the word "messianic" to describe one of those former colleagues—in his case, Herman Kahn. Yet he added, "I was extremely fond of Herman. I learned a great deal from him," and more or less justified Kahn's seemingly adventurous scenarios: "He was throwing the burden of proof on [those who advocate] avoidance [of the use of nuclear weapons]." He even praised Kahn as a "pioneer" in strategic work. In these ways the seemingly moderate strategist was accepting his immoderate colleague's position as a kind of norm—was accepting, that is, an aggressive version of "nuclear normality." We should not be surprised to learn that the "moderate" strategist at one point put forward an elaborate doctrine of *counterforce,* or concentration on the enemy's weaponry rather than cities, with a strong component of war fighting. Given the nature of institutional nuclearism at RAND and elsewhere, and the pressure from the extreme ideological end of the strategic continuum, the relative moderate moves into the role of the "decent nuclearist" whose deadly scenarios are eminently "reasonable" and "believable." Himself immersed in nuclearism, he may retain considerable admiration for the "integrity" of the very extremist he sees himself combating. For he, too, is affected by the mystical technicism at the heart of nuclearism—as were the Nazis by the mystical biologism at the heart of their vision. This man's very capacity to cover over that mysticism with apparent moderation enables him to be favorably viewed by the majority of people and therefore enormously helpful to the potentially genocidal enterprise.

Technicians of Nuclear Genocide

As "hit men" or professional killers, no nuclear group comes close to resembling the *Einsatzgruppen,* who murdered face to face with automatic weapons: virtually nobody is face to face—or even within sight of—a victim or an enemy; and nobody at this time is killing anybody else. In the Nazi case, the SS professional killers could combine intense immersion in ideology with the powerful "corps spirit" of members of an élite organization expected to undergo heroic numbing, or "hardening," in order to carry out their country's most demanding tasks. They nonetheless experienced a large number of psychiatric casualties;* and that was a factor in the Nazi shift to a higher technology of killing, that of gas chambers, which would diminish the psychological burden of the killers. In Auschwitz, for instance, that technology required special training for a group of medical corpsmen known as *Desinfektoren*, or "disinfectors," in the handling and insertion of cyanide gas. While some of these artisans, or technicians, of killing experienced psychological conflict, on the whole they carried out their function efficiently.

The nuclear technicians of potential genocide are the specially trained military personnel responsible for maintaining the weapons either in silos (where they spend extended periods of time) or on submarines at sea. But as compared even with the Nazi "disinfectors," they are much more removed from any suggestion of killing, much more detached from cause-and-effect, and can readily see themselves as little more than cogs in a highly complex technological structure. Yet in their case as well, the military has had to be concerned about their capacity to function and has instituted the Nuclear Weapons Personnel Reliability Program, which seeks to reject or remove those considered medically or psychologically unfit, including those thought to lack a positive attitude about their work. But there is evidence that at least some of them experience inner questioning about their task and concern about their potential for dangerously unstable behavior, perhaps especially among those responsible for nuclear weapons on submarines. However their function has been technicized, they, too,

---

*A German neuropsychiatrist who had treated large numbers of *Einsatzgruppen* personnel estimated that 20 percent of those engaged in the actual killing experienced psychological symptoms resembling combat reactions (anxiety, nightmares, tremors, and bodily complaints). The neuropsychiatrist was evasive about the assignments given these men after his treatment, but his professional function was clear enough: helping them to be strong enough to return to duty, to resume killing Jews. The technicians of genocide, that is, require the support of professionals of higher standing.

are human beings specially trained for carrying out the technical requirements of a genocidal system.

The Passion for Problem Solving

> There was the H bomb, which was a fascinating problem; there is SDI, and SDI is full of extremely intricate, difficult, technical problems, and it's very difficult to solve them. Take the problem, How do you make a laser beam which is direct to one part in ten million? Hitting a millimeter target at a ten-kilometer distance? A fascinating problem.
>
> —A PHYSICIST

It is difficult for many people to appreciate the emotional intensity a scientist or would-be scientist can bring to problem solving. Moreover, that activity—no matter what project one is involved in—can enable one to feel engaged in constructive professional work.

The Scientists

An extraordinarily gifted physicist declared that, scientifically speaking, the atomic bomb and the hydrogen bomb are "not very interesting . . . as real science, . . . not important." But he further explained, "It's a great satisfaction to create, even if you don't discover any fundamental principles of physics." When asked the nature of the satisfaction, he unhesitatingly answered, again with passion, "Well, you have made something that works." He was saying that bomb making, while not basic science, can involve profoundly absorbing intellectual struggles in the application of science to demanding technological problems.

One can experience solving those problems as a form of scientific creativity, which can in turn provide powerful experiences of transcendence. Then, "what works" becomes part of the self, and the self part of it. Spouses of scientists understand this process all too well. This physicist told of a series of conversations with a colleague charting their opposition to the Strategic Defense Initiative and their refutation of its scientific claims; afterward, his "wife would say from time to time, 'Just watch out, you are going to solve it [make SDI work].' " For, as he went on to explain, "these problems, even if you are against it, grow on you and challenge you."

Another physicist, particularly gifted at precisely these applications of scientific principles to technological problems, conveyed the excitement of envisioning that which has never been envisioned:

> So, you do a sketch. You estimate what is a reasonable configuration and it involves all kinds of things. . . . *It's like designing a building when you've never seen a building.* . . . I know about what yield it would give, and knew that if you had a ten-megaton bomb that it would destroy an area which was larger . . . by [a multiple of] the two thirds of the yield . . . and so that would be almost one hundred times the area. Whether it would be deliverable or not actually [I couldn't say]. I designed these things.

He emphasized that this working principle was purely technical and had nothing to do with moral considerations: "You know, it's like a surgeon taking out somebody's appendix or replacing his heart or whatever. . . . You don't ask, Is this person a gangster or a philosopher? You just do the best job you can." And he, too, brought up Star Wars (he was also a strong opponent of the program) to suggest how the passion for problem solving can melt away moral considerations:

> I was trying to explain [to a colleague] how the space mines, the counter–Star Wars weapons, would be smart enough to handle these things. But then, of course, once you do that, then you ask yourself, "Well, can't you make smarter decoys?" So I was helping them make smarter decoys. Once you're involved in one of these questions, you forget which side you were on, and pursue the argument whichever way it's going to go.

The intensity of collaborative work, in contrast to ordinary professional loneliness, could also have enormous appeal. One physicist—referring mostly to work on the atomic bomb but also, to some extent, to that on the hydrogen bomb—spoke of "this feeling of working together, . . . of belonging to one project that ought to succeed. The feeling of comradeship, I might say. Here [at my university] I work very much by myself." That camaraderie, intense male bonding—especially when probing into arcane, forbidden areas—can provide a rare intimacy and ease of being.

As in ordinary scientific work, there can be fierce competitiveness. Bethe, for example, although minimizing his work on the hydrogen bomb, did admit "satisfaction in making certain calculations" that demonstrated Teller, who had become antagonistic to Bethe's group, to be wrong on a particular issue. Such "satisfaction" could derive from many levels of antagonism. The competition between laboratories could reach the point where as one physicist put it, "at a test series the 'we' was Los Alamos or Livermore—not the United States. . . . I remember distinctly . . . that . . . during those early years, if Livermore set off a bomb . . . and it failed, we in Los Alamos felt ready to celebrate." He said that much of the antagonism developed from the Oppenheimer hearing (Oppenheimer was associated with Los Alamos, of course, and Teller increasingly with Livermore); but beyond that, the laboratories in relationship to each other came to resemble two hotly competing physics departments at rival universities.

Close connections with the weapons world could offer enormous material rewards, including large-scale financial support for basic research in physics. When Luis Alvarez became excited about building a large hydrogen bubble chamber, he discovered that it "would cost $2.5 million" (in 1955 dollars), so that "it was clear that a special AEC [Atomic Energy Commission, which sponsored weapons building and testing] appropriation would be required." He went to his friend Ernest Lawrence for help: "Ernest and I went to Washington and talked in one day to three of the five AEC commissioners." One of those commissioners was John von Neumann, who was a good friend and strong weapons advocate: "At a cocktail party at Johnny's home that evening, I learned that the commission had voted the same afternoon to award the laboratory the $2.5 million." On the basis of experiments done with that hydrogen bubble chamber, Alvarez was later awarded the Nobel Prize in physics.

Making a creative breakthrough can bind one to weapons work, as was the case with Peter Hagelstein, whose "brilliant idea in physics" made possible the creation of the X-ray laser, a key component of the Star Wars constellation. The central idea, which came as a "flash of insight," enabled President Reagan to make his famous Star Wars speech of 23 March 1983. Hagelstein, though unaware of the weapons work at Livermore when originally accepting a generous fellowship to go there, came to be fascinated by the problem of creating an X-ray laser as a means of contributing to biomedical discoveries. Since facilities were unavailable elsewhere, he became absorbed in the work and felt impelled to solve the problem even when the weapons aspect became clearly paramount. Hagelstein summed up his own change of heart: "Until 1980 or so I didn't want to have anything to do with nuclear anything. Back in those days I thought there was something fundamentally evil about weapons. Now I see it as an interesting physics problem." He eventually returned to the Massachusetts Institute of Technology, but he had been at the weapons laboratory long enough, and was sufficiently intrigued scientifically while there, to achieve a breakthrough that affected American and world nuclear policies. A close friend of his, also a scientist, said that Hagelstein had been a brilliant and idealistic young person but "events overtook him."

Sometimes a scientist could, professionally speaking, "find himself" in weapons work. A physicist explained how, upon learning of the use of the atomic bombs while completing his undergraduate degree, he had told his family, "One thing I was sure about, . . . I would never work on these things." Yet four years later he found himself "totally immersed in it [weapons work], with total enthusiasm." Having failed the oral examinations for his Ph.D. (for psychological rather than intellectual reasons), he had been severed from his graduate program. Recently married with a young child, he was "frantic." His professor, who respected his ability, told him to "calm down, and I'll get you a job at Los Alamos." There he discovered that he was extraordinarily talented at weapons designing, and his abilities were enthusiastically recognized by some of America's most outstanding physicists. In turning out designs that became important weapons, he experienced a sense of transcen-

dence combining strong creative satisfaction with feelings of individual power: "Here's this guy, . . . this twenty-five-year-old sitting
at a desk in Los Alamos changing the face of the world."

A young antinuclear scientist, strongly opposed to weapons
work, described an experience that epitomized the contradictory
feelings that could arise. A colleague dropped in at her office one
day and began to suggest how her research might have applicability to a certain kind of weapons-related work: "We had one of the
most thrilling, exciting, and creative collaborative discussions I
have ever had, filling pages with diagrams and equations." During
the conversation itself, she thought only of the science at hand, but
so chagrined was she upon realizing, after he left, how fascinated
she had been with nuclear-weapons questions that she cried bitterly for more than an hour.

The Strategists

Strategists obtained similar satisfactions from what they also
took to be scientific problem solving. One strategist-scientist told
how thinking strategically is "for me . . . like doing a lot of little
puzzles," and how he had been fascinated by puzzles from the age
of seven. Those solutions could have the further attraction of
mathematical precision.

A strategist trained in international relations and diplomatic
history spoke of undergoing a "second education at RAND,"
where he worked with economists and engineers and developed
"more appreciation for quantitative work." Having "loved mathematics as a boy," he was excited by the RAND method of working
from mathematical models, seeking always to be "more rigorous"
and to counter the "mushiness problem" (essentially nonmath-
ematical discourse) whether manifested by opponents of nuclear
weapons or pro-nuclear generals. Intellectually he felt himself "a
student of knowledge and ideas [that were] exploring entirely new
territory." The awesome consequences of his work also held an
appeal ("I had never dealt with anything this visionary before.
. . . So there was a sense of adventure"). A close student of strategy
and strategists spoke of this man as having "remained static . . .

because [of being] too enamored with analytic operations without questioning fundamental relationships between states and between people."

As professionals, strategists have at times brought considerable intelligence to combating blatantly erroneous statements of unthinking militarists, and in this restraint assume the role of a "decent nuclearist"—of taking the kind of "acceptable" position that indirectly enhances nuclear-weapons development. But often their claim to professionalism has led strategists into theoretical models and "worst case" scenarios that contribute directly to more extensive and complex weapons arrangements. What is remarkable is that these professional "solutions" to stated "problems" have been based on such sparse data. While one knows something about weapons that already exist and have been tested, there is no experience either with nuclear weapons being used by both adversaries or with projected future weapons. There is a parallel here, limited but important, to those Nazi scientists who promulgated the biomedical vision on the basis of scanty findings in physical anthropology and genetics having to do with racial characteristics and transmissible human traits.

Doubts have always arisen concerning this approach to strategic problem solving, but have usually been beaten down by the claim that "these sorts of studies were scientific, . . . there were numbers, calculations, rigorously checked," in contrast to the unscientific "essay tradition of the past." Strategists could experience the heady illusion of reducing ultimate human questions of destruction and survival to "a problem of physics which only trained scientists can address." Ironically, the attempt to reduce world problems to pure physics and mathematics resulted in something closer to "pure theology."

Psychological Patterns in Nuclearism

I felt more at home in the laboratory than at home.
—THEODORE TAYLOR

The ideology of nuclearism, before long, became a powerful socializing force for physicists and strategists and a master narrative of American society. Though occurring in a democratic environment and with motives vastly different from those of Nazi doctors, there was nonetheless a parallel sequence to be seen from professional socialization, to socialization to government and institutional work (nuclearism), to specific work on a particular weapons system. And performing that work required a certain amount of dissociation, including patterns of psychic numbing and doubling.

Socialization of Scientists

> These guys take a lot of satisfaction in knowing they're going to be consulted over whether civilization will be destroyed or not. . . . It's a hubris, or arrogance, which says, "We are really bright guys and we can keep the country from doing ridiculous things." . . . And they're totally unaware that they're just being used by some little, puddin'-headed guy in the Pentagon.
> —A CRITIC OF JASON

PHYSICISTS

As we have already seen, socialization of physicists made possible the highly significant step from atomic-bomb work (on behalf of defeating an evil enemy in the midst of a war, however unfortunate one might consider the project in retrospect) to work (initiated during peacetime, to deter another "evil enemy") on the hydrogen bomb, which physicists knew to be a genocidal weapon. These steps took place within a pattern of overall socialization to the nation. A physicist could tend toward unquestioning national loyalty in ways that resemble, but have greater consequences than, that of ordinary Americans. Herbert York has described himself as "down deep . . . a patriotic country boy" whose father "repeatedly told me never to let the flag touch the ground." Emigré physicists have experienced equally strong national loyalties, in their case related to gratitude to their new country for providing a refuge from Nazi mass murder and an opportunity to practice their profession here.

And certainly our whole society has seemed to support the weapons enterprise, as Theodore Taylor wrote (referring to designing improved fission weapons but with applicability to the hydrogen bomb as well): "Our work at Los Alamos was strongly encouraged by the President of the United States, the Congress, the entire military establishment, and most of the general public." Although at the time, as we know, many physicists had the gravest of doubts concerning work on the hydrogen bomb, Herbert York recalls that "there was no one . . . that I was in touch with . . . who had any doubts about it." (York, then a young physicist, was completely under the influence of the California group headed by Ernest Lawrence, whose affiliations with the government in weapons work had been longstanding and very strong.)

That kind of socialization in general was greatly enhanced by two widespread attitudes among pro-bomb physicists. One was the strong conviction, shared with their fellow Americans, that their nation is good, very special, even blessed. These physicists could readily extend that American mythology to questions of technology, making it impossible to believe that America could build a bad machine—the kind of image Jeff Smith, an observer of American popular culture, sees as animating Ronald Reagan's and many Americans' SDI obsession. The other attitude was that they had an absolute right to do any scientific and technological work since they were essentially probing natural phenomena. The physicists' socialization to military production of an ultimate weapon could, then, be experienced as socialization to nature itself.

The socialization is in no way monolithic. Many physicists have made a point of distancing themselves from the military, and those who work or consult on weapons designs have passionately disagreed. But with much of the profession steadily engaged with weapons, large numbers of physicists have come to associate work with the military as simply a part of their professional self. Whether working in groups or, at moments, by themselves, they can actively engage in weapons work while feeling, as one scientist put it, "alone with their physics." And here it is well to consider a mordant observation by Müller-Hill concerning Nazi scientists: "The more you understand of science, the less you [want to] understand of the rest of the world." This socialization *as a scientist* readily creates a sense of routine—indeed, inevitability—until continuing participation in the genocidal project becomes, as a Nazi doctor in Auschwitz put it, "like the weather."

There is a darker personal side to this weapons socialization which Theodore Taylor described as "fascination with a sense of power, of extraordinary power, personal power, over global events." He spoke of personally experiencing that power "in a brute way, by just contemplating the numbers that had to do with the destructive capacity of these things, and occasionally seeing one go off." And he said, "One gets very possessive about these things," experiencing unspoken feelings such as "Yeah, that's my bomb that destroyed this island." Taylor associated that special sense of power with an "addiction" he developed to weapons making, becoming "dependent on doing it, the equivalent of drinking alcohol." This addiction may be to the "high states" Taylor spoke of, having to do with extraordinary power and influence—as was evident in Nazi doctors and scientists, especially in relation to the "heroic" early days of experiencing and disseminating the visionary biomedical project.* Physicists collectively experienced elements of this transcendence: first, during the Manhattan Project; and then, on the return to Los Alamos for hydrogen-bomb work, which many experienced (as one of them put it) "as another great time of the lab."

That experience of transcendence, however, can be accompanied by disturbing perceptions, as York suggests in connection with two powerful experiences. The first occurred while on the island of Eniwetok, where he was involved in an early thermonuclear test explosion, when Edward Teller appeared one night and drew on a blackboard, in one of the temporary aluminum buildings, a diagram of the projected hydrogen bomb. York remembers feeling, "That was it"—human existence had been changed in a dangerous way. He had a similar response to the first actual test of a hydrogen bomb on 2 November 1952, when he exchanged coded signals over the telephone with Edward Teller. Upon hear-

---

*This addiction to high stakes also occurs in many drug users and in members of certain religious and political cults.

ing Teller's confirmation that the test had been successful, York had the awesome sense that "they pushed the trigger. . . . That's when it happened, and that's when this world we live in was created." York choked up when describing these two events, and said, "It's just difficult to get through the whole story," and especially to tell the two stories to students. For they were associated with the dark side of the project, with early forebodings that were quickly suppressed as well as with later glimmers of guilt and sustained arms control advocacy.

The very intensity of weapons socialization can fix one to immediate experience and block out other considerations. Bethe has recently stated that during the early days of weapons making scientists never dreamed there would be so many bombs in the future—a lack of foresight that puzzled one scientist-strategist: "Well, you know you could have [imagined the 25,000 warheads] because you had the plants churning this stuff out, and it never dies—it never decays away, so if you run these plants out [calculate their production] . . . the numbers come out big like that. But we weren't thinking about that."*

The path from socialization to desocialization can pose difficulties. Once one is fully admitted into this realm of power and mystery, efforts to criticize it or extricate oneself may meet with official denunciation, or worse. In the notorious Oppenheimer hearings, the label of "security risk" followed upon the desire not even to leave the weapons fraternity but only to oppose the making of a particular weapon, the "super" or hydrogen bomb. (Oppenheimer had come to favor smaller, tactical nuclear weapons instead.) The McCarthyite paranoia of the time affected physicists involved with the military; "I was afraid that they might go after all of us" is the way Bethe put it.

SOCIALIZED CRITICS

Some scientists, who can be called "socialized critics," have retained connections with the official world of weapons designing

---

*York states that John von Neumann was one of the first to grasp the changing situation, declaring to a meeting of the Air Force Science Advisory Board in 1954, "Nuclear weapons are no longer expensive, . . . no longer scarce, . . . no longer . . . the hardest part of the problems involved in the weapons systems."

while opposing many of its policies. The three we will discuss have in common a combination of early active involvement in building nuclear weapons, subsequent opposition to the nuclear arms race, and a policy of continuing to consult professionally at weapons laboratories. The weapons (and, to a degree, the laboratories) are in some sense theirs: they have created them, designed them, promoted them, opposed them, put forward various views about them—to the point where they cannot seem to imagine their professional identity as being fundamentally removed from them. Far from being unreflective nuclearists, they are all sensitive people who worry greatly about the world. But in their more or less permanent professional bond with the weapons, these compassionate scientists retain elements of nuclearism—a sense that they can somehow find a way, via work on the weapons, to make things better, to solve the problems presented by the weapons.

Among these "socialized critics," Richard Garwin, though in recent years a leading voice for arms control, still consults on "almost all government [nuclear-weapons] programs." On prospective projects, he offers advice on technical feasibility, on whether the system would put America at a disadvantage, and whether it would create instability: "When you make something that you're sure works, you've developed it for *them* [the Soviets], too. And so you really shouldn't bring these things into the world, unless you think it's better if both sides have them." In regard to already existing weapons programs, such as the making of hydrogen bombs, Garwin said, "I review what they're doing, and I give them some suggestions as to how to do it better as long as they're doing it." At the same time he has "big arguments" with Defense Department officials over his advocacy of a comprehensive test ban treaty, during which he points out the advantages of a situation in which neither the United States nor the Soviets could "develop any new kind of nuclear weapon."

Concerning Star Wars, which he has publicly opposed vehemently, Garwin has described himself as "an enemy of the program," but added, "Oh, I've given them some very good ideas, . . . major inventions—which fortunately they don't pay any attention to." He further explained that, while a fuller development of Star Wars would be "a very bad thing" for relations between the

Soviet Union and the United States, he justifies working with the
program on three counts: first, even if he could give them "really
good ideas," these still could not make the program work; second,
because he thinks that a certain amount of development in some
SDI areas (such as sensors) could be useful "for seeing what's
going on on the other side" and therefore stabilizing; and third,
that since the government is determined to spend heavily on the
program, "you need a way out [an alternative to more harmful
directions of work] that costs money." He does draw the line at
working on certain projects: when someone from RAND tele-
phoned him about a project for developing antimatter* for defense or for small weapons, his answer was "Look, we don't need
it"—because "there's no reason to believe that, when we and the
other side has it, it would be to our advantage." And he added a
motto, "If it's not worth doing, it's not worth doing well."

Garwin made very clear his sense of the importance of remaining
an insider:

I think it adds credibility. . . . I think that it helps me to help other
people [in opposing weapons buildup] if I know about these things.
. . . I couldn't do a good job if I were ignorant. I would have to be quiet
because there are things there that I didn't know about and when I was
saying something I would be thinking, "Well, how do I know this is
true?" . . . If I didn't do it according to my standards, I would just be
a person who was taking a political position.

A scientist with particular brilliance in the realm of technology,
he is fundamentally drawn to that realm, and only from work and
observation in it can he feel comfortable about expressing his
position of restraint on nuclear weapons. It is also true that he has
been involved in, and superlative at, certain kinds of weapons
designing since his graduate school days, so that his socializations
as physicist and weapons designer merge.

Hans Bethe also fits into the category of socialized critic, having
ambivalently agreed to work on the hydrogen bomb while hoping

*Antimatter is a hypothetical form of matter consisting of antiparticles—those having
a set of characteristics identical with those of corresponding particles as well as a set of
opposite ones. Within physics there is a phenomenon known as "annihilation" which takes
place when a particle and an antiparticle disappear, with a resultant release of energy
approximately equivalent to the sum of their masses.

it could not be made (see pages 116–17). Bethe's exclusive focus on technical matters was threatened by the direct enthusiasm of others; but his socialization to the overall weapons-producing environment prevailed in his suppression of the impulse to tell the military officers "what a horrible thing we were working on." Similarly, this strong advocate of arms control continues to consult on the weapons; when asked why, he smiled somewhat uneasily and answered, "Old habit." His reasons are similar to Garwin's. Bethe wants "to know what's going on," which requires that he be on the inside; in these consultations, he listens" to people and [tells] them . . . this idea is nonsense and that idea may be useful and that third idea I don't like at all because it might work and it makes the tension worse." In that way he can "very clearly" express his reservations about certain weapons and at the same time carry out his strong "sense of responsibility" toward the Los Alamos laboratory and its division of pure physics which he helped to build.

Herbert York, after an unusually extensive career involved in making and setting policies about the weapons, followed by an equally extensive public commitment to promoting peace and arms control, also continues to consult on weapons. He explained simply that, having had a great deal of experience as both insider and outsider, "you can have much more influence as an insider." The title of York's book, *Making Weapons, Talking Peace,* captures well the general situation of the socialized critic.

These socialized critics of nuclearism, and other physicists as well, can experience elements of a "transfer of conscience," where conscience no longer stands between a scientist and the potential victims of the weapons he helps make but is instead directed toward loyalty to his professional group and its overall project. That transfer of conscience can be eased for some by the presence of highly respected senior physicists. Theodore Taylor, despite his initial reservations about weapons work, quickly found that, when his talent brought praise, "it was fun being patted on the head by people like Fermi and Bethe"; moreover, "the prominence of the people that were involved there . . . [helped] remove any hint of the notion that I shouldn't be doing what I was doing." The intensity of the shared enterprise, and the continuing sense of belonging to the professional group responsible for that enterprise, powerfully affect the most prominent and senior of scientists, even when they have gone far in their criticisms of nuclearism and of the arms race.

THE NEW WEAPONS PHYSICISTS

Over time, as the mainstream of physics has moved away from weapons work, the laboratories have had to depend upon a separate group of scientists who take on the specific career of weapons designing. That career has its rewards, including financial ones, and special opportunities, some of which we have observed. But, according to several scientists, physicists who work on weapons exclusively—as opposed to those of international standing who leave their universities periodically to consult or spend time at the weapons laboratories—have tended to be looked down upon or even ostracized by the profession as a whole. When the weapons physicists have been associated with Edward Teller, as many have been, some of that negative sentiment derives from Teller's conduct at the Oppenheimer hearings. In any case, full-time weapons designers tend to be isolated in their lives and work, separate from the academic side of the profession and unable to return to it because their absence puts them increasingly far behind in a competitive field. They tend to be unable to publish their work because it is top secret. And if, as one scientist-observer put it, they have been involved "on the black side of things"—in work whose very nature is not disclosable—"they have a gap in their career they can't explain. Who's going to hire them to do what?"

In addition, as another scientist close to the question explained, the individual scientist may be put under considerable pressure to produce a functional weapons product:

> It's a different situation when you're working with weapons as compared to regular physics. In regular physics, if you make your hypothesis and it turns out to be in error, you try another one and see if that will work. You go on. But in the case of the weapons makers, your whole career is threatened if you admit being wrong, you can't [be sure] what to do with the rest of your life.

Not surprisingly, weapons physicists, especially when young, form their own tight-knit communities with their own set of customs and shared experience. They often live close to one another in what an observer has called "a very closed society," and their behavior may seem strange to outsiders. Many, extremely shy and uncomfortable in social situations, can relax only with each other. They also have their own gallows humor. At the Star Wars project, Lowell Wood, the charismatic leader of the weapons group who had enormous influence over the younger scientists and was feared by some of them, was referred to as "Darth Vader" (the figure of evil from the 1977 *Star Wars* film). And the "joke" about him was that a plan to take up a collection to buy a Darth Vader costume for him had to be abandoned because they knew he would wear it. Likewise, Nazi scientists and doctors made fun of the more bizarre Nazi racial theories, while they themselves, of course, carried out the "rational" work of the regime. Mocking the bizarre extreme of the genocidal system thus helps one to do the work of the system in a "sensible" and "balanced" manner.

But another scientific observer close to these matters insisted that such scientists in the Soviet Union are still more isolated: "Talk about the isolation of Livermore, but with those guys [the Soviet scientists], it's a separate world." Not surprisingly, then, Livermore scientists could feel a certain identification with their Soviet counterparts—much more so, according to the observer, than with many American physicists or nuclear strategists. Moreover, despite the isolation of both groups, there has been a certain amount of visiting of each other's laboratories. On one such occasion, Soviet weapons scientists came into the "green [classified] area" for a joint seminar. There had been some cooperation between the two countries on general matters of fusion; and when a Soviet scientist who presented made certain points considered classified in America, the Americans had to be silent as the Soviets went on talking about this classified material. This particular form of American-Soviet "affinity" attests to the military and nuclear socialization of both groups, to the special quality of that socialization no matter where it occurs—and, we must add, to the absolute absurdity of the genocidal stance of both nations.

THE JASON GROUP

Aside from physicists' individual connections to nuclear-weapons programs, there has been a specific mechanism for keeping outstanding civilian scientists actively involved in military questions. The Jason Group was initiated during the late 1950s, primarily by senior physicists with extensive weapons experience: John Wheeler, Eugene Wigner, and Marvin Goldberger from Princeton; and Herbert York, then with the Defense Department, who arranged to integrate it with the military. From the beginning this group sought to engage "our best scientists with a strong interest in the defense of the country," especially young scientists, and to have them "work on problems connecting the most advanced ideas and results in the physical sciences with the current problems of defense." The group has since come together regularly for "long summer study" and at other briefer meetings over the winter, and did succeed in engaging such brilliant younger scientists as Richard Garwin, Sidney Drell, and Freeman Dyson; of the approximately one hundred people who have "seriously participated" in Jason over its first twenty-five years, as York proudly recounts, eight have received the Nobel Prize. The Jason Group thus enabled many of America's most gifted younger scientists to maintain their fundamentally academic identities while becoming socialized to a privileged status within the defense hierarchy. The group was said to take on a physicists' version of the "Kennedy style"—a sense of intellectual and personal élan as the scientific "best and brightest,"* of being in an exclusive club: "We were all bright young men together; we were all precocious thirty years ago," as Freeman Dyson later wrote.

In much of what they have done, Jason members have seen themselves as countering extreme, and scientifically untutored, military positions, as "shooting down" lethal plans or harmful ideas. Some members, for instance, provided influential opposition to the antiballistic missile, and thus encouraged some of the

---

*Their meetings in attractive summer areas (La Jolla or Cape Cod) included social evenings with humorous skits (on one occasion, a mock striptease number by one of the wives to the tune of the song, "My Heart Belongs to Daddy," recast as "My Heart Belongs to IDA," the acronym standing for Institute for Defense Analysis, the military-sponsored structure to which Jason was attached).

younger scientists to join the group. Similarly, many within Jason were opposed to the Vietnam War, and it is said that the group's deliberations and papers contributed to the end of the bombing and to heading off the use of nuclear weapons in that war. But it is also true that members of the group put forward plans for the infamous "electronic battlefield" which, had it been carried out, was to have been a 20-by-100-kilometer strip of the Laos-North Vietnamese border in which anyone attempting to pass would be "killed, maimed, or blown up." And concerning Jason's opposition to the war in Vietnam, when a group of its members was asked whether any of them had expressed that opposition to General Maxwell Taylor when he briefed them, one answered, "No, you don't confront generals"—a reaction reminiscent of Bethe's sense that he had to remain quiet before the generals who were waxing poetic about the hydrogen bomb he knew to be genocidal.

That socialization to the military also applies to weapons designing, where Jason has served the cause of nuclearism all too well: pioneering work on beam weapons (for SDI) of all kinds; contributions to a variety of strategic issues "ranging from basing modes (as for the MX)* to the interaction between nuclear explosions and detective systems"; and probing the alleged "window of vulnerability," a concept of vulnerability to a first strike invoked in the 1970s and 1980s to justify expanded nuclear-weapons development in order to close that window. The bold judgment of one critic (see epigraph on page 133), however harsh, makes the crucial point concerning the nature of socialization to weapons making.

Socialization of Strategists

The socialization of nuclear strategists began with Air Force sponsorship of the RAND corporation, and from the beginning was bound up with the principle of strategic or saturation bombing. Rather than to the Air Force or even the military in general, RAND strategists and their successors have most fundamentally

---

*The MX ("missile experimental") is a highly controversial intercontinental ballistic missile meant to destroy the "hard [most protected] targets" of the enemy, but presenting a notoriously difficult basing problem in terms of its own protection from enemy attack, leading to "various schemes for moving the missile around on airplanes, trucks, trains, and even canal boats."

been socialized to the ideological juggernaut of nuclearism which they themselves did much to create. Their real "hosts" to whom they have maximum "responsibility" have been the weapons themselves, the strategists having created since 1945 a tradition of constant promulgation of institutional nuclearism—in their own places of work (such as the RAND Corporation) and in the institutions they serve (the Defense Department, the presidency). In the process an impressive galaxy of American leaders, some of whom were later to become highly influential critics of nuclearism, were initially caught up in that tradition. Thus, an engineer-strategist emphasized that those now thought of as "noble souls" in the sense of being antinuclear (he mentioned George Kistiakowsky, Jerome Weisner, and Robert McNamara) "were at one time working hard on building weapons against the Russians." His point was that the existence of a real threat out there from the Russians gave weapons programs sufficient "credibility" to attract men of that caliber, a very different situation from that of Nazi science.* Though surely right about the reality of the threat, he was also revealing the extent of American individual and institutional nuclearism at the highest levels.

Having known and worked with many of these people, he could also stress their decency: "I just couldn't imagine them doing anything on a personal level that would be comparable [to the Nazi doctors] in any way. . . . They're pussycats individually." He did, in fact, attribute some of his own participation in the strategic enterprise to the sense that "working with such people, you think you are somehow part of . . . an ultimate civilization." Yet he quickly backtracked by stating, in rapid succession, that he had been "rather impressed" to hear about the ordinariness of Nazi doctors and could recall all too well the nasty behavior, during the McCarthy years, on the part of ordinary Americans, some of them people from whom he expected much more.

Like the physicists with whom their socialization has been interwoven, the strategists' identification of self with both weapons and nation can extend to feelings of immortalizing power—to a "he-

---

*While he is basically correct about the difference from Nazi science, that science was also given great legitimacy by the leading German biologists and physicians who participated in it.

roic sense" of their own existence, as one former strategist put it, in combating the Soviet threat which has preoccupied them. In the process, as he explained, they become "enchanted" with the closeness to the corridors of power. In that sense, they experience high states bound up, not with the making of weapons, as in the case of physicists, but with a sense of the all-consuming power of the nuclearistic community, of being importantly involved with "big events."

But everything depends upon remaining an insider—a member of the group that holds the weapons or makes the strategy. In order to maintain one's own nuclearistic views, one must be part of the process by which (as the same strategist put it) "outsiders are rejected"—that is, by which those who question the prevailing views are relegated automatically to outsider status so that questions can be dismissed.

Insider status also became associated with what a leading decision maker described as "a macho side to nuclear weapons." He told how members of the Defense Department's inner circle would meet privately on policy matters and, when issues of conventional forces arose, "all of the military people at the table felt constrained to say that, of course, if a war came, we ought to use everything we've got, especially our nuclear weapons." Their psychological situation was such that "in order to ask for conventional forces they had to first . . . make it clear that they were not afraid of nuclear weapons." There seemed to be two psychological requirements: "They didn't want to appear to be too different—I mean they didn't want to appear to be weak."* The group-psychological need (he called it "some kind of 'group-think' ") was to demonstrate one's socialization to nuclearism and to the requisite "toughness" or brutalization.

Some of their gallows humor has a special tonality, developed particularly by Herman Kahn, that can be called "omnicidal whimsy." In order to "clarify a good deal of current strategic thinking," Kahn developed not only the concept of the "Doomsday Machine" (programmed [see pages 5–6] to be set off in a way that would destroy all of human life if a certain number of nuclear

---

*There have, of course, been occasions on which military men have been more cautious than civilians, and urged nuclear restraint.

bombs exploded over the United States), but also the "Doomsday-in-a-Hurry Machine" (which would do the same should the Soviets or the Chinese violate a code of behavior the United States would unilaterally legislate) and the "Homicide Pact Machine" (a computerized arrangement that would bring about "automatic mutual homicide" as a consequence of a failure of deterrence). Kahn did not actually advocate these "machines"; but, granting the unacceptability of a doomsday machine that would risk the lives of three billion inhabitants of the earth, he did ask, "Then *how many people would we be willing to risk?*" and in answer speak of "the *possibility* of one or two hundred million people (i.e., about 5 times more than World War II deaths) dying from the immediate effects, even if one does not include deferred long-term effects due to radiation." The psychological function of omnicidal whimsy is to establish a moral universe in which the mass murder of more than two hundred million people is acceptable as a preferred alternative to an imagined machine that would "blow up the world." Thus, a doomsday machine is for Kahn by no means a *complete* caricature.* His faint humor and playfulness in discussing these devices serve to socialize the strategic community, and to some extent the general public, to highly brutalized forms of nuclearism.

Strategists' language is crucial to their continuing socialization, as Carol Cohn has concluded from her own experience: "Learning the language is a transformative, rather than an additive, process. When you choose to learn it you are not simply choosing to add new information, new vocabulary, but to enter into a mode of thinking—a mode of thinking not only about nuclear weapons, but also, de facto, about military and political power, and about the relationship between human ends and technological means." We shall have more to say about that language (see chapter 7), but here we need only emphasize its importance for unconsciously internalizing the nuclearistic standards of the strategic group and buttressing one against doubt.

Strategists can vary in their attitudes from nuclear fatalism—a

---

*Kahn speaks of them as "almost caricaturized." The "Doomsday Machine" made its way into the film *Dr. Strangelove*, where it is portrayed, correctly we believe, as a logical extension of Kahn's and others' deterrence policies.

deep sense of the inevitability of nuclear war and even at moments
a mystical desire to witness it—back to optimistic insistence that
their work on deterrence will prevent nuclear war from ever taking
place. Many come to sense the tenuousness of their project and the
hollowness of the claim sometimes made that they are doing "empirical work" in the absence of empirical data. The unreality felt
by strategists when away from RAND suggests that they require
continuous reinforcement of their socialization from their own
reference group. There they can be confirmed in a specific way, as
a former strategist explained: "If there is just a modest chance that
[any particular weapons planning] will serve its purpose without
. . . ever having to be used, that rationalization becomes available
to you, . . . an indeterminate chance that the deterrent works, and
it never gets used—you've got a way out." That "way out"
becomes what is called "conservatism," which can amount to cling-
ing to a stance of aggressive nuclearism that includes potential use.
A former Defense Department official recognized the paradox:
"You could say it's not 'conservative' to suppose you would use
nuclear weapons. And yet it's conservative in the sense that we're
not going to make any big changes that we don't know the result
of."

The road to socialization can be paved with civility. A former
strategist who came from a family of education and means said
in quiet tones, "I've always had a distaste for nuclear weapons."
He was probably telling the truth, but leaving out his considerable attraction for strategic work involving them. Unlike some
strategists, he spoke modestly of his work and stressed its limitations, declaring, "We would be kidding ourselves to say we had
enough data to be completely confident about any of our reports." He stressed the computer's dependency upon human intelligence: "Garbage in, garbage out." And he spoke of how
difficult it is in nuclear work to "bind the uncertainties" and
"control the variables"; and while "you work hard to safeguard
the system, . . . there's a limit about how much you can guaran-
tee precautions won't fail—especially under extreme stress."
And "you just do not know where [the work] is going to lead."
Yet precisely this civility and relative restraint helped sustain

him during his decades of work on nuclear strategy. His apparent moderation—his seeing himself as combating cruder and more hawkish voices and minds around him—gave authority to the dangerously "flexible" nuclear strategies he came to advocate, and enabled him to remain socialized to the strategic endeavor.

Strategists may come to view the weapons as a permanent and necessary part of cosmic balance. One has to go on building, deploying, and imagining scenarios for the weapons because "that's the way things are." The larger nuclear-weapons "system" can, for many, resemble the cosmos or God in seeming infinitely greater than any individual or group of individuals. They can see themselves as among the closest to that mystical system—rendered simultaneously all-powerful by that association and at the same time helpless before its power. (Here there is a parallel to the mixture of omnipotence and impotence characteristic of Nazi doctors.) The strategists' socialization includes holding fast to a sense of harmony with the system and, at the same time, pursuing what can become an equally mystical "contest" with the Soviets for leadership or dominance of the system. They can in the process experience themselves as part of an élite group specially empowered to violate taboos. Their situation is reminiscent of Thomas Mann's description, in his novel applying the Faust legend to the Nazi historical experience, of the diabolical quest of the Nazi self for unlimited "creative power"—the promise of absolute breakthrough, of conquest of time and death, if the new self will "dare to be barbaric, twice barbaric indeed."

Nuclear Doubling

The process of doubling in weapons designers and strategists is less extreme than in Nazi doctors, but is just as functional in enabling the former to do their work. For example, Theodore Taylor, the physicist who described feeling "more at home in the laboratory than at home" (see epigraph, page 132), went on to talk about "some kind of split" in himself, a split encouraged, he felt, by attitudes of his family: "They knew I was working on atomic bombs, and they simply didn't care [to know] what I was doing. It's just that my wife didn't want to hear about it. The kids didn't want to hear about it." He contrasted the ordinariness of his domestic life and doubts about himself as a husband and father with his extraordinary recognition and "sense of uniqueness" in the laboratory.

Actually, he knew that his wife *did* care what he was doing and was proud of his accomplishments, but was at the same time "wishing I was doing something else." His work at the laboratory became "the skeleton in the closet," by implication something shameful that had to be hidden. And it was kept almost completely separate: "Physically I was behind the fence in the complex, and so the two tended generally not to get mixed. . . . It really . . . was not only a skeleton in the closet, but the door was pretty much locked." His wife and children came to refer to the laboratory as "Daddy's workpen"—a phrase that suggested its walled-off separateness, childishness (parallel with the children's "playpen"), and perhaps the dubious nature of what went on there. Despite the division, both his wife and his mother would sometimes ask, "Why are you working on trying to find new ways to kill as many people as possible?" To which he would answer that he and the others in Los Alamos and their counterparts in the Soviet Union "were in fact the world's front line of peacemakers, . . . making war obviously insane." But the two women began to ask the question less frequently because "they didn't see how it had any effect on me."

Taylor's separation of his laboratory self from his family self broke down, at least in part, in response to civil defense arrangements about which he was required to inform his family in the event that "a bomb went off above us in Los Alamos." His wife and children were clearly "terrified" by his description of "what would happen." And it was clear that nobody, himself included, was much reassured by either evacuation plans or shelters. Now his laboratory self, including the bomb, was very much in the home, and so was his and his family's moral conflict. The doubling was also undermined by later work at the Pentagon which convinced him that "there were dangerous situations in the handling of nuclear materials," and revealed "how out of control things were" in regard both to the war in Vietnam and to nuclear weapons. He found that "people were lying," and that no one was paying much attention to what he considered a great danger: "the possibility that criminals or terrorists might swipe weapons or nuclear material to make weapons."

Yet the doubling, even when precarious, was supported by the "addiction" to weaponry mentioned earlier; and years later—even after he had turned antinuclear (see page 271)—when asked to write an article for a magazine about new generations of nuclear weapons, "I found myself drawn into the excitement. I was disappointed when the damage done by . . . a bomb . . . was less than I had originally thought. . . . And every once in a while I'd tap myself and say, 'What's going on with you?' " Now he could recognize his past doubling in connection with weapons making and his participation in targeting Soviet cities and their inhabitants:

> And never that I can remember [did I have] a daydream about those people . . . as individuals, what they might look like, how many of them one would see slammed up against the walls of the nearest building and splattered all over the place. You don't think about that. . . . If you start thinking about that too much, you are not going to be able to think . . . very creatively about new ways of making bombs.

Hans Bethe experienced similar inner division while he was working on the hydrogen bomb. He reported keeping his time in the laboratory "very separate" from his time with his family, and that "the content of my brain was totally different." It was a particularly enjoyable time in his personal life, as his family was close, his children were growing up "nicely," and there were several good friends whom he saw regularly. The separation between work and family was made easier by the fact that the basic breakthrough in making the weapon had been achieved: "It was more like most people doing a job during the day and then relaxing at home." The classified nature of the work also helped sustain the barrier, so that "it was just the technical issues" he needed to be concerned with. That was in contrast to the earlier time at Los Alamos when, working on the atomic bomb, he threw himself passionately into the problem and thought about it day and night. He summed up the situation this way: "In spite of hating the hydrogen bomb, I remember the year 1952 as a happy year"—then a long pause—"personally." He was saying that the hydrogen bomb required more doubling on his part than did the atomic bomb because of the greater need to keep his weapons-laboratory self separate from his more humane, family self; and that the doubling was generally, but not entirely, effective.

Another scientist-strategist told of a poignant struggle against dissociation and doubling. Having left weapons work in mid-career because of his increasingly critical view of weapons and his strong feeling that "it didn't make sense to talk about fighting a nuclear war," he is still involved in teaching on the subject. And he is troubled to find that he "remains deeply interested in specific kinds of questions, 'Does the MX missile make more sense than the Midgetman missile?' " even though he knows that these have no real importance compared with problems of getting rid of weapons and preventing nuclear holocaust. He described himself as still engaging in "two kinds of thinking," and even as feeling himself close to being two different people. One kind is quantitative-analytic and technical, in which he approaches problems precisely and, when possible, mathematically—focusing on "puzzle solving." He gives a course on such questions, which he believes he can deal with "as well as anybody in the United States"—precisely because "it is like doing a lot of little puzzles."

This scientist-strategist also gives another course "doing just the opposite," a course in which "we raise all the fundamental questions" about the human dimensions of nuclear threat and engage in "a critique of the thinking of others." When preparing ideas for the second course, he finds it hard to concentrate for more than a few minutes at a time and can be distracted by almost anything. He falls asleep while reading, looks for interruptions (sharpening pencils, making phone calls, and so on), and views the entire enterprise as very difficult. In general, he continues to experience "a lot of anxiety" not only in connection with nuclear threat but "particularly about my role in it—because of this ambivalence, this schizophrenia." This man's struggle has had considerable success, given his present convictions and activities. Yet even now he finds himself (in the manner of Theodore Taylor who spoke of his "addiction") all too susceptible to the lure of weapons technicism and its accompanying dangers of dissociation and doubling.

Steven Kull's descriptions of his interviews with strategists and decision makers reveal repeated evidence of splitting and probable doubling (see pages 13–14 and chapter 7). A RAND analyst told him of personally believing in a restrained policy based on minimal need, but professionally advising continuing nuclear buildup because of its importance for *perceptions* of superpower balance. He thought it necessary to manifest such a split: "Well, you have to distinguish between what *you* think . . . and what you would instead, *as a policy analyst,* advise."

Concerning the idea of winning a nuclear war, Kull told of the common belief that "there's someone else, . . . someone in the Pentagon [who] really believes it," though each Pentagon official he interviewed claimed not to be the one who held such a belief. The inner contradiction is revealed by one former high Pentagon official, who dismissed statements about winning a nuclear war as "primarily for the American audience," but a little later, in a deeper, slower tone, commented, "Yeah, we're tough. We're prepared to carry through American policies"—now making it clear that he and others were indeed prepared to fight and win a nuclear war. Kull referred to the second statement as "cheerleading," meaning a kind of bravado rather than a serious military statement. But the "team" for which he is "cheerleading" could well represent his own nuclear-weapons self—the constellation of self that struggles to hold on to a conviction that it is part of a nuclearized structure capable of fighting and winning. Another former high Pentagon official commented more candidly on how the necessity of "always dealing with contradictory audiences" leads to "inherent contradictions if you want to appear gentle and thoughtful to your own public, and tough—and just a touch irrational—to your adversary." He explained that "you usually do that with two personalities, and you kind of move them forward or back depending on the circumstances." The "two personalities," we believe, inevitably take on a certain breadth and autonomy to the point where they have separate realities for the individual.

And it is possible to lose track of which self is the appropriate one to call forth, as apparently happened to George Bush during the 1980 election campaign. In an interview with the journalist Robert Scheer, Bush stated that he did not believe that there was no such thing as a winner in a nuclear exchange, and spoke of winning being made possible by such things as survivability of command and control, and of industrial potential, and by a "capability that inflicts more damage on the opposition than it can inflict on you"; he added that the Soviets' planning is based on "the ugly concept of a winner in a nuclear exchange." But when a newspaper headline appeared the next day saying, "Bush thinks he can win a nuclear war," he called an urgent press conference to deny that statement and explain that he meant, "It's the Soviets who think they can win a nuclear war." In commenting on this sequence, Kull noted that Bush was attempting to appeal both to the constituency who believes you can win a nuclear war (and would assume his denial was made only for political reasons) and those who believe you cannot win a nuclear war (and would assume that Bush was clarifying his position to take that view). Kull rightly pointed out that "this creates . . . a split within the person himself," and added, "I doubt that George Bush knows what he really thinks." But from another perspective, Bush does know what he really thinks: he really thinks we *can* win a nuclear war (the view put forward by one constellation of self); and he really thinks that we *cannot* win a nuclear war (the view put forward by another constellation of self).

Other evidence of this tendency are the decision makers' frequent "flip-flops" Kull described between aggressive and restrained nuclear-weapons advocacy or between belief and disbelief in the necessity of a particular weapons system for a particular strategic purpose. As Kull observed, these flip-flops, including Bush's, "speak to the two parts of the person." A former high government official could say to Kull, "You know, I envy you guys in academics. You get to tell the truth. When you're a public figure, it's different." He was referring not just to what he took to be conscious deception, but to the inner divisions in officials associated with public contradictions and private confusions. One former member of the Joint Chiefs of Staff, for instance, found it difficult to reconcile the beliefs that we would "seek an advantage" in a nuclear war (in effect, seek victory), on the one hand, and that "everybody will lose in a nuclear war," on the other. Finally, almost in despair, he declared, "Very little thought has been given to how to fight a nuclear war. We don't really think about it.

Nobody can come up with any realistic situation as to what would happen during a nuclear war. We are groping in the unknown." And a former National Security Council official, when asked whether stated war-fighting policies were merely declaratory (designed for some political effect) or represented actual intent, paused and then answered, "I don't think we even know that ourselves."

Dissociation, Doubling, and Failed Mysticism

Those in the highest offices feel pressures of socialization to the weapons and can engage in dissociation and doubling. A scientist who had enjoyed advisory positions in several administrations described the division in Eisenhower from his "public face" of advocating only *defensive* weapons deemed necessary for national security, while at the same time silently and secretly encouraging "the building of first-strike weapons." Eisenhower emerged as a man who really did believe in weapons restraint and at the same time really did wish first-strike weapons to be built. Other presidents, this scientist added, had the same inner division. The former tendency has to do with a president's deep sense of responsibility for avoiding nuclear war; and the latter, with his inability to extricate himself from the predominant institutional nuclearism.

And that institutional nuclearism is, in turn, maintained, as the prominent British science adviser Solly Zuckerman put it, by "the man in the laboratory . . . who at the start proposes that for this or that arcane reason it would be useful to improve an old or to devise a new nuclear warhead, . . . a new missile, . . . a new system within which it has to fit." To which we would add that dissociation and doubling enable "the man in the laboratory" and the strategists to keep creating and imagining uses of the weapons. One knowledgeable observer, referring to nuclearists and weapons, declared, "They can never have enough of them," and of Edward Teller specifically, "He loves those things—it is partly the magic of it, . . . to control nature."

The weapons mysticism made possible by the dissociative process is a failed mysticism. The weaponry is equated with nature, with the cosmos, and with ultimate forces that guide our destiny.

Yet beliefs are choppy, unformed, and bound up with ultimate helplessness and ignorance: "Nobody believes it but the system believes it"; and, "Only the system knows how the system reacts." Above all, the mystical system becomes allied with the imperatives of one's own group. Just as the Nazi doctor who first opposed experiments on human beings came to engage in these experiments once convinced that they were required by his people and his movement, so might American or Soviet nuclearists blow up the world for their own group's "higher purposes." The nuclearists' dissociative mysticism also has parallels with the Nazi biologists' vision of taking over the evolutionary process in order to purify the Nordic race and ultimately redeem the world. One observer, noting the technicism and detachment of many nuclearists, commented that they could "destroy the world without malice." But they could also destroy the world out of naïve mystical passion.

That mysticism can enable nuclearists to disclaim responsibility. A leading weapons designer, when asked about his sense of the future, answered quickly, "It's not in the hands of the physicists." Though his overt point was, "It's in the hands of the politicians," he conveyed the sense of a larger force that neither physicists nor anyone else can hope to stand up against. There is a partial resemblance to the Auschwitz doctors' claim that they could not be held responsible for what happened in the camp: it was not they but the politicians who brought the prisoners there, so that all they, the doctors, could do was to perform their duty and render the killing more "humane." As nuclear participants maintain their creative momentum via their adaptive dissociation and doubling, as well as their urgent socialization to both their professional and national groups, it becomes all too easy to say of weapons involvement: "It's a terrible thing but we have to do it"—or simply, "We have to do it."

Chapter 6

Momentum toward Genocide

A vicious spiral has been created that gives the
arms race a "mad momentum" of its own and
drives it forward blindly.

—HERBERT YORK

The easiest [message] to get through . . . is "go."
—THOMAS POWERS

WHEN AND how does a group or a society cross the threshold into
genocide? When and how, that is, does the genocidal mentality
become converted into the genocidal act? To answer these questions, we must examine the collective and institutional momentum
that presses toward genocide.

In using the term *behemoth* for Nazi Germany, the distinguished
German-born social theorist Franz Neumann combines the biblical
"great or monstrous beast" with the sense in which Hobbes used
the term to describe the chaos, lawlessness, and disorder of seven-
teenth-century England during its civil war. But Nazi Germany,
whatever its chaos and lawlessness, also possessed deadly order
and murderous law*ful*ness.

The spirit of this entity was prefigured in the Nuremberg rallies,
with their merging of the individual into the mystical collectivity,
their esthetic and ideological transcendence, and their message of

irresistible power. The Nazi behemoth became, then, an organic force of destruction—in psychohistorical terms, a collection of institutions that, however disparate and antagonistic, were effectively integrated in the common pursuit of genocide. The nuclear behemoths of the United States and the Soviet Union follow most of that description, though their relation to genocide is never one of overt pursuit.

Commentators have referred regularly to "the problem of momentum" as having haunted the nuclear arms race from the time of the decision to drop the atomic bombs on Hiroshima and Nagasaki (or of the inability to make a decision *not* to drop them) to the subsequent decades of nuclear-weapons development by the United States and the Soviet Union. That is what Herbert York (see chapter epigraph, page 156) means when he speaks of the arms race as driven "blindly" in a "vicious spiral" of "mad momentum."

Always contributing to the momentum toward genocide is the spirit of nuclear crusade. That deformed spirit flourishes in the presence of manichean dualisms, the division of the world into light (American goodness) and dark (Soviet evil); or on the Soviet side, the same dualism in reverse. In each case, the weaponry took shape in a country long involved in an ideological crusade against the other, a crusade that, whatever its episodic lulls, has intensified weapons building and general embrace of nuclearism. Increasing that momentum are the irrepressible creative energies of individuals and groups—scientists, engineers, and nuclear strategists—which both contribute to and draw upon ever-accelerating technological developments with their "unforeseen" and "irreversible" and "unintended" consequences "that turn out to be not entirely unintended."

This combined momentum—ideological, creative, and technological—is perceived by the weapons community of each superpower and leads to fears (genuine, exploited, and usually both) that the momentum of the other behemoth is still greater (the nature of nuclear behemoths will be discussed later in the chapter). The resulting action-reaction dynamic persists even during periods of political détente, in relation to a weapons technology that is "extremely open-ended." The "endless generations" of weapons development become bound up with perpetual genocidal momentum in each behemoth unless decisions are made to interrupt the cycle. "The men in the laboratory" are, in proposing and developing technologies for new weapons and for improving old ones, "a prime source" of this momentum, as Zuckerman stressed. But laboratory scientists are just one group who increasingly depend upon active involvement in this momentum toward genocide as a form of self-definition. Herbert York speaks of a larger community of defense intellectuals for whom this intensified arms race is a source not only of regular income and important consultant fees but of solving "psychic and spiritual needs," since "a very large part of their self-esteem [derives] from their participation in what they believe to be an essential—even a holy—cause." There is a kind of equilibrium between the *active inertia* of the arms race (*inertia* here meaning the tendency of something in motion to stay in motion) with a more *passive psychological inertia* (the tendency of something at rest to stay at rest—in this case the dependency of the self on the arms race).

Momentum extends readily into the impulse to use the weapons, especially when close to the threshold. As Thomas Powers has pointed out, "once war has become inescapable, there is something to be gained by going first" as "with glacial inexorability the fear of war is . . . pushed aside by the fear of being caught on the ground" (see pages 4–5). Different as their situation was, the Nazis' irresistible momentum toward genocide—developing out of the interplay between organizational (and ideological) energies and new technology—has some relevance for nuclear danger. Very important for Nazi genocidal momentum was the wartime situation which enormously intensified both feelings of threat and impulses toward the most violent forms of national rejuvenation. In the nuclear case also, should there arise any possibility of war, a point could be readily reached at which, as Powers tells us, the easiest message to get through is go. One recalls Brodie's early reading of such a situation—"Be quick on the draw and the trigger squeeze, and aim for the heart"—while recognizing that "you will probably die too!"

The Nazi Behemoth

> In the final analysis the destruction of the Jews was
> not so much a product of laws and commands as it
> was a matter of spirit, of shared comprehension, of
> consonance and synchronization.
> —RAUL HILBERG

Recent historical studies suggest that it is virtually impossible to determine the precise moment when the Nazis crossed the genocidal threshold. These studies also suggest that many different forces contributed to that step, including (as the historian Saul Friedländer explains) "the interaction of entirely heterogeneous phenomena: messianic fanaticism and bureaucratic structures, pathological impulses and administrative decrees, archaic attitudes and advanced industrial society." But all observers agree that prior Nazi attitudes and actions had long been setting the stage for such genocide, though no straight line of intent led inevitably to it. What the genocide required was a particular ideology and mind-set, considerable institutional and bureaucratic momentum, and finally a set of immediate historical circumstances that contributed to the crossing of a macabre threshold.

Ideology and Meaning

Nazi ideology provided not a blueprint for, but a structure of thought, a tone, and a mentality fully consistent with, genocide. Nazi political and biomedical ideology, that is, rendered the genocide an act that "had meaning to its perpetrators." The totalistic ideology and its "leader principle" provided a justification for destroying any individual or group considered undesirable or otherwise threatening to Nazi goals. From the beginning, the regime killed those judged to be opposed to it or otherwise threatening.

Indeed, the Nazis mobilized great ideological energy by rendering their cause a life-and-death struggle for Germany and for the Nordic race. They focused strongly, especially during the early days of the movement, on their survivor mission from the First World War, claiming to be carrying out their unfinished work in avenging their "betrayers" and restoring German glory. They powerfully invoked the theme of sacrifice, pressing for the ultimate if unrealizable ideal: "Everybody is ready to die for everybody else." The killing of designated enemies then became part of a quest for "more life" for the German people and more health for the Nordic race, a quest that required "a continuous search for an increasingly radical solution to the Jewish question."

Yet despite the fierce anti-Semitism of Hitler and the ideologues around him, most historians are convinced that there were no plans for mass murder until "the end of 1940 at the earliest" or, as most believe, some time in the middle of 1941. Before that, consistent Nazi policy had sought "removal" (Entfernung), or forced "emigration" of Jews, to be accomplished by "ghettoization, starvation, humiliation, and persecution." Contained within such victimization, however, was the pseudoreligious impulse toward "purification of German soil and German blood."

An important step toward releasing previously suppressed "eschatological-apocalyptic tendencies inherent in Nazism" was the event the Germans called Kristallnacht—the systematic, government-instigated national pogrom of 9 November 1938 in which Jews were beaten, humiliated, and arrested, and synagogues and Jewish-owned stores destroyed. Kristallnacht was an attempt to reinvigorate the Nazi revolution, to maintain the active energy of "a movement" rather than to risk becoming merely a "traditional right-wing dictatorship." It was in that sense both a "culmination" of existing ideological passions and at the same time "a dividing line" because it clearly increased the momentum of Jewish victimization. The Nazis were approaching the threshold to genocide.

Another important step was Hitler's first public threat to bring about "the annihilation of the Jewish race in Europe," a threat made in January 1939 in connection with his blaming the Jews for the impending war. The threat, though not backed by any concrete plan, had considerable psychological importance as a preliminary statement of an imagined act. The invasion of Poland in September 1939 provided a further "release" for true believers not yet quite able to acknowledge—or at least to state publicly—the extent of their own murderous inclinations. That is, they embraced an ideology that enabled them to view all Jews as evil and criminal, and inwardly wished to destroy the Jews, but had not yet reached a mind-set of planning and carrying out the mass murder of an entire people. Indeed, as we have noted, certain Nazis (including many Nazi doctors) never became convinced that the genocidal project was right or necessary, but participated in it nonetheless with the help of only partial, even fragmentary, ideological convictions. Over time, increasingly radical and destructive Nazi policies contributed to an overall shift in mind-set that made leaders more bold, and followers more compliant, in relation to genocide.

Hitler was at the center of this ideological process, a "fighting prophet" whose anti-Semitism was crucial to his world view from the beginning but became "ever more salient" to his visions and actions. Hitler's anti-Semitism combined passion, in the form of "violent threats and fantasies of mass murder," with racial *theory* within which "mass murder of the Jews was a small 'logical' deduction." He could, with his extraordinary charismatic talent, become a "psychopathic god" and legitimate these feelings in others; he also created an immediate circle of leaders who came to share his conviction that in translating these fantasies into actions by annihilating the Jews, they were "restoring the meaning of history."

Nazi Genocidal Institutions

A nation carrying out genocide must create new institutions and alter existing ones. The Nazis did both. Their institutions, far from being passive conduits, contributed greatly to the genocidal dynamic. The actual killing institutions fell into two categories: police-military (*Einsatzgruppen*) and medical (the "euthanasia" killing centers). From the beginning, there was a relationship between the two sets of institutions, and the death camps combined these police-military and medical elements. The SS was the organization primarily responsible for the actual killing—completely in the case of the first category, and in collaboration with medical and pseudomedical groups in the second.

The *Einsatzgruppen** were employed for special missions dealing with intelligence work and tracking down suspected enemies at the time both of the annexation of Austria in 1938 and of the dismemberment of Czechoslovakia the following year. But it was in Poland that these mobile SS units began to take on a genocidal function. There in 1939 the *Einsatzgruppen* were charged with the task of annihilating Polish aristocrats, intellectuals, and priests—essentially destroying the entire Polish educated class.†

Significantly, an attempt was made to hide the murderous policy from the *Wehrmacht* (the regular German army), to which the action was described as "suppression of all anti-Reich elements . . . in particular counter-espionage." A second wave of *Einsatzgruppen* concentrated on murdering Poles and Jews in certain areas, and in others forcibly deported large numbers of Jews into the interior of Poland. Some *Wehrmacht* leaders expressed unease or even horror (the secret could hardly be kept) at SS actions, but tended to be relieved rather than resentful when Hitler cleverly rearranged governance of occupied areas to place more power in the hands of the SS—"an example of the curious military schizophrenia which so greatly facilitated the work of the *Einsatzgruppen.*" This particular form of organizational numbing on the part of the *Wehrmacht* was characteristic throughout the bureaucracy. Also operating here was the Nazi policy of giving the lethal work to those who, ideologically and organizationally, were most inclined to do it—rather than leaving it in the hands of those who did not.

Thus, there was an existing *Einsatzgruppen* tradition for genocidal behavior when new units were organized for the invasion of the Soviet Union. In addition, volunteers for these units were encouraged to feel that they were engaged in a holy war, a "war of destruction" *(Vernichtungskrieg)* and—in Hitler's equation of Jews and Bolsheviks—"a final, Armageddonlike struggle against evil" and "the crowning point of his anti-Jewish policy."

---

*The term *Einsatzgruppen* means "task forces" but can also be translated as "special-duty groups" or "striking force" and can convey an overtone of self-sacrifice, dedication, and willingness to stake one's life for one's cause. *Einsatzgruppen* leaders came to include "a curious collection—highly qualified academics, ministerial officials, lawyers, and even a Protestant priest and an opera singer."

†Hitler apparently took encouragement from a previous "successful" genocide: when briefing his SS generals, he raised the rhetorical question "Who still talks nowadays of the extermination of the Armenians?"

Enhancing the momentum toward genocide was the ideological mystification contained in Hitler's early directive that "the Bolshevist/Jewish intelligentsia" must be eliminated in the service of liquidating "all Bolshevist leaders or commissars." That mystification provided a political rationale for murdering Jews while rendering amorphous additional categories of victims, which eventually included "many millions of Poles, Russians, Ukrainians, Byelorussians, and others"; indeed, the overall total of murder victims "may have surpassed even the Final Solution." The expanding brutality helped the Nazis muster the psychological and political will to murder *all* Jews. Commanders were clearly aware of their mission, and their reports were "couched in cold, official language as if recording production figures for refrigerators or numbers of vermin destroyed."

When men in the *Einsatzgruppen* units showed resistance or exhibited psychological conflicts, a commander might invoke the concept of the necessary ordeal for the Nazi "higher purpose," and also insist that each man in his unit "overcome himself"—share in the killing and thereby form a bond of "blood guilt" that could hold the group together. The struggle to overcome such conflicts contributed to the extreme ferocity and grotesque thoroughness of the mass murder. Applying unrestrained energy to the assignment enabled one to avoid taking in psychologically the meaning of one's actions. As in the case of Nazi doctors (and probably of most genocidal perpetrators), conscientiousness came to replace conscience. At every level, the momentum and the psychological environment of the killing institution enabled individual men to mobilize a sense of dedication to, and even enthusiasm for, the task, which in turn enabled them to suppress whatever horror they might otherwise have felt.

The institutions within the medicalized killing channels included the hereditary health courts of the sterilization program, the various components of the "euthanasia" project culminating in the "killing centers," and (in part) the death camps themselves. The hereditary health courts included practicing physicians, district judges, and administrative health officers, all of whom tended to be sympathetic to Nazi projects (see chapter 2). These "courts" made decisions for sterilization which could be appealed but were rarely reversed. Backed by the police power of a totalitarian state, the courts provided an important institutional beginning of the visionary biomedical scenario the Nazis were to play out. At the same time, the courts received additional professional support from another institution favored by the Nazis: the various centers for "racial hygiene" established at universities throughout Germany, where genetically minded physicians and biologists helped formulate, develop further, and provide sanction for the biomedical vision.

That sanction was important for the jump from coercive sterilization to the direct medical killing of the "euthanasia" project, which required institutions of its own. These included mental hospitals and mental homes (both of which served regularly as a source of victims and at times as a place where they were killed), transportation arrangements (crucial to a secret program, and usually run by the SS), transitional institutions (to which patients were often sent from mental hospitals before being killed), and the actual killing centers. There were also institutional procedures for reporting of cases and for "expert evaluation" (by prominent Nazi psychiatrists who served as "experts" and "higher experts" in fraudulent review processes). All these institutions had such medical-sounding names as "The Reich Committee for the Scientific Registration of Serious Hereditary and Congenital Diseases" for listing victims or "The Reich Work Group of Sanatoriums and Nursing Homes" for the overall arrangements for killing adults. Children were killed mainly on the wards of general hospitals or children's homes; and the six adult killing centers were converted from former nursing homes, mental hospitals, or prisons, all surrounded by high walls (some had been castles in the distant past) and in isolated locations. Thus, the special institutions required for genocide were created from bits and pieces of existing institutions, with added arrangements for killing; each element in the overall structure had its professional euphemisms.

The killing centers were run by physicians, usually psychiatrists, who were required to open the gas cock, in accordance with the slogan "the syringe belongs in the hands of a physician" (see page 99). This was the final common pathway of both the killing and its medicalization. But the medicalized structure in general conveyed to outsiders, particularly families of patients, the image of institutions that would heal rather than kill; and constant falsifications (including death certificates) maintained that illusion. Medicalization could also contribute psychologically to a doctor's capacity to kill. One psychiatrist told how gradually increasing the dosage of barbiturates with very young children, so that they became progressively lethargic until they died, could give one the feeling that "there was no killing. . . . This is not murder, it is a putting-to-sleep." While no such illusion could be maintained in the killing of adult patients with carbon monoxide gas, the briefings arriving doctors received from leading psychiatrists on the principle of "life unworthy of life" also had a medical aura. And when protests, mainly from Protestant and Catholic clergy, brought about the closing of adult killing centers, the murders could nonetheless be actively continued because of the existence of these medicalized arrangements. Now adults, too, were killed in hospitals or nursing institutions. Instead of gassing, with its telltale evidence of smoke and smells, killing was accomplished by injection or starvation, methods used all along in children's programs which required no modification.

The six Nazi death camps combined military-police and medicalized elements. As institutions, they were derived from the hundreds of ordinary "concentration camps" instituted almost from the moment the Nazis seized power for "protective custody" of a wide array of political enemies, including Jews; there was consistent cruelty and considerable killing but no policy of or machinery for systematic mass murder. The medicalized component helped provide that machinery in the form of equipment (notably gas chambers) and personnel transferred from the "euthanasia" killing centers in Germany to serve as the foundation of the death camps. Whether or not physicians were present to supervise the actual killing, as in Auschwitz, the killing method had been essentially developed within medical structures. Phenol injections, another form of killing either administered or ordered by doctors, can be said to have derived from both components, having been utilized as a means of killing on medical blocks in earlier concentration camps. Significantly, the first commandant of Treblinka, where the number killed was exceeded only by

Auschwitz, was a physician transferred from a "euthanasia" killing center.

Both "euthanasia" collecting centers and ordinary concentration camps, then, were *pre-genocidal* institutions—those that readily become or can be converted to genocidal function. Also important pre-genocidal institutions were the ghettos where Jews were confined prior to being sent to death camps. First established in 1940, the ghettos began primarily as a police action in persecuting Jews, but also had a "medical" source in the Nazi insistence upon the necessity of isolating Jews in order to prevent their spreading typhus to German personnel. The high Jewish death rate in the ghettos from brutal treatment, direct killing, disease, and increasingly extreme conditions of starvation came close to actual genocide. As in other pre-genocidal institutions, the big step to full-blown genocide came to seem almost natural.

Nazi Bureaucratic Initiative

> At every stage they displayed a striking pathfinding ability in the absence of directives, a congruity of activities without jurisdictional guidelines, a fundamental comprehension of the task even when there were no explicit communications.
> —RAUL HILBERG

As Raul Hilberg has pointed out, the active German bureaucrats' "pathfinding ability" was demonstrated not only in their overcoming all technical and organizational obstacles but also in their having the ingenuity necessary for getting the overall killing project under way. The competitive confusions of the Nazi "bureaucratic and administrative jungle" led to a struggle on the part of all to achieve "fidelity to the Hitlerian vision." The competition became particularly fierce in the all-important realm of persecuting and killing Jews, and one reason for the enormous power achieved by the SS in the Nazi state was its repeatedly demonstrated capacity for initiative greater than anyone else's in this realm.

In the Nazi bureaucracy, "careerism could be exploited to harness ordinary people in the service of mass murder." Moreover, the technical achievements within that careerism played a major role in developing genocidal procedures and policies and maintaining their momentum. For instance, the development of the mobile gassing unit or gas van depended upon contributions of medium- and low-level bureaucrats working closely with an array of scientists and automotive technicians who "adapted both their talents and psyches to the new task at hand." A chemist from the SS "Criminal Technical Institute," Albert Widmann, performed animal tests with chemically pure carbon monoxide that enabled him to recommend gas as the killing agent for the general "euthanasia" project. When it was found impossible to produce and transport sufficient amounts of that gas for the large-scale killing of Jews in the East, an alternative method was developed of producing carbon monoxide from the exhaust of special vehicles, within which Jews could be gassed. That innovation required, first, the imagination of the head of the same SS crime laboratory who suggested the idea; then, an elaborate sequence of collaboration and testing involving laboratory criminologists, chemists, and technicians from the "euthanasia" program; and, finally, experiments carried out by an *Einsatzgruppen* unit comparing the killing efficiency of the new gas van (favorably) with explosives also being considered at the time.

The social dynamic of genocide was fed by competition not only among segments of the hierarchy for dominant roles in dealing with the Jews, but also among advocates of rival technologies. Rudolf Höss, under whose Auschwitz leadership the cyanide gas method was developed, was bitterly at odds with Christian Wirth, the designer of the carbon-monoxide gas chamber: both were ardent enough Nazis, but each felt his career depended on which technology was deemed superior. Such professional competition contributed not to better bridges or transportation systems, as it might have under ordinary conditions, but to more efficient death camps and higher totals of mass murder.

The Complicity of German Society

> The destruction process required the cooperation
> of every sector of German society. The bureaucrats
> drew up the definitions and decrees; the churches
> gave evidence of Aryan descent; the postal authori-
> ties carried the messages of definition, expropria-
> tion, denaturalization, and deportation; business
> corporations dismissed their Jewish employees and
> took over "Aryanized" properties; the railroads
> carried the victims to their place of execution, a
> place made available to the Gestapo and the SS by
> the *Wehrmacht*. To repeat, the operation required
> and received the participation of every major so-
> cial, political and religious institution of the Ger-
> man Reich.
>
> —RICHARD RUBENSTEIN

Nazi genocide took on the quality of a silent, collective crusade,
involving not just the bureaucracy of killing but German society as
a whole. As Hitler anticipated, many within German society "were
eagerly prepared to take the initiative" in carrying the program
out, many more would take part "as long as their participation
could be made part of an unthinking routine or job," and still more
"were prepared to acquiesce in or shut their eyes to what their
government was doing." Raul Hilberg conveys the extent and
insidiousness of this societal complicity when he speaks of "a mosaic of small pieces, each commonplace and lusterless by itself,
. . . [a] progression of everyday activities, . . . file notes, memoranda, and telegrams, embedded in habit, routine, and tradition,
. . . ordinary men . . . perform[ing] extraordinary tasks, . . . a
phalanx of functionaries in public offices and private enterprises."

Certain groups among the older élites had particularly important functions: the Foreign Office, in fending off international criticism of the regime's persecution of Jews; the Interior Ministry, in
writing most of the anti-Jewish legislation; and the intelligentsia,
in its extensive contributions to the idea structure and the technology for the mass killing.

The Ministry of Economics promulgated policies of taking from
the Jews vast economic spoils, including personal wealth and be-
longings, property, businesses, and professional positions and

practices, as we have especially noted in relation to medicine. In this way, for Germans at every level of society the prospect of enriching themselves was a significant motivation for justifying persecution of Jews or their participating in it. Doctors who took over coveted appointments, former rivals able to absorb Jewish holdings or former workers in Jewish enterprises who were given portions of the loot, and families able to move into Jewish apartments or obtain ownership of Jewish homes—all of these groups and many more had no less at stake than party officials who acquired personal coffers of gold and art. Intellectuals and professionals in general were an important "transmission belt" between the fierce ideologues at the center of the regime and the general population, rendering genocidal principles into "rational" historical requirements and, as we have seen, matters of shared health and hygiene.

In this purposeful momentum of destruction, the Nazi behemoth absorbed "every profession, every skill, and every social status." And once that momentum was under way, "German bureaucracy was so sensitive a mechanism that . . . it began to function almost by itself" and "did not have to be told what to do." This is the realm of automatism—of what observers have described, in relation to the technological and bureaucratic nuclear-weapons arrangements, as the more or less autonomous "system," whose reactions can only be understood by itself.

Ordinary Germans sensed the existence of the behemoth, or killing machine, and, feeling helpless in relation to it, readily disclaimed responsibility for its actions. Even if one were directly part of it, one could feel oneself merely a cog in a wheel whose motion one had not initiated and could not possibly stop. As a Nazi doctor put it, "Auschwitz was an existing fact. One couldn't really be against it, you see. One had to go along with it whether it was good or bad."

Further, the behemoth created conditions previously unimaginable. As Höhne wrote of the *Einsatzgruppen,* "the deeds demanded of them took place in the vast expanses of Russia, so far distant from their normal environment that the whole business seemed like a dream; those who had such a thing as a conscience could pretend, by a process of self-deception, that what occurred had never really taken place." Similarly, both Nazi doctors and prisoners have said that Auschwitz was so strange, so removed physically and spiritually from the rest of the world, that what one did on that "separate planet," perpetrators could feel, did not really count. The behemoth came to be perceived on all sides as a mystical force—not only all-powerful, impossible to resist, and proceeding in certain inevitable directions, but almost supernatural.

Crossing the Threshold

For the Nazis, crossing the threshold was less a matter of a specific event taking place at a particular moment than of the point at which the momentum toward genocide became irreversible. Thus, as Browning states, "By the summer of 1941, . . . the Nazis had long crossed the 'moral Rubicon' of mass murder." Internal political repression, bloody occupation policies in Poland, "euthanasia" programs, and the initiation of the "war of destruction" against the Soviet Union all helped to "create a continuity and momentum behind the killing process from which there was no turning back." So powerful had that momentum become that the Nazis were able "to get the Final Solution under way even before the death camps equipped with stationary gas chambers were ready."

The actual threshold may well have been crossed late in 1940 or in early 1941 with the significant expansion of *Einsatzgruppen* actions in Poland, the accelerated "euthanasia" killings and the extension of the project into the camps, and the general radicalization of ideological consciousness among Nazi leaders in anticipation of the invasion of the Soviet Union. Yet as Browning, like others, points out, "there was no written order for the Final Solution nor any explicit reference to a verbal order other than the assertions of Himmler and Heydrich that they were acting with the Führer's approval." Hitler seemed deliberately to follow a policy of "maximum ambiguity," encouraging underlings to act on what they knew to be his desires. But that confusion does not alter the evidence that from the summer of 1941 "Hitler, Göring, Himmler, and Heydrich knew what they were trying to do."

The immediate situation bearing on the crossing of the threshold was the Nazi quandary after the invasion of the Soviet Union: what to do with the increasingly large numbers of Jews under their control? In that sense, the Final Solution developed, as one German historian puts it, "not solely as the result of an ostensible will for extermination but also as a 'way out' of a blind alley into which the Nazis had maneuvered themselves." But, in maneuvering themselves into that "blind alley," the Nazis were indeed expressing something close to a "will to extermination." They needed to press the situation to its limits—to ghettoize the Jews and bring them close to starvation—in order to reach the point at which mass killing could seem to be the *only* solution. They could then do what the extreme ideologues wanted to do, while viewing their action as necessary, logical, and even humane. An SS major, for instance, summing up the findings of a series of local conferences in Poland on the problem, spoke of the danger that the Jews "can no longer be fed," and asked whether "it would not be the most humane solution to dispose of the Jews, insofar as they are not capable of work, through a quick-acting agent." Another aspect of the situation was the widespread sense that all other attempted "solutions" had been failures—including forced immigration or the plans for massive "resettlement" in Madagascar or in Lublin (Poland). At some point in the spring of 1941, according to the historian Christopher Browning, "Hitler decided to break this vicious circle." Any such decision could be all too readily made because the Jews had no voice and were "protected by no countervailing force." Hence, "radicalization rather than paralysis followed." Since the Nazi invasion seemed at first dramatically successful, Browning suggests that "the euphoria of victory in the summer of 1941 and the intoxicating vision of all Europe at their feet," rather than later defeats and frustrations, contributed to the Nazis' setting the full genocidal project in motion.

The Nazis apparently made two separate decisions—the first in early (possibly March) 1941 to kill the Russian Jews, and the second in the form of a plan (a few months later) to kill *all* Jews. The complexity of the second decision is reflected in a July order that authorized a "total solution" of the Jewish question in German-occupied territories, signed by Göring, written by Eichmann, and believed to be initiated by Heydrich, who had spent the previous months organizing the *Einsatzgruppen* for the extermination of the Russian Jews. Heydrich and Himmler, in the forefront of the extermination process, "surely needed little more than a nod from Hitler to perceive that the time had come to extend the killing process to the European Jews." Eichmann later testified that, in July or August, "Himmler and Heydrich began to act on the assumption that Hitler had given them the 'green light' to prepare an extermination program." There followed a dissemination of that intention to "a gradually widening circle of Nazi Jewish experts." By the time of the Wannsee Conference (which dealt mainly with implementation) on 20 January 1942, the extermination camps had been constructed, and the gassing had begun.

Nazi genocide, then, was not from the beginning inevitable, however purposefully it was carried out. Intention was implicit in the genocidal mentality, in the increasingly radical mind-set that governed the interactions between leaders and followers and among representatives of various bureaucratic and institutional structures. Widely shared intent was first mobilized and then released—by an affirmation from the leader and by increasingly brutal and murderous behavior, with no significant countervailing forces. At a certain point, the process became irreversible: the genocidal mentality held sway, both because of its increasing strength and because it required continuing killing in order to maintain a momentum that would justify all the killing already done. Concerning Hitler's actual order for genocide, the historian Michael Marrus is undoubtedly correct in declaring that "what finally precipitated this decision is likely to remain a mystery." There is little doubt that the decision was meant to "break . . . the log jam" caused by an ill-defined policy, that it was meant to be a mystical "solution." It was a step that could not have been taken without a lengthy buildup of genocidal readiness, without a broadly entrenched genocidal mentality, and without the active contribution to that mentality by professionals and bureaucratic institutions in extending it to the general population.

The Nuclear Behemoth

> The nuclear threshold is a place where war by the
> rules ends. . . . For beyond that threshold there are
> no rules.
> —Thomas B. Allen

Permanent Threshold

Nuclear-weapons policies keep Americans and Russians—in
fact, all human beings—constantly at the threshold of genocide,
with a willingness to cross that threshold being equally constantly
asserted. Just as the Nazi genocidal intent, prior to crossing the
threshold, was a good deal less clear than many people have believed, so is genocidal intent in nuclearism greater than meets the
eye. A chilling lesson, though rarely drawn, of the Cuban missile
crisis of 1962 is that the superpowers not only reached "the brink,"
the absolute threshold, but when there, were willing to take risks
that could result in crossing the threshold into genocide or pro-
voking the adversary to do the crossing. The superpowers took
these risks, *even as they sought to avoid nuclear holocaust,* because they
were entrapped by policies and mind-sets resulting from long-
standing nuclearism. That entrapment at the nuclear threshold has
been little recognized—possibly because it is so alarming.

While the Nazis kept their relationship to the genocidal threshold a dark secret, nuclear policy makers, in contrast, loudly sing the
praises of the threshold they maintain. That threshold is, they tell
us, precisely what protects us from our great adversary and prevents nuclear war. They further mystify the genocidal threshold by
telling us that we avoid crossing it by preparing to cross it. In the
next chapter, we shall relate that mind-set of deterrence to various
forms of dissociation; our concern here is with threshold elements
and the danger of actually crossing over into oblivion.

Where technological improvements were crucial to the Nazi
threshold, they dominate the nuclear threshold to the point of
displacing the human element. Where the Nazis viciously dehumanized their victims by viewing them as vermin or bacteria or
transmitters of bad genes, nuclear dehumanization of potential

victims is quietly achieved by means of a predominantly technological structure. And while Nazi killing technology could enhance
numbing and limit guilt, nuclear technology can virtually eliminate
the latter in favor of the former. Also important in muffling emotions is the relative niceness of things—the civilized demeanor of
many individual nuclearists and their democratic convictions—as
contrasted with the murderous hatreds and persecutions manifest
in Nazi behavior.

Nuclear Ideology

The ideology of Nazism, with its draconian principles and extreme authoritarianism, required a dictatorial regime. The ideology of nuclearism, in contrast, can arise anywhere and emerges in
America in a democratic, relatively open society.* The Nazis could
name as enemies and then kill Jews, Gypsies, Poles, Russians, and
others; nuclearism also requires enemies, but its radius of killing
includes everyone, however that truth is muted by euphemisms or
claims of "national security." Nuclearism presses toward the genocidal threshold by misleadingly associating itself with military tradition, within which one prepares for and wins wars. Nuclearism,
while containing a vision of purification (of eliminating Soviet evil
or the like), is more fundamentally associated with the symbolism
of national power.

Whatever their differences, the two ideologies share an apocalyptic dimension—a vision of ultimate means and ends. For that
reason, each can evoke a form of extreme obedience to national
authority. In the Nazi case, that obedience was rendered sac-
rosanct, so that Rudolf Höss was said to declare, "My God is
Germany."† But in a democratic country, mind-sets toward authority can be more complex and more difficult to evaluate. For
example, in the United States, the Jeffersonian ideal of always
questioning authority blends with an intense nationalism, ren-

*All that is required is the capacity to produce the weapons (as in the cases of Great
Britain, France, China, Israel, India, and South Africa) or the intense desire for the weapons
as a solution for national problems (as can occur all too readily in virtually any country).

†While authority could never be directly confronted, one could at times evade it by
means of certain language and ploys, such as declaring oneself "unable" to perform a
particular act.

dered fragile and at times fierce by the nuclear insecurities—vulnerabilities—of the national-security state. And it is of some significance that the classical study of obedience to authority was done in the United States on Americans and was horrifying because it showed that many people are willing to press a switch that they have been led to believe could result in others' being harmed or even killed. Even if the obedience demonstrated was primarily associated with the *scientific* status of the researchers rather than with authority in general, as some critics have claimed, that provides scant reassurance, given the awesome scientific authority claimed for nuclear-weapons policies. And beyond obedience as such, democracies can harbor a special sense of entitlement having to do with "defending" one's free institutions, even entitlement to genocidal weapons and their use.

With nuclearism, technological distancing renders brutalization more insidious than in the case of the the overtly brutal Nazis. The projection of more and more millions of victims comes to have less and less actuality. The distancing and the numbers create a realm of unreality that is both absorbed into everydayness and at the same time maintained as a special arena of experience so radically different from the ordinary that what one does or says within it cannot be bound by ordinary moral considerations. Within that nuclear realm, weapons designers and strategists imagine in targeted detail the destruction of the Soviet Union; and these acts of imagination, repeated daily, are themselves normalized. This realm is nuclearism's equivalent to the "separate planet" of Auschwitz. And there is another still more disturbing parallel to the Nazi sequence, especially in Hitler, of first imagining the destroying of the Jews in some fashion and only later acting on those images: without requiring Hitler's fierce hatreds and vicious threats, nuclearists, too, imagine extreme forms of destruction, theirs often associated with creative satisfactions concerning new weapons and new uses for them.

Indeed, such creative "play" becomes associated with the daily enactment of nuclear holocaust by means of elaborate scenarios and "war games." The games are meant to enable decision makers to anticipate and master possible crises, but there are at least two potentially grave psychological consequences. One is that by means of its enactment within a "game," nuclear holocaust becomes more imaginable in a particular way, as something one can actually initiate. One might do so more readily in the real situation, having "practiced" the act under conditions that "felt real." Second, war games run the risk of deepening existing confusions concerning "rules" ostensibly governing the weapons and their use. While "in life . . . games have rules," a dispassionate examination of a war game makes clear that "the nuclear threshold is a place where war by the rules ends," as stated in the epigraph on page 173. Yet players can cross that threshold in a game because, aware that it is a game, they need not be restrained by conscience as actual leaders would be. War games, therefore, run the danger of contributing to a mind-set of relatively conscienceless crossing of the nuclear threshold.*

This silent brutalization spreads outward as American society becomes ever more economically and politically involved in a collusion in nuclearism. And the whole process takes on the moral obfuscations of an American business culture that "turns principles into guidelines, ethics into etiquette, . . . personal responsibility into an adroitness at public relations, and notions of truth into credibility." Given these dangers, there is a temptation to institutionalize a "nuclear priesthood." With reference to the virtual eternity of plutonium danger, Alvin Weinberg, a strong nuclear-power advocate, suggests such a *permanent* body as part of a world-wide community modeled after the Catholic church with "a *central authority* that *proclaims* and to a degree *enforces* doctrine." The genocidal materials are, that is, to be created and maintained by a mystical body of experts—the guardians of both the nuclearistic ideology and its products.

Nuclear Genocidal Institutions

The first American nuclear genocidal institution, the Strategic Air Command (SAC), emerged from the revolutionary escalation

---

*Defense intellectuals have pointed out that war games can have the opposite effect: they can enable the players to recognize the virtual impossibility of any constructive action once nuclear war begins, thereby increasing their inclination toward caution in their policy recommendations. This constructive effect can undoubtedly occur; but that does not diminish the danger created by the opposite effect we have described here.

of air warfare during the Second World War, but did not become part of a separate institution (the Air Force) independent of the Army until 1946. While the strategic bombing survey at the end of the war had mixed conclusions concerning the effectiveness of that policy, the impact of Hiroshima and Nagasaki as a "dramatic finale of World War II . . . rescued the doctrine of strategic bombardment." Indeed, the choice of the word *strategic* for the name of the new institution suggested the extent to which the concept of military strategy had become identical with the saturation bombing of cities. As images developed of "strategic capability," "strategic bombardment," "strategic bombers," and finally Strategic Air Command, the word came full circle to describe the kind of nuclear bombing that destroys everything and therefore has nothing to do with, yet has virtually replaced, the classical military concept of strategy as the art or science of military command.

Curtis LeMay, who quickly became SAC's "living personification," had achieved fame and notoriety, when commanding the Eighth Air Force during the latter part of the Second World War, as the world's most accomplished destroyer of cities. LeMay infused SAC with his swashbuckling charisma and old-fashioned aggressiveness. There was a widespread perception that "LeMay owned the bomb," and that "to LeMay, demolishing everything was how you win a war." That attitude lent itself to rampant nuclearism, the demand for full stockpiles to make available a "SAC Sunday punch" and, within a few years, the concept of "killing a nation."

Three technological breakthroughs greatly affected SAC's relationship to potential genocide. The development of the hydrogen bomb rendered SAC the first possessor of agents of truly limitless destruction, and therefore the first institution that could be said to be technologically genocidal. The SAC leaders were ambivalent about another development, that of the ICBM (the intercontinental ballistic missile), because it called into question the élite human role of the pilot behind the SAC mystique. Inevitably, SAC absorbed the pilotless weapon into its mystique and came to "own" the missiles as well. In that way, nuclearism was extended from the air age (with a human pilot) to the robot missile age. And with radical extension of that development in the form of MIRVs, SAC could further expand its weapons stockpiles both in the possession of, and in the struggle against vulnerability to, these still more destructive genocidal robots.

The third technological breakthrough involved developments that extended nuclear weapons to military service units outside of SAC: Polaris missiles on Navy submarines, and smaller tactical nuclear weapons for the Army. This initiated bitter institutional conflicts, what one observer called "the real rivalry," meaning the determination of each of the three services to outdo the other two in gaining newer and better nuclear weapons. The absurdity of the rivalry is revealed in shifts in service lines of argument—the Navy first opposing nuclear weapons as abhorrent in their random destruction of cities but, with the development of the submarine-launched Polaris missiles, seeking "to supplant the Air Force from the strategic arena altogether." While there had always been fierce service rivalries for weapons spoils, these now became struggles for what can only be called genocidal hegemony, for status as the primary genocidal institution—somewhat parallel to Nazi struggles among institutions and individuals to take control of the persecution of Jews. The combination of politics (each service had to get something) and technology (land-based missiles, submarine-based Polaris missiles, and tactical weapons; each does something the others cannot do) made it certain that there would be a division of weapons functions among the three services. But that apportionment can never be settled once and for all; rather, it is part of a continuously dynamic political and technological process involving not just the services but their advocates and critics in Congress, the executive branch, and the general population.

With these developments, the genocidal institutional structure became multilayered to include not only SAC but significant elements of all three services. Nuclear strategists (defense intellectuals in general) play a crucial role providing important conceptual fuel to this institutional dynamic. They may provide analytic arguments supporting weapons policies of their affiliate service or employer; or they may suggest further studies of weapons and strategy that enhance their research funding and general status (in the case of nonprofit think tanks); or they and their companies may make considerable money from lucrative contracts (in the case of profit-making think tanks). But even when they present arguments that go against the position of a particular service, or against unlimited stockpiling in general, they remain part of the genocidal dynamic of institutional nuclearism. By their constant connection of nuclear threat with American vulnerability, they seize upon a fear and a truth in providing nuclearistic solutions. And even when these solutions are less and less believed, versions of them tend to be retained as the most "expert" opinions around. As in the Nazi institutions associated with "euthanasia" and the Final Solution, American and Soviet genocidal institutions draw upon intellectuals and professionals for technological improvements and claims of logic and meaning.

SAC shares with the SS the mystique of an élite institution with unlimited power to destroy, an institution where the most draconian actions or plans become part of a cosmic destiny. That is what strategists conveyed to Steven Kull when referring to the constantly escalating nuclear-arms race as an inexorable process that is, by implication, beyond human control and, in a mystical sense, "the way things are." The SS mystique depended upon secrecy concerning its more grotesque actions, and Himmler could manipulate that mystique to expand SS functions until it became the most powerful institution within the Nazi state. SAC, in contrast, having emerged within a democracy, has had to weather political and military crosscurrents concerning its power and influence; and has never functioned independently of higher authority, as the SS frequently did. Yet SAC has had its own areas of secrecy, especially concerning aggressive first-strike plans; and by the time details of these became known, institutional nuclearism had proceeded so far that weapons arsenals and the rate of weapons development became virtually impossible to reduce.

Nuclear Bureaucratic Momentum

Within the nuclear bureaucracy, a weapons-seeking dynamic operates on many levels. One observer calls it a "directional force for the drift and thrust toward World War III." The dynamic is maintained by the "revolving door" practices of military people and civilians moving back and forth between each other's camps, by the never-ending interservice rivalries already mentioned, and by the continuous use of "worst-case analysis" of enemy intention as the main guidepost for policy. And there is an overall bureaucratic tendency "to promote formal rather than substantive rationality, that is, the kind of thinking that emphasizes efficiency rather than moral or contextual considerations." Drawing upon Max Weber's metaphor of the "iron cage" to suggest the self-enclosed independence of bureaucracy, a contemporary sociologist speaks aptly of our present-day "nuclear cage." But that nuclear cage is in constant bureaucratic motion, subject to such factors as the corporate marketplace, the commercial corruption that has been exposed recently in relation to Pentagon purchases, and that is probably inevitable owing to the special arrangements associated with the nuclear-weapons world and its aura not only of patriotism and national security but of mystical priority.

In that atmosphere, ardent nuclearists like Edward Teller can apply constant pressure toward the genocidal threshold, pressure that remains influential even when their views are rejected as too extreme by both government officials and ordinary people. The bureaucracy, in resisting some of this pressure, can call forth a "team spirit" in taking a more "practical" direction and focusing on technical issues, just as Nazi doctors in Auschwitz worked together to establish the most efficient arrangements for "selections." That momentum can be seen as consistent with "moderation," as can a sense of constant emergency within which there is no peacetime.

Two examples of the way in which this pattern draws in "moderates" or "decent nuclearists" (see pages 124–25) are Bernard Brodie and Robert McNamara. Brodie was a sharp early critic of post-Second World War Air Force reliance on strategic bombing with nuclear weapons, and advocated instead "sample attacks" against selected Soviet targets so as to induce anarchy and intensify the "distaste of the Russian people for the regime which covers them." Brodie's relatively "restrained" position and his opposition to "indiscriminate slaughter" enhanced the collective sense that the grotesque destructiveness of nuclear weapons was somehow being overcome or taken care of. Similarly, Robert McNamara, as the epitome during the early 1960s of the new "defense intellectual" committed to cost-effective rationality and flexibility, constantly opposed the Curtis LeMay policies of unrestrained "massive attack." But doing that required "continuous political bartering of weapons" which not only undermined arms-control efforts but required McNamara and Kennedy to raise the ICBM total "far beyond the levels they knew were adequate."

What was considered good sense and moderation—the blunting of the most extreme demands for weapons stockpiles—produced the kind of compromise that created a sustained, politically functional form of nuclearism. The bureaucracy moves the whole process along under the dissociative principle of "speaking of it but not calling it by name." Or as Henry Nash described his group of Defense Department employees engaged in targeting, "I and my colleagues, with whom I shared a large office, drank coffee and ate lunch, never experienced guilt or self-criticism. Our office behavior was no different from that of men and women who might work for a bank or insurance company."

The Complicity of American Society

> The convoys [carrying weapons and weapons parts] glide by unnoticed on the freeways, the unmarked trailer trucks blending into the traffic flow and their escort vans looking much like campers off for a weekend jaunt.
> —LESTER R. KURTZ

The propulsion toward genocide can involve the entire nation. What has been described as the national security state amounts, in our terms, to a state religion of nuclearism. The genocidal system encompasses institutions and bureaucracies throughout the society, which in turn interact to release social energies in the direction of the genocidal threshold. Both the national economy and the broadly defined body politic become part of the genocidal structure. In an article entitled "The Nicest People Make the Bomb," a leading American editor tells of visits to weapons laboratories and plants where "instead of Dr. Strangelove I found Mr. Clean. And instead of a reluctant society I found a contented one." All

nuclear weapons are assembled at the Pantax plant in Amarillo,
Texas. The men driving the convoys (described in the preceding
epigraph) are, though heavily armed and linked by radio to each
other and to a national command post, part of nationwide routine:
"The atomic bomb factory is like the collection in a museum. It is
growing with America, and it is blending into the landscape." And
not only in America. The economic and political connections extend outward and pervade our world.

In the United States, the nuclear system takes on the configura-
tion of a vast industrial corporation, sprawling and loosely connected but centrally animated by a deadly purpose in the form of
end products. Profit making is at the heart of most of the separate
elements of the system, together with such social ingredients as
labor unions and concerns about jobs and the workplace, political
power supporting and being supported by commercial institutions, and vast interlocking arrangements for dividing the economic spoils. Of great significance is the tendency of Pentagon
purchase policy to "reward failure"—to subsidize in various ways
companies whose inability to get certain contracts endangers their
standing or existence. In that way, the expanding subculture of
weapons making maintains its mutually supportive elements. The
man called "the Czar of nuclear weapons" is "the perfect example
of the technical professional civil servant" who maintains "a pun-
ishing schedule that includes heavy travel to his far-flung empire."
There is "little sign that he worries much about what his arsenal
might be called upon to do," but rather "regards himself primarily
as manager of an enterprise 'very much like an industrial organization—with perhaps higher standards.' " That "industrial organization" spans much of American society, and the "higher standards"
of control and development intensify the genocidal dynamic.

Summing up society's participation, the *New York Times* journal
ist William J. Broad, writing in 1985, noted that "in the United
States, the development, production, storage, and planning for the
use of nuclear weapons involves well over 200,000 people and an
annual budget of more than $35 billion. . . . Every working day
about eight new warheads roll off the assembly line." And in projecting plans for the Strategic Defense Initiative, Broad and his
colleagues state, "If Congress, the White House, and the American

public one day agree that a Star Wars system should be built and deployed, [it would be] an undertaking whose initial cost has been estimated to range between $100 billion and more than $1,000 billion." The dimensions of that project, in terms of both research and production, would leave few important sectors of American society uninvolved and, even in its preliminary form, has already cast an extraordinarily wide economic, intellectual, and social net. Movement of the whole system toward the genocidal threshold can be brought about by "achievements" from within any of its components—not only by the scientific and technological advances contributing to weapons systems but also by improvements in their industrial production.

A System of Nonresponsibility

> The button is set so finely it could push itself.
> —SAMUEL H. DAY

Most American presidents have tended to avoid focusing on actual war plans: "With the arguable exception of Jimmy Carter, no American president has ever acquired more than passing knowledge of how we planned to use nuclear weapons in war." Furthermore, as Thomas Powers has observed:

Representatives and Senators I have talked to seem vaguely sure *somebody* must be briefed on these matters [actual war plans]. . . . This confidence that somebody has these matters well in hand is not limited to Congress. The whole National Security establishment, from the President on down, seems to share it. But when you get particular, and look around for the people in charge, you find that no body no agency or committee, no appointed or even self-appointed group in the White House, the Pentagon, or the Congress, has been asked to question the SIOP [Single Integrated Operational Plan] and its implications for the planet in rigorous detail on a regular and continuing basis.

Thus, without the president, the Congress, or any agency in real control, "the buck has gone around, stopping nowhere." Powers's statement that "in a sense the system built itself, and only the system knows how it would respond to insult," involves two issues: the increasing inertia of the technobureaucracy toward genocidal stances, with which we are familiar; and what we may call the avoidance of awesome responsibility on the part of individuals and groups who have the need to imagine a "higher authority" somehow in charge.

As in the Nazi case, where interaction between individuals and bureaucracies obscured issues of responsibility, so with nuclear-weapons systems—a principle, in fact, carried further by the nature of those systems. In the absence of an overall "brain" exerting knowledgeable control of all combined nuclear structures, can *anyone* be responsible for starting or joining in a nuclear holocaust? The answer that comes to mind, at least in regard to the nuclear superpowers, is that, yes, ultimate responsibility does lie with the American president or the Soviet premier. But that answer does not take into account factors that could render that responsibility nonfunctional or even nonexistent. The institutional momentum already discussed in this chapter could sweep into weapons use any leader who felt overwhelmingly threatened and without other options, or who lacked the time or information necessary for a decision for restraint, or who was notified that a nuclear "exchange" was actually under way or about to occur. Even in the absence of such an emergency, the dominance of high technology and the technobureaucracy within the nuclear system radically skews the entire question of responsibility. When the general perception is that only "the system" can understand "the system," no one—no person or group—*feels* responsible.

The practice of war games—it is estimated that fifty "nuclear wars" take place daily—may further this absence of responsibility by "producing a high-tech military élite that may not be able to distinguish the games from reality" (see pages 175–76). The "many officers [who] . . . prefer the war games because the wars are clean and fought according to plan," may be learning that numbed nonresponsibility, whatever the consequences. And that lesson passes down to the culture at large by means of parlor games available to everyone, so that one can play "Nuclear War" or "Nuclear Escalation" as one plays "Monopoly." Or one can go into a video parlor and do the same thing electronically—and much more dazzlingly, as one experiences the exuberance of making hit after hit.

Roger Molander has recalled how, during his days in the White House with the National Security Council, "those people above me who were supposed to be thinking about the Big Questions were relying on me to think about those things." But, as a relatively junior person, it was difficult for him to accept "the fact that nobody else around the White House seemed to understand nuclear war issues better than I did" because "knowing my limitations, that did not reassure me." Though he longed for higher authority to rely on, "the organized chaos at the White House, the haphazard way decisions were often reached," and "the minimum amount of time the President had to spend on nuclear war issues, his ultimate responsibility"—all led Molander to feel in the position of a former science adviser who, after making similar observations, asked, "Where are the grown-ups?" Molander was describing not only great diffusion of responsibility but something close to a "system of nonresponsibility," the phrase used by the distinguished Japanese political scientist Masao Maruyama to describe much of Japanese military and political decision making at the time of the Second World War. The nuclear system apparently requires at least some of this nonresponsibility in order to keep going. It also seems to require "the seeming lack of understanding of just how great the chance of nuclear war really [is]." The illusion of there being somewhere a higher authority who is mature, knowledgeable, and responsible permits people at all levels to accept their immediate perception of the absence of these qualities.

Information obtained in the late 1980s about the Cuban missile crisis, largely from Soviet participants, throws into question whether, under such circumstances, any superpower leader can assume full nuclear "responsibility." Although James Blight and his colleagues have termed the handling of that crisis a "masterpiece of owlish diplomacy," of cautious management, on the part of the American team, the recent evidence suggests otherwise. Apparently there was considerable conflict between the Cubans and the Russians; and in the middle of the crisis, an American U-2 observer plane was shot down because of a decision by a Soviet commander that went *against* Khrushchev's order that no U-2s be attacked. The Russian premier apparently became conciliatory largely because he was unable to control the very missiles he had ordered brought into Cuba: he was unable to be "responsible" in any other way.

Thus, when Herbert York warns about the danger of what he calls the "ultimate absurdity" (see page 8)—the automatized movement toward crossing the threshold ("a state of affairs in which the determination of whether or not doomsday has arrived will be made either by an automatic device designed for the purpose or by a pre-programmed President who, whether he knows it or not, will be carrying out orders written years before by some operations analyst")—he is really talking about the logical outcome of the collective dynamic of the technobureaucracy. He himself speaks of "the steady transfer of life-and-death authority from the high levels to low levels, and from human beings to machines."

Genocidal Behemoths

> The dynamic of the nuclear arms race is deeply rooted in the structure of the modern world.
> —LESTER R. KURTZ

> Today's hair-trigger military technology annihilates the very moment of "politics." One exterminist system confronts another, and the act will follow the logic of advantage within the parameters of exterminism.
> —E. P. THOMPSON

Probably any genocidal behemoth is both organic and machine-like, drawing upon each of these elements in varying degree and form. The nuclear behemoth can be said to have a central "brain"—the American president or the Soviet premier together with their advisers; but the brain's control of the monster is uncertain, even quixotic. Not only are there many subcenters with enormous influence on outcome (weapons laboratories, strategic think tanks, congressional arms proponents), but there is constant agitation at all levels to enhance the monster's destructive inclinations. So much so that, at crucial moments, the central brain may lack the power to combat or control that impulse even if it wished to do so. In the Nazi case, Hitler was clearly an extremely active genocidal brain; yet, by mid-1941, even he could have had difficulty altering the course of genocide. That is why, despite having the "brain" in place, both nuclear and Nazi behemoths can become perilously close to "pea-brained dinosaurs," most so when under extreme duress but all too much so on an everyday basis as well.

In the nuclear case, there is much greater effort on the part of the United States and the Soviet Union to control and restrain their genocidal systems. But the nuclear behemoth's elaborate technological structure and its continually frustrated quest for "security" may be no more controllable—may, in fact, be even less predictable—than the Nazi behemoth. Indeed, the perception of this difficulty in self-control (that is, control of one's own nuclear system) on the part of the behemoth managers could well make them seek more aggressively to control their adversary by means of threat, and to control the outcome of a nuclear war by means of illusory scenarios of recovery. The problem of controlling the nuclear behemoth lies not only in the inevitable errors and miscalculations within any sustained interaction of human beings with technology but in the extraordinarily exaggerated *reliance* on technological arrangements (see chapters 1 and 3).

The nuclear behemoth seems outwardly to have little of the anarchic quality of the Nazi project—certainly nothing to compare with the fierce struggles among Nazi leaders to consolidate their power within the regime, or with the proliferation of new institutions and vast confusion over jurisdiction and procedure. In contrast, the nuclear behemoth seems to maintain its organizational clarity via highly sophisticated communications networks and well delimited divisions of responsibility. Yet it, too, contains considerable anarchic potential—in the sometimes bizarre contradictions surrounding interservice rivalry, and in the chaos always close at hand in relation to command-and-control systems and their ostensible function of integrating the nuclear war effort (see pages 4–5).

In both the Nazi and nuclear cases—in any genocidal behemoth—a larger organizing dynamic supersedes any specific component. The removal of an apparently significant element might have little effect. If one eliminated the Los Alamos laboratory or even the Defense Department, for instance, a new laboratory or agency could be formed to do the same things—just as with the Nazis, though the SS would have been difficult to replace as a murder agency, the storm troopers could have been reconstructed for the same purpose. Again, however, nuclearism's higher reliance on technology renders the principle of replaceable parts more striking. The British historian and peace-movement leader E. P. Thompson speaks of "exterminism" as an overall organizing principle that comes to subsume existing impulses and institutions having to do with militarism, imperialism, and related political, economic, and ideological matters: "Exterminism['s] . . . institutional base is the weapons-system, and the entire economic, scientific, political and ideological support-system to that weapons-system—the social system which researches it, 'chooses' it, produces it, polices it, justifies it, and maintains it in being."

The nuclear situation has, unlike the Nazis, not just one nuclear behemoth; rather, two of them confront each other, with five or six additional countries also posing nuclear threats. Each of the two behemoths, moreover, is self-generating, neither one ceasing to expand and grow unless curbed by some sustained action.

Furthermore, the international arrangements of the weapons-possessing powers have created a global nuclear behemoth:

The five nuclear powers [the United States, the Soviet Union, France, England, and China] have spread the arms race beyond their own soil by placing nuclear-related facilities in sixty-five countries and territories. Some 11,800 nuclear weapons are stored or deployed outside the homelands of these five powers. About 70 percent of US tactical nuclear weapons are stored in foreign countries or on ships at sea. The Soviet Union has 15 percent of its Navy at sea (presumed to be nuclear-armed) and stores nuclear weapons in four Eastern European countries. Britain has nuclear weapons in West Germany. The infrastructure extends underground and into the oceans, across the land, and into the atmosphere and space. No continent is immune; no border, river, mountain range, or political frontier divides one battlefield from another. A new geography has been created.

That overall international "nuclear infrastructure," the same authors point out, is "a complex made up of hundreds of obscure research, testing, electronic, and command facilities," within which "virtually every laboratory, test range, military base, or communications transmitter contributes to preparations for nuclear warfare." Moreover, in addition to nuclear testing, continuous military exercises, maneuvers, and communications and surveillance activities "keep the system alive." Included in this nuclear infrastructure, then, are: the arsenals (missiles, ships, aircraft guns, and warheads) and the bases involved in training and maintenance; the production complex; the research, development, and testing complex; the surveillance system (worldwide monitoring including a growing complex of satellite tracking); the early-warning and "attack-assessment" complex; the communication system linking all components; the planning and command structure; and the civil defense complex. One wonders at the degree of universal contemporary alienation—psychological, social, political, and moral—that could contribute to the embrace of such a behemoth of annihilation as a source of meaning and life power. One recalls C. Wright Mills's warning that "the immediate cause of World War III is the military preparation of it."

A physicist-strategist, involved since the Second World War on virtually every level of official and non-official work with nuclear weapons, reflected on the question whether any single person is really in control of the weapons system:

It is certainly true that nobody has a grasp of the details by a large measure, and that holds true for things like the war plan. Somebody in the White House makes up a plan that says the reason we have nuclear forces is first to deter nuclear war, second to deter aggression in general, third we want to minimize possible damage and so forth. Somebody makes a general statement like that, then somebody in the Pentagon at the Secretary's level takes four or five pages to say that in the Secretary's annual report, which then goes to the services and finally it reaches the targeting staff and they plan the attack. They tend to do it through computers and there are various factors that give certain weights and you try to optimize this and then you try to design something so that you can reprogram, and so on. And it gets to the point where it's probably true that no one really understands what's . . .

This man could not quite—perhaps did not want to—finish that thought, but his clear implication was that the behemoth defied not just human control but the imaginative grasp of any individual person.

Crossing the Nuclear Threshold

Much has been written about the kinds of situation that could bring about use of the weapons: the radical intensification of a political or military conflict between the superpowers, or between other countries with whom one of the superpowers (or other nuclear-weapons–possessing powers) is allied; a conventional war anywhere in the world in which nuclear powers see themselves as having a national interest; various forms of accident involving computers or radar screens, in which a false technological representation is interpreted to be a nuclear attack by an adversary; and actions by terrorists, such as the stealing of nuclear material and clandestine building of a weapon with little compunction about threatening to use it or actually doing so. Our concern here, however, is not with the details of any such situation but with the psychological and motivational principles likely to be involved.

The first point is simple, yet highly troubling: as with the Nazis, political or economic problems of almost *any* kind can lead to mass violence. Just as extreme demoralization pervading the society rendered the German people susceptible to the revitalizing promise of Nazi ideology, whatever its violent content, so could—as has, to some extent, occurred—American and Soviet domestic struggles contribute to belligerent nuclear stances that take the superpowers closer to the threshold.

But, in contrast to the Nazi model—where the habit of killing led, more or less piecemeal, to a genocidal point of no return—crossing the nuclear threshold is likely to be sudden and total. To be sure, there could be buildups and retreats, even prolonged threats and counterthreats without weapons use; but once the weapons were actually released, a definitive step would have been taken. At the same time, the principle of ideological and structural readiness for genocide—along with a genocidal dynamic, as in the Nazi case—applies to the nuclear in strikingly similar ways. The Nazis created their own "blind alley": the anti-Semitic policies which brought about ghettoization of Jews; and then the near insoluble problem of feeding the Jews and preventing typhus epidemics among them that could spread to German personnel—all of which motivated the Nazis to "break the vicious circle" and kill them. The "vicious circle" in the nuclear sense—the unending quest for "security" and "stable deterrence"—can be "broken" only in one or two ways: by setting the weapons off, or else by getting rid of all or most of them. And insofar as a genocidal system moves strongly toward weapons use—or perceives its adversary to be doing so—there is a powerful temptation to set off one's weapons quickly so that the command-and-control structure of the enemy, rather than one's own, can be destroyed.

A nuclear war set off by computer error or miscommunication would be "an accident in name only" because the genocidal ideology, institutions, and dynamic have long been operative and can be all too easily intensified to the ultimate point. The release of a single nuclear weapon—even the creation of circumstances under which such a weapon is likely to be released—could well be the equivalent of the Nazi "crossing of the 'moral Rubicon' of mass murder." The key is the ideological-institutional propulsion toward mass murder, toward the "blind alley" of mutual nuclear confrontation. We, too, "prepare for" genocide—by our long-held nuclearistic ideology and increasingly callous dismissal of human lives in order to maintain the protective "nuclear umbrella." The existence of a dynamic weapons system—a genocidal system—is perpetuated in nuclearism by the simple facts of technology. Whatever the safeguards taken against crossing that threshold, and these are extremely important, there can be no certainty that the threshold will not be crossed so long as the weapons and the technobureaucratic structure surrounding them remain prominent features of our landscape. To build and deploy the weapons in large numbers is to prepare for their use, to prepare to cross the nuclear threshold. Or to put the matter another way, our nuclear-weapons system creates a threshold waiting to be crossed.

Chapter 7

Deterrence and Dissociation

> This [nuclear-weapons] language does not allow certain questions to be asked, certain values to be expressed. . . . No matter how firm my commitment is to staying aware of the reality behind the words, over and over I found that I *couldn't* stay connected, couldn't keep human lives as my reference points.
> —Carol Cohn

> The deterrence paradigm has become an end game, a trap.
> —Roman K. Kolkowitz

ADVOCATES OF deterrence policies see a "bright side" to nuclear weapons: their ostensible value for preventing war while maintaining national security. But only by in some way shielding one's mind from the dark horrors the weapons would bring about "if deterrence fails," can one embrace—or, at least, accept—their beneficence. Thus deterrence requires a psychological aberration, by which the mind separates, or "dissociates," from certain of its elements.

The dark side of the Nazi project did not take long to emerge, though many Germans were reluctant to recognize it. In the nuclear case, however, that dark side is much more readily hidden with the help of the high technology and apparent human decency of the weapons system. Still, psychological maneuvers are required to defend oneself against the basic contradiction of deterrence: that is, what, for the sake of credibility, we must be willing to do (fight a nuclear war) is, in fact, undoable. Credibility in this context refers to the persuasiveness of the deterring function. And the mind that accepts deterrence policy is asked to believe in a willingness to fight the nuclear war that the policy is invoked to prevent. Our argument in this chapter is that for the mind—any mind—to do that, it must willingly suspend not so much disbelief as integration and wholeness. That loss of integration and wholeness is a manifestation of dissociation.

The term *dissociation* was originally used by Pierre Janet, the great French psychiatrist and contemporary of Freud. Janet observed in some of his patients a tendency to "sacrifice" or "abandon" certain psychological components so that these became severed, or "dissociated," from the rest of the mind and gave rise to their own symptoms or behaviors. Later psychiatric usage of the term *dissociation* has continued to emphasize this principle of separating off mental processes from the rest of the mind, sometimes from the conscious mind, as well as the separation of ideas from appropriate feelings. Dissociation constitutes a broad category of psychological mechanisms, which includes psychic numbing, doubling, disavowal, and denial, each of which bears on both Nazi and nuclear behavior; we will focus primarily on the first two mechanisms, particularly in respect to deterrence.

Fundamentally, dissociation serves as a psychological facilitator for deterrence, helping to reduce the kind of psychic stress that would be morally useful and appropriate. It is, in other words, a form of adaptation, by means of which people remain sane in the service of social madness. The dissociation required for deterrence is nothing short of a collective historical phenomenon (the kind of shared theme mentioned in the preface, page xii). Strongest in those who are closest to the weapons and who formulate plans for their use, dissociation occurs in milder versions in much of the population who accept the premises and claims of deterrence. The widening critique of deterrence, in America and elsewhere, suggests that the effectiveness of the dissociation may be diminishing. But the dissociation is not overcome easily, having been fed by the "growth by accretion" of weapons technology, a vicious circle evident in earlier air warfare, as Sherry makes clear: "Bombers could be divorced from bombing: their instrumental and symbolic virtues were separable from the destruction they threatened. Their danger was the dark side of a moon of shiny progress—something imaginable but out of view." With the development of nuclear weapons, the dissociative process called forth on behalf of psychological comfort comes to endanger the entire human future. We gain perspective on the problem by examining the kinds of dissociation required by Nazi perpetrators.

Nazi Dissociation

> We must be honest, decent, loyal and comradely to members of our own blood, but to nobody else. . . . [If] 10,000 Russian females fall down from exhaustion digging an anti-tank ditch . . . [that] interests me only insofar as the anti-tank ditch for Germany is finished.
>
> —HEINRICH HIMMLER

> I was like a man following a trail of bloodstained footprints through the snow without realizing someone has been injured.
>
> —ALBERT SPEER

Not only did Auschwitz run on doubling, as we have seen, but much of Nazi Germany also ran on various forms of dissociation. There is an important historical sequence here. Dissociation was undoubtedly widespread in pre-Nazi Germany, going back to late-nineteenth-century historical dislocation or breakdown of symbols and meanings around which life had been organized, and radically intensified by the German defeat in 1918 and by subsequent economic disasters. The Nazis came to power on a promise of revitalization and relief from that dissociation, and a considerable number of Germans did seem to experience such a relief, at least temporarily, in the form of a renewed sense of integration in relation to both self and nation.

Yet that apparent integration depended upon either embracing Nazi cruelties toward Jews and others or psychologically fending off evidence of those cruelties. In other words, the Nazi ideological project contained the seeds of a new collective dissociation.

Many Germans, however, could maintain a workable psychological equilibrium, combining feelings of vitality and an activated sense of immortality (via the "Thousand Year Reich"), on the one hand, and an array of dissociative defenses, on the other. Even in the midst of killing, as was true of the Nazi doctors, those dissociative defenses could block out the horror of the enterprise. And there were parallel patterns of dissociation in less extreme Nazi environments—doctors far removed from the killing who later recalled, with faint residual guilt, memories of respected Jewish colleagues being humiliated, forced into exile, or "deported" to camps. They would claim to have been ignorant or helpless concerning what was happening; or that this was too bad but there really was a "Jewish problem" that needed something done about it; or concerning *Kristallnacht,* that there was little persecution of Jews in their particular town or neighborhood or city. Here the dissociation included patterns of both denial and psychic numbing, each entailing withdrawal of empathy from designated victims. The withdrawal was highly selective: active Nazis were perfectly capable of retaining fellow feeling toward other "Aryans"—that is, toward everyone but Jews, Slavs, homosexuals, Gypsies, and a few other groups (as stated directly by Himmler in the epigraph on page 194).

Empathy can be defined as the capacity for "resonating with the other's unconscious affect [feeling tone] and experiencing his experience with him." While that capacity varies with individuals, the collective withdrawal of empathy from an alien group, or from one toward whom there has been long-standing historical denigration, is all too easily accomplished, especially when supported by a "scientific" official ideology. But since empathy is part of being human, any such radical withdrawal represents at least the beginnings of dissociation. When that withdrawal is accompanied by systematic brutality, the dissociation, in the form of cessation of feeling or psychic numbing, must become ubiquitous. The process can build over time: *Kristallnacht* represented for many Germans the culmination of a long dissociative process whereby Jews were not seen as human beings—a process most intense in active perpetrators whose violent inclinations it allowed to express, and justify.

Once the killing was under way, those engaged in it required further dissociation, often in the form of doubling, in order to do their jobs and still maintain their own intimate relationships and family ties. We recall the doubling in Nazi doctors, with the formation of an Auschwitz self that was relatively autonomous and sufficiently inclusive to enable them to adapt to the entire Auschwitz environment (see pages 106–7). By means of that extreme form of dissociation, a Nazi doctor could live simultaneously as a man active in mass killing and an ordinary human being.

Dissociation in various forms was also a crucial factor in the capacity of reasonably intelligent people to believe in some of the bizarre elements of Nazi racial and biomedical theory. What could appear to be stupidity in an individual is better explained as an ideological constellation, segmented from the rest of the self, within which ordinary intellectual and moral standards were negated. Numbing, denial, and doubling may all have been involved in ways that helped one hold on to many of these beliefs in the face of powerful evidence to the contrary, and even to act on them in a place like Auschwitz (performing selections and experiments) as victorious Russian armies were making their way toward the camp.

Eduard Wirths, chief Nazi doctor at Auschwitz during most of the killing, exemplifies the extreme dissociation and doubling that enabled a formerly respected doctor to establish and carry out forcefully the medicalized killing project in Auschwitz. Wirths, an able and kind physician who became passionately attracted to Nazi ideology, quickly rose within the SS medical hierarchy, was appalled by what he encountered at Auschwitz when sent there as chief camp doctor, but remained a loyal Nazi who conscientiously maintained the "selections" procedures for sending arriving Jews to the gas chamber, while at the same time attempting to improve conditions for prisoners in the camp. Wirths's doubling was particularly strong, conflicted, and effective: his Nazi-Auschwitz self served the killing process with extraordinary efficiency, while his relatively humane self, supported by loving family relationships, enabled him to remain "decent" in his own eyes as well as in those of SS colleagues and even of certain prisoners. Wirths's doubling resembled in some ways that of Kurt Gerstein, a Nazi officer who served as SS specialist on the Zyklon-B gas used for Auschwitz mass murder but also made desperate efforts to inform the outside world about the horror of the Final Solution. Most observers have emphasized Gerstein's extraordinary acts of resistance (he took great personal risks in speaking to Catholic officials and a Swedish diplomat about Nazi mass murder), while others are primarily impressed with his role in the mass-murder process. Yet Gerstein and Wirths alike demonstrate that doubling can enable a man to be a passionate advocate of both killing and healing. Wirths in particular demonstrates how a "decent Nazi" with loyalty to his national regime could, *with the help of his more admirable human qualities,* contribute enormously to the genocidal project.

Other Nazis could undergo doubling and related forms of dissociation in ways that were less dramatic and more gradual. Some Nazi doctors arriving at Auschwitz, for instance, underwent a transition period for a few weeks during which they experienced anxiety and nightmares while becoming socialized to the camp. Contributing to that socialization were such patterns as heavy drinking (during which one could express doubts that were in turn dismissed or explained away by colleagues) and mentorship from more experienced Auschwitz doctors (Wirths or Mengele) in how to perform selections and adjust to the camp. One thereby made the transition "from insider to outsider" and was then able to have "better contact" with Auschwitz colleagues. Dissociative mechanisms, that is, when called upon in certain environments, enable one to achieve more workable and pleasant relationships with peers.

The doubling process was enhanced by patterns mentioned earlier—a doctor's sense of being able to make "humane" contributions in a difficult situation, and his feeling that what one did in Auschwitz as "a separate planet" did not count. This form of dissociation can be called *disavowal:* repudiation not of the reality itself but of the meaning of that reality. (Psychic numbing, which overlaps with disavowal, is used primarily in reference to feeling.)

The Auschwitz *atmosphere of dissociation* was maintained by its always euphemistic language: "Final Solution" for mass murder; "evacuation," "transfer," or "resettlement" for taking people off to be murdered; and "medical ramp duty" for conducting selections for the gas chamber. The language contributed to the disavowal, which in turn permitted the doctors, in terms of psychological experience, to engage in "killing without killing," without *feeling* themselves to be engaged in killing. Also contributing to the general dissociative process was the "research" performed by Nazi doctors (experiments on prisoners in Auschwitz and postmortem studies in "euthanasia" killing centers), as it reinforced medical identity in a way that further suppressed awareness of killing.

This overall dissociative pattern carried to a grotesque extreme the modern tendency to separate ethics from technique. (We recall [page 103] the observation by a Nazi doctor that the word "ethical," in Auschwitz, "does not exist," and that the killing was "a purely technical matter.") That caricature of pragmatism combined with the Nazi principle of "hardness," which really meant the capacity to maintain sufficient dissociation, in the form of extreme psychic numbing, to remain impervious to the suffering or death of the designated enemy and to be capable of imposing the suffering or doing the killing oneself when necessary. That "necessity" for mass killing is ideological, "is justified not simply by the exterminators' need to have more room for themselves or to enrich themselves, but by an elaborate 'philosophy' implying that the victims *deserve* annihilation for metaphysical, historical, or moral reasons." That metaphysical justification of killing, whether secular or theological, requires minimal hatred and encourages easy dissociation—all the more so when, as with the Nazis, the metaphysical justification is understood as a form of *biological* necessity.

For many ordinary Germans, people usually designated bystanders, psychic numbing had adaptive advantages: the less one felt the better off one was in relation to the regime. Both unconsciously and consciously, at least two factors contributed to the psychic numbing of bystanders. First, the truth of mass murder was deeply disturbing, and therefore resisted. Second, the absence in one's own life of anything approaching the mass killing made it difficult to imagine such behavior on the part of any group, least of all one's own. These factors could contribute to a "need not to know," which took on strong elements of self-deception and personal corruption. Indeed, the numbing, disavowal, and doubling, along with the self-deception and corruption, enabled one to know and not feel or to both know and not know.

Similar patterns occurred in active perpetrators, as in the case of Albert Speer, Hitler's architect and confidant. Although a member of the Nazi inner circle, and for a time even thought of as Hitler's successor, Speer, in his postwar writings and interviews, repeatedly denied having specific knowledge of the systematic mass murder of Jews. When pressed, he came to recognize the extent to which he willfully avoided such knowledge: "There is no way I can avoid responsibility for the extermination of the Jews. I was as much their executioner as Himmler, because they were carried past me to their deaths and I did not see. It is surprisingly easy to blind your moral eyes."

Some see Speer as having been simply a liar, given the unlikelihood that someone in his position could remain ignorant of the specific planning of the Final Solution. He might well have combined conscious falsification with deep resistance to the significance of what he had learned. In looking back, however, he used the word *consent* for what he did: "consent taking place [in myself] in connection with these events. . . . I didn't want to know, so I didn't investigate." *Collusion* might be a better word. But Speer's dissociation could have enabled him simultaneously to know and not know: that is, to have information not just about a Jew being killed here and there but about a systematic plan to kill all Jews, while at the same to disavow that information—to numb himself to it—as to be able to feel ignorant of the project. Speer spoke of himself as having been a "split personality": one part of him mesmerized by and loyal to Hitler; another part behaving "reasonably," especially in countering Hitler's final scorched-earth order for Germany.

Men like Speer—"decent Nazis"—called forth every version of dissociation along the entire psychological grid in order to adapt themselves, and skillfully and "rationally" contribute, to Nazi genocide.

The Deterrence Trap

> Deterrence is a psychological phenomenon that de-
> pends on the beliefs of the deterree. Therefore no
> necessary consistency exists between an explana-
> tion that illuminates the thinking of the deterrer
> and one that accounts for the *results* of the actions
> he takes. The deterree may accede to threats for
> those reasons or for different ones. Both can sin-
> cerely perceive each other as the blackmailers and
> themselves as the victims.
> —RICHARD K. BETTS

Virtually all writers on nuclear deterrence policy see its theoretical beginnings in Bernard Brodie's famous 1946 statement: "Thus far, the chief purpose of our military establishment has been to win wars. From now on, its chief purpose must be to avert them. It can have no other useful purpose." And many of those same writers also quote Brodie's 1948 statement identifying the nuclear-age dilemma as being that the only way to sustain the universal convic-tion that nuclear war is too horrible to contemplate is by "making every possible effort to prepare for war and thus engage in it if need be." But few, if any, have noted the direct contradiction between these two statements—a contradiction Brodie himself was to recognize, but only much later. By initiating a theory of nuclear deterrence, Brodie also initiated, in himself and others, a form of shared dissociation allowing strategists and laymen alike to ex-clude from meaningful awareness the fundamental contradiction between stockpiling weapons *solely* for the purpose of preventing one's enemy from attacking and the necessity, as part of that deter-ring function, to be willing and ready to use those weapons.

Brodie, a thoughtful man, sought always to find ways either to prevent or greatly to limit the use of nuclear weapons. But as a political scientist and authority on military history and theory, his way of achieving these ends was to incorporate the weapons into military strategy. Deterrence was to become the thinking man's expression of nuclearism—a "reasonable" theory with an accept-able moral claim. In that sense, deterrence originally emerged as an antidote to dissociation, to the profound confusion and shared fear of extinction that followed upon Hiroshima. But the antidote, as with the Nazis, was to create much more profound and more dangerous patterns of dissociation of its own.

Since Brodie, other "decent nuclearists"—men who struggled against extreme strategic views while finding a military place for the weapon—have elaborated endless versions of a theory of nuclear deterrence. By seeming to oppose more belligerent policies, they have lent a humane tone to these theories, thereby greatly reinforcing dissociation and sustaining the "deterrence trap."

As a leading observer has explained, "nuclear protagonists . . . must be permanently ready to 'go to war' " and, in order to deter "credibly," must be ready to "strike the potential aggressor in order to limit their own damage." There has thus been created "a permanently imminent war threat," "a constant upward ratcheting of forces at ever higher levels of lethality" and "a permanent nuclear war system." Deterrence logic, moreover, imposes a closed system of thought within which efforts at modification or change are readily seen as "destabilizing." In that way, it is the mind that becomes entrapped—by means of the dissociation required by the theory.

The political scientist Roman K. Kolkowitz points out that deterrence theory is unique in having been created by civilian intellectuals in the tradition of Henri Jomini, the nineteenth-century military strategist who believed that "the study and conduct of war was a science that could be reduced to fixed rules and mathematical formulas," as opposed to Karl von Clausewitz who rejected that view and warned against a false underestimation of the pain of war and overestimation of the ability to control events. In American strategy in particular, there has been an exaggerated stress on invoking science and technology to order society and control conflict, all of which results in a nuclear "professionalism" of "overabstraction, scientism, numerology, and technical jargon." That mode of thinking invites a dissociation that maintains a radical separation between thought and feeling and enables one to make analytic calculations while remaining numbed to their consequences in pain, suffering, and death. Professionally respectable as it is, such dissociative adaptation can be sustained over years.

Dissociation is called forth to cover over and deny ignorance. Not only are we much more ignorant about what we call nuclear war than we care to admit, but "we don't know how much we do or do not know about it." Since, as the Israeli philosopher Avner Cohen points out, "we do not really know how to *conceive* of nuclear warfare as a concrete actuality, how it could be properly kept under control and how it might be brought to termination," it is less than responsible to claim how such an event could be "managed, controlled or concluded." But all evidence suggests that "no matter what nuclear war might be, it would not be the kind of rule-governed practice" often assumed on the basis of past wars. And while the principle of deterrence has a long history in political and military practice going back to the time of the Greek city-states, the consequences, should deterrence fail and the deterrer act on his threat, were always limited: after the war and destruction, there would be recovery and resumption of life. Precisely the present absence of those limits "should deterrence fail," the uncertainty or unlikelihood of any significant amount of human life remaining, radically distinguishes nuclear deterrence from that tradition. Dissociation, especially in the form of psychic numbing, helps blur that distinction by denying not only our ignorance but also what we can be expected to know.

The further but related conceptual contradiction is that the more "usable" we make the weapons for the sake of the credibility of nuclear threat, the more likely it is that they will be used. While the more we treat the weapons as "unusable," "the more incredible the threat to use them becomes, and the more likely the threat will fail." That is why Cohen describes the principle of nuclear deterrence as "incoherent" in its attempt to preserve simultaneously prenuclear assumptions and postnuclear understanding. As we have seen with the Nazis, theory that is logically incoherent can nonetheless become acceptable with the help of dissociative mechanisms.

Nor is that contradiction resolved by any conceptual distinction between "deterrence by punishment," stressing the devastation one would impose on one's adversary should the latter cross a certain line, and "deterrence by denial," which seeks only to persuade the adversary to refrain from war making because one's own military forces cannot be defeated. But the distinction weakens considerably under scrutiny, and there are many borderline cases. In addition, the very concept of "deterrence by denial" tends to be accompanied by strategies of "counterforce" (aiming at the adversary's weapons instead of cities and therefore a more feasible, because limited, nuclear war). The "denial" in that deterrence concept turns out to be best understood as a psychological defense mechanism: "deterrence by denial" then comes close to "deterrence by dissociation."

Of great importance here is the potential psychological discrepancy between intention and effects. Since there is "no necessary consistency . . . between an explanation that illuminates the thinking of the deterrer and one that accounts for the *results* of the actions he takes" (see epigraph on page 200), deterrence can be a highly solipsistic enterprise. It can even reach the point of what can be called *psychism*—that is, confusion between one's own inner images and the reality of external events, so that one believes oneself to be controlling these events while one is merely engaging in one's own intrapsychic maneuvers.

Within deterrence theory, then, dissociation operates on several levels: blocking out painful human consequences; claiming knowledge one does not have in the service of denying the fallibility of one's projections and the potential cost of that fallibility; permitting one to reject the meaning of what one knows to be true (for instance, the unlimited destructive potential of nuclear weapons, and the unacceptability of nuclear war) in the service of holding to the deterrence paradox; and encouraging the belief that one's own assumptions will be held by adversaries (the psychism just mentioned). The theorizing reveals deterrence to be something of a "doubled" concept: its bright side promises peace or at least the avoidance of nuclear holocaust, while its dark side contains plans for just such a holocaust.

Beyond its intrinsic contradiction, deterrence theory is subject to extreme confusion concerning its translation into policy. David Alan Rosenberg, an authority on such matters, declares that "there is a basic distinction between theory and reality in the field of nuclear strategy." He goes on to explain that "theoretical strategic concepts, regardless of their ingenuity and apparent validity, do not necessarily shape or control the development of plans and preparations for nuclear war. Nuclear reality does not necessarily reflect nuclear theory." That confusion tends to become dissociation when radical contradictions occur between "declaratory strategy" ("how we as a nation explain our strategic objectives to ourselves and the rest of the world") and "operational strategy" ("how nuclear weapons would really be used in war").

Rosenberg identifies several levels of nuclear policy. The top level is the "high policy" developed by the president and his advisers (in the National Security Council, the Department of State, and the Department of Defense) which combines declared policy and undeclared policy (including classified statements on actual weapons use and nuclear war), as shaped by combinations of strategic theory and immediate political and economic considerations. A second level (instituted by Robert McNamara) is programming and weapons procurement by the office of the secretary of defense. The third level is strategic planning, the drawing up by the military of "general conceptual plans [many developed by the RAND Corporation during the 1950s and 1960s] for the use of nuclear weapons in war." Finally, at the "lowest level" is operational planning, including detailed targeting, designation of weapons and delivery systems and their effects as well as "routes to and times over targets." This is the place where "the rubber meets the road," where the Strategic Air Command has been dominant in producing the National Strategic Target List and the Single Integrated Operational Plan. But as Rosenberg points out, "Each level of strategy-making responds to a different set of needs and constraints, producing contradictions and disjunctions, and a striking divergence between stated policy and operational planning."

An example of that divergence occurred in the mid-1960s when Robert McNamara, torn between the doctrine of "assured destruction" and more "flexible" policies, "talked Assured Destruction, even in Top Secret memoranda to the President; but the actual targeting strategy, which McNamara closely monitored and approved, remained mainly counterforce." For "assured destruction" was a means of "beating back the excessive demands of the military," but "in the event of war, he could still choose counterforce." Moreover, these disjunctions could also be used for deliberate obfuscation, as during the late 1940s and early 1950s, when our declared policy was to retaliate "massively" only in the event of Soviet aggression. But the added phrase, "at a time and a place of our own choosing," left open the idea of pre-emptive strike. Curtis LeMay, in fact, declared that he "could not imagine a circumstance under which the United States would go second"; and one of his high planners declared in 1954 that the "exact manner in which SAC will fight the war is known only to General LeMay." These policy contradictions reflect psychological contradictions of a dissociative kind in policy makers and, at the same time, further that dissociative process. They stem ultimately from the duality of the deterrence concept.

Dissociation in strategists can be furthered by their geographical and mental isolation. As one of them said, "Somehow or other most of us were playing games at RAND as opposed to what was going on in the Pentagon. Most of us felt very divorced from any reality in those paper calculations, so I don't think they aroused any strong emotions." He was speaking of what might have been called "planet RAND": "Isolated from the hurly-burly of the rest of the world, the men and women (mostly men) of RAND nurtured an esprit de corps, a sense of mission, an air of self-confidence and self-importance." And strategists in general, including leading decision makers and, indeed, most presidents, have tended to shy away from the terrible details of command and control—from the absurd attempt to maintain command and control in the midst of nuclear holocaust. That degree of dissociation has undoubtedly been necessary to them for maintaining the upbeat side of deterrence.

Yet the darker side has been all too well known to those at the murderous edge of the weapons. In 1957, although declared policy stressed deterrence as a means of preventing war, LeMay made clear to a small group of official visitors at the headquarters of the North American Defense Command that, "if I see the Russians are amassing their planes for an attack, I'm going to knock the shit out of them before they take off the ground." And when someone protested, "But General LeMay, that's not national policy," the general's answer was, "I don't care. It's my policy. That's what I'm going to do." Though LeMay seemed to be speaking out of turn,

he was not: he was backed by a secret SAC war plan' "separate
from war plans developed by the Joint Chiefs of Staff but signed
by the President of the United States." The problem is much
greater than that of the aggressiveness of a particular general.
Given the perception of enormous advantage in hitting "first,"
there is likely to be this kind of pre-emptive proviso in the operational warplan accompanying—and contradicting—a deterrence
policy. Hence, "the persistent, heavy emphasis on counterforce
targeting in US nuclear strategy, despite declaratory policy emphasizing deterrence or assured destruction."

Those operational planners who are fully aware of that dark side
of deterrence require their own dissociation, their extensive psychic numbing and disavowal. Their apparent cynicism involves
psychic maneuvers (as illustrated in Steven Kull's interviews) that
permit them to know very well about, and yet never really *feel,* the
drastic implications of deterrence.

At every level of nuclear strategizing—creating theoretical scenarios, forming declarative policy and high strategy, programming
weapons procurement, actual strategic or operational planning—
some form of dissociation, in some way different from that of the
other levels, prevails. Moreover, there may be a kind of dissociative
feedback system, within which the dialogue between participants
at any one level and those at the other levels tends to reinforce the
dissociation all around. For even though the projections and policies at the various levels are contradictory and disjunctive, they are
interdependent, part of a single constellation of genocidal arrangements that requires all of these components and all of their
forms of dissociation. What all actors in the process seem to have
in common is a form of dissociation that enables them to sustain
their particular roles in strategies for nuclear war fighting while
knowing at some level that any such use of the weapons is likely
to destroy most or all of the human species.

Varieties of Deterrence

> As long as nuclear threat is a part of the US diplomatic arsenal and provided that threat reflects real operational intentions—it is not a total bluff—US defense planners are obliged to think through the probable course of a nuclear war.
> —COLIN S. GRAY AND KEITH PAYNE

It is easy to get lost in deterrence terminology because of the endless subcategories put forward by strategists, but the alleged distinctions between particular categories turn out to be much less important than claimed and are at times illusory. Among the categories used are "finite deterrence," "pure deterrence," "minimum deterrence," "extended deterrence," "graduated deterrence," "war-fighting deterrence," "war-winning deterrence," "existential deterrence," and "discriminate deterrence." What unites all of these forms of deterrence, as Herbert York puts it, is the idea that "you have to think about war-fighting in order to be realistic." Whatever the category, deterrence is inseparable from readiness to use the weapons. Thus, any discussion of relevant psychological patterns should begin and end with David Rosenberg's statement: "The distinctions that have been drawn between deterrent and war fighting strategies are ephemeral and artificial ones."

We should keep that truth in mind while examining a spectrum of deterrence concepts in relation to the attitude toward usability of the weapons. At one end of the spectrum are conceptions of the weapons as having the sole purpose of preventing nuclear attack, since any war fought with them cannot be won in a meaningful sense. At the other end is a view of nuclear weapons as weapons of war, which can be used on the one hand to deter a wide range of adversarial behavior on the part of other nations and, on the other, to fight and win a nuclear war. Some writers on the subject date the distinction to the early work of two men, Bernard Brodie and William Borden, both of whom published important books on atomic-weapons policy in 1946. Brodie's approach has been called "pure deterrence" because of his initial stress on the paradox that, as the historian Gregg A. Herken puts it, "a nation had to prepare

for a war it did not intend to fight." In contrast, Borden's view was
that, as his book title *There Will Be No Time* suggests, our urgent
need was to build up our nuclear stockpiles to prepare to win the
virtually inevitable nuclear war with the Soviet Union. Only Brodie's view could be called deterrence, but many subsequent deterrence strategies were to incorporate war-fighting views similar to
Borden's. While dissociation is required all along the spectrum,
the variations in psychic maneuvers required by the different forms
of deterrence help us to grasp what is actually involved in each.

"Finite" and "Extended" Deterrence

Concepts of finite or minimal deterrence follow Brodie's original advocacy of a small number of atomic weapons aimed at the
enemy's cities. That minimum principle, though overridden by Air
Force–centered policies of massive retaliation, was reasserted in
the late 1950s in connection with Navy-centered policies based on
Polaris submarines carrying enough missiles to destroy major
urban areas. But when McNamara later advocated minimal or finite
deterrence, the inevitable war-fighting component, in order to be
considered sufficient, was required to possess the capacity for killing 25 percent of the Soviet population and for destroying half
their industrial capacity (see page 29). The dissociative direction,
then, in minimum deterrence policy is the disavowal of a war-
fighting dimension one knows to be present. In declaring one's
focus to be on deterrence and not fighting, the grotesque actuality
of the inevitable ingredient of fighting need not be significantly
experienced—at least not to the extent of understanding oneself
to be articulating a policy of potential genocide.

Deterrence tends to increase its domain; and, by 1948, America
was "preparing to use nuclear weapons not so much in defense of
the homeland, as to deter or defend against an overwhelming
attack on Western Europe by Soviet conventional forces." (The
policy would eventually mean that Europe would have to be destroyed in the name of its defense, and that the resulting escalation
would destroy much of the United States and the Soviet Union as
well.) This policy of "extended deterrence" combined with the
doctrine of massive retaliation, so that, as Eisenhower phrased it,

America could "blow hell out of them in a hurry if they start anything." Dissociation in extended deterrence is bound up with the illusion of control. The deterrer, in claiming the right to unleash nuclear destruction wherever, whenever, and in whatever fashion he deems appropriate, assumes a capacity to manage world events by means of ultimate threat. The dissociation includes an unacknowledged moral polarization: the right to summon one's virtue in launching nuclear genocide, massively or "flexibly," in order to combat the evil of one's adversary. There is also numbing in relation to the nuclear war that would be fought, as reflected by the rhetoric of massive retaliation, which combined vagueness of plan with omnipotent claim.

War-Fighting and War-Winning Deterrence

Increasingly since the mid-1970s, "war-fighting deterrence" has become the "new conventional wisdom" in American strategic thought. The approach includes a widening range of targets and of ostensible nuclear options including "no-cities strategy," or "counterforce" (focusing on enemy weapons and other military targets rather than population centers), "damage limitation," (stopping short of total destruction), and "limited nuclear options" (holding to a variety of possible nuclear responses according to the level of enemy attack and other considerations). In one sense, war-fighting deterrence can be viewed as simply a candid version of deterrence in general, which always contains war-fighting contingencies. But it is more than that as well. In its theoretical focus on limits, it makes the constant claim to be more "humane" than, say, straight "countercity" deterrence, even as it legitimates nuclear holocaust. It also leads, almost inevitably, to the "new extremist position" gaining respectability—that of "war-winning" deterrence. Colin Gray articulates the logic of the policy sequence from war fighting to war winning when he points out (epigraph, page 207) that, so long as deterrence policy "is not a total bluff," defense planners must "think through the probable course of a nuclear war." Gray's worry is that strategists exert too much restraint, too much "self-deterrence," rather than a more desirable "freedom of offensive nuclear action" and "theory of victory." He advocates planning for defeating the Soviet Union "at a cost that would not prohibit US recovery" and in a way that "could help *restore deterrence*" (italics added). The war-winning strategy is thus put forward on behalf of the deterrence that was to prevent war in the first place.

The dissociative elements in war-fighting and war-winning deterrence are staggering. Both, in fact, are contradictions in terms, oxymorons, since if there is war fighting we can hardly speak of deterrence. The dissociative pattern includes blocking out the very war fighting one is planning, while planning it in detail. As Herbert York explained, "the notion of deterrence is absolutely the dominant notion [at the laboratories]," but "there really is not much thinking about war fighting." There is a further illusion of control: first, in terms of "flexibility" and "limitation"; and then, even more extremely, in relation to "winning." Dissociation permits dangerously abstruse fantasy, including a dogged insistence, against all evidence, of a certain ordinariness and manageability of nuclear weapons even in the midst of their use by leaders of highly threatened nations. The claim of "humanity" in such policies indicates a formidable moral dissociation. And the sequence of establishing deterrence, fighting nuclear wars, winning nuclear wars, and then restoring deterrence is a dissociative end point in the overall logic of deterrence. Ironically, the advocacy of that sequence by Colin Gray exposes the ultimate contradiction in all deterrence: "As long as the United States relies on nuclear threats to deter an increasingly powerful Soviet Union, it is inconceivable that the US defense community can continue to divorce its thinking on deterrence from its planning for the efficient conduct of war." That "divorce" is a direct expression of dissociation. Gray is correct when he insists that the logic of deterrence leads to a policy of planning for victory in nuclear war—even if he requires a deeper dissociation in *advocating* that policy.

Existential Deterrence

There are two special concepts of deterrence—"existential deterrence" and "discriminate deterrence"—the first hopeful in its sensitivity to human concerns, and the second quite the reverse.

The former presidential assistant for national affairs McGeorge Bundy speaks of the "existential deterrence" created by an adversary's possession of weaponry and, above all, by the "uncertainty about what *could happen,* not in what has been asserted." Fear dominates existential deterrence, even in the absence of provocative threats, since nuclear weapons "are far more terrifying to adversaries than they are comforting to their possessors." Bundy thus speaks of "wise fear," given the actual destructive power of the weapons, while he also recognizes that "fear is bad, when it leads to action and reaction in the [nuclear weapons] procurement race." Bundy sees usefulness in existential deterrence if combined with the principle (put forward by Michael Howard) of "reassurance" and pursuit of détente, mostly "reassurance of friends and détente with adversaries." He goes on to advocate search for agreements between adversaries, and an overall shift within deterrence from threat to cooperation.

The psychological direction of existential deterrence is away from dissociation. In Bundy's usage, at least, there is less denial of nuclear-weapons effects, and the illusion of control is replaced by recognition of the truth of uncertainty. While dissociative patterns persist, since they go with the weapons, they are at least not furthered by elaborate competitive buildups or "scenarios for nuclear warfare . . . [which] reflect nothing more than the state of mind of their authors." The focus, in other words, is on the weapons' actual threat and on the dangerous uncertainties and annihilative potential consequences of those uncertainties. Existential deterrence moves sufficiently away from the extremities of dissociation to suggest the possibility of moving still further in that direction—for moving, that is, beyond the psychological and moral distortions of deterrence policy, and taking mutual steps toward nuclear, and eventually conventional-weapons, disarmament.

Discriminate Deterrence

The same cannot be said for the policy of "discriminate deterrence" announced in a report to the Defense Department and the National Security Council by an official commission on 11 January 1988. The report may well be the most elaborate overall statement of war-winning deterrence to date—and the most elaborately numbed. In providing an overall American military strategy for at least the next twenty years that is maximally "integrated" and "multifaceted," the report focuses on the idea of "discriminating responses"—nuclear, nonnuclear, and a "mix of offensive and defensive systems," so that destruction can be limited ("if we are not to invite destruction of what we are defending"). In this way the report, which gives special emphasis to American interests involving the Third World, seems to de-emphasize nuclear weapons while, in actuality, once more suggesting the kind of "flexibility" that encourages their employment. There is much focus on technologies with new "precision," "control," and "intelligence" but not a word about the policy consequences of the revolutionary dimension of potential annihilation brought about by nuclear weapons. Rather, the report advocates seizing upon every improvement in weapons and their effectiveness in order to be ready to use them at whatever level of violence we deem appropriate to the situation. One paragraph is remarkable in its dissociated approach to deterrence:

> However, there should be less ambiguity about the nature of this deterrent. The [NATO] Alliance should threaten to use nuclear weapons not as a link to a wider and more devastating war—although the risk of further escalation would still be there—but mainly as an instrument for denying success to the invading Soviet forces. The nuclear weapons would be used discriminately in, for example, attacks on Soviet command centers or troop concentrations. The Alliance's nuclear posture, like its posture for conventional war, will gain in deterrent power from new technologies emphasizing precision and control.

Here nothing seems to have been learned about the perils of aggressive "deterrence." The old psychism is merely brought up to date. Now the assumption is that "discrimination" solves all; that we can stay "discriminate" in a nuclear war, and in turn will be able to cause the Soviets to remain "discriminate" ("There would be powerful incentives for Soviet planners to make sure that any nuclear attack on NATO forces was selective and discriminate"). Only with a brief aside, quickly dismissed, is it acknowledged that "the risk of further escalation would still be there," so that the bizarre argument need never skip a beat. Once more, with deterrence, the nuclear trap snaps shut.

The Fixation on Deterrence

The psychological process of dissociation maintains everyone's adaptation to deterrence. Those dealing with the weapons become, at least in one aspect of their sense of self, potential weapons users, but that aspect remains outside their awareness, as do the consequences of such use. Though Bernard Brodie could speak of "the conviction on all sides that [nuclear] war is too horrible to ever be contemplated," in fact the act of initiating nuclear holocaust is contemplated daily, the horror of it diminishing with each scenario. And the "fixation on nuclear deterrence" provides "the hooker," as Herbert York put it, that enables one to "produce . . . the most hideous and destructive kinds of weapons." The dissociated "hooker" also enables people directly involved with weapons to avoid facing the fact, as York further explained, "that the triggering events that may lead to catastrophe are not under the control of the fellows you're hoping to deter": that war could start from sources outside the two superpowers, and "then you've created this instrument [of elaborate nuclear stockpiles] and it doesn't deal with the problem." That was what the scientist quoted earlier (see page 147) meant when he said, "If there is just a modest chance, . . . just a two percent chance that somehow this thing serves as a deterrent, or an indeterminate chance that the deterrent works, and it never gets used—you've got a way out."

The fixation on deterrence, that is, locks the mind into a narrow set of dubious assumptions and blinds it to forces outside the two-way adversarial realm of deterrence. Rather than see the world in its complexity, the dissociated-deterring mind becomes accustomed to moving back and forth between preventing war and annihilating one's adversary should that adversary cease to be deterred, until it can somehow simultaneously encompass both. The deterrence hedge as war prevention can sustain a limited form of doubling in those closest to the weapons, imbuing with virtue a nuclear-weapons self that might otherwise be perceived as tainted.

The process can extend to the very top. Eisenhower was, of course divided inwardly between his "public face" of defensive deterrence and his silent, unacknowledged encouragement of the building of first-strike weapons. This latter, aggressive self found public expression in Curtis LeMay's belligerent boasts. While struggling to control LeMay, Eisenhower also (according to the same observer referred to earlier [see page 154]) tolerated and even encouraged him. The public, peace-minded self remained authentic and extremely important, as did the unspoken nuclearistic self which presided over a crucial period of rapid American nuclear buildup. The deterrence hedge was always present as a link between the two selves.

Even when nuclear-weapons designers and strategists live ordinary lives in American society, they can live simultaneously in a collectively isolated mental and professional world located on the "nuclear planet." Each segment of that planet has its own set of absorbing problems—imagining new weapons systems at the laboratories; constructing the weapons from their various components at the Pantex plant in Amarillo, Texas; projecting scenarios for weapons use at think tanks such as RAND; and developing public policies and secret plans at the Pentagon and the White House. Within each of these segments, there is intense group discussion of these problems in ways that exclude broader human questions; each person must adapt to these group norms and the accompanying "groupthink," and the entire process serves to extend and maintain collective forms of dissociation.

The Language of Nonfeeling

Integral to the collective adaptation are the rhetoric and language of nuclear weapons. Carol Cohn, the feminist writer and teacher, has pointed out the prominence of male sexual imagery in that rhetoric. The stress on "hardness" parallels Nazi practice but has its own additional dimensions. It can include strategists' pride in "hanging tough" in threatening situations, making "tough decisions" that may entail great human risk. But there is also the idea of the "hardened target" (considered protected from destruction), "hard data" (usually meaning statistical), and a parallel contempt for "soft data" (usually meaning nonstatistical or concerned with human reactions or needs). Or at times the language can be overtly sexual, such as "orgasmic whump" to describe the simultaneous use of most of the weapons we possess. Or it can be a mixture of the sexual, technical, and obscurantist, as in "optimizing penetration dynamics." Perhaps most cruelly distorting of all is its use of birth imagery ("It's a boy!" or "Baby's satisfactorily born!") in code names for successful tests, and of "Little Boy" for the first atomic bomb—that imagery reaching a kind of apotheosis in William Lawrence's equation of the explosion of a hydrogen bomb with "the first cry of a newborn world." While this imagery can, as Cohn suggests, reflect male appropriation of the female birth function, its fundamental significance may well lie in the nuclearistic impulse to associate the bomb with a creative capacity and general revitalization.

Carol Cohn was herself to discover that the language was "racy, sexy, snappy"; that "you can get so good at manipulating the words that it almost feels like the whole thing is under control"; and that "the longer I stayed, the more conversations I participated in, the less frightened I was of nuclear war." Adopting that language, she found herself increasingly unable to express the humane concerns she originally brought with her: "The better I got at engaging in this discourse, the more impossible it became for me to express my own ideas, my own values." Here, as in the chapter epigraph ("I *couldn't* stay connected, couldn't keep human lives as my reference points"), she was describing her own sequence of doubling: the formation of a nuclear-weapons self that enabled her to become more comfortable in that environment, to experience its dissociated pleasures along with a sense of mastery of the nuclear-weapons problem, and, above all, to cease to experience the human consequences of the weapons whose use she was imagining. The whole process was enhanced by the decency of the men around her and the appeal of being accepted as an articulate and knowledgeable member of the group. No wonder that Cohn concluded that "learning the language is a transformative, rather than an additive, process." The key point about the language—as was true of Nazi euphemisms for and about the Final Solution (see page 198)—is its dissociative power, its enhancement of numbing, disavowal, and doubling. The sexual imagery, though important, is in the service of that dissociative function. Cohn, of course, interrupted and reversed the process in herself, as shown by her sensitive exposure of it.

The dissociative language readily absorbs technological developments, changes that can be generally destabilizing strategically but not psychologically to the active participant in deterrence planning. It enables weapons designers, strategists, and decision makers to remain inured to the way in which "technological exuberance . . . overwhelms the other factors that go into the making of overall national policy." That is why McGeorge Bundy can rightly state that "the internal politics of the strategic arms race has remained the prisoner of its technology"; and Lord Zuckerman can similarly claim that the arms race has been driven by "the men in the nuclear weapons laboratories of both sides." But the process would not occur without a sustained means of blocking out, in the minds of those involved with the technology, painful human truths about the weapons. And part of the way that collective dissociation operates is for participants to experience the sense mentioned earlier that someone or some group "up there" in the hierarchy is more wise and knowledgeable then they. It becomes a matter of even the experts leaving it to the experts, until that ostensibly wiser "someone" turns out to be the technology itself. Through dissociation, they turn human authority over to technology, and the technology is invested with the wisdom they themselves lack.

In psychological terms, the nuclear trap is our state of collective dissociation, our prison of numbing. We have ourselves set that trap as a barrier against our own perceived vulnerability, and we struggle to maintain effective dissociation in order to avoid taking in full knowledge of that highly vulnerable existential state. But the vulnerability emerges, as in the statement (in an interview with Steven Kull) of a former National Security Council official: "I have trouble generating scenarios because you can't generate a scenario for nuclear war that is not implausible." More frequently the pattern is that (as Thomas Powers commented in relationship to the destruction of command and control in a nuclear war) "in effect, when we no longer know what's happening, we try to bomb them back to the Stone Age."

Richard Feynman's observation that he and others "just stopped thinking," while working on the first bombs at Los Alamos, reflects a dissociated community. The tragedy, as we have already seen, is that the first nuclear-weapons–related dissociated community was also close to being a utopian community, with its "atmosphere of excitement, enthusiasm, and high intellectual and moral purpose." And the momentum of those emotions could be sustained even after the defeat of Germany and the knowledge that, because of the limited progress made by German scientists, there could be no other atomic bombs in the world at that time.* Elements of the Los Alamos model have been perpetuated in subsequent weapons communities, including the idea (especially compelling during the Second World War) that the bombs were necessary and would serve good purposes.

The dissociation has extended in all directions, making a vicious circle, with extreme dissociation at the center (for instance, doubling in weapons scientists and strategists) and less but still active dissociation at the periphery (including the numbing of ordinary people); significant in this vicious circle are the reassurances constantly made by respected nuclear "experts" concerning the safety and wisdom of their policies and scenarios. With this dissociative feedback system in place, deterrence has become associated with a deep collective fatalism ("It may not work but it's all we have, and if it fails and there is nuclear holocaust, what can you or I do?") or, worse, with renewal ("Through the strength of our deterrence, even if it fails, we reconstitute the world"). This second dissociative pattern was expressed, according to Molander, by a Navy captain: "It was wrong to assume that nuclear war would be the end of the world when, in fact, only 500,000,000 would be killed."

---

*Samuel Goudsmit, the physicist who headed the American intelligence mission during the last days of the war to track down German scientists and evaluate their progress on a German atomic bomb, told how an American major, upon learning that the Germans had never come close, commented, "Isn't it wonderful that the Germans have no atom bomb? . . . now we won't have to use ours."

Dissociative Shifts and Struggles

Many strategists and decision makers struggle against their dissociative stances and, in so doing, shift position and contradict themselves. Significantly, these dissociative flip-flops have occurred in some of the most influential thinkers and actors in the nuclear-weapons realm: Bernard Brodie, the ancestor figure of American nuclear strategy; Robert McNamara, former secretary of defense and a strong advocate, with his "whiz kids," of management techniques and civilian control over the military establishment; and Henry Kissinger, nuclear-weapons theorist and former national security adviser and secretary of state.

Bernard Brodie

> Strategic bombing does not necessarily mean mass slaughter.
>
> —BERNARD BRODIE

> Violence between great opponents is inherently difficult to control, and cannot be controlled unilaterally.
>
> —BERNARD BRODIE

Bernard Brodie's struggles had to do with the "usability" of first the atomic bomb and then the hydrogen bomb. In emphasizing the paradox that one has to avoid using them by demonstrating willingness to use them, Brodie undoubtedly blocked out at least partially some of their human consequences. He required still more psychic numbing to begin to advocate possible military uses of the weapons while opposing dropping them on cities. But then he increasingly found himself theorizing on how best to *use* the weapons, asking questions such as "how many bombs will do what? And the 'what' must be reckoned in overall strategic results rather than merely in acres destroyed." By December 1950, during the Korean War but before the Chinese entered it, he was advocating "publicizing right now the fact that strategic bombing does not necessarily mean mass slaughter." Even then, Brodie resisted the dissociative extremes of Curtis LeMay and other ardent nuclearists (whom he consistently opposed), but did so by maintaining his own dissociation sufficiently to advocate more limited or "humane" bomb employment. He was, in other words, flirting with war-fighting deterrence.

Then came the hydrogen bomb which, according to his strategist-colleagues, "sort of swamped Brodie," and "undid" him, to the point where he became pessimistic about the weaponry and wrote of "the end of strategy as we have known it." Yet he remained very much the strategist, now turning away from strategic bombing in the direction of tactical, battlefield use of nuclear weapons in order to "secure our objectives without bombing enemy cities." The "high priest of deterrence" had now developed a "bizarre infatuation" with tactical use of nuclear weapons and limited nuclear war. But after a year in France (1960), he returned to his original principle of finite deterrence in a way that included the strategic French deterrent. And then, during the early 1960s, he underwent a "series of flip-flops," reversing an earlier emphasis on non-use; he, in fact, declared that it would be "one of the grossest forms of self-disarming" to adopt a firm principle of no first use. At about that time (1961), he stated that Soviet leaders might consider it "rational" to start a nuclear war; but in 1965, he declared that it would be impossible to discover reasons for Soviet leaders to do so "unless we are dealing with utter madmen."

These confusions were part of a gradual but powerful disaffection with the profession he had done much to create, including recognition of the difficulty of controlling violence between great opponents. Brodie was strongly influenced by the failure of strategic thought during the Vietnam War. And during the last years of his life (he died in 1978), he began to dismiss efforts to impose rationality on strategic nuclear situations as "simply playing with words," and came to think of the enterprise as being (in the journalist Fred Kaplan's words) "something of an illusion." While intense hostilities toward, and rivalries with, other strategists contributed greatly to Brodie's flip-flops, as did his decreasing national influence from the early 1960s, psychological shifts away from dissociation were clearly of great importance. At the end, a sensitive man's diminishing capacity or inclination to dissociate in relation to deterrence policies contributed to his increasing wisdom, and to his disillusionment with the strategic enterprise that had been his life's work.

Robert McNamara

> We might try to knock out most of the Soviet strategic nuclear forces, while keeping Russian cities intact, and then coerce the Soviets into avoiding our cities (by the threat of controlled reprisal) and accepting our peace terms.
> —ROBERT MCNAMARA

> Nuclear weapons serve no military purpose whatsoever. They are totally useless except to deter one's opponent from using them.
> —ROBERT MCNAMARA

Robert McNamara's dissociative switches are even more impressive owing to his responsibility, as secretary of defense, for potential use of the weapons. McNamara's first stance was, like Brodie's, the doctrine of finite deterrence, as espoused in early 1961 by the U.S. Navy. Described as enthusiastic upon emerging from his briefing on that doctrine, he emerged "stunned," just a week later, from another briefing. This one, conducted by SAC Commander Thomas Power, presented the prevailing Single Integrated Operational Plan (SIOP) which involved "an all-out preemptive first-strike against the USSR, Eastern Europe and Red China, in response to an actual or merely impending Soviet invasion of Western Europe" even if that invasion involved no nuclear weapons at all. This was the first time, as Herbert York put it, that McNamara had "looked at the subject of nuclear war down the throat," and allowed himself to take in something of the *experience* of nuclear war. McNamara felt impelled to seek measures of restraint; to arrange for greater presidential control over the military, over any decision to launch the weapons; and also to find a policy less extreme than the war-fighting plan he had heard.

Those impulses were furthered by a crash of a B-52 bomber at that time, investigation of which revealed that five of six safety devices designed to prevent one of its hydrogen bombs from accidentally exploding had failed at the moment of impact ("Only a single switch prevented the bomb from detonating and spreading fire and destruction over a wide area"). Shortly afterward, a "massive false alarm" of a Soviet missile attack on the United States, at the North American Air Defense Command, impressed McNamara with the great danger of accidental nuclear war. About a month later, McNamara, exposed to counterforce doctrine promulgated by William Kaufmann and other RAND analysts, began to move toward accepting their principles of "multiple options," "flexible response," and "controlled escalation."

McNamara was, so to speak, caught in a dissociative trap. Having permitted the human horror of full-scale nuclear war to enter his consciousness and thereby break through prior psychic numbing, the only possible recourse was, he felt, to adopt a less extreme plan, but one that turned out to be a war-fighting form of deterrence which required that he now dissociate in relation to claims of control and limitation of killing and damage. McNamara, however, came to question this new mode of dissociation as well as to realize, over time, that strategies for "damage limitation" did little to limit damage. The Cuban missile crisis of October 1962 also contributed to McNamara's struggle against dissociation and toward imagining actual nuclear holocaust. He had told Kennedy during the crisis, "If one of these goddamned things was launched against New York, Washington, or Miami, it would destroy so many people that you, Mr. President, would never want to accept that risk," and later commented, "If that was the case with one, think what a limited nuclear war would look like." He came to reject war-fighting deterrence and counterforce and finally embraced his doctrine of "assured destruction," which was a version of his original position of finite deterrence. Now, having broken through the dissociation concerning control-and-damage limitation (that is, concerning war fighting), he still required the fundamental deterrence dissociation having to do with the willingness, should deterrence fail, to fight a nuclear war. Years later, when out of office, he could finally conclude that "nuclear weapons serve no military purpose whatsoever" (see epigraph, page 220).

Henry Kissinger

> What in the name of God is strategic superiority?
> —HENRY KISSINGER

Henry Kissinger's dissociative shifts are also instructive since, unlike Brodie and McNamara, he began by advocating extended and war-fighting deterrence, as expressed in his 1957 book, *Nuclear Weapons and Foreign Policy.* As a scholar, that is, he was intellectually committed to the dissociative stance of alleged control and limit. Later, as a leading decision maker in the Nixon administration, he seemed to retain that stance and even moved it to the point of war-winning deterrence: a secret 1972 White House memorandum he partly drafted defined "strategic sufficiency" as the forces necessary "to insure the United States would emerge from a nuclear war in discernibly better shape than the Soviet Union." But he developed doubts, especially when he discovered, in connection with the international crisis surrounding the 1974 Arab oil embargo, that the most limited nuclear war envisioned by the Pentagon as a response to a Soviet invasion of Iran would involve the use of at least two hundred nuclear weapons. Later that year, he was to express his frustration in a rhetorical outburst: "What in the name of God is strategic superiority? What is the significance of it, politically, militarily, operationally, at these levels of numbers? What do you do with it?"

Kissinger could never find answers for these questions. He had, in 1969, complained to McNamara that the warplan passed on to the Nixon administration was totally inappropriate for deterring Soviet nuclear attack on the United States, since it included American use of nuclear weapons to stop a Russian conventional assault on Europe, which, Kissinger pointed out, would surely result in Soviet use of the weapons on us. But some years later, Kissinger was to concede to McNamara that he, too, had been unable to evolve a U.S. nuclear strategy any more appropriate. There is, of course, no such thing as "appropriate" nuclear strategy, in that once one frees oneself of dissociation in relation to experiencing nuclear horror and renounces illusory claims of control and limit, one can no longer accept the weapons as usable.

Generally speaking, these shifts in attitude represent break-downs of dissociative arrangements within the self and can reflect, as we have observed, a decreasing capacity to block out horror and hold on to specific illusions. But, over time, these shifts can signify changes in the self-system: from a professional-strategic self built around aggressive claims of war-fighting or war-winning deter-rence to a relatively more humane and feeling self with greater commitment to maintaining human life. Serving as a decision maker while one espouses the ideology of deterrence requires, over time, some form of nuclear-weapons–centered and nuclear-weapons–using self, which in turn can become vulnerable to being overturned when, as a result of various pressures, one breaks out of that dissociation, at least in part, and permits oneself to per-ceive—and inwardly experience—terrible nuclear truths. Though a decision maker envied Kull's role as an academic ("you guys . . . get to tell the truth"), one still has to feel the truth to be able to tell it, and to find a place for that truth within the self, morally and psychologically, in order to live and act from it.

The Cult of Deterrence, and Its Decline

> The concept of deterrence retains its value as an emotive word, sparking feelings of security and safety, but has lost any precise meaning . . . [be-cause] nuclear deterrence today means whatever the speaker wishes it to mean. It is a blank check. . . . Every conceivable threat, actual or perceived, and every belief or determination in the minds of Soviet leaders, absolutely any weapons system can be justified in terms of the blank check of deter-rence.
>
> —K. D. JOHNSON

Although the claims of deterrence are accepted by great numbers of people throughout the world, its doctrine originally arose from, and is still embraced and nurtured by, groups of strategists and

defense intellectuals whose commitment to deterrence ideology is
such that they resemble a cult. A cult is characterized by an ideology whose closed logic believers cling to, whatever the larger
evidence to the contrary, and whatever the degree of dissociation
required by the cult's practices and beliefs.

Thus, however dubious the supporting scholarship, and however species destroying the potential consequences, the ideology
of deterrence is continuously put forward to justify virtually any
nuclear-weapons system, whether clearly offensive or ostensibly
"defensive." For as Kolkowitz points out,

> Far from inventing a modern science and policy for the management
> and prevention and deterrence of nuclear war, the American defense
> intellectuals have in fact, consciously or otherwise, projected an Ameri-
> can ideology in the form of strategic theory, an ideology based in part
> on some of the traditional beliefs and values of our history . . . [which]
> simply reflects the inherent preferences and values of this intellectual
> class and their traditions.

While the deterrence ideology is promulgated by those at the
center of the cult, the rest of us at the periphery remain imprisoned
by it. But the inmates are straining at the prison bars, and the
deterrence-sustaining dissociation is itself under duress.

An understanding of these dissociative processes could deepen
the critical thought on deterrence which is now emerging. For
instance, Michael MccGwire, a leading authority on national security issues, declares deterrence to be "the problem, not the solution," since "the steady buildup of nuclear weapons to deter
. . . hypothetical Soviet initiatives actually makes war more likely
through accident, miscalculation, or the increased tension and
tougher political posturing that go with such policies." He points
out that deterrence replaces "concern for the innate dangers of
nuclear weaponry" and provides "a technical solution for . . . a
political problem." He describes how deterrence has "pandered"
to an already-existing "visceral" American anticommunism and
"fostered the impression of America the magistrate, and Russia
the law-breaker." In that way, it has "stunted the development of
US foreign policy and fueled the arms race" under the principle
that "more is better." And he speaks of the "bad politics" and

"bad strategy" resulting from applying "Cartesian logic to complex problems of political psychology."

In addition, MccGwire tells us, deterrence has "encouraged unwarranted complacency and . . . [dissipated] the sudden urgency that nuclear weapons brought to the search for new ways of managing interstate relations," and has "provided a pseudo-ethical façade for policies which were inherently unethical." MccGwire believes that the claim that deterrence has prevented war with the Soviet Union "cannot be disproved," but that "neither can the counterclaim that nuclear deterrence was not responsible for keeping the peace." Kolkowitz sums up much of MccGwire's argument in a single sentence: "The very conditions and policies demanded for coping with the potential imminence of nuclear war threat also create a condition of imminence of war threat, . . . a permanent war threat."

Other leading advocates of deterrence, such as Fred Iklé and Joseph Nye, tend to question at some point the very assumptions on which they themselves have built their deterrence theories. Iklé as early as 1973, in his article "Can Nuclear Deterrence Last Out the Century," condemned the policy because it "blinds us to the fact that our method for preventing nuclear war rests on a form of warfare universally condemned since the Dark Ages—the mass killing of hostages." And in 1987, in "The Long Term Future of Deterrence," Joseph Nye stated that "the rational models of deterrence theory tend to be static and ahistorical," and "even if nuclear deterrence has lasted for nearly four decades, it is difficult to believe that it will last forever." But Nye has consistently held to his commitment to deterrence, and Iklé used his strictures against finite deterrence as reasons for adopting in its place war-fighting and war-winning forms of deterrence, as ultimately exemplified in his co-chairing the commission that produced the document "Discriminate Deterrence." Dissociation, it would seem, is hard for sensitive people to sustain, but too often their response is only to give up one version of that condition for another, and thereby to adapt to and further, rather than confront, the malignant constellation of dissociation and deterrence policy.

The Dissociative Field: Nazi and Nuclear

The diagram is mistaken for reality itself.
—LEWIS MUMFORD

Dissociation, then, by occurring consistently within individual members, envelops the various groups that contribute to the genocidal system. This collective dissociation can come to dominate interlocking institutions, as it did in Nazi Germany, and does in ways that are psychologically less extreme, but potentially just as dangerous, in the contemporary United States and Soviet Union. We can then speak of a "dissociative field," within which each person is helped to adapt, and to contribute in "normal" fashion, to the genocidal enterprise.

The Nazis' dissociation was maintained by an ideology that stressed the virtue or necessity of destroying the Jews or of at least "solving the Jewish problem." Nazis were thus motivated to avoid feeling the pain of Jewish victims. Similarly, by believing in the virtue or necessity of the weapons, nuclearists are motivated to avoid experiencing the murderous effects of their potential use. The resulting social dynamic centers on a dissociation that can permit killing in the name of therapy—the operation of the healing-killing paradox. With deterrence, there is the assumption that we must be prepared to kill hundreds of millions of people in order to prevent large-scale killing, to cure the world of genocide. With the Nazis, the assumption was that killing all Jews was a way of curing not only the Aryan race but all humankind. Involvement in a therapeutic mission helps block out feelings of the deaths one is or may be inflicting.

The collective dependency on the constellation of dissociation and genocidal ideology can approach shared addiction. People can come to feel that should they cease extending nuclear stockpiles (or killing Jews) they will not be able to sustain their collective life. The shared numbing, doubling, and disavowal must be maintained in order to avoid recognition that what one has been doing is, or could be, associated with mass killing rather than with a justified form of self-strengthening and healing. In that way, dissociation itself takes on a momentum, a pattern of necessity, that is difficult to break. The dissociation is made easier by significant improvements in the technology of killing—the switch from face-to-face shooting to gas chambers, or the sequence from nuclear weapons as scarce and special to their almost limitless profusion. The dissociative field involves those at greater remove (American university departments with weapons-related contracts), thereby extending the normalized genocidal arrangements into virtually every corner of a society.

Genocidal intent is always unclear. It was surely overtly suggested in Nazi Germany; but even there, the intent was not specific until early 1941. In nuclearism, genocidal intent, though always denied, exists nonetheless, at least as a contingency, in war-fighting plans. But in any genocide, the sequence from unclear intent to action is made possible by dissociation, which at every point prevents the self from experiencing the mass killing—removing, that is, the murderer from murder. This constellation of ideology and dissociation can become a malignant mysticism. Nazi mysticism sought perfect harmony and oneness in a world purified of Jews and other "life unworthy of life." Nuclear mysticism seeks in the weaponry, and its technology and science, a salvation for human pain, vulnerability, and struggle. Both cases assume an ultimate principle whose truth is unarguable. That mystical assumption powerfully supports the overall dissociative process, and itself (since it is justifying mass murder) requires sustained dissociation in its adherents. The killing done in the name of this dissociative mysticism can then be understood in relation to what Camus called "crimes of logic"—killing in response to visionary projects their adherents see as necessary and rational.

Dissociation can readily entrench itself in an entire population because it is part of the human repertoire, of the general psychological capacity of all of us. In the dissociative state, there is an interruption in the flow of images and forms that characterizes the ordinary symbolizing function of the self. Portions of the self act separately and antagonistically so as to interfere with the cohesion and controlling function of the self as the overall symbolic agent of the entire person. Instead, elements of experience—of self-process—are inactivated in various ways: certain kinds of feelings are blocked *(numbing)*, meaning structures are negated *(disavowal)*, or a separated element of the self functions autonomously and antithetically to the prior self *(doubling)*.

Dissociation can be adaptive in that it coexists with actively functional portions of the self in which symbolization and general emotional experience are intact. Where the situation producing the dissociation is temporary and rectifiable, the dissociation itself can readily give way to integrated function of the self, having served a limited, protective purpose. But when those external conditions (as in both Nazi and nuclear situations) are themselves lasting, so are the dissociative inner divisions of the self that harmfully interfere with the always fragile human aspiration for wholeness.

The dissociation surrounding deterrence is significantly influenced by historical attitudes toward science. Lewis Mumford speaks of the emergence, during the sixteenth century, of "the new assumption the cosmos itself was primarily a mechanical system": from that time, "not man but the machine became the central feature in this new world picture"; and, "in the acceptance of this mechanical orthodoxy man was to find his salvation." While in nuclearism the mechanical world has been replaced by the electronic feedback system, the principle holds: a "depersonalized mechanical world picture" is diagrammed, "and then the diagram [is] . . . mistaken for reality itself." While scientific thought has varied, as have attitudes about it, general developments in science over the past four centuries have been consistent with dissociated stances. The very rigor required in scientific work—that extreme intellectual abstraction be separated from the rest of psychic function—lends itself to numbing and doubling that exclude broader human consequences. Extreme versions of this state, where reason is isolated and separated from feelings (what the Indian psychologist Ashis Nandy calls "Cartesian sickness") can culminate by "placing the world in jeopardy."

Yet recognition of this dissociative process and its terrible dangers is well within our capacity. Indeed, the dissociative field itself becomes vulnerable to truths about deterrence and about victimization of any kind, actual or potential. When Bishop

Hunthausen declares that we must "speak plainly" and recognize a particular nuclear-weapons system as "the Auschwitz of Puget Sound" (epigraph, chapter 1), he is insisting that we examine the fate of past victims as part of our struggle against the numbing and dissociation that could result in still greater numbers of future victims.

Chapter 8

Victims

How securely do we live, we men of the century's
and the millennium's end?

—PRIMO LEVI

IT IS bad enough to acknowledge that ordinary people with professional training—Nazi doctors or American physicists—can engage in genocidal projects. It is worse to begin to suspect that
potential victims—the rest of us—tend to resist the truth about
these projects and, all too frequently, to collude in them. Still
worse may be our beginning recognition that the infinitely destructive power of our technology tends to break down ultimate distinctions between perpetrators and victims, or between either of these
and bystanders—in marked contrast to the Nazis, whose victims
were fundamentally distinct from their victimizers. Nuclear genocide, that is, would be human self-genocide.

Nazi and nuclear cases, then, give us very different answers to
such important questions as, Who are the victims? What steps do
they take to prevent their victimization? What are the impediments
to potential victims' taking effective action on their own behalf?
These questions lead, in turn, to ways in which psychic numbing,
in response to pressures and threat, can blunt the imagination of
victims, even to the point of their colluding in their own victimization.

Numbing of Nazi Victims and Bystanders

> I do not know . . . whether in my depths there lurks
> a murderer, but I do know that I was a guiltless
> victim and I was not a murderer. I know that the
> murderers existed, not only in Germany, and still
> exist, retired or on active duty, and that to confuse
> them with their victims is a moral disease or an
> aesthetic affectation or a sinister sign of complicity;
> above all, it is a precious service rendered (inten-
> tionally or not) to the negators of truth.
> —PRIMO LEVI

In Nazi Germany, one group, the Nazis, killed members of other groups, mostly with bullets or poison gas but also by means of hanging, beheading, injection, and starvation. These Nazi victims included those designated as political opponents (communists, social democrats, certain religious leaders, and rivals within the Nazi movement); as "life unworthy of life" (mental patients and others thrust into the "euthanasia" project); and as racially or otherwise inferior or dangerous (Jews, especially, but also Gypsies, educated Poles, Soviet functionaries and prisoners of war, homosexuals, and Seventh Day Adventists). Ultimately there was a Nazi impulse, certainly in Hitler himself, toward a national *Götterdämmerung*, in which the German people themselves were to be destroyed, ostensibly as punishment for their failure and unworthiness, but also as part of the ultimate vision of redemption or cure.

The Jews were, as we know, the Nazis' primary victims; as the ultimate source of racial "disease," their destruction had special mystical significance. Yet it has been argued that the Nazis created a "genocidal universe" requiring an ever-expanding designation of victim groups. Probably both tendencies were present: the Jews as the fundamental genocidal target, whose victimization was most necessary psychologically to the Nazis (so that *all* Jews had to be killed); and the category of "life unworthy of life," interwoven with and furthered by anti-Jewish ideology, being potentially limitless. (Indeed, the first Nazi genocide, conducted mainly from 1939 to 1941, was the hundred thousand victims of the "euthanasia" project, most of them German non-Jewish mental patients.) The Nazi experience also suggests the ready transition from genocide to *self-*genocide, as the process of purification extends to one's own people. The shared omnipotence can be bizarrely extended into a vision of immortalization via national suicide or collective self-murder. This may well be a possible end stage of any genocide. But whatever the significance of that last murderous gasp of Hitler, and whatever the behavior of collaborators and coerced victims, the distinction between the Nazis and their victims was clear enough.

Coerced Victims

"There are few more durable generalizations about the history of the Holocaust," Marrus writes, "than the characterization of Jewish passivity in the face of mortal threat." The biblical image of Jews going to their deaths "like sheep to the slaughter" has haunted Jews and non-Jews alike with its suggestion of both sacrifice and passivity. That image goes back to Jews who urged resistance in the Vilna ghetto and was taken up again by the Jewish historian Emmanuel Ringelblum, in late 1942, in his Warsaw ghetto diary: "Why didn't we resist when they began to resettle 300,000 Jews from Warsaw? Why did we allow ourselves to be led like sheep to the slaughter?" After the event, prominent Jewish writers on the Holocaust—notably Raul Hilberg and Hannah Arendt—reasserted that accusation of Jewish passivity. Hilberg spoke of "almost complete lack of resistance," along with frequent "anticipatory compliance," and attributed the Jewish response to a two-thousand-year history of subservience as a means of surviving in the Diaspora, of Jews having "learned that they could avert or survive destruction by placating and appeasing their enemies." Hilberg described the Jewish leaders in the ghettos (the *Judenrat*) as having become "implements of German will." And Arendt went even further in attacking Jewish leaders for their "role in the destruction of their own people" as the "darkest chapter of the whole dark story."

Some students of the Holocaust came to question these assessments, stressing instead the extensive, and previously unacknowledged, Jewish resistance. They pointed out that many thousands of Jews fought in resistance groups of one kind or another; that there were significant uprisings in three of the six death camps and in at least three other camps; and that various kinds of resistance took place in the ghettos, including the heroic uprising of the Warsaw ghetto. But Marrus and other historians have concluded that, despite these instances, resistance not only tended to be limited and isolated but often brought about the deaths both of resistors as well as large numbers of other Jews through vicious Nazi reprisal policies.

Jewish resistance was limited, but that limitation need not be attributed to Jewish character or the insecurities of Jewish history. Of considerable significance here is that 3,300,000 of 5,700,000 Soviet prisoners died in German custody, "most of them executed, starved, or worked to death"; yet there is no record of their engaging in any significant uprising until the very end of the war. And these were young men with military training and combat experience. This and other evidence suggests that the crucial factor in victims' inability to resist was the brutally manipulative Nazi use of its overwhelming military and police power. The Nazi talent for inducing psychic numbing in general, and for coercing collusion in particular, is crucial to any psychological or moral evaluation of their victims' behavior.

To understand what interfered with victims' taking more effective action on their own behalf, we need to imagine our way into their minds, particularly their capacity to feel. The concept of psychic numbing was developed in connection with the victims of the first atomic bomb. Hiroshima survivors said that, in response to the overwhelming horrors of the atomic bomb, they very quickly—sometimes within minutes or even seconds—simply ceased to feel. However clear their sense of what was happening around them, their emotional reactions were unconsciously turned off. This acute response is *psychic closing off,* and the longer-lasting diminution of feeling is *psychic numbing* (see pages 13–14).

Psychic numbing is a fundamental human reaction to extreme threat, and is prefigured biologically in an animal's tendency to become motionless and "freeze" when attacked by a stronger animal. Just as that stance helps the weaker animal by conveying a message that discourages the attack of the stronger, so can psychic numbing be helpful to human victims by preventing psychological breakdown and the shattering of the self. In human beings, numbing becomes a means of undergoing a partial and temporary psychic death as a means of fending off total and permanent physical or psychic death. In that sense, for people in Hiroshima as for persecuted Jews, a certain numbing was necessary for them to function well enough to survive. But pronounced numbing in either group could have the opposite effect: it could interfere with the alertness and decisive behavior required to remain alive.

For Jews, in addition to real social and economic limitations— the lack of the money and connections necessary for escape from Germany—a series of physical and psychological pressures contributed to dissociation and numbing. These included "a long, drawn-out process of attrition, in which the victims had no knowledge of, and no way of knowing, the final outcome." In other words, sufficient "terror, degradation, and spoliation" could induce psychic numbing, but no clear revelation of the plan and project to kill all Jews. For Jews, as for most people everywhere, the idea that a project so extreme and so murderous could be mounted in the middle of the twentieth century was simply unimaginable. This second form of psychic numbing derives from the inability of the mind to take in what it cannot connect with prior experience or prior imagination. Jewish survivors tell of having heard many rumors of German cruelty and murder, but also of how difficult it was to know which of them to believe. And even if accepted as truth, such stories could not begin to encompass the Nazis' project of mass murder.

Under this duress, Jews could simultaneously believe and not believe that the Nazis were murdering very large numbers of fellow Jews. This "dual belief" has been called "middle knowledge" in relation to dying patients: such patients may either say that they know they are dying while at the same time they make preparations for a personal future, or else insist they will not die while they are carefully completing their personal arrangements. Characteristic of this duality is that one has an active psychological inclination toward each side of the contradictory beliefs: thus, in the midst of Auschwitz, some people could not quite take in the truth of the gas chambers. And later, a Jewish physician-survivor told how, after about two years in Auschwitz and almost forty years of working medically with survivors, "I still cannot believe that they did it. . . . That anyone would try to round up all the Jews in Europe to kill them." So drastic is the violation of all that one has known and seen before that, as one journalist witnessing the liberation of Buchenwald put it, "you can't understand it, even when you've seen it." Which is to say that one belief system within the self takes in the evidence and knows the truth, and another belief system within the same self rejects that evidence as unacceptable and unimaginable. This pattern of dual belief overlaps with such mechanisms as "denial" and "cognitive dissonance": but rather than the mind's rejecting the unacceptable belief, as in the former mechanism, or grasping at a belief that overcomes the "dissonance" of the latter mechanism, here the mind is able to maintain both of the antagonistic beliefs over a considerable period.

These tendencies were especially strong in Jews who had become well established in Germany or other European countries, who had in the past witnessed or experienced persecution that had turned out to be only sporadic or temporary. Persons whose forebears had lived in an area for generations were especially reluctant to uproot their families in a sudden, decisive move that might turn out to have been unnecessary. In such life-threatening crises, though human beings may not disbelieve entirely in the danger, their simultaneous belief and disbelief in it combine to enable them to maintain everyday patterns of behavior rather than make a fundamental break with them. A recent Jewish commentator refers specifically to "our failure to imagine genocide." He is surely correct. But in many cases the failure may have been less an inability to imagine genocide than to act on such imagination— precisely because one simultaneously imagined an alternative, less absolute set of possibilities.

In respect to those Jewish groups thrust into the actual machinery of destruction—the *Judenrat,* the *Sonderkommando,* and various camp functionaries—the psychic numbing becomes associated with the *psychology of coerced collusion.* Generally speaking, there has been all too much evidence that victimizers, by applying ruthless methods, can involve victims in various contributions to a genocidal project.

Prisoner doctors in Auschwitz required the support of Nazi doctors in order to remain alive and to do a certain amount of actual medical work to help fellow prisoners. These prisoner doctors faced, therefore, a terrible moral dilemma when Nazi doctors came to the medical wards to make "selections," which meant choosing the weakest, most moribund individuals for the gas chamber so that they could be replaced in the camp by relatively stronger workers. Prisoner doctors preferred to have nothing to do with these selections; but the more they avoided consulting with Nazi doctors on them, the greater the danger that the latter would select for death those patients who were sufficiently intact to be able to survive instead of those who would almost certainly die in any case. The prisoner doctors tried to confer with one another about a common policy, and some ended by simply giving medical evaluations of patients, leaving the Nazi doctors to make the decisions for life or death. In this psychology of coerced collusion, a victim faces impossible choices: refusal to cooperate at all with one's captors may result not only in harm or death to oneself but in more deaths in general than does willingness to engage in a measure of cooperation.

In the case of the *Judenrat* leaders, Nazi coercion was still more sustained and systematic: "The Jews were *forced* to establish the councils [of the *Judenrat* leaders, who were responsible for running the ghettos], . . . individuals were *forced* to serve on them, and . . . the councils were *forced* to provide services for the Germans." The coercion had at least two levels of blackmail: threat to the lives of the individual council leader and his family; and insistence that the only way to make arrangements that could help Jews—save Jewish lives—was to cooperate with the Gestapo in providing lists, helping in roundups, and so on. *Judenrat* leaders varied enormously in their responses, and some made courageous attempts to save lives. But the combination of pressure and corruptibility led some to become confused dictators, and their force of "Jewish police" to become cruelly efficient in complying with Nazi requirements. None could avoid these forms of compliance.

The members of the Jewish *Sonderkommando* were in an equally tragic situation, being more directly involved in the killing sequence than any other Jewish group. Though they lived under somewhat privileged conditions, their survival depended upon doing the work of their special unit: conducting arriving Jews, usually roughly, to the selections and then to the "showers" (for the most part, actively maintaining the deception); then removing the bodies from the gas chambers and placing them in the crematoria. At the end of a specified period of time—usually six weeks— the *Sonderkommando* were themselves killed and replaced.

In such coerced collusion, the victim's numbing in relation to others being killed can be enhanced by one's own powerful impulse to survive as well as the sense that one may be helping others to live. Those involved in coerced collusion—some of the *Judenrat* ghetto leaders, for instance—might have combined their numbing with dual beliefs concerning Nazi genocide. Even evidence reaching them from Jews who had escaped from Nazi death camps could be subsumed to those dual beliefs, and to the assumption that the Nazi murders they were witnessing were expressions of "unrestrained hatred and extreme disregard for human lives," or of unwillingness to provide food for Jews, rather than manifestations of a systematic policy of extermination.

Bystanders

> Again and again, the Holocaust illustrates how difficult it was for "good" people to move from *knowledge* of what the Nazis were doing, to *comprehension* of the significance of Nazi activities, and then to *action* aimed at thwarting Nazi success.
> —JOHN K. ROTH

Nothing more facilitated the genocidal process than the numbing of bystanders, both without and within Germany. All too familiar by now is the coldness to the Jewish plight manifested by most of the world's leaders, notably those of the United States and Great Britain. Behind that refusal to take action on behalf of Jews (bomb death camps or, at least, the rail lines leading to them), or to offer significant sanctuary that might have saved the lives of large numbers of Jews, was a terrible mixture of military rigidity, bureaucratic distancing, amoral political calculations, and anti-Semitism, both veiled and overt. All contributed to a psychic numbing that was often actively sought and generally scandalous.

Another dimension of that numbing went beyond any of the elements just listed: it again had to do with incredulity as profound as it was pervasive. Just to label this pattern numbing or denial does not capture what actually happened; for that, one requires a more detailed sequence of behavior.

The Jewish writer and editor Marie Syrkin provides that sequence in her description of how the incredulity extended even to the Jewish communities of the world:

In August 1942, shortly before Doctor Stephen Wise, despite a reluctant State Department, was informed via Great Britain of the reality of the extermination program, I was summoned to a small private meeting of Jewish publicists and spokesmen in New York City at which Doctor Leon Kubowitsky gave us information that he had received about the existence of death camps and gas chambers. All those present were in the forefront of the campaign steadily waged by American Jews at the time to arouse American sentiment against the Nazi persecutions. Hence the auditors at that meeting were neither uninformed nor indifferent but they had no inkling of where these persecutions would lead. Though from the vantage point of later knowledge it has become fashionable to excoriate American Jewry for passivity during the Nazi era, every person who listened to Kubowitsky's report was passionately involved in seeking to arouse the American public and the "conscience of the world," and to discover havens for Jewish refugees. Nevertheless we left the meeting in a kind of haze in which shock was muted by disbelief. I could think of no more accurate way of describing our state of mind.

At approximately the same time Syrkin and the editor of the magazine *Jewish Frontier* had received from Jewish sources in Poland a detailed, accurate "account of the extermination of the Jews of Lodz by means of gas-filled trucks driven to the neighboring woods," in which "every monstrous detail from the initial deceptive 'bath' to the looting of the corpses was given." Syrkin is unsparing in her recollection of her and her colleague's state of mind and their actions:

I must confess to you that we read the document without the emotional capacity to accept its truth. Yet we hesitated to dismiss the report outright as an incredible horror story. So we hit on an editorial compromise for which I can give no reasonable post-facto explanation and which today I recall with shame. To assuage our misgivings, in our September, 1942 issue we printed the dread account—which now reads so matter-of-factly—in fine print, in the back of the magazine, as a story that had reached us and for which we could not vouch. The title of the article, "Murder in Poland," was not even featured on the cover.

The "reasonable post-facto explanation" she seeks has undoubtedly to do with duality of belief: to Syrkin and her colleagues, the reports were both true (because backed by evidence) and untrue (because they were simply not believable, acceptable, imaginable). Syrkin goes on to say that the second report (given at the meeting) "heightened our fear without effecting conviction." That conviction could only come a few weeks later when additional information from other sources "no longer left room for doubt." She and her editor then plunged into action by preparing an entire issue of their journal, "with heavy black borders," devoted exclusively to the reports with an editorial declaring that "a systematic extermination of European Jewry was under way"—probably the first English-language effort to alert the American public to the Nazi killing project. Even then, the American media mostly ignored the matter: "Except for the Jewish press, the silence was almost complete."

Syrkin goes on to say that these two issues of their magazine— one relegating the story to fine print in the back, the other bordered in black and devoted entirely to the subject—represented an "evolution in consciousness—the ability to think the unthinkable," and "indicates how difficult it was as late as 1942 for even the most alert and nationally sensitive sector of American Jewry to make the psychic leap from an awareness of bloody persecution to acknowledgement of the reality of the Final Solution." That "evolution in consciousness" or "ability to think the unthinkable" can be understood as a new integration of the individual selves of the various people involved, a process that gave increasing dominance to the constellation of belief in the terrible truth through undermining the other constellation of doubt and disbelief. The process was difficult precisely because it entailed a re-ordering of the self as a whole, a difficult process which one must share with a like-minded group.

In a related process, the American press in general began to print a great deal about persecution of the Jews but "persistently ignored the scope and significance of the events it described." Editors and journalists prided themselves on their skepticism and "toned down what reached them from European sources, qualifying the magnitude and ubiquity of mass murder." Incredulity not only was considered a professional virtue but had been sharpened by inflated atrocity stories of the First World War. Individually and collectively, American journalists also had to overcome gradually their inclination toward disbelief and strengthen that toward accepting the truth. That incredulity and toning down of stories had to do with the absence of a place in the imagination, journalistic or otherwise, for a systematic, scientifically run program of exterminating millions of people.

Ordinary Germans underwent similar imaginative struggles in the face of evidence closer to hand. For many, intense numbing was made possible by emotions bordering on religious enthusiasm called forth by the Nazi promise of national revitalization. While anti-Semitism was widespread among them, few Germans would have been ready to give clear support to the systematic murder of all Jews. Their numbing took the form of selective attention to ostensible Nazi virtues and achievements and selective inattention to evidence reaching them about persecutions and killings. Nazi doctors remembered their enthusiasm for early Nazi accomplishments but, when asked about persecution of Jews and about *Kristallnacht* in particular, usually answered with words to the effect that "Well, I don't remember too much about that," or, "In my area not too much happened on *Kristallnacht*." Selective inattention was more difficult for them in relation to Nazi treatment of Jewish colleagues because the whole matter was much closer; they had more trouble maintaining their numbing, as revealed in uneasy protestations about their past friendly relationships with Jewish doctors and their helplessness before what took place. They would sometimes add, in a seemingly gentle fashion, that there had been a particularly great "Jewish problem" in German medicine (too many Jewish doctors), and that even if what the Nazis did was "too extreme," *some* solution was needed. That attitude contributed greatly to numbing by rendering cruelty abstract, by distancing the speaker from it, and by portraying anti-Semitism as "reasonable."

Like some of their Jewish compatriots, some ordinary Germans viewed Hitlerism as a temporary phenomenon which would pass. Many more Germans, attracted to Hitler, attributed cruel behavior to local excess: the higher-ups would get these matters under control, and almost certainly the Führer knew nothing about them and, once informed, would surely stop them. The latter attitude enabled Germans to maintain their deification of Hitler, their obedience to authority, and their sense of righteousness. It also reflected their sense of adapting to a "consensus view"—a "moderate" position of holding reservations about certain kinds of Nazi behavior without "going too far" in that criticism. And that "moderate" position readily lent itself in turn to the idea of working from within to make things better, and with the phenomenon of the "decent Nazi" we have discussed.

But once Germans had given themselves to the regime, as most did early, their numbing in respect to its violence came to require "a need not to know"—that is, intense forms of resistance to clearly mounting evidence. Bystanders' psychic numbing became an active process on behalf of certain forms of moral and psychological passivity.

Levels of Awareness

Nazi genocide was made possible, then, by the numbing of victimizers, victims, and bystanders: victimizers could kill without feeling, victims were killed without being able to mobilize energy toward flight or resistance, and bystanders could withdraw and fend off feelings of compassion. As killing becomes more technological, the whole process is more simply achieved: victimizers are distanced from their murder, victims have less time to mobilize potential resources as they are thrust quickly and efficiently into the killing technology, and bystanders have relatively less exposure to the killing.

Each group struggled with the problem of awareness. Perpetrators, as we have seen, had first to imagine the act and then order it or carry it out; there was an in-between stage during which they could progress from confusion to murderous action, from a *fragmentary awareness* of general intent to a *formed awareness* of systematic policy.

There was a parallel struggle among victims and potentially sympathetic bystanders. Roth's point about the difficult sequence from knowledge to comprehension to action (epigraph, page 237) can be understood as bystanders' struggles between fragmentary awareness (impressions, rumors, and evidence that, however strong, is still unacceptable) and formed awareness (sufficient integration of evidence of genocide to act upon it).

One meaning of awareness has to do with being cognizant of danger, being wary; while the other includes insight, understanding, and even illumination that takes one beyond appearances. The numbing of victims and bystanders, in response to Nazi brutality and deception, interfered with both dimensions of awareness. For significant or formed awareness to take shape and become operative, Jews and bystanders required an image of possibility or hope, an imagined action that could enable them to look beyond the overwhelming immediate threat. For all too many Jews and bystanders in Germany and throughout the world, no such awareness developed. Jews behaved as they did not because they were Jews with a long tradition of nonresistance but because they were human beings in a particular situation of extreme threat and duress. Bystanders behaved as they did because human beings tend to distance themselves from, to be slow to come to formed awareness of, brutal treatment of other human beings. But nothing in this view suggests that, given insight and motivation, we cannot alter these patterns.

The Victims of Nuclear War

> If we cannot imagine a world without nuclear weap-
> ons, then we have already lost. The weapons will
> have killed our imaginations.
> —EMMA ROTHSCHILD

It would be futile to predict just who would survive a nuclear
war. Everyone is a potential nuclear victim—which is what Elie
Wiesel meant when he wondered whether "the whole world has
turned Jewish." Unfortunately, much of American society also
qualifies as "Germans." The distinction between victimizer and
victim, then, breaks down for two reasons: because everyone on
earth shares potential victimization; and because enormous numbers of people, in one way or another, are in collusion with the
victimizers. If nuclear weapons are used, most of us could say
truthfully, with Primo Levi (see page 231), that we were not murderers; we would have less right to declare ourselves "guiltless
victims."

The simple point is that all of us are hostages to deterrence:
nuclearists and antinuclearists will be annihilated in common
"should deterrence fail." People turning the keys, or giving orders to turn the keys, along with ordinary people who had nothing to do with weapons or the keys to them, would be equally
annihilated. As would the Chinese, the Danes, the Nigerians, the
Iranians, the Israelis, the Germans, and everyone else. Not only
is it hard to distinguish particular victim groups as we can in the
case of the Nazis, but it becomes misleading to distinguish, as
Freeman Dyson does, between "warriors" and "victims." While
this distinction holds in connection with activities and mind-
sets—the "warriors" concerned with bomb making and with
strategy, the "victims" opposed to the weapons and fearful of
their consequences—any such distinction vanishes with use of
the weapons.

That is why we can say that deterrence policy threatens self-
genocide in the name of "national security." The self-genocide is

not intended but is inherent in the very structure of deterrence, whomever one may attempt to designate or exclude as enemies or victims. In that sense, we victimize ourselves no less than the Soviets, and they victimize themselves no less than us. Even for bystanders, the designation loses all significance at the moment of weapons use. One can employ that category (for people in various places who have little to do with either promoting or resisting the weapons) only until that moment.*

While Jews persecuted by the Nazis contributed to their own victimization only under extreme coercion and murderous threat, under nuclearism there is no such coercion or immediate threat: collusion is voluntary, usually enthusiastic. As a people, we not only are hostages to deterrence but willingly support our own and the world's hostage status. We elect and appoint established nuclearists who maintain these arrangements by formulating and instituting deterrence policies. Not only do we install and employ our own victimizers but they, too, are potential victims. We and they deny their potential victimization by means of elaborate provisions to maintain command and control, particularly to provide special planes and the deepest bunkers and shelters for political and military leaders. In so doing, there is the illusory insistence that they will not be among the victims. It is as if a privileged group on the Titanic had claimed the lifeboats but then found themselves adrift in a completely poisoned, life-destroying sea.

Americans in general, then, resemble both the Jews in being potential victims and the Nazi professionals in colluding with the victimizers. That is especially true of those American scientists and strategists who lend their professional skills to deterrence structures, but it is also true of the rest of us in ways less direct yet all too significant. Consider the enormous involvement in weapons-related work of American universities, corporations, and overall technical and communications resources. While the role of the active nuclearists most closely parallels that of the Nazi doctors, the rest of us, also without coercion, play a part in ways that parallel lesser German victimizers, German bystanders, and Jewish

---

*The Chernobyl nuclear accident of 1986, endangering not only Russians but Poles and Germans—in fact, people throughout Europe and beyond—made clear that victimization by nuclear technology cannot be contained.

victims. Certainly, much of American society provides a support system for nuclearism no less than German society did for Nazism. In our support of the entire structure, there is a parallel to the German everyman who lent support to Nazi policies as well as to German professionals who did the same. We are a free people and they were not. Yet in the name of nation—and especially national security—we, like them, lend our energies to a genocide-ready structure—indeed, to *permanent* readiness for genocide.

We Americans have, in fact, been victimized by nuclear weapons, even without their use, and by the related militarization of society, from the time of the Second World War. That victimization without use is all too obvious in the economic plight of many areas of society, as the military-industrial complex drains desperately needed money from urban programs (including those related to jobs, housing, and drugs), from support for the homeless and the underclass in general, from education at all levels, and from vital health programs.* To these we can add the developing evidence of increased incidence of various forms of cancer among people living close to nuclear-weapons facilities, and of the dangerous methods used for disposal of nuclear waste at some of these facilities. More generally, as several writers have shown, the weapons-dominated society, with its powerful impulse toward secrecy and extreme centralization, poses a threat to the democratic process itself.

Under these conditions, and with much of the technical job market dominated by the military, those who would seem to be bystanders are drawn into the realm of perpetrators. At the moment of the bomb's use, of course, there are no longer any bystanders; but long before that, the reach of the military and its institutions will have greatly reduced the numbers of those who could be called bystanders.

Soviet society also tends to absorb its people, especially those

---

*It is often pointed out that nuclear weapons are "cheap" in the sense of providing efficient levels of destructiveness for their cost and constituting only about 15 percent of the defense budget. But the larger truth is that the weapons, and the technological and bureaucratic systems they require, constitute the heart of the American and Soviet military machines; and decisions about their construction and deployment determine policies about remaining military requirements. Hence, progress in demilitarization of either American or Soviet society, or of other nuclear-weapons–possessing countries, undoubtedly depends upon nuclear arms control agreements.

with technical skills, into a situation of genocidal readiness. A major difference, of course, has been the absence there until Gorbachev's recent reforms of anything approaching popular democracy—or free expression—in relation to those issues. We, as Americans, have had greater opportunities to refuse genocidal arrangements, and have at times taken important steps toward doing so (see chapter 9), but have far from succeeded in breaking down the numbing that pervades broad circles of national support for nuclearism.

Nuclear Numbing

> We cannot afford further failures of imagination.
> —RABBI BERNARD RASKIS

Nuclear numbing is fed from many directions. The mind rejects, and rejects again and again, the merging of victims and victimizers. By maintaining that distinction, one can continue to cover over feelings of vulnerability and helplessness in the face of nuclear weapons and draw from the weapons instead a claim of strength. The idea that it is the *others* who would be killed is consistent with a deeply ingrained dichotomy between winners and losers, whether in war, sporting events, or life itself—each of these a contest, an ordeal, or a trial, in which one is to demonstrate one's superior skill and virtue in order to triumph over those with lesser attributes. Carried over to nuclear war, that principle could mean, as one former member of the Joint Chiefs of Staff put it, "If we attack 'em at all it's going to be a major attack. It's nonsense to think you'd shoot two or three missiles and get on the telephone and say, 'how'd you like them apples?' . . . Well, that's bullshit. Most of the people who come up with these ideas have never been in a war."

Negating the distinction between victims and victimizers undermines not only the idea of the contest but another principle especially valued in democracies: that it is justifiable to use military force against aggressors. The latter principle became particularly strong during the Second World War struggle against Nazi Germany and was carried over into postwar confrontations with the Soviet Union; it does not easily give way to the morally unsatisfying idea that good and bad people (or nations)—aggressors and defenders against aggression—perish alike in nuclear holocaust. Nor is it easy for a people who pride themselves on their freedoms to recognize that a democratic nation with nuclear weapons is as capable of genocide as anyone else. Recognition of the weapons as evil has been readily fended off by the benign imagery of deterrence—of holding back an aggressor and preventing war. The nation must keep expanding the stockpiles, then, partly because of the convolutions of the deterrence argument: *we* need these additional warheads to deter those other ones *they* are now building. But there is an additional psychological factor: namely, if we don't keep building the weapons, we risk the possibility of viewing both them as evil and ourselves as having been long associated with that evil. We and the Soviets need to keep building nuclear weapons in order to maintain our and their faith in nuclear weapons. And since that expansion of deterrence means more planning for war fighting, it echoes the principle, alluded to earlier in connection with the Nazis, that atrocity begets atrocity—even if the atrocity is, so far, potential.

In its very consensus about the efficacy of nuclear weapons, American society contributes to nuclear numbing. Nuclearists do not collude with an evil regime (as did Nazi doctors) or with an evil enemy (as did some *Judenrat* leaders, under extreme duress). Rather, they collude with an evil *project,* a genocidal system, maintained within a democracy. That collusion has, as we have seen, generally been achieved with an aura of decency and professional focus—as opposed to the more intensely ideological Nazi regime within which German doctors and scientists were integrated. We recall, for example, the German doctor who first opposed dangerous experiments on human subjects but could be persuaded by the leading Nazi medical official that they were necessary for the country and its war effort—to the point of later becoming himself implicated in such experiments. He was at that point adhering to what was a consensus position in Nazi Germany. Even more chilling was the consensus Hitler achieved with the SS *Einsatzgruppen* leaders, on the one hand, and the regular German army, on the other, permitting the former to do the dirty work of systematically murdering Jews without either objection or direct participation on the part of the latter.

In respect to nuclear weapons, the original Los Alamos experience provided a heroic model that scientists later working on the hydrogen bomb could embrace. Although they have much greater freedom of choice than did Nazi doctors, and many more attractive options, they have been strongly affected by the extent to which the building and stockpiling of lethal nuclear weaponry has become normalized in American society (see chapter 1). While building the weapons, they have been able to occupy American political middle ground, a consensus position that opposes extreme nuclearism while favoring "prudent" deterrence. In nuclear America or in the nuclear Soviet Union, the consensus position means that each of us colludes in the construction and possible deployment of genocidal instruments.

Nuclear numbing is a relatively mild form of dissociation (people can remain functional and quite reactive in other areas) but is of enormous collective historical and social significance. Its consequence is simply the widespread inability to imagine nuclear genocide. Rabbi Raskis had nuclear numbing in mind when he referred to the "terribly and painfully costly" Jewish "failure to imagine [Nazi] genocide." Prospective nuclear victims—all of us—share with the Nazis' victims both a psychological resistance to taking in the most dreadful of images and the absence in past experience of anything approaching the scope of such annihilation. That event, because of the dimensions of its ahuman technology, is even more difficult for its potential victims to imagine. For all of us it remains remote.

In addition, nuclear threat has a certain persistence and unresolvability. No single critical moment determines whether we succeed or fail in our efforts to avert nuclear holocaust. Crises come and go, somehow we get through them, but the threat continues. The threat has, moreover, been around for nearly half a century, so that most people on the earth have never known a world not menaced by these instruments of annihilation. As with the Jews persecuted by the Nazis, the numbing is immediately adaptive (one cannot afford psychologically to feel much more than one does) but ultimately profoundly maladaptive (one is divested of the imaginative capacity required to understand the threat and act upon it). Just as Jews could numb themselves to Nazi intent right up to the moment of the gas chambers, so are we capable of doing the same right up to the moment of nuclear holocaust. Although periodically interrupted by ebbs and flows of feeling, that kind of numbing is diffused throughout the American and world population.

As compared, then, to the sense on the part of some Germans that the Nazi era would soon blow over, nuclear numbing applies to an unending world process. Numbing can take the form of assuming that process to be somehow "under control," because "it's in the hands of experts," because "people up there" (leaders and decision makers) are taking care of things, or because nobody would be "that crazy"—no "sane person" would ever set them off. Political and military leaders, reluctant to permit their people to experience the truth of nuclear vulnerability, reinforce those assumptions. By stressing "strength" and "security," leaders enhance everyone's numbing, including their own.

Leaders tend to resist radical shifts in consciousness. Just as generals tend to function according to the requirements of the previous war rather than of the one they are in, so do world leaders draw from the past lessons about "preparation" and "defense" that are likely to be the wrong ones. Leaders are expected to provide guidance in a nuclear world for which they have little appropriate preparation. Rather than confront the full danger, they tend to deny the threat and encourage all other prospective victims to do the same. The terrible truth is that most leaders, at least within the superpowers, have been inseparable from the genocidal mentality; indeed—perhaps until recently—they have been at its very heart.

Leaders also play a role in maintaining a politics of selective memory in regard to genocide. In the case of the United States, that may mean ignoring Hiroshima or else, on that event's yearly commemoration, 6 August, employing the occasion to defend our use of the weapon. That selective memory also tends to exclude, or in various ways mute, earlier American genocidal behavior in relation to black slavery and to the treatment of Native Americans. Relevant here also is our inadequate response to Nazi genocidal behavior—during the Nazi era, in refusing to admit significant numbers of Jews; and after the Second World War, in harboring certain prominent contributors to Nazi killing in order to enlist them for either scientific work or anticommunist activities.

Principles developed at the Nuremberg trials concerning crimes of war and "crimes against humanity" have enormous importance in terms of establishing a body of international legal thought concerning mass killing. But that tribunal, in its failure to examine Allied culpability for Hiroshima and Nagasaki and previous strategic bombing, can never fully escape the label of "victor's justice." The politics of selective memory extends to America's official reluctance to condemn *as* genocide the Turkish slaughter of Armenians in 1915 because of our present military alliance with Turkey. All of this matters because failure to confront historical examples of genocidal killing, committed by one's own country or by another, contributes to contemporary nuclear numbing—to the inability to acknowledge the nuclear threat to our species and to mobilize the new ethical requirements for confronting that threat.

Nuclear numbing is easily accomplished by narrowing one's psychological field or vantage point. One can, for instance, focus strongly on defense economy, on "More bang for the buck" as the bomb-centered slogan of the 1950s had it. Or one can remember oneself as an American soldier during the Second World War who, having already seen much bloody combat, was scheduled to take part in what promised to be the still more bloody invasion of Japan. Spared that fate, one could understandably feel, "Thank God for the atomic bomb!" The numbing would be present not in the original sentiment but in the subsequent inability to subsume that sentiment to a broader psychological and ethical perspective. Among the economically privileged, nuclear numbing has been enhanced by a preoccupation with maintaining one's living standard and with consumerism in general. And numbing in relation to the desperate situation of the American underclass and the homeless has promoted a general psychological isolation from actual or potential human suffering which in turn reinforces nuclear numbing. In keeping with Elie Wiesel's comment that the great human problem is that of indifference, we may say that ours is an age not of anxiety but of numbing.

Nuclear numbing is enhanced by confusions about intent. Unlike the Nazi situation, we have no clear ideology of nuclear victimization. Though we may sometimes seem to approach one in labeling the Soviets as the "evil empire," even then only at the ideological fringes do Americans view the Soviets (or they us) with the clear victimizing imagery characteristic of the Nazis in respect to Jews. Nuclear genocidal impulses (war-fighting plans) exist but are more hidden, muted by euphemisms having to do with the "failure" of deterrence. This quality of intent divested of intent has a certain parallel, limited but telling, to Nazi situations in which killing became psychologically divested of killing. Moreover, precisely that numbed blurring of intent is crucial to our moral sense of ourselves.

Enclosed in a circle of numbing (see pages 217, 226–27)—or in a series of concentric circles—are those most closely involved with the bomb (Strategic Air Command officers and men, submarine crews, Defense Department officials, strategists, and weapons designers) at the center; a variety of planners, university research divisions, and corporations involved in manufacturing and synchronizing key nuclear elements between the center and the periphery; and the rest of the American population at the periphery. Numbing emanates from the center and proceeds outward, then back and forth between and among the three concentric circles: the behavior and status of weapons designers and strategists enhances the numbing of ordinary people, the activities of universities and nuclear corporations enhance the numbing both of nuclear strategists and ordinary people, and the numbing of ordinary people contributes to the numbing of military guardians of the bomb and of university nuclear researchers.

The principles of nuclear normality (discussed in chapter 2)—the equation of nuclearism with proper psychological and moral adjustment—contribute greatly to maintaining this equilibrium. Nuclear normality is constantly questioned—as, for instance, by the nuclear-freeze movement—but seems only to recede temporarily and then return in new guise. For instance, following the modest but important INF treaty of 1987 (see page 36), the elaborate official restatement and extension of ostensibly "flexible" uses of nuclear and conventional weaponry under the concept of "discriminate deterrence" (see chapter 7) flew in the face of virtually every concept of non-use of nuclear weapons so painfully developed over the last few decades. Nuclear normality keeps coming back to dominate prospective victims' discourse because we as a society and especially our leaders—in spite of any beginning change in consciousness—have simply not abandoned the ideology of nuclearism. The collective imagination is blunted by the technology of weapons-centered deterrence rather than enlarged by the human truths of Hiroshima. In "living with nuclear weapons," we turn out to have them too much with us: we hold on to them, viewing them through the "thick glass" of nuclear numbing.

Deep Shelters—Deep Illusions

> We too are so dazzled by power and prestige as to forget our essential fragility. Willingly or not we come to terms with power, forgetting that we are all in the ghetto, that the ghetto is walled in, that outside the ghetto reign the lords of death, and that close by the train is waiting.
>
> —PRIMO LEVI

Among the illusions put forward by potential nuclear victimizers is the expectation that they themselves cannot be counted among the victims. As late as the 1980s, we were still being told that, since "ants eventually build another ant hill," it follows that "with enough shovels" everybody will be able to dig their way out of the ruins. From the standpoint of the present discussion, the advocacy of civil defense is an attempt to retain the separateness of victims and victimizers. It is presented in terms of "preparedness," its message that individuals and nations who are prepared (who make their evacuation plans and build their shelters) will survive, and those who are not will die. It is thus a vision of the prepared as a kind of "elect" chosen for salvation. In that way, it is suggested, one ceases to be a victim. But the truth is that the active promotion of civil defense, which has always met with much skepticism, is a desperate embrace of an illusory prenuclear world in which moral and military categories seemed clear and one could call forth one's most powerful weapons on behalf of virtue without being consumed by them together with one's enemies.

The deepest civil defense bunkers—those allocated to leaders—encourage the deepest illusion. These, the ultimate hubris of élite victims, are echoed by Primo Levi's account of the tragedy of Chaim Rumkowski, the head of the *Judenrat* of the Lodz ghetto. Rumkowski, becoming drunk with power, formed a Jewish police force to protect himself and gave demagogic speeches in the manner of Hitler or Mussolini; when the ghetto was liquidated and he, too, was to be deported to Auschwitz, he succeeded in gaining the right to go to his death in a private car for himself and his family. Where Rumkowski's hubris emerged under a situation of extreme persecution, nuclearists voluntarily and willfully embrace the uniquely lethal weapon, which persecutes us all, while fostering the illusion that they themselves thereby remain immune. They behave, that is, as if they were not part of the human species and did not share with us what Levi called "our essential fragility."

At the end of one of his essays, Levi attempts to convey the difficulty of anticipating the future, and speaks of "willed incredulity, mental blocks, generally exchanged with self-catalyzing consolatory truths." It is then that he asks, "How securely do we live, we men of the century's and the millennium's end?" and, "Why aren't we leaving our country? Why aren't we fleeing 'before'?" In the case of Nazi threat, the extreme persecution interfered greatly, at every stage, with the capacity of victims for awareness. In the nuclear case, we have much greater possibilities for moving from fragmentary to formed awareness, to knowledge that becomes integrated, however painfully, into the self. But that step requires that we accept the merging of victims and victimizers in nuclear holocaust; that we shift from the numbed stance, justifying a good nation stockpiling nuclear weapons to deter bad aggressors, to a recognition of the common human interest in preserving our species.

Chapter 9

A Species Mentality

I know the enemy's brother.
—W. S. MERWIN

THE GENOCIDAL mentality is neither biologically ordained nor intractable. It is part of a malignant historical direction that extends into general realms of technology, ultimate power, and, finally, illusion. But there are other ways of thinking and feeling, already well under way, that reject this "dangerous attachment" to the world. They propel us, in fits and starts, toward a change in consciousness, toward a new narrative.

What we suggest here is not a precise formula or an exact policy program. Yet neither is it a superficial shift in a few attitudes. At issue is an expansion of collective awareness, an altered sense of self, that embraces our reality as members of a single species and thereby opens up new psychological, ethical, and political terrain. It is, in a sense, a "moral equivalent" to the genocidal mentality: an alternative that serves similar psychological needs in ways that are life enhancing.

Reversing the Genocidal Mentality

> Don't make any more bombs. Don't think of them
> as anything but . . . tools of the devil. They repre-
> sent nothing but danger, not one tiny bit of secu-
> rity.
>
> —THEODORE TAYLOR

While working on this book, we, as individuals, have traveled
widely—in the United States, Western and Eastern Europe, Asia,
and the Middle East—and have encountered a worldwide hunger
for species consciousness. Whatever the more narrow and destructive tendencies around them, significant minorities articulate a
form of humanity suggested by the Vietnamese Buddhist monk-
poet who asks, "Please call me by my true names so that . . . the
door of my heart be left open."

In that spirit, we can suggest at least the seeds of a moral antithe-
sis to each of the elements of the genocidal mentality. To begin
with, our universal entrapment in a world genocidal system, and
the radical absurdity of that system and of the "nuclear normality"
sustaining it, have been recognized early and sharply criticized by
certain individuals and groups. Indeed, making public the dangers
and absurdity of nuclear normality was at the intellectual heart of
the early scientists' movement, the SANE-Freeze movement, the
physicians' movement, and the statements on the weaponry by the
American Catholic bishops, the American Methodist leaders, and
other religious groups.

Similarly, concerning nuclearism as a "cure" for nuclear fear,
there has been rapidly expanding recognition that "possessing
such power is, more than a little, to be possessed in turn." That
"possession" is seen to be a form of nuclearism, which is itself
unraveling as an idea system with a claim to moral necessity. The
weapons have not, after all, "killed our imagination," as the writer
Emma Rothschild feared. From within science and most other
professions, there are important moral and intellectual critiques of
nuclearism and its social reach. There is awareness of the principle
expressed by a German physician after reflecting on the activities

and choices of his brother, originally considered a good man, as chief Nazi camp doctor in Auschwitz: "The only thing to do in a situation like this is to say, 'No, I won't do it!'" Saying no to professional involvement in genocide is the beginning of saying yes to the requirements of the human species.

Halting society's momentum toward genocide means reclaiming human agency and reasserting control over our destructive technologies and their related bureaucracies. Radical reductions in weaponry will have to be accompanied by clear-cut efforts to halt "technological drift" with its unintended and not-quite-unintended consequences. We are capable of resisting the powerful temptation to plunge ahead merely because a weapons system is "technically sweet." All of these constructive alternatives depend upon a deepening awareness of the experiences of human beings in Hiroshima and Nagasaki to serve as a basis for nuclear truth rather than the disembodied technical exercises of scenarios and war games.

At the psychological and material heart of the transformation in consciousness we are suggesting is the replacement of dissociatied deterrence with an integrated mind-set and a policy of national defense that is neither genocidal nor threatening. This reversal of mind-set and policy would be based on precisely those human truths blocked out by existing patterns of numbing, disavowal, and doubling. While these dissociative tendencies can hardly be eliminated entirely, their collective expression in weapons policies can be radically diminished. This goal requires the rejection of the entire *deterrence system* because that system is inherently genocidal. To reject the genocidal system requires breaking out of its closed reasoning and recognizing that destroying the world in response to a perceived attack is neither politically nor morally acceptable. Thus, we must look critically at our ways of symbolizing through "high-order abstraction that remains too severely or too long detached from its existential content." For, indeed, it is our extraordinary capacity to symbolize, and symbolize wildly, that renders the human mind special both in its gifts and in its vulnerabilities. We are all too capable of symbolizing the world-destroying retaliation of deterrence as necessary to peacekeeping, but we are also capable of correcting ourselves when our symbolizing process has gone awry. That correction is what George Kennan had in mind when he spoke of arms competition "taking possession of men's imagination and behavior, becoming a force in its own right, detaching itself from the political differences that initially inspired it." But, in reconnecting means and ends, we are also reconnecting the elements of the self that have become dissociated from one another in adhering to this deadly nuclear symbolization. While we shall have more to say about how much deterrence must or should be retained, here we wish to suggest the kind of transformation of mind-set, now partially under way, that is necessary if people are to face the full significance of the phrase "should deterrence fail" and get rid of a policy whose consequence is annihilation.

The final reversal is a movement toward formed awareness of the actuality of nuclear threat by its prospective victims—that is, everyone on earth. Only by accepting the difficult truth that, in a nuclear attack, there would be complete merging of perpetrator and victim—of generals and presidents and premiers in deep shelters and ordinary people everywhere—can we create the responsibility and cooperation necessary to preserve the world.

Species Consciousness and Species Self

> I helped because a human being ought to help another.
>
> —HELA HORSKA

These moves away from the genocidal mentality replace it with a species mentality: that is, full consciousness of ourselves as members of the human species, a species now under threat of extinction. Indeed, that very threat may evoke the larger possibilities of the species self.

Species consciousness contributes to a sense of self that identifies with the entire human species. But the self cannot live, so to speak, on the human species alone. Its traditional forms of immediate identification—other people, family, work, play, religion, ethnic group, and nation—give substance to the species identification and are necessary to it. As in many things, only by holding to the particular can one have access to the universal—as George Kateb (paraphrasing Nietzsche) means when he speaks of becoming "attached to the particulars in one's life in a new way, without narrowness, exclusiveness, and obsession, in order to make room for a nonparticularist attachment to existence as such." For "existence as such" is inseparable from survival of the human species.

At issue is a modest yet far-reaching realignment of elements of the self. Whatever the capacity of an individual self for concern, caring, loyalty, and even love can now be extended in some degree to the human species as a whole—though one need in no way cease being concerned, about caring for, loyal to, or loving any smaller unit of human beings or any single human being. However flawed and partial, the species self is likely to advocate moral and political policies attuned not to only a single group or nation but to all humankind. Only by so doing can we take in and experience larger human realities of threat and suffering and resist numbing and brutalization. We can then speak of a continuous mutual strengthening of species consciousness and species self on the one hand, and confrontation of genocide and genocidal threat on the other.

In telling himself, "Somebody has to care for the planet!" Richard Garwin was expressing his shift from the nation-based competitiveness and weapons-based illusions of the arms race to a combination of species consciousness and individual humanity. The same combination is present in the actions and words of a Polish woman, Hela Horska, who saved many Jews from being murdered by the Nazis and cared for them warmly at great personal risk: "It did not matter who it was. If someone needed help I had to give it. . . . I believed that the world became such a horrible place and someone had to counteract the cruelties of the world." This is the kind of commitment Erikson had in mind when he spoke of "a truly wider identity [which] . . . includes . . . the capacity for empathic identification . . . especially with people at first perceived as incomprehensively 'other'—but also the willingness to understand the otherness as well as the all-too-familiar in ourselves."

Strong antagonism to species consciousness is likely to result from fear—fear of altering a world one has come to know, fear of change in general, or fear of being weakened if one gives up reliance on nuclear weapons. This "anti-species backlash" seems to occur whenever there is any strong possibility of movement toward species consciousness and the species self. In 1989, for example, Iran's Ayatollah Khomeini called for the death of Salman Rushdie not only in response to the latter's novel *Satanic Verses,* and its alleged insult to sacred Islamic religious concepts, but also because Khomeini wanted to counter tendencies in his own country away from fundamentalism and in the direction of adaptation to the rest of the world—that is, mildly in the direction of species consciousness.

The philosopher Gunther Anders likens contemporary man to "an inverted Faust: whereas Faust had infinite anticipations and boundless feelings, and suffered because his finite knowledge and power were unequal to these feelings, we know more and produce greater things than we can imagine or feel." Anders refers to our vast gap between knowledge and feeling; the species self enables us to become aware of the gap, narrow it somewhat, and render it less dangerous. In doing that we begin the alteration in collective mentality that Albert Einstein was calling for in his famous observation that "the splitting of the atom has changed everything, save our ways of thinking."

The Shift in Symbolic Immortality

> To be attached to existence is to want human and
> natural existence on earth to go on forever.
> —GEORGE KATEB

The species self involves a psychological rearrangement concerning larger human connectedness. One moves not from one mode of symbolic immortality to another—say, from the biological to the creative mode, or from the religious to the natural mode—but, rather, *within* the biological, or biosocial, mode. In addition to the feeling that "I live on in my children and their children, in my people, in my nation," one now has the sense that "I live on in humankind." One feels oneself a link not only in these traditionally circumscribed chains but in the all-inclusive and endless human chain.

The other modes of symbolic immortality are also affected by the species principle. For instance, the species self of a religious believer requires that the spiritual principles one embraces remain, beyond one's death, illuminating to human beings in general as opposed to belligerently promoting one group over another. And the same universalizing principle applies to lasting works, identification with eternal nature, or even one's relationship to high states or experiences of transcendence.

Consider the striking phenomenon of very old people joining actively in the antinuclear movement. One might wonder at their doing so, since they appear to have so little time left in their lives to be concerned about. But in actuality, as they approach death, older people can be deeply concerned about what will remain of their fundamental human connections: Will their family, people, tribe, nation—and now species—continue to thrive? Will something of their works or influence survive in a human society sufficiently intact to absorb and make use of them? Older people raise these questions about modes of symbolic immortality, at whatever level of consciousness, because they feel the meaning of their entire lives to be at issue. They may therefore have more at stake psychologically than anyone else in keeping the species going.

The emergence of the species self is a collective historical process. As such, it must be uneven; it can be, like species awareness, fragmentary. But with greater integration of self and world and the achievement of formed awareness, we can speak of a process of social evolution, of "an ascent towards consciousness." There seems to be a strange historical parallel here between the extreme, unfeeling intellectual abstraction producing the threat of extinction on the one hand, and the species-embracing sense of self in response to that threat on the other. Both developments emerge from eighteenth-century Enlightenment struggles with science: the first, from the exclusion of human beings from the scientific landscape; the second, from the exhilarating science-based Enlightenment motto "Dare to know!" In living up to that motto, the species self seeks to break out of what Anders has called the "freezing point of human freedom" created by the threat of extinction.

But rather than view ourselves, as he does, as becoming "a new species," we do better to understand our situation as a struggle for a new relationship to our present species.

That new psychological and moral relationship allows us to focus on the well-being of all of humankind by means of the species ethics and politics mentioned earlier, and of species economics as well. A species model could enable us to transform our preoccupations from nuclear weapons to planetary preservation—a transformation that certain nuclear physicists have made individually but that has yet to be realized in broad policy terms. Again the refrain, "somebody has to care for the planet." That refrain, as we know, required the confronting of atrocity, the principle of looking into the abyss in order to see beyond it.

Important here is the pattern of "retirement syndrome" (or "retirement wisdom") on the part of a number of American political and military leaders: having long actively espoused nuclearism, at the moment of retirement they have felt impelled to condemn it and expose its dangers. Dwight Eisenhower's famous warning of the dangers of the military-industrial complex, which his administration had done so much to build up, was a retirement speech. With a deepening general critique of nuclearism, we may hope that this wisdom—or shift to a species mentality—can be expressed by leaders long before their retirement.

The shift in symbolic immortality, then, involves confrontation with absurd collective death and, inevitably, with questions of one's own individual death. Indeed, one reclaims one's own individual death from the grotesqueness and absurdity of collective nuclear destruction. At the same time, one affirms one's larger human connectedness (or symbolic immortality) as bound up with the continuity of the human species, and lives out the ideology of the species self.

Traditions of Species Consciousness

> I refuse to accept the cynical notion that nation
> after nation must spiral down a militaristic stairway
> into the hell of nuclear destruction. I believe that
> unarmed truth and unconditional love will have the
> final word in reality.
>
> —MARTIN LUTHER KING

Species consciousness has been advocated over the centuries by spiritual traditions of moral and intellectual power. In their humane, nonviolent struggles, Mohandas Gandhi and Martin Luther King, and the movements they inspired, drew heavily upon Christian tradition, and Gandhi upon Hindu and Muslim tradition as well. But we can also include such modern Jewish figures as Martin Buber and Abraham Joshua Heschel. Indeed, all of the world's great religions contain principles of universalism or species consciousness, however these have been violated by religiously inspired conflicts, wars, and massacres. The evolution of monotheism in Jewish tradition, for instance, suggests the principle of one God for all people. (It has been argued that monotheism has in some ways divided people by its stress on the exclusiveness of the true God, while polytheism tends to be more open and in some ways more universal; but one can associate polytheism with universalism only after monotheism has made its appearance.) That principle was revitalized in Christianity and given vivid expression in the teachings of Jesus. In the Sermon on the Mount ("Blessed are the poor in spirit: for their's is the kingdom of heaven. Blessed are they that mourn: for they shall be comforted. Blessed are the meek: for they shall inherit the earth"), Jesus meant *all* the poor in spirit, *all* who mourn, and *all* the meek—and "the earth" is our planet.

While this species principle has often been overwhelmed by human cruelties and bitter sectarian struggles, it has been kept alive by those few who, against the grain of their times, chose to take it seriously. Now our technology of both extinction and communication makes it available to massive numbers of people everywhere.

We also have available the great modern secular syntheses that are species oriented, notably those of Marx and Freud. Freud laid out a series of psychological concepts concerning instinct and defense, sexuality and childhood, and dreams and unconscious motivation, to be applied to all human beings. In the best of his sweeping cultural studies of his later years, *Civilization and Its Discontents,* Freud declared, "The fateful question for the human species seems to me to be whether and to what extent their cultural development will succeed in mastering the disturbance of their communal life by the human instinct of aggression and self-destruction." In a parallel way, Marx meant his principles of economic determinism, dialectical materialism, class struggle, and alienation to apply to all human beings on this earth. He even developed the concept of man as a "species-being," one who "relates to himself as to a universal and therefore free being," and "to the species as to himself and to himself as to the species." Marx and Freud, though frequently antithetical in their politics and assumptions about human behavior, both saw themselves as exposing contradiction and hypocrisy in the service of overall human liberation. That universalism survives the limitations and overgeneralizations of both great visions as well as the rigidities and distortions of their followers. Indeed, both men were deeply influenced by the universalistic claims of the modern scientific tradition to which they attached themselves, and by the equally universalistic claims of the Judeo-Christian tradition of which they were radically critical.

The excesses associated with the Second World War—the Nazi death camps and the atomic bombings of Hiroshima and Nagasaki—brought about a new wave of species consciousness. The trials at Nuremberg were an attempt to establish universalistic principles for such things as "crimes against humanity." While the judgments inevitably took on aspects of victors' justice—from which the bombings of Hiroshima and Nagasaki were exempt—they retain great importance for us at least in the ideal they sought to represent. Robert H. Jackson, the chief U.S. prosecutor at Nuremberg, invoked in his opening statement the Charter of the United Nations as the basis for the trial and declared, "While this law is first applied against German aggressors, the law includes, and if it is to serve a useful purpose it must condemn, aggressions by any other nations, including those who sit here now in judgment." And precisely that idea—the principle of "crimes against humanity"—has been raised by thoughtful legal groups in relation to the genocidal system created by the mere stockpiling and deployment of nuclear weapons.

Yet it was Hiroshima and Nagasaki that were mainly responsible for the intense, collective feeling of "One World or None" so widely expressed in the United States immediately after the Second World War. That phrase was the title of a slim paperback volume published by the Federation of American Scientists in March 1946, which, remarkably, became a best seller. In it the physicist Philip Morrison, after a vivid description of a hypothetical atomic-bomb attack on New York City, declared, "If we do not learn to live together so that science will be our help and not our hurt, . . . the cities of men on earth will perish." Arthur Compton similarly posited that the only alternative to total destruction is "adjusting the pattern of our society on a world basis." And Leo Szilard advocated a long-term goal of world government and shorter-term arrangements for inspection and exchange of scientists and their families. Although these scientists' comments reflect the sudden rush of species consciousness at the time, there was much confusion about what to do with that consciousness, confusion probably aggravated rather than relieved by the tendency to insist on world government as the only solution. Since then, those early impulses toward species consciousness have been developed in connection with principles of "global citizenship," "planetary identity," and "the citizen pilgrim," in the research and writings of Saul Mendlovitz and Richard Falk in association with the World Policy Institute.

There have also been what may be called perverse species quests: movements that claim or possess a species vision but in actuality take on totalistic qualities that sharply—and sometimes destructively—divide the world into absolute versions of good (their own ideological camp) and evil (their designated enemies, in some cases everyone but themselves). Included here are political and religious fundamentalist movements, among them the Nazis. As much as one may resist the idea, the Nazis had their species vision—the claim that, in strengthening and rendering healthy the Nordic race, the only culture-creating race, and annihilating the "Jewish race," the only culture-destroying race, they were purifying the world and performing a great service to humankind. Since that service *required* destroying the Jews and other groups, their species claim was corrupt from the beginning. The same may be said of world communism, at least from the time of its Leninist direction. Originally conceived as a means of liberating all of humankind from economic and social chains, communism, too, took totalistic directions and became increasingly preoccupied with designated enemies to the point of killing more people than the Nazis did. The Nazi movement was fundamentalist from the start, claiming to possess, and then literalizing, sacred truths from the German historical and racial past. Communism, by no means fundamentalist in its origins, became so all too readily, especially under Stalin in the Soviet Union and under Mao in China. Herculean efforts can be required to shake off that fundamentalist legacy, as in the case of Gorbachev's reform movement in the Soviet union.

Fundamentalism in general seems to require what Erik Erikson has called "pseudospeciation"—the viewing of those outside one's cultural or ideological orbit, and especially of one's designated enemies, as members of a different species, as other than human. They are deprived of human traits, or "dehumanized"; the Nazis could, from that standpoint, kill Jews without feeling they were killing human beings. Indeed, those designated enemies are likely to be chosen from among groups tending toward a species orientation, since fundamentalists view that orientation as a profound threat. The perceived "cosmopolitan" nature of Jews, for instance, was a factor in their genocidal persecution by the Nazis, as it has been in their persecution by the Soviets as well. The act of genocide itself tends to be associated with a fundamentalist bent toward eliminating either species consciousness or at least the kind of openness that could lead to it.

Common Security

Yet, as we have mentioned, at this time a call to the species self is not going unheard—as has been acknowledged in recent international awards—the Nobel Peace prizes, for instance, to the U.N.

Peacekeeping Forces, Amnesty International, the International Physicians for the Prevention of Nuclear War, Elie Wiesel, Desmond Tutu, and Mother Teresa, all are strongly identified with universalistic principles. Of comparable importance have been the Right Livelihood awards given at the same time and place to lesser known figures—in 1987 to Hans-Peter Dürr, director of the Heisenberg Institute of Physics in Munich "for his profound critique of SDI and work to convert high-technology to peaceful uses." More and more people throughout the world recognize that their individual and national future depend upon greater species awareness: they recognize their shared fate.

The trend toward species awareness expresses itself in the advocacy of what is called "common security." To act on the idea that the United States is not secure unless the Soviet Union is—indeed, unless all other countries of the world are—is a form of species politics that in no way requires world government. This principle of common security has been put forward by world leaders and commentators on nuclear threat, as well as by various religious groups offering moral comment on our nuclear entrapment. Consider, for instance, the following two statements—the first by Cyrus Vance, secretary of state under President Jimmy Carter; and the second by Mikail Gorbachev, the leader of the Soviet Union:

> There is one overriding truth in this nuclear age: No nation can achieve true security by itself. To guarantee our own security, we must face these realities and work together with other nations to achieve common security. For security, in the nuclear age means common security.

> The nations of the world today resemble a pack of mountaineers tied together by climbing rope. They can either climb on together to the mountain peak or fall together into an abyss. This new political outlook calls for the recognition of one simple axiom: security is indivisible. It is either equal security for all, or none at all.

Enormously important in this context is Ronald Reagan's reversal from the doctrine during his early presidency of fighting and winning nuclear wars, to a position at the end of that presidency that there can be no winners at all in a nuclear war. In the United States, the Soviet Union, and other countries in various parts of the world, people have advocated plans to diminish nuclear and non-nuclear danger, using such terms as "nonoffensive defense," "nonprovocative defense," "defensive defense," "reasonable sufficiency," "mutual defensive superiority," and "defense without aggression." However varied in content, these plans all transcend narrow interests in favor of species concerns. That same mentality entered strongly into the Intermediate Nuclear Force agreement of 1987, however limited the agreement was in what it covered, and whatever the additional motivations, political and economic, that influenced Reagan and Gorbachev.

The crux of a species-oriented policy lies in ending the confrontation of rival genocidal systems we call deterrence, and replacing it with arrangements conducive to genuine security and peace. Michael MccGwire—anticipating that the "final defence of the deterrent dogmatist is to ask, 'What would you put in its place?' "—declares, "The short answer is, 'Nothing.' " His point is that "the immediate objective is to reduce the salience of deterrence dogma in the formulation of policy," so that it can be replaced by negotiation and diplomacy "enriched by a more subtle understanding of the classic concepts of deterrence and reassurance, and by a deeper awareness of human frailty under stress in crises." MccGwire speaks from species awareness when he adds, "We should recognize that it is world war, however it starts, not Soviet aggression, that poses the greatest threat to all our people," and should therefore "pay less attention to developing the military means to deter the onset of war, and concentrate more on developing the political means of averting those situations that make war more likely." MccGwire also points out that "mutual deterrence is an objective fact," and that we need to reduce radically the existing number of nuclear weapons and "block . . . new avenues for arms racing, rather than seek . . . to shape the arsenals to deter, or, if necessary, control nuclear war."

There are many plans for radical nuclear-arms reduction, and for including conventional arms reduction as well: the all-important principle here is the well-being of all members of the human species in formulating and carrying out such policies. Holding to that principle means mutual rejection of any possibility of nuclear "exchange" as a means of dealing with American-Soviet—or any other international—conflict. Arrangements could enable parties to negotiate aggressively, to cajole or compete with one another, and at times to resort to economic pressures, but never to threaten—or have in place the means to threaten—the human species with nuclear extinction. We would have to put aside the present preoccupation with maintaining the biggest nuclear stockpile and, together with all other countries, focus on the means by which danger to all people might be averted. Within this common project, there exists a measure of alliance among all countries. And from that minimal alliance, built as it is on a sense of shared fate, stronger forms of cooperation can develop. The principle is that "cooperation breeds cooperation," through "more and better information about one another's capabilities and intentions," as well as "realistic empathy" in the form of appreciating the legitimacy of each other's interests. It is then possible for both parties to redefine both their interests and their policies.

Indeed, precisely that kind of cooperation is actively under way in response to the Gorbachev initiative of the late 1980s. And it includes mutual efforts to explore ways of avoiding nuclear war and of ending the arms race. These efforts include genuine intellectual collaboration, joint satellite television programs on the arms race, and discussions by various professional groups at a level that can be called "species-oriented." For the first time in decades, serious talk is coming from both sides about ending the cold war. Species awareness, that is, allows us to question the nuclearism and the technological mysticism that have dominated American-Soviet relations since the Second World War.

Species Advocacy in the Professions

> We . . . need to reorient our sense of citizenship toward the position that it is disloyal for citizens to abet the crimes of their government.
> —RICHARD FALK

> Profess not the knowledge . . . that thou hast not.
> —ECCLESIASTICUS

A gifted poet, who has read his works and met his counterparts in many countries, once said, "All poets the world over are brothers and sisters." He was saying that people with certain common concerns or struggles can come together and identify strongly—as members of a particular group within the broader human species—in ways that transcend governments and their repressive or genocidal projects. To be a professional—as to be a citizen—is, in the broadest definition and experience, to be a species advocate.

That requires us to recover the ethical core in each profession—for instance, medicine as healing, law as justice, and science and scholarship as quest for knowledge—so readily covered over by the inflated claims and narrowly technical focus of professional*ism*. To be true to that universalistic principle requires an ethical focus on the *projects* to which professionals attach themselves. Neither the professions themselves nor society at large can permit the "reckless, even fatal delegation of power" by which "we leave the issue of nuclear arms, their control and their consequences, to the men who make horror their everyday occupation." We are ready for a new focus on the neglected species principle at the heart of each profession, a principle that does not permit one, as a member of any profession, to (in Feynman's phrase) "just stop thinking."

One may start with science and the sciences. More than any other enterprise, science has an international language and always proceeds from the principle that its method of approach and criteria for evaluation apply equally in all cultures. Victor Weisskopf, long an articulate antinuclear spokesman from the scientific community, makes the ironic point that there was something to learn about scientific universalism from Los Alamos. Pointing to the "deep common bond among the scientists that was stronger than any national bond," he envisions "the great idea of science as a concern for all men together, as supernational activity, the idea of science as the spearhead of human cooperation across national and political frontiers"; but, as Weisskopf surely knows, the Los Alamos source of his model matters. Species awareness in the nuclear age requires scientists to consider the nature and sponsorship of their work and its likely effect on fellow human beings. The exclusion of these ethical and species considerations, whatever the universality of method and intellectual understanding, permits science to be used for virtually anything at all, including species annihilation. Also necessary for a species orientation is scientists' clear rejection, from within science, of scientism and technicism, including the "Cartesian sickness" that encourages continuing separation of knowledge and feeling. In other words, a species-oriented science would call into question its own tendencies to require or encourage dissociation and numbing.

Many individual scientists and groups of scientists have begun to embrace these species principles, sometimes specifically in relation to nuclear and environmental threat. More than a few have turned from working on weapons to militant public opposition to weapons policies. The process can be said to have begun with the Chicago group of scientists who, toward the end of the Second World War when they had completed their bomb-related work (which was still going on at Los Alamos), launched an effort to prevent the United States from exploding an atomic weapon on a populated city. Though the effort failed, it was of the deepest historical significance. That group, including Franck, Rabinowitch, and Szilard, constituted the beginnings of the scientists' antinuclear movement that was to flourish in the early postwar years. And the way in which the group came to its ethical stance, as Rabinowitch makes clear, directly confirms the principle of insight via confrontation of holocaust—in this case, confronting a holocaust that had not yet occurred: "In the summer of 1945, some of us walked the streets of Chicago suddenly lit by a giant fireball, the steel skeletons of skyscrapers bending into grotesque shapes and their masonry raining into the streets below, until a cloud of dust arose and settled over the crumbling city." And it was, as he put it, "from this vision" that scientists began their effort "to stop the hands of the clock before it struck the first hour of the atomic age."

Scientists have also made that shift after considerable involvement with later weapons systems. The shift could be clear and absolute, as in the case of Theodore Taylor whose doubling, we recall, enabled him to feel "more at home in the laboratory than at home" (see pages 148–49). After some years of maintaining a pattern close to doubling that enabled him radically to separate his laboratory life from his home life, he became alienated from his work as he came to observe what he called "misbehavior" on the part of the military in relation both to nuclear weapons and to the Vietnam War. He decided to leave weapons making and to work on life-enhancing technologies, all of these feelings culminating, as he reported, in the experience he had in the mid-1980s when visiting the Soviet Union for the first time:

> Walking in Red Square in Moscow, Taylor saw many young people in wedding parties visiting Lenin's tomb and the Tomb of the Unknown Soldier and was impressed by how happy they looked. He experienced a flashback to the night of the birth of one of his children years before when, rather than being with his wife, he was at the Pentagon poring over intelligence data, including aerial photographs of central Moscow, in connection with potential plans for nuclear attack. Standing in Red Square, he began to weep uncontrollably: "It was seeing those happy-looking, specific people, going around, working their way up to the mausoleum. For any human being to contemplate setting off a bomb on top of all this, these people, is insane, . . . a symptom of insanity." He had experienced such feelings before, but now for the first time "I literally set foot in the Soviet Union to see what it was that I was doing with all the details filled in." Before that, Moscow had been no more than "a set of lines at various levels of rads [units of energy] and . . . pressures and calories [units of heat from an explosion] per square centimeter" that one had to "match" with "the bombs with those numbers."

Of enormous importance here is the breakdown of dissociative patterns and the emergence of feeling—about what the bomb would do to human beings in a city he had helped target, and about his own relationship to his wife and child. The delayed guilt over having not been at his wife's bedside when she gave birth became associated with guilt over having strayed from her loving influence in his weapons work in general. Thus, the recovery of feeling can become a recovery of moral imagination: Taylor returned to his early anti-bomb feelings and to deeper commitment as a husband and father.

Weapons designers and strategists have parallel journeys away from nuclearism and toward feeling and life enhancement. Taylor's story, in one sense unusual—there have rarely been experiences as dramatic as his in Red Square—in another sense epitomizes the human capacity, under certain circumstances, to emerge from the dissociation connected with weapons work to achieve a particularly intense combination of moral imagination and species responsibility in the service of combating the weapons' danger.

Also in Moscow, in the mid-1980s, a very different event occurred during a visit of American doctors associated with the International Physicians for the Prevention of Nuclear War for joint meetings and activities with their Soviet counterparts. One day in a Moscow hospital, the cardiologists Evgueny Chazov and Sidney Alexander, the respective heads of the Soviet and the American delegations, were examining a sick cardiac patient. To those who later saw the incident on film, it was clear that, as each man applied his stethoscope in turn, both had lost all awareness of Russians and Americans, even of the nuclear-weapons question, and were totally focused on how they might find a way to maintain the life of the desperately ill human being before them. In observing the two doctors, one witnessed an affirmation, as simple as it was profound, of the universal—that is, species—principle of healing.

Writers, artists, filmmakers, and various critics have great importance for us in enhancing our capacity to take in the threat and act appropriately toward it. Berthold Brecht and Samuel Beckett may well be our most valuable resources here, not in addressing nuclear war directly—neither has—but in their insistence that we must experience, as a precondition for hope, the despair and confusion appropriate to our age of holocaust. Beckett tells us, for instance, "The confusion is not my invention. . . . It is all around us and our only chance is to let it in. The only chance of renovation is to open our eyes and see the mess. . . . There will be new form, and . . . this form will be of such a type that it admits the chaos and does not try to say that it is really something else." Both the artist's confrontation and the cultural comment on it are necessary to nuclear-age wisdom. Though creative responses occur in fits and starts, their profound and extensive development is no less important than our political response.

The theological profession has powerfully, if belatedly, handed down a moral condemnation of nuclearism. The 1983 pastoral letter of the American National Conference of Catholic Bishops, "The Challenge of Peace: God's Promise and Our Response," for instance, begins with a quotation from the opening of the Second Vatican Council: "The whole human race faces a moment of supreme crisis in its advance toward maturity," and goes on to state specifically that "nuclear weaponry has drastically changed the nature of warfare and the arms race poses a threat to human life and human civilization which is without precedent." The letter is notable for its ethical denunciation of the arms race as "one of the greatest curses on the human race, . . . to be condemned as a danger, an act of aggression against the poor, and a folly which does not provide the security it promises." It calls forth traditional Catholic just-war policy to reject concepts of limited nuclear war and, in fact, any use of the weapons at all. Because of both its sponsorship and its content, the letter had a profound effect on American consciousness. But it nonetheless hedged on deterrence, seeing it as "not an adequate strategy as a long-term basis for peace" and in need of replacement but at the same time as granting "a strictly conditioned moral acceptance of deterrence" as a transitional means of holding back nuclear war.

The United Methodist Council of Bishops, in 1986, went much further in a declaration of species awareness, as evident in their document's ringing introductory sentences:

> We write in defense of creation. We do so because the creation itself is under attack. Air and water, trees and fruits and flowers, birds and fish and cattle, all children and youth, women and men live under the darkening shadows of a threatening nuclear winter. We call the United Methodist Church to more faithful witness and action in the face of this worsening nuclear crisis.

The Methodist report goes on to declare that "nuclear deterrence has too long been reverenced as the idol of national security. In its most idolatrous forms it has blinded its proponents to the many-sided requirements of genuine security." The report rejects any moral case for deterrence, "even as an interim ethic," because of that policy's association with "unrelenting arms escalation" and of its serving as a "dogmatic license for perpetual hostility between the superpowers and for their rigid resistance to significant measures of disarmament." The report insists, "The *ideology* of deterrence must not receive the church's blessing, even as a temporary warrant for holding on to nuclear weapons." And it declares that mutual efforts of states "to eliminate their nuclear weapons" constitute "an ethic . . . shaped by a realistic vision of *common security* and the escalation of mutual trust rather than mutual terror" (italics added). The document is remarkable not only in its moral clarity but in its careful evaluation of principled positions concerning nuclear weapons, and in its insistence on "nurture in the ways of peacemaking" as "the prime alternative to hostility and violence." The overall document may, in fact, be understood as a sustained call to planetary peacemaking.

Here and in some of the previous examples, the professions, or at least significant minorities within them, take on the role of promulgators and guardians of species awareness. That role becomes possible only with a protean openness to divergent ideas and images for the creation of the species-related symbolizations crucial for human survival. Not just professionals, but people in general can then "make and unmake their arrangements and make them again" in quest of the new narrative for which we hunger.

Global Consciousness

> You must go on a little more, you must go on a long
> time more, you must go on forever more.
> —SAMUEL BECKETT

Species awareness inevitably extends to the habitat of all species, to the earth and its ecosystem. Our awareness of our relationship to the sun, to the oceans, to the earth's resources of food, energy, and materials of every kind, to all animals and plants—becomes intensified as both we and that ecosystem are simultaneously threatened. We experience a deepened respect for all animals that inhabit the greater ecosystem with us, and we question assumptions of human entitlement that permit us to abuse these fellow inhabitants of ours. Yet whatever our efforts at greater empathy for other species, we remain aware that the problems we confront are those of the *human* imagination. Here, too, the threat comes most directly from nuclear weapons but also from nuclear power and the many chemical and bacteriological agents derived mostly from industrial waste or industrial products themselves, and also from medical waste and general garbage. Increasingly, the problem is seen to be global: the "greenhouse effect," destruction of the ozone layer, poisoning of oceans and other international waterways, and deadly infectious diseases, most of which have been mentioned earlier. Awareness of our interdependency on our global environment has been dramatically increasing, even if insufficiently translated into political, corporate, and individual practice. The phenomenal worldwide success of Carl Sagan's television series *Cosmos* attests to the universal hunger for a synthesis of humanity, earth, solar system, and cosmos.

Much of this development has been summed up under the concept *global ecopolitics,* which focuses on environmental issues that include control over natural resources, questions of scarcity, and related issues of social justice in ways that throw into question or "overturn" international political arrangements and "related system of rules established during the period of industrial expansion." Also involved in the concept is a shift in "social paradigm," "a period of transformation of great consequence, . . . an entirely new way of looking at the world and a new set of values, ethics, and survival rules." The shift includes "a growing realization that all states and individuals share a finite ecosphere and that there are limits to the burdens that can be imposed on that ecosphere." And new political and moral questions concern the apportionment of global resources and the collective responsibility toward maintaining the health of the ecosphere. An important related movement is *ecofeminism,* which seeks similar goals while focusing on "the planet . . . not [as] an environment, but a living home, where everyone can explore and realize . . . natural potentialities; and there is an accompanying stress on the body in nature or embodied politics." These various developments lay powerful stress on psychological and moral relationships of the evolving human self with the creatures and natural elements of its *entire* habitat.

Exploration of space contributes to this profound global-ecological consciousness. Despite the abuse of this exploration through its link with weapons development, it contains a potential for expanding human awareness in ways we cannot yet fully grasp. Much has been said about one remarkable photograph of Earth taken from space, a photograph justly celebrated for its rendition of our planet as no more than a small sphere. But there is something else to note that has not been much talked about. The photo, taken as it was from *outside* Earth, suggests a new kind of relationship human beings are now able to have with the earth. We continue to live on it, but we can at the same time step outside it and look down at it. We can—astronauts in actuality and the rest of us in our imaginations—move in and out of our earthly connection. We can become *participant-observers*—the term used for anthropologists when they enter into the life of a particular tribe or group the better to understand its rituals and mores. The analogy is far from exact, since we remain earthlings, and those anthropologists can never become actual members of the essentially alien tribe in whose life they participate. But the more general point is that we gain a new perspective on our overall human tribe and recognize it as a single tribe, as a species to which all of us as earthlings belong. Unlike the anthropologist, we are responsible for the tribe because we *are* the tribe. As we see the earth whole literally for the first time, we reconnect with its entirety. We assert our expanded sense of immortality in accordance with Archibald MacLeish's poetic vision: "To see the earth as it truly is, small and blue and beautiful, in that eternal silence where it floats, is to see ourselves as riders on the earth together, brothers on that bright loveliness in the eternal cold—brothers who know now they are truly brothers"—and, we must add, sisters who know they are truly sisters.

A Species Moment

> Strange dreams occur,
> For dreams are licensed as they never were.
> —Louis Simpson

Can we geniunely act as "riders on the earth together"? There are historical turning points—times described by the Greeks as *Kairos*, or decisive moments in human experience during which crucial actions may be taken, actions that can determine the collective future.

There were *Kairos* moments in relation to genocidal danger: the Nazi policy of systematic mass murder of Jews and others; the dropping of the atomic bombs on Hiroshima and Nagasaki; the post–Second World War embrace of atomic weapons for military purposes rather than of a worldwide effort to abolish them; and the 1950 decision to make the hydrogen bomb. Much of this book has, in fact, been about psychological participation in such genocidal moments. They have resulted in a form of nuclear eschatology—a perception of "last things" that leaves us hopeless in our deep resignation to a "nuclear end."

The opposite *Kairos* potential, the worldwide call to species consciousness, may be today little more than a strongly felt aspiration. That call begins with a self-imposed demand: "Don't kill the species!" The demand extends to the insistent alternative: "Help the species to live—to thrive!" Present in the call is our growing awareness that we do not have unlimited time. The sense that everything could suddenly end sharpens our recognition that time can run out on our efforts to reverse our course. It is not a question of the world achieving sudden purity of heart or spirit: there is little expectation that violence within and between nations will suddenly disappear. Rather, there is growing recognition that we have permitted the human capacity for violence to become entrenched in genocidal structures—a recognition that we can no longer afford the resulting genocidal mentality and its potential consequences, any more than we can afford to continue the many-sided destruction of our global environment.

Species awareness means awareness of human choice: "This is not the End of Time—unless we choose to make it so. We need not accept the death sentence. . . . We are not powerless." By choosing instead a human future, we are—in the words of the Polish Solidarity leader Adam Michnik—"defending hope." And "hope is important. Perhaps more important than anything else." Hope is greatly enhanced—as is the acceptance of individual mortality—by the sense of reasserting the immortality of the species. The task is intensified by the psychological upheavals we can expect in connection with the millennial transition of the year 2000. Whatever the millennial imagery, we must recognize that the hopeful future is not an apocalyptic heavenly peace but rather expanded awareness on behalf of human continuity.

This adaptation will not eliminate people's need to define themselves in relation to otherness, but it can begin to subsume that otherness to larger human commonality. It must include struggles against widespread oppression and drastic human inequities by invoking the kind of "originality in political action" that has taken place in the Solidarity movement in Poland—and in related movements in Hungary, East Germany, Czechoslovakia, and Bulgaria—and was so cruelly frustrated in the student movement in China: "Political action that enlarges, rather than blights or destroys, human possibilities." This species-oriented approach would "defy the given models of defiance."

No one can claim knowledge of a single, correct path. Rather, there must be endless combinations of reflection and action and, above all, the kind of larger collective adaptation we have been discussing. At the same time, we must remain aware of persisting genocidal arrangements and expressions of genocidal mentality. We cannot afford to "stop thinking." Nor can we wait for a new Gandhi or Saint Joan to deliver us. Rather, each of us must join in a vast project—political, ethical, psychological—on behalf of perpetuating and nurturing our humanity. We are then "people getting up from their knees" to resist nuclear oppression. We clear away the "thick glass" that has blurred our moral and political vision. We become healers, not killers, of our species.

Notes

Chapter 1. "If Deterrence Fails": Confronting Nuclear Entrapment

PAGE

1 The chapter epigraph is from Elie Wiesel, *Viewpoint* (ABC television news program), 20 November 1983, transcript.

2 This definition of "deterrence" is from the *Oxford English Dictionary*.

2 Dulles's analogy is from Lawrence Freedman, *The Evolution of Nuclear Strategy* (New York: St. Martin's Press, 1983), pp. 87–88.

2–3 Ibid., for Dulles's analogy as misleading.

3 The "omnicide" label can be found in Berel Lang, "Genocide and Omnicide: Technology at the Limits," in A. Cohen and S. Lee, eds., *Nuclear Weapons and the Future of Humanity: The Fundamental Questions* (Totowa, N.J.: Rowman & Allenheld, 1986), pp. 115–30.

3–4 The description of the "improved weapons" and the "calls" are from Robert C. Toth, "The U.S. Strategy for a Nuclear War," *Los Angeles Times*, July 1989, p. 1.

4 George Kennan's quote is from his *The Nuclear Delusion: Soviet-American Relations in the Atomic Age* (New York: Pantheon, 1982), p. 176.

4 Brent Scowcroft was quoted in *Viewpoint*, 20 November 1983, transcript.

5 The comment on "brinkmanship" is from Daniel Ford, *The Button: The Pentagon's Strategic Command and Control System* (New York: Simon & Schuster, 1985), p. 240.

5 Ibid., pp. 91–92, for the comments on Carter, Nixon, and Reagan.

5 Kennan's "You are mortal men . . ." in "A Modest Proposal," *New York Review of Books*, 16 July 1981, p. 14.

5 *Dr. Strangelove* recalled in Ford, *The Button*, p. 28.

5 Ibid., p. 53, for Herres on the "hair-trigger posture."

5 Ibid., p. 166, for ". . . pea-brained dinosaurs."

6 Kahn on the Doomsday Machine in Herman Kahn, *On Thermonuclear War* (Princeton: Princeton University Press, 1961), pp. 145, 147.

6 The former member of the Joint Chiefs of Staff quoted in Steven Kull, "Mind-Sets of Defense Policy-Makers," *Psychohistory Review* 14 (1985): 30.

6 The "emergency action messages" and "significant event[s] or incident[s]" in William M. Arkin, "Nuclear War in Triplicate," *Bulletin of the Atomic Scientists* 42 (December 1986): 6–7.

PAGE

6–7   For nuclear weapons proliferation, see Leonard S. Spector, *The Undeclared Bomb: The Spread of Nuclear Weapons, 1987–88* (Cambridge, Mass.: Ballinger, 1988); David Albright and Tom Zamora, "India, Pakistan's Nuclear Weapons: All the Pieces in Place," *Bulletin of the Atomic Scientists* 45 (5 [June 1989]): 20–26; and Leonard S. Spector, "New Players in the Nuclear Game," *Bulletin of the Atomic Scientists* (1 [January–February 1989]): 29–32. For chemical weapons, see the writings of Brad Roberts: for instance, "U.S. and Chemical Arms Control," *New Technologies for Security and Arms Control,* American Association for the Advancement of Science, Autumn 1989. And for bacteriological weapons, see Nicholas A. Sims, *The Diplomacy of Biological Disarmament: Vicissitudes of a Treaty in Force, 1975–85* (New York: St. Martin's Press, 1988).

7   For the authority on command and control, see Thomas Powers, "How Nuclear War Could Start," review of Paul Bracken, *The Command and Control of Nuclear Forces,* in *New York Review of Books,* 17 January 1985, pp. 33–35.

7   "The mechanism," in Langdon Winner, *Autonomous Technology: Technics-Out-of-Control as a Theme in Political Thought* (Cambridge, Mass., and London: MIT Press, 1978), pp. 28–29.

8   York's quotes from Herbert York, *Race to Oblivion: A Participant's View of the Arms Race* (New York: Simon & Schuster, 1970), pp. 228–32.

8   "Nobody believes it . . ." from Steven Kull, personal communication.

8   The section epigraph is from the manuscript of Archbishop Raymond G. Hunthausen's speech "Faith and Disarmament," delivered at Pacific Lutheran University, Tacoma, Washington, 12 June 1981.

9   Samuel Pisar's commentary from his *Of Blood and Hope* (Boston: Little, Brown, 1980), pp. 262–63.

9   Rabi's "And now . . ." from I. I. Rabi, "How Well We Meant," speech delivered at Los Alamos in 1983, at the fortieth anniversary reunion of atomic scientists.

10   Maier's quote in Charles S. Maier, *The Unmasterable Past: History, Holocaust, and German National Identity* (Cambridge, Mass.: Harvard University Press, 1988), p. 69.

10   The observer on nuclear weapons arrangements is Ronald Bee, personal communication.

11   The "leading authority" on genocide is Leo Kuper, *Genocide: Its Political Use in the Twentieth Century* (New Haven: Yale University Press, 1981), p. 46.

11   " 'An' act . . . like omnicide," from Gary Stahl, "Remembering the Future," in A. Cohen and S. Lee, eds., *Nuclear Weapons,* p. 111.

11   "Plausible basis" through "a human illness," in Maier, *Unmasterable Past,* pp. 69–70.

12   "Entire human groups," from Kuper, *Genocide,* pp. 19–23.

PAGE

12   Genocide defined by U.N. General Assembly, in ibid., p. 210.

12   "An old practice in its modern development," Kuper's paraphrase
        of Lemkin, in ibid., p. 22. See also Lemkin, "Genocide as a Crime
        Under International Law," *American Journal of International Law* 41
        (1947): 146.

12   The "biomedical vision," from Robert Jay Lifton, *The Nazi Doctors:
        Medical Killing and the Psychology of Genocide* (New York: Basic Books,
        1986).

12   The ideology of nuclearism is discussed in Robert Jay Lifton, *The
        Broken Connection: On Death and the Continuity of Life* (New York: Basic
        Books/Harper Colophon, 1983 [1979]), chap. 23; and Robert Jay
        Lifton and Richard Falk, *Indefensible Weapons: The Political and
        Psychological Case Against Nuclearism* (New York: Basic Books, 1982).

13   See discussions of these psychological mechanisms in Lifton, *Nazi
        Doctors;* and Robert Jay Lifton, *Death in Life: Survivors of Hiroshima*
        (New York: Basic Books/Harper Colophon, 1983 [1968]).

14   Maier on the Holocaust, *Unmasterable Past,* p. 97.

14   Collingwood's quote from R. G. Collingwood, "Autobiography," in
        Encyclopaedia Britannica, 15th ed. (1943–73), vol. 8, p. 964.

15   Mumford's passage from Lewis Mumford, *The Transformations of Man*
        (London: Allen & Unwin, 1957), p. 138.

Chapter 2. The Evolving Genocidal Mentality

16   Lindbergh's statement in the chapter epigraph is quoted in Michael
        Sherry, *The Rise of American Air Power: The Creation of Armageddon*
        (New Haven and London: Yale University Press, 1986), pp. 209–10.

16   The quote beginning "an accretion . . ." is from ibid., p. 363.

17   The section epigraph is from ibid., p. 2.

18   Douhet quoted in Lee Kennett, *A History of Strategic Bombing* (New
        York: Charles Scribner's Sons, 1982), p. 179.

18   Ibid., for "merciful substitute for the hell . . ." See also Sherry, *The
        Rise,* pp. 21, 24.

18   "Of all the belligerents of World War II . . ." quoted from Kennett,
        A History, p. 180.

18   "Piecemeal evolution . . ." quote from Sherry, *The Rise,* p. 96.

18   "Blind" bombing and "depended for effectiveness . . ." quote from
        Wesley F. Craven and James L. Cate, *The Army Air Forces in World
        War II,* vol. 1 (Chicago: University of Chicago Press, 1948), pp.
        596–97.

19   The "primary objective" is from Charles Webster and Nobel
        Frankland, *The Strategic Air Offensive Against Germany,* vol. 1 (London:
        Her Majesty's Stationery Office, 1961), p. 157.

PAGE

19   The "four furious assaults" and "a bonus" are from Sherry, *The Rise*, pp. 153, 154.

19   Billy Mitchell's quotes are from ibid., p. 58.

19   Ibid., p. 156, for "with an eye . . ."

19–20   The source for the statement about generals Hansell and LeMay is Kennett, *A History*, pp. 168–69.

20   Sherry, *The Rise*, p. 283.

20   Ibid., pp. 149, 201, 201, respectively, for the quotes about ongoing technological advances.

20   Dyson quotes in both text and footnote from ibid., p. 199.

20–21   Ibid., pp. 146, 147, for quotes on Americans at home.

21   Ibid., p. 260, for estimates of Dresden bombings.

21   Vonnegut's quote from his *Slaughterhouse 5* (New York: Laurel, 1988 [1966]), p. 173.

21   The quote about Hamburg, from Sherry, *The Rise*, p. 153.

21   Ibid., pp. 276–77, for the quotes on Tokyo bombing. See also Fred Kaplan, *The Wizards of Armageddon* (New York: Simon & Schuster, 1983), p. 42; and Hoito Edoin, *The Night Tokyo Burned: The Incendiary Campaign Against Japan, March–August, 1945* (New York: St. Martin's Press, 1987).

21   The "distinction" quote is from Sherry, *The Rise*, p. 323.

22   Ibid., p. 349, for Truman's quote.

22   Ibid., pp. 243–46, on attitude toward the Japanese.

22   American and Japanese racist attitudes from John Dower, *War Without Mercy: Race and Power in the Pacific War* (New York: Pantheon, 1986).

23   Oppenheimer's quotes on poisoning the German food supply, in Richard Rhodes, *The Making of the Atomic Bomb* (New York: Simon & Schuster, 1986), pp. 510–11.

23   Ibid., p. 419, for Oppenheimer's conclusion.

23   Ibid., p. 664, for Fermi's wager on the bomb igniting the atmosphere.

23   Bard quoted in Martin Sherwin, *A World Destroyed: Hiroshima and the Origins of the Arms Race* (New York: Vintage, 1987 [1975]), p. 217.

24   Figures and estimates on Hiroshima death and destruction from: Robert Jay Lifton, *Death in Life: Survivors of Hiroshima* (New York: Basic Books, 1982 [1967]), p. 20; Rhodes, *The Making*, pp. 714–34; and Averill A. Liebow, "Encounter with Disaster—A Medical Diary of Hiroshima," *Yale Journal of Biology and Medicine* 37 (60 [1965]): 235.

24   Hiroshima survivors' quotes from Lifton, *Death in Life*, pp. 22, 29.

25–26   The "science of city-burning" quote from Kennett, *A History*, p. 171.

25   Churchill quoted in Sherry, *The Rise*, p. 325.

25   Fermi and Rabi in the section epigraph are quoted in Herbert York, *The Advisors: Oppenheimer, Teller, and the Superbomb* (San Francisco: W. H. Freeman, 1976), p. 158.

PAGE

25–26 Details on hydrogen bomb from Kosta Tsipis, "The Physics of Nuclear Weapons," in *The Nuclear Almanac: Confronting the Atom in War and Peace* (Reading, Mass.: Addison-Wesley, 1984), chap. 10, p. 199.

26 "Fusion" quote from Rhodes, *The Making,* pp. 775–76; see also York, *The Advisors,* pp. 20–21.

26 The General Advisory Committee's report quoted in York, *The Advisors,* pp. 156–57.

26 "Like saying 'no' to a steamroller" from David Lilienthal quoted in Gregg Herken, *Counsels of War* (New York: Alfred A. Knopf, 1985), p. 58.

27 Information on warplan Trojan from David Alan Rosenberg, "The Origins of Overkill: Nuclear Weapons and American Strategy, 1945–1960," *International Security* 7 (Spring 1983): 15–16.

28 LeMay's revelation in Kaplan, *Wizards,* pp. 133–34.

28 For overviews of the evolution of nuclear strategy, see Lawrence Freedman, *The Evolution of Nuclear Strategy* (New York: St. Martin's Press, 1983); Kaplan, *Wizards;* Herken, *Counsels;* and Desmond Ball and Jeffrey Richelson, eds., *Strategic Nuclear Targeting* (New York: Cornell University Press, 1986).

28 The massive U.S. response in Samuel F. Wells, Jr., "The Origins of Massive Retaliation," *Political Science Quarterly* 96 (1 [Spring 1981]): 34.

28 Radford quoted in Kaplan, *Wizards,* pp. 183–84.

28–29 The high-ranking air force officer was General James Walsh, director of SAC Intelligence, quoted in ibid., pp. 211–12.

29 "Just exactly as you would use a bullet . . ." from Eisenhower quoted in Freedman, *Evolution,* pp. 77–78.

29 McNamara and "controlled escalation" from Herken, *Counsels,* pp. 138–39.

29 McNamara and *assured destruction* from Freedman, *Evolution,* pp. 246–47.

29–30 The acronym MAD and its preference from Herken, *Counsels,* p. 248.

30 On the Cuban missile crisis, see, for example, J. Anthony Lukas, "Class Reunion: Kennedy's Men Relive the Cuban Missile Crisis," *New York Times Magazine* 135 (30 August 1987): 22ff.; James G. Blight, Joseph S. Nye, Jr., and David A. Welch, "The Cuban Missile Crisis Revisited," *Foreign Affairs* 66 (Fall 1987): 170–89.

30 MAD as "a policy of genocide" from Iklé quoted in Herken, *Counsels,* p. 249.

30 Information on Schlesinger in Jerome H. Kahan, *Security in the Nuclear Age: Developing U.S. Strategic Arms Policy* (Washington, D.C.: Brookings Institution, 1975), p. 161.

31 Carter on "the elimination of all nuclear weapons" quoted in Herken, *Counsels,* p. 279.

PAGE

31   Information on Carter's presidential directives from Thomas
          Powers, "Choosing a Strategy for World War III," *Atlantic Monthly*
          250 (May 1982): 84.

31   Ibid., p. 83, for Brzezinski on *ethnic targeting.*

31   The briefer's reply to Brzezinski in Powers, "Choosing," p.
          83.

32   Quotes on ethnic targeting as genocide in David T. Cattell and
          George H. Quester, "Ethnic Targeting: Some Bad Ideas," in Ball
          and Richelson, *Strategic Nuclear Targeting*, p. 281.

32   Ibid., p. 84, for the commentator on "the logic of the situation."

33   Information on "B-team" in Herken, *Counsels*, p. 277.

33   "To Reagan . . ." in Kaplan, *Wizards*, p. 386.

33–34   "Crazier analysts" from Herbert York quoted in Robert Scheer,
          With Enough Shovels: Reagan, Bush, and Nuclear War (New York:
          Random House, 1982), p. 269.

34   "Armageddon syndrome" in Herken, *Counsels*, p. 310.

34   Quotes from Gray's articles in Colin S. Gray and Keith Payne,
          "Victory Is Possible," *Foreign Policy* 39 (Summer 1980): 14–27; and
          Colin S. Gray, "Nuclear Strategy: A Case for a Theory of Victory,"
          International Security 4 (1 [Summer 1979]): 54–87.

34   The "watershed" in strategic thinking, in Herken, *Counsels*, p.
          318.

34   Reagan and Star Wars in Phillip M. Boffey et al., *Claiming the
          Heavens: The New York Times Complete Guide to the Star Wars Debate*
          (New York: Times Books, 1987).

35   On the INF treaty, see, for example, Gerard C. Smith, "The INF
          Treaty: A Reason for Hope," *Arms Control Today* 18 (1
          [January/February 1988]): 3–5.

35   Ellsberg on the U.S. threat to use nuclear weapons, from Daniel
          Ellsberg, "Introduction: Call to Mutiny," in E. P. Thompson and D.
          Smith, eds., *Protest and Survive* (New York and London: Monthly
          Review Press, 1981), p. i.

35–36   Ibid., p. xi, for Ellsberg's additional point.

36   On the Soviet threats, see, for example, William T. Lee, "Soviet
          Nuclear Targeting Strategy," in Ball and Richelson, *Strategic Nuclear
          Targeting*, pp. 84–108.

37   The section epigraph is from Albert Carnesale et al., *Living with
          Nuclear Weapons* (New York: Bantam Books, 1983), p. 255.

37   Information on Hiroshima survivors in Lifton, *Death In Life*, pp.
          15–56.

37–38   The "duck and cover" drills study in Michael J. Carey,
          "Psychological Fallout," *Bulletin of the Atomic Scientists* 38 (January
          1982): 20–24. See also Paul Boyer, *By the Bomb's Early Light: American
          Thought and Culture at the Dawn of the Atomic Age* (New York:
          Pantheon, 1985); and Robert Jay Lifton, *The Future of Immortality and
          Other Essays for a Nuclear Age* (New York: Basic Books, 1988), pp.
          136–47.

PAGE

38–39   Kahn on "rationality" and on the dialogue with the president in
         Herman Kahn, *On Thermonuclear War* (Princeton: Princeton
         University Press, 1961), pp. 641–42.
39   Ibid., p. 86, for Kahn and radiation meters.
39   Incident at Kahn's lecture described to Robert Jay Lifton.
39   The "quasi-official campaign" in Boyer, *By the Bomb's*, p. 316.
39   Ibid., pp. 316–17, for Parsons's quotes.
40   The formation of a special panel in William F. Vandercook,
         "Making the Very Best of the Very Worst: The 'Human Effects of
         Nuclear Weapons' Report of 1956," *International Security* 11
         (Summer 1986): 184, 188.
40   Ibid., pp. 191–92, for quotes from the "Human Effects" report.
41   Blake quoted in William Barrett, *The Illusion of Technique* (New York:
         Doubleday/Anchor, 1979), p. xv.
41–42   "Civil defense education" and "duck and cover" drills in Michael J.
         Carey, "The Schools and Civil Defense: The Fifties Revisited,"
         Teacher's College Record 84 (Fall 1982): 115–127.
42   Teller's minimization of fallout dangers in Edward Teller, with
         Allen Brown, *The Legacy of Hiroshima* (Garden City, N.Y.: Doubleday,
         1962), pp. 180–81.
42   Teller's quotes in ibid., pp. 288–89.
42   Ibid., p. 244, for "save perhaps 90 percent . . ."
43   Harvard Study Group's quotes in Carnesale et al., *Living with Nuclear
         Weapons*, pp. 253–55, 233–35, 156, 62, xvii.
43–44   On evolution of *Dr. Strangelove* from book to film, see Paul Brians,
         Nuclear Holocausts: Atomic War in Fiction (Kent, Ohio: Kent State
         University Press, 1987).
44   For the Harvard Study Group on *Dr. Strangelove* and Tom Lehrer,
         see *Living with Nuclear Weapons*, p. 13.
44–45   Discussion of "hawks, doves, and owls" in Graham T. Allison,
         Albert Carnesale, and Joseph S. Nye, Jr., eds., *Hawks, Doves, and
         Owls: An Agenda for Avoiding Nuclear War* (New York: W. W. Norton,
         1985), pp. 209–13.
45   For doves' stress on controlling nonrational factors, see, for
         instance, Jerome Frank, *Survival and Sanity in the Nuclear Age* (New
         York: University Press of America, 1988 [1982]); Lester Grinspoon,
         "Crisis Behavior," *Bulletin of the Atomic Scientists* 40 (April 1984):
         27–31; and Dietrich Fischer, *Preventing War in the Nuclear Age*
         (Totowa, N.J.: Roman & Allenheld, 1984).
45   The owls' focus on a "credible nuclear deterrent" in Allison,
         Carnesale, and Nye, *Hawks, Doves, and Owls*, p. 244.
45   Nye's remarks from Joseph S. Nye, Jr., *Nuclear Ethics* (New York:
         Free Press, 1986), pp. 52, 111, 12.
46   The quotes on Star Wars in Paul Boyer, "How S.D.I. Will Change
         Our Culture," *The Nation* 244 (10 January 1987): 16.
46   Civil defense propaganda in Edward Zuckerman, *The Day After World
         War III* (New York: Viking Press, 1984), pp. 91–92, 100–101, 118.

PAGE

46–47   T. K. Jones quoted in Scheer, *With Enough Shovels*, pp. 18, 138.

47   Information on T. K. Jones in Kaplan, *Wizards*, p. 388.

47   "To anyone . . ." from Boyer, "How S.D.I.," p. 20.

47   Reagan's quotes in Boffey et al., *Claiming the Heavens*, p. 271. See
         also Robert Karl Manoff, "Modes of War and Modes of Social
         Address: The Text of SDI," *Journal of Communication* 39 (Winter
         1989): 59–84; and H. Bruce Franklin, *War Stars: The Superweapon and
         the American Imagination* (New York: Oxford University Press, 1988).

48   The comment about conditioning the public, from Boyer, "How
         S.D.I.," p. 17. See also Jeff Smith, "Reagan, Star Wars, and
         American Culture," *Bulletin of the Atomic Scientists* 43
         (January–February 1987): 19–25.

48   "The fantasies lay the psychic groundwork . . ." from Boyer, "How
         S.D.I.," p. 17.

48   Ibid., p. 17, for "in a world of nuclear menace . . ."

49   "This is a President . . ." from Kull, "The Mind-Sets," p. 28.

49   Colin Gray's "raise the flag . . ." quote from Colin S. Gray,
         "Nuclear Strategy: A Case for a Theory of Victory," *International
         Security* 4 (Summer 1979): 71.

49   Reagan's characterization of the superpowers in Boffey et al.,
         Claiming the Heavens, p. 22.

50   "Organized peacelessness" from Dieter Senghaas in Bradley Klein,
         "Strategic Discourse and its Alternative" (Occasional Paper no. 3,
         Center on Violence and Human Survival, John Jay College of
         Criminal Justice, City University of New York, 1987), p. 6.

Chapter 3. Genocidal Ideology: Trauma and Cure

51   The first epigraph in John Bartlett, ed., *Familiar Quotations*, 14th ed.
         (Boston: Little, Brown, 1968), p. 125b.

51   Second epigraph from William L. Laurence, *Men and Atoms* (New
         York: Simon & Schuster, 1959), p. 197.

51   Berlin quoted on nationalism in his "Nationalism: Past Neglect and
         Present Power," in *Against the Current: Essays in the History of Ideas*
         (Harmondsworth, Eng.: Penguin, 1982 [1979]), p. 349.

52   Hitler's quote in section epigraph from *Hitler's Mein Kampf*, with an
         introduction by D. C. Watt, trans. Ralph Manheim (London:
         Hutchinson, 1977 [1933]), p. 209.

52   "Oppressive with doom . . ." from Robert C. Cecil, *The Myth of the
         Master Race: A Study in the Rise of German Ideology* (New York: Dodd,
         Mead, 1972), p. 93.

PAGE

52   "Cultural despair" from Fritz Stern, *The Politics of Cultural Despair: A Study in the Rise of the Germanic Ideology* (Berkeley: University of California Press, 1961).

53   Hitler on curing "this . . . inwardly sick and rotten" era, in *Mein Kampf,* (Boston: Houghton Mifflin, 1943 [1925–26]), p. 435.

53   Ibid., pp. 300–308, 312–13, for Hitler's remarks on race. See also Robert Jay Lifton, *The Nazi Doctors: Medical Killing and the Psychology of Genocide* (New York: Basic Books, 1986), p. 16; Eberhard Jäckel, *Hitler's Weltanschauung: A Blueprint for Power* (Middletown, Conn.: Wesleyan University Press, 1972 [1969]), p. 58.

53   Hitler on "the removal of the Jews" in Jäckel, *Hitler's Weltanschauung,* p. 51.

53–54   Hitler's quotes on the racial cure from *Mein Kampf,* pp. 397–98. See also, Lifton, *Nazi Doctors,* p. 17; Jäckel, *Hitler's Weltanschauung,* p. 77.

54   Rudolf Hess on National Socialism as "applied biology" quoted in Lifton, *Nazi Doctors,* p. 31.

54   The Nazi doctor in Auschwitz quoted by Ella Lingens-Reiner, *Prisoners of Fear* (London: Gollancz, 1948), pp. 1–2.

54–55   "Totalistic" ideologies in Robert Jay Lifton, *Thought Reform and the Psychology of Totalism* (Chapel Hill, N.C.: University of North Carolina Press, 1989 [1961]).

54–55   The Nazis' "political principle of totalitarianism" from Martin Brozat, "The Concentration Camps, 1933–1945," in Helmut Krausnick et al., *Anatomy of the SS State* (New York: Walker, 1968 [1965]), p. 430; see also pp. 400–420, 429–30. See, more generally, Fred Weinstein, *The Dynamics of Nazism: Leadership, Ideology, and the Holocaust* (New York: Academic Press, 1980).

55   The eugenics quote from Daniel J. Kevles, *In the Name of Eugenics* (New York: Alfred A. Knopf, 1985), p. ix.

55   Quotes on racism, nationalism, and degeneration from George L. Mosse, *Toward the Final Solution: A History of European Racism* (New York: Harper & Row, 1980 [1978]), pp. 34, 82.

55   Fritz Lenz quoted in Helmut Krausnick, "The Persecution of the Jews," in Krausnick et al., *Anatomy,* pp. 16–17.

55   The "final solution" and "applied biology" from Lifton, *Nazi Doctors,* p. 31.

55–56   The Nazis and millenarian movements in Joseph M. Rhodes, *The Hitler Movement* (Stanford, Calif.: Hoover Institution Press, 1980), pp. 45, 49.

56   The ideological dichotomy in Lifton, *Nazi Doctors,* p. 205.

56   Ibid., pp. 129–30, for the medical administrator.

57   Ibid., p. 434, on "ideological fragments" of Nazi doctors.

57–58   Ibid., pp. 22–79, 147, for the "five identifiable steps" and the Nazi "euthanasia" programs.

PAGE

58   The sacred function of the SS, in Heinz Höhne, *The Order of the Death's Head: The Story of Hitler's SS* (New York: Ballantine, 1971 [1966]), pp. 26, 175.

58   Himmler quoted in Lucy S. Dawidowicz, *The War Against the Jews, 1933–1945* (New York: Holt, Rinehart and Winston, 1975), p. 149.

58   SS officers on need to "overcome" oneself quoted in Lifton, *Nazi Doctors*, p. 436.

59   Edward R. Murrow in section epigraph quoted by Paul Boyer, *By the Bomb's Early Light: American Thought and Culture at the Dawn of the Atomic Age* (New York: Pantheon, 1985), p. 7.

59   Ibid., pp. 181–95, for Hiroshima-related American fear.

59   Rutherford's quotes in epigraph and text from Richard Rhodes, *The Making of the Atomic Bomb* (New York: Simon & Schuster, 1986), p. 44.

59–60 Soddy and Wells quoted in John Dowling, *Fictions of Nuclear Disaster* (Iowa City: University of Iowa Press, 1987), pp. 44–45.

60   Szilard's story and quote in Rhodes, *The Making*, pp. 281, 331, 442.

61   The section epigraph quoted from Ulam, in Rhodes, *The Making*, p. 677.

61   Ibid., pp. 673–77, for reactions of Los Alamos scientists to the Trinity test.

62   Farrell quoted by Leslie R. Groves, *Now It Can Be Told: The Story of the Manhattan Project* (New York: Harper, 1962), pp. 437–38.

62   Farrell on the "longhairs" in Spencer Weart, *Nuclear Fear: A History of Images* (Cambridge, Mass.: Harvard University Press, 1988), p. 101.

62   The co-pilot, Lewis, quoted in Rhodes, *The Making*, p. 710.

62   McCormick quoted in Boyer, *By the Bomb's*, p. xix.

62   Ibid., p. 6, for quote from the *New York Herald Tribune*.

62   Ibid., p. 5, for Kaltenborn's quote.

63   Ibid., for quote from the *St. Louis Post-Dispatch*.

63   For quote from the *New York Times*, Spencer Weart, "The Atomic Age: The Heyday of Myth and Cliché," *Bulletin of the Atomic Scientists* 41 (August 1985): 43.

63   America's "free security" and Americans' obsession with "national security" in Richard Smoke, *National Security and the Nuclear Dilemma* (New York: Random House, 1984), p. 23–24.

63   Childs's comments in Norman A. Graebner, *The National Security: Its Theory and Practice, 1945–1960* (New York: Oxford University Press, 1986), p. 7.

64   "That henceforth" quote in Richard Rubenstein, *The Cunning of History* (New York: Harper/Colophon Books, 1978 [1975]), p. 2.

64   "A time of cultural crisis" from Boyer, *By the Bomb's*, p. 25.

65   Survey quotes from Leonard S. Cottrell and Silvia Eberhart, *American Opinion on World Affairs in the Atomic Age* (New York: Greenwood Press, 1969 [1948]), pp. 21, 89, 28.

65   End-of-the-world images quoted from Boyer, *By the Bomb's*, p. 14.

PAGE

65   Ibid., pp. 15, 11–12, 20, for array of cultural responses.

65   Ibid., p. 15, for "years before. . . ."

65   Section epigraph from Norman Moss, *Men Who Play God: The Story of the H-Bomb and How the World Came to Live with It* (New York: Harper & Row, 1968), pp. 211–213.

66   Vannevar Bush quoted in Gregg Herken, *The Winning Weapon: The Atomic Bomb in the Cold War, 1945–1950* (New York: Alfred A. Knopf, 1980), p. 127.

66   Ibid., pp. 114–136, for Canadian "atom spies."

66   Boyer's comments on "a population . . . in the grip of atomic fear" in Boyer, *By the Bomb's,* pp. 102–3.

67   On the Rosenbergs and atomic-bomb espionage, see, for instance, Ronald Radosh and Joyce Milton, *The Rosenberg File: The Search for the Truth* (New York: Vintage, 1984); and Joseph Sharlitt, *Fatal Error: The Miscarriage of Justice that Sealed the Rosenbergs' Fate* (New York: Charles Scribner's Sons, 1989).

67–68   On the politics of paranoia in the 1950s, see David Caute, *The Great Fear: The Anti-Communist Purge Under Truman and Eisenhower* (New York: Simon & Schuster, 1978).

67–68   Shils on Americans' fears in Edward Shils, *The Torment of Secrecy: The Background and Consequences of American Security Policies* (Glencoe, Ill.: Free Press, 1956), pp. 64–65; 71.

68   Ibid., for the "secret" of "hidden Communists."

68   Sputnik and "a new dimension of fear" in Eric Goldman, *The Crucial Decade—And After; America: 1945–1960* (New York: Vintage, 1960 [1956]), pp. 307–10.

68   "The very word was enough to send shivers . . . " in Fred Kaplan, *The Wizards of Armageddon* (New York: Simon & Schuster, 1983), pp. 135–36.

68   Ibid., pp. 141–42, for Gaither Committee report.

69   "Mood of diminished awareness" from Boyer, *By the Bomb's,* p. 352.

69   *On the Beach* discussed in Paul Boyer, "From Activism to Apathy: America and the Nuclear Issue, 1963–1980," *Bulletin of the Atomic Scientists* 40 (August/September 1984): 15.

69   On the Cuban missile crisis and wave of fear, see, for example, Barton J. Bernstein, "The Week We Almost Went to War," *Bulletin of the Atomic Scientists* 32 (February 1976): 12–21; David Detzger, *The Brink* (New York: Crowell, 1979); James G. Blight, Joseph S. Nye, Jr., and David A. Welch, "The Cuban Missile Crisis Revisited," *Foreign Affairs* 66 (Fall 1987): 170–89; and David A. Welch and James G. Blight, "The Eleventh Hour of the Cuban Missile Crisis: An Introduction to the Excomm Transcripts," *International Security* 12 (3 [1987–88]): 3–92.

69   "Most Americans . . ." quoted in Boyer, "From Activism to Apathy," p. 23.

70   On early 1980s psychological and social studies, see Daniel Yankelovich and John Doble, "The Public Mood: Nuclear Weapons

PAGE

and the USSR," *Foreign Affairs* 63 (Fall 1984): 33–46; and Daniel Yankelovich, "Voter Options on Nuclear Arms Policy." *The Public Agenda Foundation and the Center for Foreign Policy Development at Brown University* (1984). See also Milton Schwebel, ed., *Mental Health Implications of Life in the Nuclear Age* (special issue), *International Journal of Mental Health* 15 (Spring–Summer–Fall, 1986).

70   The section epigraph is from Martin Amis, *Einstein's Monsters* (New York: Harmony Books, 1987), p. 2.

71   "The dread destroyer . . . " quote is from Boyer, *By the Bomb's*, p. 349.

71   The "questionable assumption . . . " quote is from Harold P. Ford, "Politics, Ethics, and the Arms Race," in H. P. Ford and F. X. Winters, eds., *Ethics and Nuclear Strategy* (Maryknoll, N.Y.: Orbis Books, 1977), p. 58.

71–72 Teller's attitude toward arms control, from interview with nuclear physicist.

72   Teller's quote from Edward Teller, with Allen Brown, *The Legacy of Hiroshima* (Garden City, N.Y.: Doubleday, 1962), p. 312.

72   Oppenheimer's higher purpose and "shaking mankind free" is from Nuel Pharr Davis, *Lawrence and Oppenheimer* (New York: Simon & Schuster, 1960), p. 221.

72   Oppenheimer, Bohr, and "complementarity" in Rhodes, *The Making*, p. 132.

72   Oppenheimer and the physicists' relation to "sin" quoted in Peter Goodchild, *J. Robert Oppenheimer: Shatterer of Worlds* (London: British Broadcasting Corporation, 1980), p. 174.

72–73 The dangerous psychological essence of nuclearism expressed in letter of Robert Oppenheimer to James Conant, in Stanley A. Blumberg and Gwinn Owens, *Energy and Conflict: The Life and Times of Edward Teller* (New York: G. P. Putnam, 1976), p. 207.

73   "Weapons of death" and "weapons of life" quoted in William F. Broad, *Star Warriors: A Penetrating Look into the Lives of the Young Scientists Behind Our Space Age Weaponry* (New York: Simon & Schuster, 1985), p. 47.

73   Distinctions made by ideological factions vs. atomic bomb survivors in Robert Jay Lifton, *Death in Life: Survivors of Hiroshima* (New York: Basic Books, 1982 [1967]), pp. 290–305.

74   Forrestal quote in section epigraph is from Graebner, *The National Security*, p. 8.

74   Raskin on the concept of national security in Marcus Raskin, *The Politics of National Security* (New Brunswick, N.J.: Transaction Books, 1979), p. 32.

74   Ibid., p. 33, for ideology of "the national security state."

75   "Appeasement phobia" discussed in Martin Sherwin, "The Sources of American Conduct," in *Socialist Review* 15 (2 [March–April 1985]): 8.

PAGE

75   Steel quoted in Robert Borosage, "The Making of the National Security State," in L. S. Rodberg and D. Shearer, eds., *Pentagon Watchers* (Garden City, N.Y.: Doubleday, 1970), p. 5.

75   "A certain omnipotence and hubris" quoted from Raskin, *The Politics*, p. 38.

75   "Burgeoning reliance" quote in Graebner, *The National Security*, p. 24.

75   "A qualitative edge . . . " quoted in Herbert F. York, *Making Weapons, Talking Peace: A Physicist's Odyssey from Hiroshima to Geneva* (New York: Basic Books, 1987), p. 77.

75   Mills quoted in Borosage, "The Making," p. 12.

75   "The country had no choice . . . " quoted in Graebner, *The National Security*, p. 25.

75–76   York's description of the first SIOP in York, *Making Weapons*, p. 185.

76   Increasingly destructive war-fighting plans discussed in Borosage, "The Making," pp. 49, 50, 51.

76   York's "treason" quote is from his *Making Weapons*, p. 120.

76   "If the Jew did not exist . . . " quote from Hitler, attributed to Hermann Rauschning, former Nazi head of their Danzig government; cited in Leon Poliakov, *Harvest of Hate: The Nazi Program for the Destruction of the Jews of Europe,* rev. and expanded ed. (New York: Holocaust Library, 1979 [1951]), p. 2.

Chapter 4. Science, Technology, and Totalism

77   The first chapter epigraph is from Henry Adams, *The Education of Henry Adams* (New York: Modern Library, 1931), p. 380.

77   The second chapter epigraph is from E. L. Doctorow, "The State of Mind of the Union," *The Nation* 242 (22 March 1986): 330–31.

79   The section epigraph is from Langdon Winner, *Autonomous Technology: Technics-Out-of-Control as a Theme in Political Thought* (Cambridge, Mass.: MIT Press, 1980 [1977]), p. 73.

79   Mumford and the "mechanical world-picture" quoted in Lewis Mumford, *The Pentagon of Power: The Myth of the Machine,* vol. 2 (New York: Harcourt Brace Jovanovich, 1969), p. 265.

79   Ibid., p. 248, for his quotes about Hitler and the "megamachine."

79   Ibid., p. 267, for Mumford on our present megamachine.

79   White's image of the "defense intellectual" quoted from Fred Kaplan, *The Wizards of Armageddon* (New York: Simon & Schuster, 1983), p. 257.

PAGE

79   "Silent secularization" described in Fritz Stern, *Dreams and Delusions:
         The Drama of German History* (New York: Alfred A. Knopf, 1987).

80   Technique as its own mystical truth in William Barrett, *The Illusion
         of Technique* (New York: Doubleday/Anchor, 1979); and Jacques
         Ellul, *The Technological Society* (New York: Alfred A. Knopf, 1964).

80   The Nazis and "reactionary modernism" discussed in Jeffrey Herf,
         *Reactionary Modernism: Technology, Culture, and Politics in Weimar and the
         Third Reich* (Cambridge: Cambridge University Press, 1984). See
         also Albert Speer, *Inside the Third Reich* (New York: Macmillan,
         1970).

80   "A combination of reactionary politics . . . " quote is from Michael
         Sherry, *The Rise of American Air Power* (New Haven: Yale University
         Press, 1987), p. 66.

80   Unpredictability of technological developments described in Winner,
         Autonomous Technology, p. 97.

80   For attitudes of technological destiny and deliverance, Steven Kull,
         personal communication, and *Minds at War: Nuclear Reality and the
         Inner Conflicts of Defense Policymakers* (New York: Basic Books, 1988),
         pp. 208–22; William F. Broad, *Star Warriors: A Penetrating Look into
         the Lives of the Young Scientists Behind Our Space Age Weaponry* (New
         York: Simon & Schuster, 1985), pp. 47–71; Winner, *Autonomous
         Technology*, pp. 70–71, 73.

80   Heisenberg quoted in Winner, *Autonomous Technology*, p. 70.

81   Teller quote is from interview with physicist, 1987.

81   "Technically sweet" from Oppenheimer in testimony before the
         U.S. Atomic Energy Commission in 1954, quoted in *In the Matter
         of J. Robert Oppenheimer* (Cambridge, Mass.: MIT Press, 1971), p.
         251.

81   The "rhetoric of the technological sublime" is from Leo Marx,
         "Does Improved Technology Mean Progress?" *Technology Review* 90
         (January 1987): 38.

81   The "nuclear sublime" quoted from Frances Ferguson, "The
         Nuclear Sublime," *diacritics* 14 (2 [Summer 1984]): 9.

81   On nuclearism and the illusion of technological wisdom, see
         Barrett, *The Illusion*, p. 218.

81   For a discussion of *psychism*, see Robert Jay Lifton, *Revolutionary
         Immortality: Mao Tse-tung and the Chinese Cultural Revolution* (New York:
         Random House, 1968), p. 32.

81   "Cosmic emptiness" quoted in Barrett, *The Illusion*, p. 218.

82   The section epigraph is from William L. Laurence, *Men and Atoms*
         (New York: Simon & Schuster, 1959), p. 118.

82   Adams quoted in Winner, *Autonomous Technology*, pp. 44–45.

82–83   Laurence's description of the Trinity test is from Laurence, *Men and
         Atoms*, pp. 116–19.

83   Ibid., p. 118, for Kistiakowsky quote.

83   "This rising supersun . . . " quoted in Laurence, *Men and Atoms*, p.
         197.

PAGE

83   From annihilation to worship in Robert Jay Lifton, *The Broken Connection: On Death and the Continuity of Life* (New York: Basic Books/Harper Colophon, 1983 [1979]), pp. 373–75.

83   Ibid., p. 424, nuclearism discussed as *heroic scientism*; the myth of the hero discussed in Joseph Campbell, *The Hero with a Thousand Faces* (New York: Meridian, 1956). See also Edward Teller, with Allen Brown, *The Legacy of Hiroshima* (Garden City, N.Y.: Doubleday, 1962).

84   Teller's false claims are discussed in Frank von Hippel, "The Myths of Edward Teller," *Bulletin of the Atomic Scientists* 39 (March 1983): 6–12.

84   Teller's statements on radiation in Teller, *The Legacy*, p. 180.

84   The "faith-state" described in William James, *The Varieties of Religious Experience: A Study in Human Nature* (London and New York: Longmans, Green & Co., 1952), pp. 421–22.

84   "Faith-state" in strategists and decision makers, Steven Kull, personal communication.

84   "See themselves as channels . . . " from James, *The Varieties*, p. 99.

84   Nuclear fundamentalism described in A. G. Mojtabai, *Blessed Assurance: At Home with the Bomb in Amarillo, Texas* (Boston: Houghton Mifflin, 1986), pp. 167–68. See also Robert Jay Lifton, *The Future of Immortality and Other Essays for a Nuclear Age* (New York: Basic Books, 1987), pp. 122–24; and Grace Halseol, *Prophesy and Politics: Militant Evangelists on the Road to Nuclear War* (Westport, Conn.: Lawrence Hill & Co., 1986).

85   Pentecostal preacher and nuclear Armageddon quotes from Lifton, *Future of Immortality*, pp. 122–23.

85   On millennial movements, see Norman Cohn, *Pursuit of the Millennium: Revolutionary Messianism in Medieval and Reformation Europe and Its Bearing on Modern Totalitarian Movements*, 2d ed. (New York: Harper Torch Books, 1961).

85   "A millenarian-gnostic revolution . . . " quote from James Rhodes, *The Hitler Movement* (Stanford, Calif.: Hoover Institution Press, 1980), p. 18.

85   On von Liebenfels, see Ewa Kuryluk, "The Other Vienna," *Formations* 2 (2 [Fall 1985]).

85   On the Aryan Nation and similar groups, see James Coates, *Armed and Dangerous: The Rise of the Survivalist Right* (New York: Noonday Press, 1987).

86   Evidence of lure of Armageddon in some strategists, Kull, personal communication. See also Kull, "Nuclear Arms and the Desire for World Destruction," *Political Psychology* 4 (1983): 563–91.

86   See Arthur Kopit, *End of the World: With Symposium to Follow*, International Creative Management, typescript.

87   Section epigraph from Doctorow, "The State of Mind," p. 330.

87   Bolshevism as "the highest stage of Judaism" quoted from John W. Herz, "Power Politics or Ideology? The Nazi Experience," in

George Schwab, ed., *Ideology and Foreign Policy: A Global Perspective* (New York: Cyrco Press, 1978), p. 18.

87   "Godless monsters" and "focus of evil" from a Ronald Reagan speech to National Association of Evangelicals, 8 March 1983.

87–88   NSC-68 report quoted from "NSC-68: A Report to the National Security Council," *Naval War College Review* 38 (May–June 1985): 53–79; Samuel F. Wells, Jr., "Sounding the Tocsin: NSC-68 and the Soviet Threat," *International Security* 4 (Fall 1979): 116–58.

88   "Deliberately hyped" from Kaplan, *Wizards,* p. 140; "amazingly incomplete . . . " from Wells, "Sounding the Tocsin," p. 139.

88   York's comments on weapons work and the defense department in Herbert F. York, *Making Weapons, Talking Peace: A Physicist's Odyssey from Hiroshima to Geneva* (New York: Basic Books, 1987), p. 327–28.

88   "Totalistic projects" discussed in Robert Jay Lifton, *Thought Reform and the Psychology of Totalism: A Study of "Brainwashing" in China* (Chapel Hill, N.C.: University of North Carolina Press, 1989 [1961]), esp. pp. 419–37.

88   "Metaphors of power, . . . " quote in Paul Chilton, "Metaphor, Euphemism, and the Militarization of Language," *Current Research on Peace and Violence,* vol. 10 (Finland: Tampere Peace Research Institute, 1987), pp. 7–19; quote on p. 16.

89–90   Powers on the General Advisory Committee report, from Thomas Powers, personal communication.

90   Himmler, quoted in Lucy S. Dawidowicz, *The War Against the Jews, 1933–1945* (New York: Holt, Rinehart and Winston, 1975), p. 149.

90   Ibid., for Himmler's quote about the SS.

91   On routinization of mystique, see, for example, Max Weber, *On Charisma and Institution Building,* ed. with an introduction by S. N. Eisenstadt (Chicago: University of Chicago Press, 1968), esp. chap. 6; and Ronald M. Glassman and William H. Swatos, Jr., eds., *Charisma, History and Social Structure* (New York: Greenwood Press, 1986).

91   On bizarre nuclear "scenarios," see Lawrence Freedman, *The Price of Peace* (New York: Henry Holt, 1986), p. 38.

91   A former missile combat crew member quoted in Lloyd J. Dumas, "Human Fallibility and Weapons," *Bulletin of the Atomic Scientists* 36 (November 1980): 17–18.

91   "You just do not know" from interview with a senior strategist, 1987.

92   A German medical professor in Lifton, *Nazi Doctors,* p. 393.

93   On the moral justification for the atomic bombing of Japan, see, for examples, Rufus E. Miles, "Hiroshima: The Strange Myth of Half a Million American Lives Saved," *International Security* 10 (1985): 123–35; and Charles B. Strozier, "Unconditional Surrender and the Rhetoric of Total War: From Truman to Lincoln," Occasional Paper

PAGE

        no. 2, Center on Violence and Human Survival, John Jay College of Criminal Justice, City University of New York, 1987.

93   American "folk culture of nuclear weapons" in Alan Wolfe, "Nuclear Fundamentalism Reborn," *World Policy Journal* 2 (1 [Fall 1984]): 92.

93   York's interpretation of Oppenheimer quoted in York, *Making Weapons*, p. 326.

93   Ibid., p. 327, for quote on GAC report.

94   Nye's response to Schell quoted from Joseph S. Nye, Jr., *Nuclear Ethics* (New York: Free Press, 1986), pp. 63–64.

94   Phyllis Schlafly, quoted in Lynn Rossellini, "Victory Is Bittersweet for Architect of Amendment's Downfall," *New York Times*, 1 July 1982, p. A12.

95   The "legitimation crisis" and "de facto legitimacy of indiscriminate killing" are discussed by Brian D'Agostino, "War and Strategic Weapons in American Politics: Changing Attitudes and Legitimation Crisis," typescript.

96   Stimson quoted in Lifton, *Broken Connection*, pp. 377, 379.

96   Ibid., pp. 419–20, for Szilard.

96   Ibid., p. 380, for view held by Truman and others.

96   Lowell's "And I am a red arrow . . . " from "Where the Rainbow Ends," *Lord Weary's Castle* (New York: Harcourt, Brace, and World, 1946), p. 69.

96–97   Lowell quoted in A. Alvarez, "A Talk with Robert Lowell," *Encounter* 24 (2 [February 1965]): 39–46.

Chapter 5. Professionals

98   The first chapter epigraph is from Primo Levi, *The Drowned and the Saved* (New York: Summit Books, 1988), p. 123.

98   The second chapter epigraph is from Richard Feynman, Obituary by James Gleick, *New York Times*, 17 February 1988, p. A1.

99   The section epigraph is from a Nazi physician, quoted in Robert Jay Lifton, *The Nazi Doctors: Medical Killing and the Psychology of Genocide* (New York: Basic Books, 1986), p. 71.

99   On *Gleichschaltung* and the German medical profession, see Karl Dietrich Bracher, *The German Dictatorship* (New York: Praeger, 1970), p. 247. See also Michael Kater, *Doctors under Hitler* (Chapel Hill: University of North Carolina Press, in press); and Lifton, *Nazi Doctors*, pp. 22–44.

100   Lenz quoted in Kater, *Doctors under Hitler*, in press.

100   Lorenz, quoted in Lifton, *Nazi Doctors*, p. 134.

101   The central theorist described in Benno Müller-Hill, *Murderous*

PAGE

Science: Elimination by Scientific Selection of Jews, Gypsies, and Others in Germany 1933–1945 (Oxford, New York, Tokyo: Oxford University Press, 1988), p. 12.

101   Ibid., p. 6, for "What a special and rare joy. . . ."

101   On killing centers as places of advanced therapy, see Lifton, *Nazi Doctors*, pp. 45–79.

101   "Life unworthy of life" from Karl Binding and Alfred Hoche, *Die Freigabe der Vernichtung lebensunwerten Lebens: Ihr Mass und ihre Form* (Leipzig: F. Meiner, 1920).

101   Ibid., pp. 61–62, for "one hundred percent certainty. . . ."

101–2   On leading doctors and biomedical ideology, see Lifton, *Nazi Doctors*, pp. 103–33.

102   Ibid., p. 104, for "scientific tradition."

102   Ibid., pp. 105–7, 269–78, for discussion of brain dissections and sterilization experiments.

102–3   Ibid., pp. 169–79, 255–68, for description of Auschwitz doctors and the killing process.

103   Ibid., p. 178, for "purely a technical matter."

103   Auschwitz as "a monument . . . " in Müller-Hill, *Murderous Science*, p. 15.

103–4   Socialization to killing, discussed in Lifton, *Nazi Doctors*, pp. 193–213.

104   Ibid., p. 71, for Brandt, Conti, and "responsibility."

104   Ibid., pp. 123–25, for Eberl quotes.

104–5   Ibid., pp. 114–17, for Brandt on the gas method as more "humane."

105   Ibid., pp. 143, 453, for the second consultation.

105   Ibid., pp. 172–79, 445–46, 452–53, on "medical responsibility" and language in Auschwitz.

105–6   Ibid., pp. 178–79, for quotes on Auschwitz life for Nazi doctors.

106   Ibid., pp. 200, 446–47, for doctors' double sense of Auschwitz.

106   Ibid., pp. 446–47, for "a separate planet."

106   Ibid., pp. 418–65, for psychological *doubling*.

106   Ibid., p. 425, for "internal environment."

107   Ibid., p. 198, for "the Auschwitz weather."

107   Section epigraph is from Hans Bethe, personal interview, 1987.

108   Haber, Franck, Hahn, and Immerwahr discussed in Richard Rhodes, *The Making of the Atomic Bomb* (New York: Simon & Schuster, 1986), pp. 92–95.

108   Oppenheimer in the early 1930s described in Daniel Kevles, *The Physicists* (New York: Vintage, 1979), p. 218.

108   *Ibid.*, p. 282 for "the United States leads the world. . . ."

108   Ibid., p. 286, for "big physics" and "expensive machines. . . ."

109   Ibid., p. 293, for "how best. . . ."

109   Ibid., p. 303, for "radiation laboratory."

109   Ibid., p. 308, for "the atom bomb only ended the war. . . ."

PAGE

110   Interview with Hans Bethe at Cornell University, 14 December 1987.

110   Interview with Herbert York in New York City, 1 June 1987.

110   Wilson on "survival of the democratic world," from telephone interview, 24 February 1988.

110   Bethe's recollection of physicists from interview, 14 December 1987.

110   Ibid. for Bethe on scientists viewing photographs of Hiroshima bombing.

111   Section epigraph from Rhodes, *The Making,* p. 572.

111   Ibid., p. 539, for Teller on Oppenheimer.

111   Ibid., p. 445, on Oppenheimer's arrogance and impatience.

111   Ibid., p. 570, for first Bethe quote on Oppenheimer.

111   Oppenheimer as "intellectually superior," from interview with Bethe, 14 December 1987.

111–12   For this kind of charismatic leader, see especially Erik H. Erikson, *Young Man Luther* (New York: W. W. Norton, 1958); *Gandhi's Truth* (New York: W. W. Norton, 1969); and *Life History and the Historical Moment* (New York: W. W. Norton, 1975).

112   Oppenheimer and *Trinity* discussed in Rhodes, *The Making,* p. 572.

112   Ibid., p. 132, for Segrè on complementarity.

113   "Oppenheimer became a symbol . . . " from Philip Rieff, quoted in Kevles, *The Physicists,* p. 377.

113   Ibid., p. 336, for *Time* quote.

113–14   Ibid., p. 308, for physicists and the American military. See also I. B. Holley, Jr., "The Evolution of Operations Research and Its Impact on the Military Establishment: The Air Force Experience," in *Science, Technology and Warfare,* Lt. Col. D. Wright and L. J. Paszek, eds. (Washington, D.C.: Office of Air Force History, 1970), pp. 89–109.

114   "Without definite knowledge . . . " quoted from Franck report on "The Political Implications of Atomic Weapons" (11 June 1945), in Martin Sherwin, *A World Destroyed: Hiroshima and the Arms Race* (New York: Vintage, 1987 [1973]), p. 329.

114–15   "My main wish . . . " "very exciting time . . . " and ". . . a pleasant place, . . . " from interview with Bethe, 14 December 1987.

115   On the Baruch plan, see McGeorge Bundy, *Danger and Survival* (New York: Random House, 1988), pp. 155–76; Paul Boyer, *By the Bomb's Early Light: American Thought and Culture at the Dawn of the Atomic Age* (New York: Pantheon, 1985), pp. 53–56; Herbert F. York, *Making Weapons, Talking Peace: A Physicist's Odyssey from Hiroshima to Geneva* (New York: Basic Books, 1987), p. 42; and Gregg Herken, *Counsels of War* (New York: Alfred A. Knopf, 1985), p. 55.

115   York's "*Who's Who* of American physics . . ." noted in York, *Making Weapons,* p. 52.

116   York's observation about Lawrence quoted from interview with York, 1 June 1987.

116   Teller's visit to Bethe from interview with Bethe, 14 December 1987.

PAGE

116   Ibid., for Bethe's response.

116   "This weapon of total annihilation" quoted from Hans Bethe, "The Hydrogen Bomb," *Bulletin of the Atomic Scientists* 6 (4 [April 1950]): 99–104.

117   Bethe's change of heart, from interview, 14 December 1987.

117   Ibid., for Bethe's feelings on official visit.

118   Bethe as mentor at Los Alamos quoted in Freeman Dyson, *Disturbing the Universe* (New York: Harper & Row, 1979), p. 51.

118   On post–Los Alamos period and honorable "sin," see Rhodes, *The Making*, pp. 749–88; and Kevles, *The Physicists*, pp. 334–53.

118   Lawrence's defiant reply to Oppenheimer quoted in Herbert F. York, *The Advisors* (San Francisco: W. H. Freeman, 1976), p. 64.

118   York quoted in Karyn Gladstone, *The Unfolding of the Nuclear Age: A Psychohistorical Investigation into the Lives of Ten Men*, vol. 1., Ph.D. diss., Union Institute, Cincinnati, Ohio, 1987, p. 193.

118–19   Alvarez's summation quoted in Luis W. Alvarez, *Alvarez: Adventures of a Physicist* (New York: Basic Books, 1987), p. 181.

119   Garwin's comments on Los Alamos from interview with Richard Garwin in New York City, 7 May 1987.

119   Ibid., for Teller's remark.

119   Garwin as "a wizard" from interview with Bethe, 14 December 1987.

119   "High-intensity involvement . . . " from interview with Garwin, 7 May 1987.

119–20   For a description of subsequent generations of physicists, see William F. Broad, *Star Warriors: A Penetrating Look into the Lives of the Young Scientists Behind Our Space Age Weaponry* (New York: Simon & Schuster, 1985), pp. 28–36; 50–51.

120   Taylor's recollections of Teller from interview with Theodore Taylor in Baltimore, Maryland, 3 December 1987.

120   Brodie quoted in Fred Kaplan, *The Wizards of Armageddon* (New York: Simon & Schuster, 1983), pp. 9–10.

121   Ibid., pp. 32–33, for Brodie's quotes on deterrence.

121   Ibid., p. 59, for description of RAND.

121–22   Ibid., p. 73, for RAND and *game theory*.

122   Ibid., p. 62, for RAND's "freewheeling . . . atmosphere."

122   RAND and *systems analysis* described in Bradley S. Klein, "Strategic Discourse and Its Alternatives," Occasional Paper no. 3, Center on Violence and Human Survival, John Jay College of Criminal Justice, City University of New York, 1987, p. 8.

123   See Kaplan, *Wizards*, pp. 119–32 for a discussion of Kahn; see Herken, *Counsels*, pp. 309–12, for a discussion of Gray.

123   Gray, Brennan, and "Armageddon syndrome" from Herken, *Counsels*, pp. 310, 342–43; quote on p. 310.

123   Breakthrough élite who "would attempt . . ." and "condition an entire generation . . ." in Kaplan, *Wizards*, p. 10.

123   "Intractable uncertainties" and "realistic tactical experience . . ."

quoted from Holley, "The Evolution of Operations Research," pp. 101–2.

124–25   York's remarks about Teller from interview with York, 1 June 1987.

125   Kahn as "messianic" and a "pioneer," from interview with a prominent nuclear strategist, 1987.

125–26   For a discussion of *Einsatzgruppen* and *Desinfektoren*, see Lifton, *Nazi Doctors*, pp. 159–62.

126   Ibid., p. 15, for the German neuropsychiatrist.

126   Nuclear Weapons Personnel Reliability Program discussed in Lester Grinspoon, "Crisis Behavior," *Bulletin of the Atomic Scientists* 40 (April 1984): 27–32; see also Lloyd J. Dumas, "Human Fallibility and Nuclear Weapons," *Bulletin of the Atomic Scientists* 36 (September 1980): 15–19.

127   Section epigraph from interview with physicist, 1987.

127   Ibid., for quotes about the atomic and the hydrogen bomb.

128   Ibid., for quotes on SDI.

128   Scientific principles and technological applications from interview with physicist, 1987.

129   "This feeling of working together . . ." from interview with a different physicist, 1987.

129   Bethe's "satisfaction" from interview, 14 December 1987.

129   Alvarez and the AEC, quoted from Alvarez, *Alvarez*, p. 189.

130   Hagelstein and Star Wars, from Broad, *Star Warriors*, p. 117.

130   Ibid., for Hagelstein's change of heart.

130   "Events overtook him," from interview with scientist, 1987.

130   Quotes on a young scientist at Los Alamos, from interview with physicist, 1987.

131   Contradictory feelings described in interview with physicist, 1987.

131   Quote on problem solving, from interview with strategist, 1987.

131   "Second education . . ." and following quotes, from interview with strategist, 1987.

131–32   Strategist as having "remained static," from interview with student of strategy, 1987.

132   "These sorts of studies . . ." quoted from Kaplan, *Wizards*, p. 121.

132   "A problem of physics . . ." from Klein, "Strategic Discourse," p. 14.

132   "Pure theology," in Kaplan, *Wizards*, pp. 139–40.

132   First section epigraph from interview with Theodore Taylor, 1987.

133   Second section epigraph, from Deborah Shapley; "Jason Division: Defense Consultants Who Are Also Professors Attacked," *Science* 179 (4072 [2 February 1973]): 460.

133   York's description of himself quoted in York, *Making Weapons*, p. 295.

134   "Our work at Los Alamos . . ." quoted from Theodore B. Taylor, "From Bomb Designer to Disarmament Activist," typescript, pp. 3–4.

PAGE

134   "There was no one . . ." quoted from interview with York, 1 June
           1987.

134   Reagan and SDI, in Jeff Smith, "Reagan, Star Wars, and American
           Culture," *Bulletin of the Atomic Scientists* 43 (November 1987): 19–25.

134   "Alone with their physics," from interview with scientist, 1987.

134–35   "The more you understand . . ." from Müller-Hill, *Murderous Science*,
           p. 15.

135   "Fascination with a sense of power, . . ." and following quotes,
           from interview with Taylor, 3 December 1987.

135   "Another great time . . ." from interview with Bethe, 14 December
           1987.

135–36   York's disturbing perceptions described in interview, 1 June
           1987.

136   Early days of weapons making recalled by Bethe, interview, 14
           December 1987.

136   Puzzling lack of foresight quoted from interview with
           scientist-strategist, 1987.

136   von Neumann quoted in York, *Making Weapons*, pp. 91–92.

136   "I was afraid . . ." quote from interview with Bethe, 14 December
           1987.

137   Garwin on government programs from interview, 7 May 1987.

137–38   Ibid., for comments on Star Wars.

138   Information on antimatter from the *American Heritage Desk Dictionary*
           (Boston: Houghton Mifflin, 1981).

138   Garwin and "credibility," from interview, 7 May 1987.

139   Bethe's remarks on weapons consulting from interview, 14
           December 1987.

139   York's quote ("you can have much more influence . . .") from
           interview, 1 June 1987.

139   Taylor's "it was fun . . ." and "the prominence . . ." quoted from
           interview, 3 December 1987.

140   "The black side of things . . ." quoted from interview with
           strategist, 1987.

140   "It's a different situation . . ." quoted from interview with scientist,
           1987.

141   Weapons physicists in "a very closed society," from interview with
           another scientist, 1987.

141   Wood as "Darth Vader," from Broad, *Star Warriors*, p. 116.

141   "Sensible" and "balanced" manner, from Lifton, *Nazi Doctors*, p.
           434.

141   American-Soviet "affinity" described in interview with scientist,
           1987.

142   The Jason group discussed in Deborah Shapley, "Jason Division,"
           pp. 459–505, quote ("our best scientists") on p. 460; see also York,
           Making Weapons, p. 234, for "work on problems . . . of defense."

142   Jason group and Nobel Prize recounted in York, *Making Weapons*, p.
           153.

PAGE

142   Meetings in attractive areas and Dyson quote in Shapley, "Jason Division," p. 460.

143   Ibid., p. 461, for description of "electronic battlefield."

143   Ibid., for "you don't confront generals."

143   "Ranging from basing modes . . ." and "window of vulnerability," from York, *Making Weapons,* p. 234.

143   The MX described in Herken, *Counsels,* p. 289.

144   Kistiakowsky, Weisner, McNamara, as "noble souls" with "credibility," from interview with engineer-strategist, 1987.

144   Ibid., for quotes that stress their decency.

144–45   "Heroic sense" and "enchanted" with "big events," described in interview with former strategist, 1987.

145   Ibid., for "outsiders are rejected."

145   Insider status, "a macho side," and "group-think" discussed in interview with leading decision maker, 1987.

145   "Omnicidal whimsy" and Doomsday Machines in Herman Kahn, *On Thermonuclear War* (Princeton: Princeton University Press, 1961), pp. 145–52.

146   Ibid., p. 149, for "Then *how many people . . . ?*" and "the *possibility. . . .*"

146   Ibid., p. 145, for Doomsday Machine "almost caricaturized."

146   "Learning the [nuclear] language . . ." quote from Carol Cohn, "Slick'ems, Glick'ems, Christmas Trees, and Cookie Cutters: Nuclear Language and How We Learned to Pat the Bomb," *Bulletin of the Atomic Scientists* 43 (5 [June 1987]): 17–24, quote on p. 24. See also Carol Cohn, "Sex and Death in the Rational World of Defense Intellectuals," *Signs* 12 (4 [Summer 1987]): 687–718.

147   "—you've got a way out" quoted from interview with engineer-strategist, 1987.

147   The paradox of "conservatism," quoted from interview with high-ranking decision maker, 1987.

147   "A distaste for nuclear weapons," "garbage in, garbage out," and other quotes, from interview with former strategist, 1987.

148   "That's the way things are," from Steven Kull, personal communication.

148   On mystical system, and mystical "contest," see Steven Kull, *Minds at War: Nuclear Reality and the Inner Conflicts of Defense Policymakers* (New York: Basic Books, 1988), esp. chap. 10.

148   "Dare to be barbaric, . . ." quote from Thomas Mann, *Doctor Faustus: The Life of the German Composer Adrian Leverkühn as Told by a Friend* (New York: Alfred A. Knopf, 1948 [1947]), p. 243.

148–49   "Some kind of split" encouraged by family, described by Taylor, interview, 3 December 1987.

149   Ibid., for "Daddy's workpen" and effect on Taylor's family.

149   Ibid., for his description of "what would happen."

149–50   Taylor at the Pentagon, quoted in David Scheff, "About Face"

PAGE

(interview with Theodore B. Taylor), *Rolling Stone,* 24 September 1987, p. 145.

150   Taylor on magazine article quoted from interview, 3 December 1987.

150   Bethe on separation between work and family, quoted from interview, 14 December 1987.

151   Poignant struggle against dissociation and doubling and "two kinds of thinking" and other quotes, from interview with scientist-strategist, 1987.

151   Ibid., for second course and "schizophrenia."

152   Kull's interviews with strategists and decision makers described in Steven Kull, "The Mind-Sets of Defense Policy-Makers," *Psychohistory Review* 14 (1985): 21–37.

152–53 Ibid., p. 29, for Bush interview with Scheer.

153   Ibid., p. 25, for decision makers' "flip-flops."

154   Division from "public face" in Eisenhower and others, from interview with scientific advisor, 1987.

154   "The man in the laboratory . . ." quoted from Solly Zuckerman, "Science Advisors, Scientific Advisors, and Nuclear Weapons," *Proceedings,* The American Philosophical Society, 124 (4 [August 1980]): 10–11.

154   "They can never have enough . . ." and comments on Teller, from interview with knowledgeable scientific observer, 1987.

155   "Only the system . . ." is from Thomas Powers, "How Nuclear War Could Start," review of Paul Bracken, *The Command and Control of Nuclear Forces,* in *New York Review of Books,* 17 January 1985, p. 35.

155   "Destroy the world without malice" quoted from Charles B. Strozier, personal communication.

155   "It's not in the hands of . . ." from interview with leading weapons designer, 1987.

Chapter 6. Momentum toward Genocide

156   The first chapter epigraph is from Herbert F. York, *Race to Oblivion: A Participant's View of the Arms Race* (New York: Simon & Schuster, 1970), p. 237.

156   The second chapter epigraph is from Thomas Powers, "How Nuclear War Could Start," *New York Review of Books,* 17 January 1985, p. 35.

156   Term *behemoth* described in Franz L. Neumann, *Behemoth,* 2d ed. (New York: Octagon Books, 1963 [1944]).

157   "The problem of momentum," from Lawrence Freedman, *The*

PAGE

Evolution of Nuclear Strategy (New York: St. Martin's Press, 1983 [1981]), p. 337.

157   "Vicious spiral . . ." quote is from York, *Race to Oblivion,* p. 237.

157   "Unforeseen," "irreversible," and "unintended" consequences, quoted from Langdon Winner, *Autonomous Technology: Technics-Out-of-Control as a Theme in Political Thought* (Cambridge, Mass.: MIT Press, 1980 [1977]), pp. 89–93.

157–58   Weapons technology "extremely open-ended" and "endless generations," from Theodore B. Taylor, "Endless Generations of Nuclear Weapons," *Bulletin of the Atomic Scientists* 42 (November 1986): 12.

158   "Psychic and spiritual needs . . . holy—cause" from York, *Race to Oblivion,* p. 235.

158   "Once war has become inescapable" quoted from Thomas Powers, "Spontaneous Combustion," review of Daniel Ford, *The Button,* in *The Sciences* 25 (September–October 1985): 51, 52.

158   Brodie's early reading, quoted in Gregg Herken, *Counsels of War* (New York: Alfred A. Knopf, 1985), p. 38.

159   The section epigraph is from Raul Hilberg, *The Destruction of the European Jews,* vol. 1 (New York: Holmes & Meier, 1985 [1961]), p. 55.

159   Friedländer quoted in Gerald Fleming, *Hitler and the Final Solution* (Berkeley: University of California Press, 1985 [1982]), p. xxxi.

159   Genocide an act that "had meaning . . ." quoted from Hilberg, *The Destruction,* vol. 3, p. 993.

160   "Everybody is ready to die . . ." from J. P. Stern, *Hitler: The Führer and the People* (Glasgow: Fontana/Collins, 1975), p. 195.

160   "More life . . ." quote from Christopher Browning, *Fateful Months: Essays on the Emergence of the Final Solution* (New York and London: Holmes & Meier, 1985), pp. 15–16.

160   No plans for mass murder until "the end of 1940 . . ." and other quotes in Yehuda Bauer, "The *Kristallnacht* as Turning Point: Jewish Reactions to Nazi Policies," in L. Letgers, ed., *Western Society After the Holocaust* (Boulder, Colo.: Westview Press, 1983), p. 42.

160   Ibid., for "purification of German Soil. . . ."

160   Ibid., pp. 39–55, for description of *Kristallnacht.*

160   Hitler and "the annihilation of the Jewish race in Europe" from Michael R. Marrus, *The Holocaust in History* (Hanover and London: University Press of New England, 1987), p. 37.

161   Hitler a "fighting prophet," from Fleming, *Hitler,* p. 69.

161   Quotes on Hitler's anti-Semitism from Eberhard Jäckel in Marrus, *The Holocaust,* p. 15; see also Robert G. L. Waite, *The Psychopathic God: Adolf Hitler* (New York: Basic Books, 1977).

162   *Einsatzgruppen,* or "task forces," from Lucy S. Dawidowicz, *The War Against the Jews, 1933–1945* (New York: Holt, Rinehart and Winston, 1975), p. 114.

162   "A curious collection . . ." quote from Heinz Höhne, *The Order of*

the Death's Head: The Story of Hitler's SS (New York: Ballantine Books, 1984 [1971]) (originally published in German in 1966), p. 405.

162   Hitler quoted on "the extermination of the Armenians" in Browning, *Fateful Months*, p. 5.

162   The "suppression of all anti-Reich elements . . ." quote from Höhne, *The Order*, p. 337.

162   Ibid., p. 403, for "an example of the curious military schizophrenia. . . ."

162   The "war of destruction" and following quotes, from Bauer, "The Kristallnacht," p. 41.

163   Hitler's early directive quoted from Höhne, *The Order*, p. 401.

163   "Many millions . . . may have surpassed even the Final Solution," from Marrus, *The Holocaust*, p. 53.

163   Commanders' reports, "couched in cold, official language . . ." from Höhne, *The Order*, pp. 407–8.

163   Ibid., p. 415, for Nazi "higher purpose."

163–64   For a general discussion of Nazi sterilization and "euthanasia," see Robert Jay Lifton, *The Nazi Doctors: Medical Killing and the Psychology of Genocide* (New York: Basic Books, 1986), pp. 22–144.

165   "There was no killing . . ." quoted from ibid., p. 57.

165   Ibid., pp. 152–62, for development of Auschwitz killing method.

165–66   Ibid., pp. 123–25, for the first commandant of Treblinka.

166   See Hilberg, *The Destruction*, vol. 1, pp. 155–270, for a discussion of ghettos as pre-genocidal institutions.

166   The section epigraph is from Hilberg, *The Destruction*, vol. 3, p. 993.

166   "Bureaucratic . . ." and "fidelity . . ." quotes from Marrus, *The Holocaust*, p. 42.

167   "Careerism could be exploited . . ." in Browning, *Fateful Months*, p. 58.

167   Ibid., for "adapted both their talents . . ." and the SS "Criminal Technical Institute."

168   The section epigraph is from Richard L. Rubenstein, *The Cunning of History: The Holocaust and the American Future* (New York: Harper & Row, 1978), p. 4.

168   Many "were eagerly prepared . . ." and following quotes, from Browning, *Fateful Months*, p. 4.

168   "A mosaic of . . . enterprises" quoted from Hilberg, *The Destruction*, vol. 3, pp. 993–94.

169   Intellectuals and professionals as "transmission belt," from Yehuda Bauer, personal communication. See also Eric Markusen, "Professions, Professionals, and Genocide," in I. W. Charny, ed., *Genocide: A Critical Bibliographic Review*, vol. 2 (New York: Facts on File, 1990).

169   "Every profession, every skill . . ." quote from Hilberg, *The Destruction*, p. 1011.

PAGE

169 "German bureaucracy . . . did not have to be told . . ." quoted in Browning, *Fateful Months,* p. 11.

169 "Auschwitz was an existing fact . . ." quoted in Lifton, *Nazi Doctors,* p. 196.

169–70 "The deeds demanded of them . . ." quote from Höhne, *The Order,* p. 412.

170 " 'Moral Rubicon' " quote in Browning, *Fateful Months,* p. 86.

170 Ibid., p. 87, for "war of destruction . . . no turning back."

170 Ibid., p. 7, for "to get the Final Solution under way. . . ."

170 Ibid., p. 36, for "there was no written order. . . ."

170 Ibid., p. 37, for Hitler's "maximum ambiguity" and following quote.

171 Final Solution "not solely as the result . . ." quoted in Marrus, *The Holocaust,* p. 41.

171 "Jews 'can no longer be fed,' . . ." and following quotes, from Browning, *Fateful Months,* p. 16.

171 Ibid., p. 32, for "the euphoria of victory. . . ."

171–72 Ibid., pp. 22–23, for July order and "total solution."

172 Ibid., p. 22, for quotes on Heydrich and Himmler.

172 On the Wannsee Conference, see Martin Gilbert, *The Holocaust: A History of the Jews of Europe During the Second World War* (New York: Holt, Rinehart and Winston, 1985), pp. 280–93.

172 Hitler's actual order for genocide, discussed in Marrus, *The Holocaust,* quotes on pp. 45–46.

173 The section epigraph is from Thomas B. Allen, *War Games* (New York: McGraw-Hill, 1987), p. 350.

173 On the Cuban missile crisis and "the brink," see, for example, J. Anthony Lukas, "Class Reunion: Kennedy's Men Relive the Cuban Missile Crisis," *New York Times Magazine* 135 (30 August 1987): 22ff.; James G. Blight, Joseph S. Nye, Jr., and David A. Welch, "The Cuban Missile Crisis Revisited," *Foreign Affairs* 66 (Fall 1987): 170–89.

174 On the capacity to produce weapons or the desire for weapons, see, for example, Leonard S. Spector, *The Undeclared Bomb: The Spread of Nuclear Weapons, 1987–1988* (Cambridge, Mass.: Ballinger, 1988).

174 "My God is Germany," from German documentary on Rudolf Höss.

174 For means of evading Nazi authority, see Lifton, *Nazi Doctors,* pp. 108, 110, 308–9.

175 For the classical study of obedience, see Stanley Milgram, *Obedience to Authority: An Experimental View* (New York: Harper & Row, 1974).

175–76 On war games and "rules," see Allen, *War Games,* pp. 349–50.

176 American business culture that "turns principles into guidelines . . . truth into credibility," from Robert Jackall, *Moral Mazes: The World of Corporate Managers* (Oxford: Oxford University Press, 1988), p. 204.

176 "Nuclear priesthood" and quote by Weinberg in J. Gustave Speth, Arthur R. Tamplin, and Thomas B. Cochran, "Plutonium Recycle:

PAGE

The Fateful Step," *Bulletin of the Atomic Scientists* 30 (9 [November 1974]): 20 (emphasis in original).

176–77 For the emergence and development of SAC, see K. C. Hopkins, *Development of the Strategic Air Command, 1946–1976,* Office of the Historian, Headquarters Strategic Air Command, 21 March 1976.

177   Hiroshima and Nagasaki a "dramatic finale . . . " quoted from Lawrence Freedman, *The Evolution of Nuclear Strategy* (New York: St. Martin's Press, 1983 [1981]), p. 22.

177   Ibid., pp. 23–30, on the evolution of the concept "strategic."

177   "Living personification" and "LeMay owned the bomb . . . killing a nation" quoted from Fred Kaplan, *The Wizards of Armageddon* (New York: Simon & Schuster, 1983), pp. 41–45.

178   Ibid., p. 235, for "the real rivalry," and following quote.

179   "The way things are," quote from Steven Kull, personal communication.

179–80 "Directional force for the drift . . ." "revolving door" practices . . . to promote formal . . . rationality, . . . " and "iron cage . . . nuclear cage," from Lester R. Kurtz, *The Nuclear Cage: A Sociology of the Arms Race* (Englewood Cliffs, N. J.: Prentice-Hall, 1988), pp. 105. See also Henry Jacoby, *The Bureaucratization of the World* (Berkeley: University of California Press, 1973 [1969]).

180   Brodie and "sample attacks" to intensify the "distaste . . . for the regime . . . " quoted in Gregg Herken, *Counsels of War* (New York: Alfred A. Knopf, 1985), p. 28.

180   Ibid., p. 31, for Brodie's relatively "restrained" position.

181   McNamara and Kennedy, discussed in Nick Kotz, *Wild Blue Yonder: Money, Politics, and the B-1 Bomber* (New York: Pantheon, 1988), pp. 76–77.

181   Defense Department employees described in Henry T. Nash, "Bureaucratization of Homicide," *Bulletin of the Atomic Scientists* 36 (April 1980): 24.

181   The section epigraph is quoted from Samuel H. Day, "The Nicest People Make the Bomb," in J. Rowen, ed., *Time Bomb: A Nuclear Reader from the Progressive* (Madison, Wis.: Progressive Foundation, 1980), p. 59.

181   Ibid., p. 56, for "instead of Dr. Strangelove . . ."

182   Ibid., p. 61, for "the atomic bomb . . . landscape."

182   Pentagon policy to "reward failure," in Kurtz, *Nuclear Cage,* pp. 91–101.

182   "The Czar of nuclear weapons" and following quotes, from Robert D. Hershey, Jr., "The Czar in Charge of Nuclear Arms," *New York Times,* 12 December 1981, p. 20.

182   "In the United States, the development . . . " quote from William J. Broad, *Star Warriors: A Penetrating Look into the Lives of the Young Scientists Behind Our Space Age Weaponry* (New York: Simon & Schuster, 1985), p. 15.

182–83 "If Congress, the White House . . . Star Wars . . . more than $1,000 billion" quoted in Phillip M. Boffey, William J. Broad et al., *Claiming the Heavens: The New York Times Complete Guide to the Star Wars Debate* (New York: Times Books, 1987), p. 251. See also Mary Kaldor, *The Baroque Arsenal* (New York: Hill and Wang, 1981), for a discussion of the "weapons system."

183   The section epigraph is from Thomas Powers, "Spontaneous Combustion," review of Daniel Ford, *The Button*, in *The Sciences* 25 (September–October 1985), p. 49.

183   "With the arguable exception of Jimmy Carter . . ." and "Representatives and Senators I have talked to . . ." quoted by Thomas Powers, "What's Worse than MX?" *Washington Post*, 31 March 1985, pp. K4, K1.

183   Ibid., p. K4, for "the buck has gone around. . . ."

183–84   "In a sense the system built itself . . . " from Thomas Powers, "How Nuclear War Could Start," review of Paul Bracken, *The Command and Control of Nuclear Forces*, in *New York Review of Books*, 17 January 1985, p. 35.

184   Fifty "nuclear wars" take place daily, "producing a high-tech military élite . . . " and "many officers . . . prefer the war games . . ." from Josh Martin, "Fighting World World III with Quarters," *Washington Monthly*, October 1984, p. 49. See also Gary D. Brewer and Bruce D. Blair, "War Games and National Security with a Grain of SALT," *Bulletin of the Atomic Scientists* 35 (June 1979): 18–26; Albert Gross, "Armageddon Under the Christmas Tree," *Technology Review* 89 (February–March 1986): 73–74; and Allen, *War Games*.

185   "Those people above me who were supposed . . ." and other quotes from Roger Molander, "How I Learned to Start Worrying and Hate the Bomb," *Washington Post*, 21 March 1982, p. D5.

185   "System of nonresponsibility" used by Maruyama, quoted in Ivan Morris, ed., *Thought and Power in Modern Japanese Politics* (London: Oxford University Press, 1963).

185   On Cuban missile crisis and American "owlish diplomacy," see James D. Blight, Joseph S. Nye, Jr., David A. Welch, "The Cuban Missile Crisis Revisited," *Foreign Affairs* 66 (Fall 1987): 170–88. See also Graham T. Allison, Albert Carnesale, Joseph S. Nye, Jr., eds., *Hawks, Doves, and Owls: An Agenda for Avoiding Nuclear War* (New York: W. W. Norton, 1985), chap. 8.

186   Khrushchev's inability to be "responsible" discussed in Joseph S. Nye, Jr., "Cuban Graffiti," *New Republic*, 13 March 1989, pp. 16–18.

186   The "ultimate absurdity . . ." quoted in York, *Race to Oblivion*, p. 232.

186   Ibid., p. 231, for "the steady transfer of . . . authority . . . to machines."

186   The first section epigraph is from Kurtz, *Nuclear Cage*, pp. 60–61.

186   The second epigraph is from E. P. Thompson, *Beyond the Cold War* (New York: Pantheon, 1982), pp. 49–50.

187   "Pea-brained dinosaurs" quoted from Daniel Ford, *The Button: The*

Pentagon's Strategic Command and Control System (New York: Simon & Schuster, 1985), p. 166.

188   "Exterminism['s] . . . being" from Thompson, *Beyond the Cold War,* pp. 64–65.

188   "The five nuclear powers. . . . A new geography has been created," from William M. Arkin and Richard W. Fieldhouse, *Nuclear Battlefields: Global Links in the Arms Race* (Cambridge, Mass.: Ballinger, 1975), p. 4.

189   Ibid., pp. 65–66, for quotes on international "nuclear infrastructure."

189   "The immediate cause of World War III . . ." from C. Wright Mills, *The Causes of World War III* (Westport, Conn.: Greenwood Press, 1976 [1958]), p. 82.

189   "It is certainly true that nobody has a grasp . . ." quoted from interview with physicist-strategist, 1987.

Chapter 7. Deterrence and Dissociation

192   The first chapter epigraph is from Carol Cohn, "Slick'ems, Glick'ems, Christmas Trees, and Cookie Cutters: Nuclear Language and How We Learned to Pat the Bomb," *Bulletin of the Atomic Scientists* 43 [(5 (June 1987)]:22.

192   The second chapter epigraph is from Roman K. Kolkowitz, "Intellectuals and the Nuclear Deterrence System," in R. Kolkowitz, ed., *The Logic of Nuclear Terror* (Boston: Allen & Unwin, 1986), p. 39.

193   On *dissociation,* see Pierre Janet, *The Major Symptoms of Hysteria* (New York: Macmillan, 1907), and *Psychological Healing* (New York: Macmillan, 1923). See also Leston Havens, *Approaches to the Mind* (Boston: Little, Brown, 1973), pp. 34–62; and Henri F. Ellenberger, *The Discovery of the Unconscious* (New York: Basic Books, 1970), pp. 364–417.

193   For later psychiatric usage of *dissociation,* see Sigmund Freud and Josef Breuer, *Studies on Hysteria,* in James Strachey, ed., *Standard Edition of the Works of Sigmund Freud,* vol. 2 (London: Hogarth Press, 1955 [1893–95]), pp. 3–305. See also Edward Glover, *On the Early Development of Mind: Selected Papers on Psychoanalysis,* vol. 1 (New York: International Universities Press, 1956 [1943]), pp. 307–23; Melanie Klein, "Notes on Some Schizoid Mechanisms," *International Journal of Psychoanalysis* 27 (1946): 99–110; Otto F. Kernberg, "The Syndrome," in O. Kernberg, ed., *Borderline Conditions and Pathological Narcissism* (New York: Jason Aronson, 1975), pp. 3–47; Paul W. Pruyser, "What Splits in Splitting?" *Bulletin of the Menninger Clinic* 39 (1975): 1–46; Jeffrey Lustman, "On Splitting," in Kurt Eissler et al.,

PAGE

eds., *The Psychoanalytic Study of the Child,* vol. 19 (New Haven: Yale University Press, 1977), pp. 19–54; and Charles Rycroft, *A Critical Dictionary of Psychoanalysis* (New York: Basic Books, 1968), pp. 156–57.

193   On social madness, see Ronald Aronson, "Social Madness," in I. Wallimann and M. N. Dobkowski, eds., *Genocide and the Modern Age: Etiology and Case Studies of Mass Death* (New York: Greenwood Press, 1987), pp. 125–41.

194   "Growth by accretion," in Samuel F. Wells, Jr., "Sounding the Tocsin NSC-68 and the Soviet Threat," *International Security* 4 (Fall 1979): 119.

194   "Bombers could be divorced . . . " quote from Michael Sherry, *The Rise of American Air Power: Creation of Armageddon* (New Haven and London: Yale University Press, 1987), p. 23.

194   The first section epigraph is from Heinrich Himmler, quoted in Roger Manvell and Heinrich Fraenkel, *Heinrich Himmler* (London: Heinemann, 1965), pp. 135–36.

194   The second section epigraph is from Albert Speer, quoted from interview in *Playboy Magazine,* 18 June 1971, p. 72.

194–95   On dissociation and pre-Nazi Germany, see, for instance, Ronald Gray, *The German Tradition in Literature, 1871–1945* (Cambridge: Cambridge University Press, 1977 [1965]), pp. 46–77; and John H. Hanson, "Nazi Aesthetics," *Psychohistory Review* 9 (1981): pp. 251–81.

195   *Empathy* defined, in Michael Franz Basch, "Empathic Understanding: A Review of the Concept and Some Theoretical Considerations," *Journal of the American Psychoanalytic Association* 31 (1 [1983]): 101–26; quote on p. 104.

195–96   For a discussion of collective withdrawal of empathy, see Helen Fein, *Accounting for Genocide: National Responses and Jewish Victimization During the Holocaust* (New York: Free Press, 1979), pp. 4, 60–69.

196–97   On Wirths's extreme dissociation and doubling, see Robert Jay Lifton, *The Nazi Doctors: Medical Killing and the Psychology of Genocide* (New York: Basic Books, 1986), pp. 384–414, 424–25.

197   On Gerstein and doubling, see C. Pierre Joffroy, *A Spy for God: The Ordeal of Kurt Gerstein* (New York: Harcourt Brace Jovanovich, 1971), pp. 207–9; see also Saul Friedländer, *Kurt Gerstein: The Ambiguity of Good* (New York: Alfred A. Knopf, 1969).

197   Nazi doctors arriving at Auschwitz, in Lifton, *Nazi Doctors,* pp. 194–99.

197–98   Ibid., pp. 442–47, for disavowal and euphemistic language.

198   Ideological "necessity" for mass killing and quote, from Leszek Kolakowski, "Genocide and Ideology," in Lyman H. Letgers, ed., *Western Society After the Holocaust* (Boulder, Colo.: Westview Press, 1983), p. 8.

199   "Need not to know," phrase used by Daniel Ellsberg, *Papers on the War* (New York: Simon & Schuster, 1972), p. 301.

PAGE

199 "There is no way that I can avoid . . ." quote from Speer interview, *Playboy*, p. 72.

199 Speer's "consent" and "split personality," quoted from interview with Albert Speer in Heidelberg, 1978.

200 The section epigraph is from Richard K. Betts, *Nuclear Blackmail and Nuclear Balance* (Washington, D.C.: Brookings Institution, 1987), pp. 133–34.

200 "Thus far, the chief purpose . . ." quoted in Bernard Brodie, ed., *The Absolute Weapon* (New York: Harcourt Brace, 1946), p. 76.

200 "Making every possible effort . . ." quoted in Gregg Herken, *Counsels of War* (New York: Alfred A. Knopf, 1985), p. 39.

201 The "deterrence trap" quoted in Roman K. Kolkowitz, "Intellectuals and the Nuclear Deterrence System," in R. Kolkowitz, ed., *The Logic of Nuclear Terror* (Boston: Allen & Unwin, 1986), p. 36.

201 Ibid., pp. 37–39, for "nuclear protagonists. . . . "

201 Ibid., p. 40, for "the study and conduct of war . . . numerology, and technical jargon."

202 "We don't know how much we do . . . " and following quotes, from Avner Cohen, "Deterrence, Holocaust and Nuclear Weapons: A Nonparochial Outlook," in L. R. Beres, ed., *Security or Armageddon: Israel's Nuclear Strategy* (Lexington, Mass.: Lexington Books, 1986), pp. 178–79.

202 Ibid., pp. 181, 183, 185, for "usable" and "unusable" weapons.

202–3 "Deterrence by denial" and "counterforce" discussed in Robert Jervis, "Strategic Theory: What's New and What's True," in R. Kolkowitz, ed., *The Logic of Nuclear Terror* (Boston: Allen & Unwin, 1986), pp. 47–81.

203 For a discussion of the psychological discrepancy between intention and effects, see Robert Jervis, Richard Ned Lebow, and Janice Gross Stein, *Psychology and Deterrence* (Baltimore: Johns Hopkins University Press, 1985); and Michael Charlton, *From Deterrence to Defense: The Inside Story of Strategic Policy* (Cambridge, Mass.: Harvard University Press, 1987).

203 On the concept of *psychism*, see Robert Jay Lifton, *Revolutionary Immortality: Mao Tse-tung and the Chinese Cultural Revolution* (New York: Random House, 1968), pp. xv, 32, 114–122, 129–35.

203–4 "Declaratory strategy," "operational strategy," and preceding quotes, from David Alan Rosenberg, "Reality and Responsibility: Power and Process in the Making of United States Nuclear Strategy, 1945–1968," *Journal of Strategic Studies* 9 (March 1986): 35–52; terms on p. 35.

204 Ibid., p. 37, for "general conceptual plans . . . over targets."

204 Ibid., p. 38, for "each level of strategy-making. . . ."

204 McNamara and "assured destruction" from Fred Kaplan, *The Wizards of Armageddon* (New York: Simon & Schuster, 1983), p. 319.

205 LeMay and massive retaliation, quoted in Herken, *Counsels*, p. 97.

PAGE

205   "Somehow or other most of us . . ." quoted from interview with experienced strategist, 1987.

205   "Planet RAND . . . isolated from the hurly-burly . . ." quoted in Kaplan, *Wizards*, p. 51.

205   Ibid., p. 134, for LeMay, "if I see the Russians . . ." and following exchange.

206   Ibid., for a secret SAC war plan.

206   The "persistent, heavy emphasis . . ." is from Rosenberg, "Reality and Responsibility," pp. 49–50.

207   The section epigraph is from Colin S. Gray and Keith Payne, "Victory Is Possible," *Foreign Policy* 39 (Summer 1980): 16–17.

207   "You have to think about . . ." from interview with York, 1987.

207   Rosenberg's statement in "Reality and Responsibility," p. 50. See also Phillip K. Lawrence, *Preparing for Armageddon: A Critique of Western Strategy* (New York: St. Martin's Press, 1988).

207–8   "A nation had to prepare for a war . . ." quoted from Herken, *Counsels*, p. 14.

208   See William Borden, *There Will Be No Time: The Revolution in Strategy* (New York: Macmillan, 1946).

208   McNamara and finite or minimal deterrence, in Kaplan, *Wizards*, pp. 316–17.

208   America "preparing to use nuclear weapons . . ." quote from Rosenberg, "Reality and Responsibility," p. 39.

208–9   Eisenhower, quoted in Herken, *Counsels*, p. 103.

209   On "war-fighting deterrence" as the "new conventional wisdom," see Robert C. Gray, "The Reagan Nuclear Strategy," *Arms Control Today* 13 (March 1983): 1–2, 9–10.

209   Ibid., for widening range of ostensible nuclear options.

209–10   Colin Gray on war-fighting and war-winning, from Colin S. Gray, "Nuclear Strategy: The Case for a Theory of Victory," *International Security* 14 (Summer 1979): 54, 87, 78; Gray and Payne, "Victory Is Possible," 16, 21, 24.

210   "The notion of deterrence . . ." in relation to "winning," from interview with York, 1 June 1987.

210   "As long as the United States relies on nuclear threats . . ." from Gray and Payne, "Victory Is Possible," p. 27.

210–11   "Existential deterrence" and quote, from McGeorge Bundy, "Existential Deterrence and its Consequences," in D. MacLean, ed., *The Security Gamble: Deterrence Dilemmas in the Nuclear Age* (Totowa, N. J.: Rowman & Allenheld, 1984), p. 9.

211   Ibid., p. 10, for "are far more terrifying. . . ."

211   Ibid., p. 9, for "wise fear," "reassurance," and other quotes.

211   Ibid., p. 8, for "scenarios for nuclear warfare. . . ."

211–12   "Discriminate deterrence," report of the Commission on Integrated Long-term Strategy. Co-chairmen: Fred Iklé and Albert Wohlstetter. Members: Ann L. Armstrong, Zbigniew Brzezinski, William P. Clark, W. Graham Claytor, Jr., Andrew J. Goodpaster, James L. Holloway,

III, Samuel P. Huntington, Henry A. Kissinger, Joshua Lederberg, Bernard A. Schriver, and John W. Vessey. (Washington: U.S. Government Printing Office, January 1988).

212   Ibid., pp. 1, 2, 3, 30, 31, and 49, for following discussion and quotes.

212   Ibid., p. 30, for "However, there should be less . . . new technologies emphasizing precision and control."

212   Ibid., for "there would be powerful incentives . . ." and following quote.

213   "The conviction on all sides . . ." from Brodie quoted in Herken, *Counsels,* p. 39.

213   York on "the hooker" and following quotes from interview with York, 1 June 1987.

213   "If there is just a modest chance . . ." from interview with a scientist-strategist, 1987.

214   On "groupthink," see Irving L. Janis, *Groupthink: Psychological Studies of Policy Decisions and Fiascoes,* 2d ed. (Boston: Houghton Mifflin, 1982).

214–15   See Cohn, "Slick 'em, Glick'ems," for prominence of male sexual imagery in nuclear rhetoric.

215   Ibid., p. 22, for Cohn's quotes about the language as "racy, sexy, snappy."

216   Ibid., p. 31, for ". . . a transformative . . . process."

216   "Technological exuberance . . ." quote from Herbert F. York, *The Advisors: Oppenheimer, Teller, and the Super Bomb* (San Francisco: W. H. Freeman, 1976), p. ix.

216   "The internal politics . . ." quoted in McGeorge Bundy, "To Cap the Volcano," *Foreign Affairs* 48 (October 1969): 13.

216   "The men in the nuclear . . . laboratories . . ." quote from Lord Zuckerman, "Science Advisers, Scientific Advisers and Nuclear Weapons," *Proceedings,* The American Philosophical Society, 124 (4 [August 1980]): 10–11.

216   "I have trouble generating scenarios . . ." from Steven Kull, *Minds at War: Nuclear Reality and the Inner Conflicts of Defense Policymakers* (New York: Basic Books, 1988), p. 179.

217   ". . . bomb them back to the Stone Age," quote from Thomas Powers, "How Nuclear War Can Start," review of Paul Bracken, *The Command and Control of Nuclear Forces,* in *New York Review of Books,* 17 January 1985, pp. 33–36.

217   "Atmosphere of excitement, . . ." quote from I. I. Rabi et al., *Oppenheimer* (New York: Charles Scribner, 1969), p. 8.

217   "Isn't it wonderful . . ." quoted in Samuel A. Goudsmit, *Alsos,* History of Modern Physics Series, 1800–1950, vol. 1 (Los Angeles: Tomash, 1983), p. 76.

217   Navy captain quoted in Roger Molander, "How I Learned to Start Worrying and Hate the Bomb," *Washington Post,* 21 March 1982, pp. D1, D5.

PAGE

218   Brodie's quotes in the section epigraph are from Kaplan, *Wizards,* pp. 47–48, 340.

218   Brodie's "How many bombs will do what? . . ." quoted in Kaplan, *Wizards,* p. 46.

219   Brodie "swamped," and quotes and discussion in remainder of paragraph, are from Herken, *Counsels,* pp. 35, 38, 100; and Kaplan, *Wizards,* pp. 80, 339–40.

219   "Simply playing with words" and "something of an illusion" quoted in Kaplan, *Wizards,* pp. 341–42.

220   First section epigraph quoted in Kaplan, *Wizards,* p. 316.

220   Second section epigraph from Robert McNamara, "The Military Role of Nuclear Weapons," *Foreign Affairs* 62 (Fall 1983): 79.

220   McNamara "stunned" from briefing, in Kaplan, *Wizards,* pp. 262, 271. *Ibid.* for "an all-out preemptive first-strike. . . ."

220   York on McNamara quoted in Herken, *Counsels,* p. 139.

221   Ibid., p. 137, for "only a single switch. . . ."

221   See Kaplan, *Wizards,* pp. 277–85, for "massive false alarm" and McNamara's response to RAND analysts.

221   McNamara to Kennedy during Cuban missile crisis, quoted in Herken, *Counsels,* p. 167.

222   Ibid., p. 266, for the section epigraph by Kissinger.

222   Ibid., p. 266, for quotes on Kissinger's dissociative shifts.

222   Ibid., pp. 266–67, for Kissinger-McNamara exchange on appropriate nuclear strategy.

223   Decision maker to Kull, quoted in Steven Kull, "Mind-Sets of Defense Policy-Makers," *Psychohistory Review* 14 (3 [Spring 1986]): 25.

223   The section epigraph is from K. D. Johnson, "The Morality of Nuclear Deterrence," in G. Prins, ed., *The Nuclear Crisis Reader* (New York: Vintage, 1984), pp. 144–45.

224   "Far from inventing a modern science . . . " quoted in Kolkowitz, "Intellectuals," pp. 42–43.

224–25   MccGwire's quotes on deterrence, from Michael MccGwire, "The Insidious Dogma of Deterrence," *Bulletin of the Atomic Scientists* 10 (December 1986): 24–29.

225   Ibid., pp. 26–27, for deterrence "encouraged unwarranted complacency . . ." and following quotes.

225   "The very conditions and policies . . ." quote from Kolkowitz, "Intellectuals," p. 38.

225   ". . . the mass killing of hostages," quoted from Fred Iklé, "Can Deterrence Last Out the Century?" *Foreign Affairs* 51 (January 1973): 267–85.

225   "The rational models of deterrence theory . . ." and "even if nuclear deterrence . . ." quoted in Joseph S. Nye, Jr., "The Long-Term Future of Nuclear Deterrence," in R. Kolkowitz, ed., *The Logic of Nuclear Terror* (Boston: Allen & Unwin, 1986), pp. 233, 234.

PAGE

226   The section epigraph is from Lewis Mumford, *The Pentagon of Power: The Myth of the Machine*, vol. 2 (New York: Harcourt Brace Jovanovich, 1969), p. 37.

227   "Crimes of logic" in Albert Camus, *The Rebel* (New York: Alfred A. Knopf, 1954), p. 11.

228   On the fragile human aspiration for wholeness, see Erik Erikson, "Wholeness and Totality: A Psychiatric Contribution," in C. J. Friedrich, ed., *Totalitarianism* (Cambridge: Cambridge University Press, 1954), pp. 156–71, 161–62.

228   Mumford on sixteenth-century "mechanical world picture," quoted in Mumford, *Pentagon of Power*, pp. 33–37.

228   "Cartesian sickness" in Ashis Nandy, *Traditions, Tyranny, and Utopias: Essays in the Politics of Awareness* (Delhi: Oxford University Press, 1987), p. 32.

228   "Placing the world in jeopardy," quoted from Langdon Winner, *Autonomous Technology: Technics-Out-of-Control as a Theme in Political Thought* (Cambridge, Mass.: MIT Press, 1980 [1977]), p. 73.

229   "The Auschwitz of Puget Sound" quoted from Archbishop Raymond G. Hunthausen, "Faith and Disarmament," speech delivered at Pacific Lutheran University, Tacoma, Washington, 12 June 1981.

Chapter 8. Victims

230   The chapter epigraph is from Primo Levi, *The Drowned and the Saved* (New York: Summit Books, 1988), p. 165.

231   Ibid., pp. 48–49, section epigraph, for ". . . whether in my depths there lurks a murderer. . . ."

231   For Nazi and Hitler *Götterdämmerung* impulse, see Albert Speer, *Inside the Third Reich* (New York: Macmillan, 1970), pp. 440, 457; see also Donald M. McKale, *Hitler: The Survival Myth* (New York: Stein and Day, 1981).

231   A "genocidal universe" from Alan Rosenberg, "The Genocidal Universe: A Framework for Understanding the Holocaust," *European Judaism* 13 (1979): 29–34.

231–32 For the killing of mental patients as the first Nazi genocide, see Robert Jay Lifton, *The Nazi Doctors: Medical Killing and the Psychology of Genocide* (New York: Basic Books, 1986), pp. 45–144.

232   "There are few more durable generalizations . . ." and "like sheep to the slaughter" quoted from Michael R. Marrus, *The Holocaust in History* (Hanover and London: University Press of New England, 1987), p. 108.

232   Ibid., pp. 108–9, for Ringelblum's Warsaw ghetto diary.

PAGE

232   Hilberg on the Jewish leadership as "implements of German will" in Raul Hilberg, *The Destruction of the European Jews,* vol. 3, rev. and def. ed. (New York: Holmes & Meier, 1985), pp. 1030–31, 1038–39.

232   Arendt's attack on the Jewish leadership for their "role in the destruction of their own people" in Hannah Arendt, *Eichmann in Jerusalem: A Report on the Banality of Evil,* rev. and enlarged ed. (New York: Penguin Books, 1976 [1964]), pp. 117–18.

233   "Most of them executed, starved, or worked to death," quoted in Marrus, *The Holocaust,* p. 140.

233–34   On *psychic closing off* and *psychic numbing,* see Robert Jay Lifton, *Death in Life: Survivors of Hiroshima* (New York: Basic Books, 1982 [1967]), pp. 31–34, 500–516.

234   "A long . . . process of attrition . . . terror, degradation, and spoliation," quoted in Marrus, *The Holocaust,* pp. 112–13.

234   On "middle knowledge," see Avery Weisman and Thomas Hackett, "Predilection to Death: Death and Dying as a Psychiatric Problem," *Psychosomatic Medicine* 33 (3 [1961]).

234–35   "I still cannot believe that they did it . . ." quoted from interview with survivor-physician, 1978.

235   "You can't understand it . . ." quote in Marrus, *The Holocaust,* p. 158.

235   For "cognitive dissonance," see Leon Festinger, *A Theory of Cognitive Dissonance* (Evanston, Ill.: Row, Peterson, 1957).

235   "Our failure to imagine genocide," quoted from Rabbi Bernard S. Raskas, "Swords into Ploughshares: The Jewish Responsibility to Work for Nuclear Disarmament," typescript.

235–36   On the psychology of coerced collusion, see Lifton, *Nazi Doctors,* pp. 214–38.

236   The *Judenrat* leaders, "*forced* to establish the councils . . ." quote from Marrus, *The Holocaust,* p. 113.

236–37   On the *Sonderkommando,* see Jadwiga Beswinska and Danuta Czech, eds., *Amidst a Nightmare of Crime: Notes of Prisoners of Sonderkommando Found at Auschwitz* (Oswiecim, Poland: Polish State Museum at Oswiecim [Auschwitz], 1973).

237   Dual beliefs and "unrestrained hatred . . ." quote in Marrus, *The Holocaust,* pp. 119–20.

237   The section epigraph is from John K. Roth, "Comment: Foreboding and Melancholy," in L. H. Legters, ed., *Western Society After the Holocaust* (Boulder, Colo.: Westview Press, 1983), p. 25.

237–38   See Marrus, *The Holocaust,* pp. 156–83, for summary discussion of the behavior of bystanders. See also David S. Wyman, *The Abandonment of the Jews: America and the Holocaust, 1941–45* (New York: Pantheon, 1984).

238   "In August 1942, shortly before Doctor Stephen Wise . . ." quoted from Marie Syrkin, "Comment: Holocaust and Genocide," in Legters, ed., *Western Society,* p. 57.

318   *Notes*

PAGE

238-39 Ibid., p. 58; for the "account of the extermination . . . of Lodz . . ."
"I must confess . . . " and " . . . the silence was almost complete."

239 Ibid., for "evolution in consciousness" and ". . . the reality of the
Final Solution."

240 American press "persistently ignored the scope . . ." and
". . . qualifying . . . mass murder," quoted in Marrus, *The Holocaust*,
pp. 161–62.

240 For a discussion on Nazi selective inattention, see Lifton, *Nazi
Doctors*, pp. 17–18, 35–38, 41–42, 434, 438, 439, and research
interviews.

241 "A need not to know," from Daniel Ellsberg, *Papers on the War* (New
York: Simon & Schuster, 1972), p. 28.

241 On the role of technology in facilitating mass killing, see Eric
Markusen, "Genocide and Total War: A Preliminary Comparison,"
in I. Wallimann and M. Dobkowski, eds., *The Age of Genocide: Etiology
and Case Studies of Mass Death* (New York: Greenwood Press, 1987),
pp. 97–123.

242 On *fragmentary* and *formed awareness*, see Robert Jay Lifton,
"Imagining The Real," in Robert Jay Lifton and Richard Falk,
*Indefensible Weapons: The Political and Psychological Case Against
Nuclearism* (New York: Basic Books, 1982), pp. 111–25.

243 The section epigraph is from Emma Rothschild, "A European
Strategy for Peace," in "A World without Nuclear Weapons?"
(Symposium), *New York Times Magazine*, 5 April 1987, p. 48.

243 Wiesel quote, see epigraph, chap. 1.

243 "Warriors" and "victims," in Freeman Dyson, *Weapons and Hope*
(New York: Harper & Row, 1984), p. 316.

244 On Chernobyl, see, for examples, Lynn R. Anspaugh, Robert J.
Catlin, and Marvin Goldman, "The Global Impact of the Chernobyl
Reactor Accident," *Science* 242 (16 December 1988): 1513–20; and
Thomas Powers, "Chernobyl as a Paradigm of a Faustian Bargain,"
Discover 7 (June 1986): 33–36.

245 On militarization of society and neglect of human needs, see Ruth
Leger Sivard, *World Military and Social Expenditures, 1987–1988*
(Leesburg, Virginia: World Priorities, 1988).

245 On threat to democracy posed by nuclear weapons, see Richard
Falk, "Contra Secular Absolutism," in Lifton and Falk, *Indefensible
Weapons*, pp. 260–65; and Falk, "Taking Stands," in ibid., pp.
128–43. See also Eric Markusen and John B. Harris, "Nuclearism
and the Erosion of Democracy," in J. B. Harris and E. Markusen,
eds., *Nuclear Weapons and the Threat of Nuclear War* (San Diego, Calif.:
Harcourt Brace Jovanovich, 1986), pp. 366–76; and Robert Karl
Manhoff, "The Media: Secrecy vs. Democracy," *Bulletin of the Atomic
Scientists* 40 (1 [January 1984]): 26–29.

245-46 On Soviet genocidal readiness, see Thomas B. Cochran, *Soviet
Nuclear Weapons: Nuclear Weapons Databook*, vol. 4 (New York: Harper
& Row, 1989); David Holloway, *The Soviet Union and the Arms Race*

PAGE

    (New Haven: Yale University Press, 1983); and Honore M. Catudal, *Soviet Nuclear Strategy from Stalin to Gorbachev: A Revolution in Soviet Military and Political Thinking* (Atlantic Highlands, N. J.: Humanities Press International, 1989).

246   The section epigraph is from Raskis, "Swords into Ploughshares," typescript.

246   "If we attack 'em at all . . ." quoted in Steven Kull, *Minds at War: Nuclear Reality and the Inner Conflicts of Defense Policymakers* (New York: Basic Books, 1988), p. 75.

248   "Terribly and painfully costly . . . failure to imagine . . ." quote from Raskis, "Swords into Ploughshares," typescript.

249   "Under control . . . hands of experts" and other quotes, from Fred Kaplan, *The Wizards of Armageddon* (New York: Simon & Schuster, 1983), p. 319.

249–50   On American selective memory, see Leo Kuper, *Genocide: Its Political Use in the Twentieth Century* (New Haven and London: Yale University Press, 1981), pp. 40–41.

250   For Nuremberg principles, see, for instance, discussions by Richard Falk in Richard Falk, Gabriel Kolko, and Robert Jay Lifton, eds., *Crimes of War* (New York: Random House, 1971), pp. 3–10, 73, as well as opening statements by Robert F. Jackson at Nuremberg expressing the principle of universalism (p. 85). See also F. J. P. Veale, *Advance to Barbarism: How the Reversion to Barbarism in Warfare and War-Trials Menaces Our Future* (Appleton, Wis.: C. C. Nelson, 1953 [1948]).

250   On U.S. alliance with Turkey and genocide, see, for example, Richard G. Hovannisian, "The Armenian Genocide," in I. W. Charny, ed., *Genocide: A Critical Bibliographic Review* (New York: Facts on File, 1988), pp. 89–102.

250   For "thank God for the atomic bomb," see Paul Fussell, *Thank God for the Atomic Bomb and Other Essays* (New York: Summit Books, 1988).

251   Indifference as the great human problem, paraphrased from Elie Wiesel, "One Must Not Forget," *U.S. News & World Report,* 27 October 1986, p. 68.

252   "Thick glass" quoted from Czeslaw Milosz, *Bells in Winter* (New York: Ecco Press, 1978), p. 64.

252   The section epigraph is from Levi, *The Drowned,* p. 69.

252   "Ants eventually build another anthill . . . with enough shovels," quoted in Robert Scheer, *With Enough Shovels: Reagan, Bush, and Nuclear War* (New York: Random House, 1982), p. 3.

253   On civil defense bunkers for leaders, see Edward Zuckerman, *The Day After World War III: The U.S. Government's Plans for Surviving a Nuclear War* (New York: Viking Press, 1984), pp. 211–38.

253   See Levi, *The Drowned,* p. 69, for his account of Rumkowski.

253   Ibid., for "our essential fragility."

253   Ibid., pp. 165–66, respectively, for "willed incredulity, mental blocks . . . why aren't we fleeing . . . ?"

Chapter 9. A Species Mentality

PAGE

255   The first chapter epigraph is from W. S. Merwin, "For Now," in *The Moving Target* (New York: Atheneum, 1971), p. 95.

255   "Dangerous attachment" paraphrased from George Kateb, "Thinking About Human Extinction (1): Nietzsche and Heidegger," *Raritan* 6 (2 [Fall 1988]): 1.

255   "Moral equivalent" quoted from William James, "The Moral Equivalent of War," in R. A. Wasserstrom, ed., *War and Morality* (Belmont, Calif.: Wadsworth, 1970), pp. 4–14 (James originally published in 1910).

256   The section epigraph is from interview with Theodore Taylor, 3 December 1987.

256   "Please call me by my true names . . ." quoted from Thich Nhat Hang, "Non-Violence: Practicing Awareness," *Stauros Notebook* (May–June 1987): 1.

256   "Possessing such power . . . " quote from Terrence Des Pres, *Praises and Dispraises: Poetry and Politics, the 20th Century* (New York: Viking Press, 1988), p. 8.

256   "Killed our imagination," quote by Emma Rothschild, "A European Strategy for Peace," in "A World without Nuclear Weapons?" (Symposium), *New York Times Magazine*, 5 April 1987, p. 48.

257   "The only thing to do . . ." quoted in Robert Jay Lifton, *The Nazi Doctors: Medical Killing and the Psychology of Genocide* (New York: Basic Books, 1986), p. 412.

257   "High-order abstraction . . . " quoted in Robert W. Gardiner, *The Cool Arm of Destruction: Modern Weapons and Moral Insensitivity* (Philadelphia: Westminister Press, 1974), p. 72.

258   "Taking possession of men's imagination . . ." from George Kennan, "A Modest Proposal," *New York Review of Books*, 16 July 1981, p. 14.

258   The section epigraph is from Hela Horska, quoted in Nechama Tec, *When Light Pierced the Darkness: Christian Rescue of Jews in Nazi-Occupied Poland* (New York: Oxford University Press, 1986), p. 166.

259   Nietzsche paraphrased, in Kateb, "Thinking About Human Extinction," p. 10.

259   "Somebody has to care for the planet!" quoted from interview with Richard Garwin, New York City, 7 May 1987.

256   "It did not matter who it was . . . ," Hela Horska quoted in Tec, *When Light Pierced the Darkness*, pp. 165–66.

259   "A truly wider identity . . ." quoted from Erik Erikson, "Remarks on the 'Wider Identity,' " in S. Schlein, ed., *A Way of Looking at Things: Selected Papers of Erik H. Erikson from 1930 to 1980* (New York: W. W. Norton, 1987), p. 502.

PAGE

260 On Rushdie, see, for instance, Youssef M. Ibrahim, "Khomeini's Judgment," *New York Times,* 16 February 1989, p. A1.

260 "An inverted Faust . . ." quote from Gunther Anders, "Reflections on the H-Bomb," *Dissent* 3 (2 [Spring 1956]): 152.

260 Einstein quote in Paul C. Warnke, "Prospects for International Arms Control," in M.I.T., ed., *The Nuclear Almanac: Confronting the Atom in War and Peace* (Reading, Mass.: Addison-Wesley, 1984), p. 337.

260 The section epigraph is from Kateb, "Thinking About Human Extinction," p. 1.

260–61 On modes of symbolic immortality and historical shifts, see Robert Jay Lifton, *The Broken Connection: On Death and the Continuity of Life* (New York: Basic Books, 1983 [1979]), pp. 13–112, 283–92.

261 "An ascent towards consciousness" from Teilhard de Chardin, quoted in Roger Walsh, "A Psycho-Evolutionary Analysis," in S. Grof and M. L. Valier, eds., *Human Survival and Consciousness Evolution* (Albany, N. Y.: State University of New York Press, 1988), p. 3.

261–62 "Freezing point . . ." and "a new species," quoted in Anders, "Reflections on the H-Bomb," pp. 153, 146, respectively.

262 Eisenhower's famous warning, from Dwight D. Eisenhower, "Liberty Is at Stake," *Vital Speeches* 27 (8 [1 February 1961]): 228–31.

263 The section epigraph is from Martin Luther King, speech accepting Nobel Peace prize, 11 December 1964.

263 Monotheism and polytheism, discussed by Harvey Cox, personal communication.

264 "The fateful question for the human species . . ." quoted in Sigmund Freud, *Civilization and Its Discontents,* in J. Strachey, ed. and trans., *The Standard Edition of the Complete Psychological Works of Sigmund Freud,* vol. 21 (London: Hogarth Press and the Institute of Psycho-Analysis, 1961 [1929]), p. 145.

264 Marx on "species-being," quoted in David McLellan, ed., *Karl Marx: Selected Writings* (Oxford: Oxford University Press, 1977), pp. 81, 82.

264 Jackson quoted in Richard A. Falk, Gabriel Kolko, and Robert Jay Lifton, eds., *Crimes of War* (New York: Random House, 1971), p. 85.

265 Morrison, Compton, and Szilard, in Paul Boyer, *By the Bomb's Early Light: American Thought and Culture at the Dawn of the Atomic Age* (New York: Pantheon, 1985), pp. 76–81. See also *One World or None* (Freeport, N. Y.: Federation of American Scientists, March 1946).

265 On "global citizenship" and similar principles, see, for examples, Richard A. Falk, *A Study of Future Worlds* (New York: Free Press, 1975) and *The Promise of World Order: Essays in Normative International Relations* (Philadelphia: Temple University Press, 1987); Saul H. Mendlovitz, ed., *On the Creation of a Just World Order: Preferred Worlds for the 1990's* (New York: Free Press, 1975); and Harry B. Holions, Averill L. Powers, and Mark Sommer, *The Conquest of War: Alternative Strategies for Global Security* (Boulder, Colo.: Westview Press, 1989).

PAGE

265   With respect to death tolls under Stalin, James Mace ("Genocide in
the U.S.S.R.," in I. W. Charny, ed., *Genocide: A Critical Bibliographic
Review* [New York: Facts on File, 1988], p. 116) states that "serious
demographic estimates range from 9.1 million in 1926–39 to over
28.6 million and perhaps as many as 32.4 million in 1929–49."

266   "Pseudospeciation" from Erik H. Erikson, "Evolutionary and
Developmental Considerations," in L. Grinspoon, ed., *The Long
Darkness: Psychological and Moral Perspectives on Nuclear Winter* (New
Haven: Yale University Press, 1986), pp. 63–72.

266   On dehumanization see Herbert C. Kelman, "Violence Without
Moral Restraint: Reflections on the Dehumanization of Victims and
Victimizers," *Journal of Social Issues* 29 (4 [1973]): 25–61.

267   Award to Dürr, quoted in the Right Livelihood Foundation
brochure and press release, from Research Office, School of Peace
Studies, University of Bradford, United Kingdom, 9 October 1987.

267   Vance and Gorbachev, quoted in Mark Sommer, "An Emerging
Consensus: Common Security Through Qualitative Disarmament,"
Alternative Defense Project (pamphlet) 1 (1988): 2–3.

268   On "nonoffensive defense" and similar terms, see, for instance, Hal
Harvey et al., "Nonoffensive Defense" (a special section of articles),
Bulletin of the Atomic Scientists 44 (7 [September 1988]): 12–54. See
also D. Carlson and C. Comstock, eds., *Securing Our Planet: How to
Succeed When Threats Are Too Risky and There's Really No Defense* (Los
Angeles: Jeremy P. Tarcher, 1986); and Anatoly Gromyko and
Martin Hellman, eds., *Breakthrough: Emerging New Thinking* (New
York: Walker and Co., 1988).

268   "Final defence of the deterrent dogmatist . . . " and following
quotes, from Michael MccGwire, "Deterrence: The Problem—Not
the Solution," *International Affairs* 62 (Winter 1985/86): 55–70.

268   On principle of mutual rejection of possibility of nuclear
"exchange," see, for examples, Jonathan Schell, *The Abolition* (New
York: Alfred A. Knopf, 1984); and James N. Miller, Jr., "Zero and
Minimal Nuclear Weapons," in J. S. Nye, Jr., G. T. Allison, and A.
Carnesale, eds., *Fateful Visions: Avoiding Nuclear Catastrophe*
(Cambridge, Mass.: Ballinger: 1988), pp. 11–32. See also Theodore
B. Taylor, "Go Cold Turkey," and Sidney D. Drell, "Not So Fast,"
in an exchange entitled "Why Not Now? Debating a Nuclear-free
Millennium" (held at the March 1989 annual national meeting of
Physicians for Social Responsibility, Palo Alto, California), *Bulletin of
the Atomic Scientists* 45 (July–August 1989): 25–31; and Rajni Kothari
et al., *Towards a Liberating Peace* (New York: New Horizons Press,
1988).

269   "Cooperation breeds cooperation" and following quotes, from Sean
M. Lynn-Jones and Stephen R. Rock, "From Confrontation to
Cooperation: Transforming the U.S. Soviet Relationship," in Nye et
al., eds., *Fateful Visions*, pp. 111–31; quote is on 125–26. See also
Thomas R. Rochon, *Mobilizing for Peace: The Antinuclear Movements in*

Western Europe (Princeton: Princeton University Press, 1988); and Robert Axelrod, *The Evolution of Cooperation* (New York: Basic Books, 1984).

269   On ending the cold war, see John Lewis Gaddis, "How the Cold War Might End," *Atlantic Monthly* (November 1987): 88–100; and symposium, "The 'End' of the Cold War?" *Deadline,* a bimonthly research and press review published by the Center for War, Peace, and the News Media, New York University, vol. 4, Summer 1989.

269   The first section epigraph is from Falk, "The Question of War Crimes," in Falk et al., eds., *Crimes of War,* p. 10.

269   The second epigraph quoted from Ecclesiasticus, Sir. 3:25.

270   "All poets the world over . . ." quoted from Stanley Kunitz, personal communication.

270   "Reckless . . . delegation of power," from John Kenneth Galbraith quoted in John Ernst, "A Call to Conscience of the University Community," *The Center Magazine* (January–February 1982): 4.

270   Weisskopf, quoted in in I. I. Rabi et al., *Oppenheimer* (New York: Charles Scribner, 1969), pp. 26, 28, respectively.

271   "In the summer of 1945 . . ." and next quote, from Eugene Rabinowitch, "Five Years After," in M. Grodzins and E. Rabinowitch, eds., *The Atomic Age* (New York: Basic Books, 1963), p. 156.

271–72   "Misbehavior" and "Walking in Red Square . . ." quoted from interview with Taylor, 3 December 1987.

273   For writers', artists', and critics' responses, see Paul Brians, *Nuclear Holocausts: Atomic War in Fiction, 1895–1984* (Kent, Ohio: Kent State University Press, 1987); Des Pres, *Praises and Dispraises;* David Dowling, *Fictions of Nuclear Disaster* (Iowa City: University of Iowa Press, 1987); and Jan Caputi, "Films of the Nuclear Age," typescript.

273   Beckett quotes, from Lawrence Shainberg, "Exorcising Beckett," *Paris Review* (1987): 108.

273–74   Pastoral letter, quoted from American National Conference of Catholic Bishops, "The Challenge of Peace: God's Promise and Our Response," special supplement to the *Chicago Catholic,* 24 June and 1 July 1983, p. 2a.

274   Ibid., p. 3a, for "one of the greatest curses . . ." and following quotes.

274   "We write in defense . . . " quoted from The United Methodist Council of Bishops, *In Defense of Creation: The Nuclear Crisis and a Just Peace* (Nashville: Graded Press, 1986), p. 11.

274–75   Ibid., pp. 14–15, for "nuclear deterrence . . . " and following quotes.

275   "Make and unmake their arrangements . . . " quote from George Kateb, "Thinking About Human Extinction (II)," *Raritan* 6 (3 [Winter 1988]): 17.

PAGE

275   The section epigraph is from Beckett, quoted in Shainberg, "Exorcising Beckett," p. 108.

276   See Carl Sagan, *Cosmos* (New York: Random House, 1980), also the basis for the PBS television series *Cosmos,* aired in 1980.

276   On *global ecopolitics* and "social paradigm," see Dennis Pirages, *The New Context for International Relations: Global Ecopolitics* (Monterey, Calif.: Brooks-Cole, 1978), introduction.

276   *Ecofeminism,* quoted from Ynestra King, "The Common Ground for the Person," paper presented at "Peacemaking and Species Consciousness" conference, John Jay College of Criminal Justice, City University of New York, New York City, 23 February 1989; and Carolyn Merchant, *The Death of Nature: Women, Ecology, and the Scientific Revolution* (New York: Harper & Row, 1980).

277   "To see the earth as it truly is . . . " quoted from Archibald MacLeish, "Riders on the Earth Together," *New York Times,* 25 December 1969, p. 1.

277   The section epigraph is from Louis Simpson, *Collected Poems* (New York: Paragon House, 1988), p. 83.

278   "This is not the End of Time. . . . We are not powerless," quote from Patricia Mische and Gerald Mische, *Toward a Human World Order: Beyond the National Security Straightjacket* (New York: Paulist Press, 1977), p. 350.

278   "Defending hope . . ." from Adam Michnik, *Letters from Prison and Other Essays* (Berkeley: University of California Press, 1985), p. 10.

279   Ibid., p. xvii, for Jonathan Schell's quotes on "originality in political action."

279   "Defy the given models of defiance," from Ashis Nandy, *Traditions, Tyranny and Utopias* (Delhi: Oxford University Press, 1987), dedication.

279   "People getting up from their knees," from Michnik, *Letters,* p. 10.

Index